Relevance, Pragmatics and Interpretation

Bringing together work by leading scholars in relevance theory, this volume showcases cutting-edge research within the theory and demonstrates its influence across a range of fields including linguistics, pragmatics, philosophy of language, literary studies, developmental psychology and cognitive science. Organised into broad thematic strands that represent the latest research and debates, the volume shows the depth of analysis now possible after nearly 40 years of intensive work in developing and applying the principles of relevance theory. The breadth of influence of the framework is reflected in the chapters of the volume, in some cases moving beyond the traditional realms of semantics and pragmatics to include discourse analysis, language acquisition, media and education. The volume will be essential reading for researchers in these fields, as well as for those already working within relevance theory or with other pragmatic theories.

KATE SCOTT is a Senior Lecturer in English Language and Linguistics at Kingston University, London. Her research focuses on the pragmatics of reference, with a special interest in the nature and role of procedural meaning.

BILLY CLARK is Professor of English Language and Linguistics at Northumbria University. His research covers a wide range of topics in linguistics and stylistics, with a particular focus on semantics and pragmatics.

ROBYN CARSTON is Professor of Linguistics at University College London. Her main research interests are in pragmatics, semantics, relevance theory, metaphor, and word meaning.

T0370886

Relevance, Pragmatics and Interpretation

Essays in Honour of Deirdre Wilson

Edited by

Kate Scott
Kingston University

Billy Clark
Northumbria University

Robyn Carston
University College London

CAMBRIDGE
UNIVERSITY PRESS

University Printing House, Cambridge CB2 8BS, United Kingdom

One Liberty Plaza, 20th Floor, New York, NY 10006, USA

477 Williamstown Road, Port Melbourne, VIC 3207, Australia

314-321, 3rd Floor, Plot 3, Splendor Forum, Jasola District Centre, New Delhi - 110025, India

103 Penang Road, #05-06/07, Visioncrest Commercial, Singapore 238467

Cambridge University Press is part of the University of Cambridge.

It furthers the University's mission by disseminating knowledge in the pursuit of education, learning and research at the highest international levels of excellence.

www.cambridge.org
Information on this title: www.cambridge.org/9781108407618
DOI: 10.1017/9781108290593

First published 2019
First paperback edition 2022

A catalogue record for this publication is available from the British Library

Library of Congress Cataloging in Publication data
Names: Scott, Kate, 1976– editor. | Clark, Billy, editor. | Carston, Robyn, editor.
Title: Relevance, pragmatics and interpretation / edited by Kate Scott,
Billy Clark, Robyn Carston.
Description: New York, NY: Cambridge University Press, 2019. |
Includes bibliographical references and index.
Identifiers: LCCN 2019000690 | ISBN 9781108418638 (hardback) |
ISBN 9781108407618 (paperback)
Subjects: LCSH: Relevance. | Pragmatics. | Semantics. | Semiotics.
Classification: LCC P99.4.R44 R449 2019 | DDC 401/.45–dc23
LC record available at https://lccn.loc.gov/2019000690

ISBN 978-1-108-41863-8 Hardback
ISBN 978-1-108-40761-8 Paperback

Contents

Contributors

NICHOLAS ALLOTT, Senior Lecturer in English, University of Oslo, Norway.

AXEL BARCELÓ ASPEITIA, Professor of Philosophy, National Autonomous University of Mexico (UNAM), Mexico.

ANNE BEZUIDENHOUT, Professor of Philosophy and Linguistics, University of South Carolina, USA.

DIANE BLAKEMORE, Professor of Linguistics (1998–2014), University of Salford, UK.

RICHARD BREHENY, Reader in Linguistics, University College London, UK.

ROBYN CARSTON, Professor of Linguistics, University College London, UK.

BILLY CLARK, Professor of English Language and Linguistics, University of Northumbria, UK.

VICTORIA ESCANDELL-VIDAL, Professor of Linguistics, National Distance Education University (UNED), Spain.

INGRID LOSSIUS FALKUM, Researcher, Department of Philosophy, Classics, History of Art and Ideas, University of Oslo, Norway.

THORSTEIN FRETHEIM, Emeritus Professor of Linguistics, Norwegian University of Science and Technology (NTNU), Norway.

ANNE FURLONG, Associate Professor of English, University of Prince Edward Island, Canada.

ELENI GREGOROMICHELAKI, Visiting Assistant Professor, Heinrich Heine University, Germany; Visiting Research Fellow, King's College London, UK.

MYRTO GRIGOROGLOU, PhD Candidate, Department of Linguistics and Cognitive Science, University of Delaware, USA.

ELLY IFANTIDOU, Professor of Language and Linguistics, National and Kapodistrian University of Athens, Greece.

MARK JARY, Professor of Linguistics and Philosophy, University of Roehampton, UK.

RUTH KEMPSON, Emeritus Professor of Linguistics, King's College London, UK.

MIKHAIL KISSINE, Associate Professor of Linguistics, Université Libre de Bruxelles, Belgium.

TOMOKO MATSUI, Professor of Linguistics, Tokyo Gakugei University, Japan.

JACQUES MOESCHLER, Professor of Linguistics, University of Geneva, Switzerland.

EUN-JU NOH, Professor of English Language and Literature, Inha University, South Korea.

ANNA PAPAFRAGOU, Professor of Psychology and Linguistics, University of Delaware, USA.

ANNE REBOUL, Senior Researcher, Institute for Cognitive Sciences-Marc Jeannerod (CNRS, UMR 5304), France.

KATE SCOTT, Senior Lecturer in English Language and Linguistics, Kingston University, UK.

NEIL SMITH, Emeritus Professor of Linguistics, University College London, UK.

DAN SPERBER, Professor of Cognitive Science and Philosophy, Central European University, Hungary.

ROBERT J. STAINTON, Distinguished Professor of Philosophy, University of Western Ontario, Canada.

CLAUDIA STREY, Assistant Professor, Escola Superior de Propaganda e Marketing (ESPM), Brazil.

CHRISTOPH UNGER, Postdoctoral Fellow, Department for Language and Literature, Norwegian University of Science and Technology (NTNU), Norway.

TIM WHARTON, Principal Lecturer in Linguistics, University of Brighton, UK.

Cover Acknowledgements

Cover image and illustrations by Apoa Falby Clark

Couple dancing the Twist: H. Armstrong Roberts / Retrofile RF / Getty Images

Portrait of George Eliot: DEA PICTURE LIBRARY / De Agostini / Getty Images

UK - London - Gordon Square in Bloomsbury: Mike Kemp / Corbis Historical / Getty Images

The Last Remaining Cabmen's Shelters in London: Chris J Ratcliffe / Stringer / Getty Images News / Getty Images Europe

Poached egg on toast: Tornadoflight / iStock / Getty Images Plus / Getty Images

Noam Chomsky: Rick Friedman / Corbis Historical / Getty Images

Human head skull phrenology study: ilbusca / DigitalVision Vectors / Getty Images

Queen Elizabeth II and Prince Philip en route to Eagle Farm Airport, Brisbane, Queensland, 1954: State Library of Queensland

Deirdre Wilson: Photograph by Theodore Zeldin

Dan Sperber: Photograph by Denis Tatone

Introduction

Robyn Carston, Billy Clark and Kate Scott

The publication of *Relevance: Communication and Cognition* by Dan Sperber and Deirdre Wilson in 1986 initiated a new phase in the study of the human capacity for communication and comprehension (i.e. pragmatics), with significant implications for cognition and interpretation more broadly. It was named as one of the most important and influential books of the decade in the *Times Higher Educational Supplement*. Since then, the ideas that Sperber and Wilson presented in this very influential book have been considerably refined and developed, by both Sperber and Wilson themselves and many others. A number of subsequent publications (Carston & Uchida 1998; Rouchota & Jucker 1998; Padilla Cruz 2016) have presented updates on the achievements of the relevance-theoretic research programme. Our collection demonstrates the ongoing influence of the ideas presented in the 1986 book and the diversity and range of research it continues to inspire. It contains twenty chapters, each focused on a specific topic or issue, by researchers at the forefront of current research who come from a range of disciplines (including linguistics, philosophy, literary studies and developmental psychology).

In recent years, there have been some major developments and new directions within the framework. A key methodological development was the experimental turn in the early 2000s, which is now central to the discipline, with theoretical claims being routinely subjected to empirical testing and the gathering of experimental data on utterance processing guided by theoretical hypotheses. Relevance theorists were pioneers in this regard, more or less inventing the field of 'experimental pragmatics' (for overviews by leaders in this field, see Noveck & Sperber 2004; Breheny 2011). Significant new areas of content, investigated both theoretically and empirically, include the human capacity for epistemic vigilance and its interaction with information conveyed communicatively (e.g. Sperber et al. 2010; Mazzarella 2013, 2015; Reboul 2017), lexical pragmatics and the nature of word meaning (e.g. Wilson & Carston 2007; Carston 2012, 2013; Kolaiti & Wilson 2014), the relation between pragmatics and theory of mind (e.g. Sperber & Wilson 2002; Breheny 2006), the relation between pragmatics and the evolution of language (Reboul 2015; Scott-Phillips 2015), the pragmatics of non-verbal communication (e.g. Wharton

2003a, 2009), pragmatics and the stylistic analysis of texts (e.g. Caink & Clark 2012; Chapman & Clark 2014, in press), the pragmatics of aspects of online social networking (e.g. Scott 2015, 2018), children's developing pragmatic abilities (e.g. Papafragou & Tantalou 2004; Pouscoulous 2013; Zufferey 2015). Many of these new developments are represented in this volume.

We have divided the twenty chapters into three thematic parts. In the first part, 'Relevance Theory and Cognitive Communicative Issues', the chapters focus on questions that arise within the core domain of the theory, namely, 'ostensive-inferential' communication and comprehension, and its cognitive underpinnings. The second part, 'Pragmatics and Linguistic Issues', addresses the implications of relevance-theoretic pragmatics for various components of the stable (encoded or conventional) meaning of specific linguistic elements (words, particles and structures). In the third part, 'Figurative Language and Layered Interpretations', the chapters include discussion of aspects of non-literal communication, of various ways in which communication can involve 'layers' of meaning and of the expression of non-propositional effects, including emotional ones. It would, of course, be possible to structure the chapters in a number of other ways, as the themes and topics often interface and even overlap. For instance, several of the chapters address issues in children's pragmatic development as part of their investigation of a specific phenomenon. The organisation we eventually settled on highlights the ongoing contribution of ideas from relevance theory to theoretical issues in the study of communication, to work on the interface of pragmatics with linguistic meaning, and to broader questions about communication and interpretation of different kinds and levels (social, personal, practical and emotional).

The first part, on cognitive communicative issues, starts with a chapter by Nicholas Allott, which considers how relevance theory can be seen as responding to doubts about the possibility of any kind of systematic pragmatic theory. He considers three sceptical positions: Fodor's argument that pragmatic processes are not amenable to scientific study because they are unencapsulated (highly context sensitive), Chomsky's claim that human intentional action is a mystery rather than a scientifically tractable problem, and a third view which maintains that intentional communication is too complex for systematic study. Allott argues that work in relevance theory can be seen as successfully challenging these sceptical views and he gives concrete examples of its achievements.

Richard Breheny's chapter begins by pointing out one particular success of relevance theory: its account of anticipatory processes in language comprehension and of the effects of stress placement on these processes. Breheny aims to build on this by investigating pragmatic processes which anticipate the source of relevance (the intended context) rather than components of linguistic form or content. He reviews recent empirical work on the processing of questions and negation, and draws out its implications for the issue of how the source of relevance is represented in utterance processing. He finds in favour of the relevance-theoretic account and against the currently popular view in formal pragmatics that representations of context take the form of 'questions under discussion'.

In their chapter, Axel Barceló Aspeitia and Robert Stainton focus on the interpretation of a group of expressions which they term 'quasi-factives', an area in which the recurring issue of the relative contributions of linguistically encoded meaning and pragmatic inference is especially striking. In line with Deirdre Wilson's early work on presupposition (Wilson 1975), they argue that the factive conclusions which these expressions seem to support are not to be explained semantically. Rather, they are components of the speaker's meaning and their derivation by the addressee depends on the kind of cost–benefit trade-off that is central to relevance theory.

The topic of Victoria Escandell-Vidal's chapter is 'explicature', a notion which has been central to relevance theory from its inception and which introduced a radically new way of thinking about explicitly communicated meaning and about the semantics–pragmatics distinction. Escandell-Vidal focuses here on how utterances of particular expressions in Spanish (some occurrences of the verb *estar* and some uses of 3rd-person imperfective forms) lead to 'higher-level' explicatures expressing a speaker's evidential commitment. She argues that the evidential meaning does not arise from the semantic composition of linguistically encoded content but rather emerges as the optimal solution to a 'feature mismatch' between two components of encoded meaning.

In his chapter, Jacques Moeschler addresses some complex issues about negation, metarepresentation and their interaction. He identifies three distinct uses of negation, namely, descriptive negation and two kinds of metarepresentational negation (one metalinguistic, the other presupposition-cancelling), which differ in their semantic entailments. His key claim is that all three of them have what he calls 'representational' (or propositional) effects on the context, specifically the elimination and/or the strengthening of existing assumptions, albeit different for each of the uses.

Anne Reboul's chapter makes a significant contribution to relevance-theoretic discussions of the phenomenon of 'free indirect discourse', by developing a pragmatic account of the appropriate use and interpretation of pronouns in this special kind of discourse (which typically occurs in literary texts). She first reviews current semantic accounts of pronouns in this kind of discourse and finds that they have problems with certain non-transparent referential uses of pronouns and their presuppositions. Her alternative account, which employs the relevance-theoretic notion of pragmatic enrichment together with the account of singular concepts developed within François Recanati's mental files framework, avoids the problems of the semantic accounts.

In the final chapter of this first part of the book, Myrto Grigoroglou and Anna Papafragou explore what seems to be a paradox about the development of pragmatic abilities: while very young children are able to perform tasks which demonstrate what is required for pragmatic reasoning, certain areas of their pragmatic performance do not become adult-like until much later. Focusing on the much-discussed topic of scalar implicature, they propose that performance in tasks designed to elicit the derivation of such an implicature is significantly affected by the nature of the contextual material provided. When, for example, children appear not to understand an utterance of the form *'some X are Y'* as suggesting *'not all X are Y'*, it may be because they have not seen the potential relevance in the particular context of the thought that *all X are Y*.

The theme of the second part of the book is 'relevance-theoretic pragmatics and linguistic issues' and the chapters in this part demonstrate how giving the human pragmatic capacity primacy of place in the interpretation of linguistic utterances encourages a new perspective on aspects of linguistically encoded meaning and even on the nature of syntax. In the first chapter in this part, Mark Jary and Mikhail Kissine examine the meaning of imperative sentences, taking the existing relevance-theoretic semantic analysis, in terms of the desirability and potentiality of the described state of affairs, as their point of departure. In their view, a complete account of the interpretation of imperatives has to explain how they can result in the addressee forming an intention to perform an action and this requires the theory to make room for 'action representations' (in addition to factual representations, such as assumptions). They claim that the imperative form is uniquely specified to interface with such action representations.

A very different kind of linguistic form is investigated in the next chapter, which is by Eun-Ju Noh: the Korean sentence-final suffix *ci*. The analysis here builds on a body of work in relevance theory on discourse markers or particles, which are typically non-compositional elements of form that do not affect propositional content, but rather indicate something about the speaker's attitude towards or evidence for that proposition. With regard to *ci*, Noh argues that existing treatments of it as an epistemic or attitudinal marker are unable to account for the full range of cases, and that it is better analysed as a metarepresentational marker indicating that the propositional form represents not a state of affairs in the world but rather the speaker's own representation of that state of affairs.

The focus of Diane Blakemore's chapter is two kinds of linguistic phrase which seem to be inherently expressive, nominal epithets such as *The idiot* and small clauses such as *You angel*. She argues against accounts that treat these structures as linguistically encoding the property of expressiveness and in favour of a relevance-theoretic account according to which they communicate a particular conceptual content that guides the addressee in identifying the attitude the speaker holds towards the target individual. Expressiveness arises when the main relevance of the utterance comes from this information about speaker attitude.

The next two chapters contribute to an area of considerable current interest in semantics and pragmatics, that is, the nature of polysemy (the representation and processing of words with multiple related senses). In her chapter, Robyn Carston discusses the relevance-based on-line construction of ad hoc concepts (or occasion-specific senses) as the source of much semantic polysemy (where words are stored with a cluster of related senses). In an attempt to give a full account of polysemy, one that marries the pragmatics of word meaning with the demands of grammar, she advocates a split view of the lexicon, with one part narrowly linguistic and computational, and the other an ever-evolving store of communicational units.

Thorstein Fretheim discusses a particular Norwegian modal adverb, *gjerne*, which he maintains is polysemous, in that it has two related meanings, both of which are conventionalised and stored in the lexicon. This case of polysemy seems to be different from the polysemy of open-class words (nouns, verbs, adjectives), which is typically explained in relevance-theoretic terms as involving pragmatic adjustments of an encoded concept. He argues that the two meanings of *gjerne* are better analysed as encoded procedures, so as constraining the hearer's interpretation process rather than contributing a concept to that interpretation.

In her chapter, Anne Bezuidenhout shows how the meaning of noun-noun compounds cannot be predicted by linguistic rules but must allow for a component of context-specific relevance-based inference. She reviews several approaches which attempt to provide semantic and/or statistical (bigram frequency-based) accounts of the meaning of compounds but finds none of these fully adequate. She concludes that such accounts inevitably have to be supplemented by local pragmatic processes of concept narrowing and broadening (ad hoc concept construction), such as those developed within the relevance-theoretic framework.

This linguistically oriented part of the book ends with what is perhaps the most radical account of the relation between pragmatics and the linguistic system. In this chapter, Eleni Gregoromichelaki and Ruth Kempson present a range of arguments and data, including cases of split utterances, in support of their position that even syntax should be construed in terms of the linguistic underspecification of utterance content and incremental context-relative processing. This approach to language (which they call 'Dynamic Syntax') is fundamentally different from orthodox generative grammar and conceptualises syntax as procedures for interaction.

The third and final part of the volume focuses on more creative uses of language and their interpretation. The chapters in this part include several that discuss new questions arising for long-standing topics within pragmatics, specifically, metaphor, metonymy and irony, and some that address new emerging concerns in the field, including the communication of emotions and the communicative nature of adaptations from one medium into another.

The part begins with a chapter by Ingrid Lossius Falkum in which she uses data from young children's communicative development to argue that metaphor and metonymy rely on different pragmatic mechanisms. Metaphor and metonymy have certain characteristics in common: they both target individual words or phrases, they both contribute content to the proposition expressed, and they both lie on a continuum of literal and figurative uses. However, developmental data suggests that early metonymic uses may be the result of a more basic process than metaphorical uses, one in which the child exploits salient associative relations to compensate for gaps in vocabulary.

The chapter by Elly Ifantidou also discusses aspects of the interpretation of metaphor. However, her focus is specifically on issues arising for the understanding of metaphors in a second language learning context. She presents an empirical study in which native Greek-speaking learners of English were presented with a selection of metaphors from British newspapers. The results of this comprehension task suggest that even when second language learners are confronted with a metaphor whose intended propositional content they cannot fully grasp, the literal content of the metaphor may still trigger images, sensorimotor processes and emotional attitudes which provide them with a partial interpretation.

The next two chapters focus on some other kinds of non-literal language use, specifically irony and allegory. Tomoko Matsui takes a developmental perspective on ironical language use and considers the role of epistemic vigilance and mind-reading mechanisms in children's understanding of irony. She discusses evidence that indicates that children as old as 9 years may misinterpret instances of irony as deliberate lies and suggests that this is a result of their developing epistemic vigilance mechanisms (specifically, a sensitivity to the truth or falsity of information) together with a not yet fully mature appreciation of how information can achieve relevance.

In his chapter on allegory, Christoph Unger first outlines the pragmatic mechanisms employed in the processing of metaphor and irony, and then compares them with those that seem to be required for the understanding of allegories. Building on ideas of Sperber and Wilson (1987b), he argues that allegories are like fictions more generally in that they require the capacity to process multi-layered intentions. As such, processing allegory differs radically from metaphor comprehension (which involves ad hoc concept construction) but uses some of the same abilities as irony comprehension, specifically the ability to process utterances on two levels in parallel and the capacity to process interpretive resemblances between representations.

The somewhat neglected topic of emotion in communication is the focus of the chapter by Tim Wharton and Claudia Strey, who argue that it is time to develop an account of how emotions are expressed and communicated and to fully integrate it into pragmatic theory. They discuss the descriptive ineffability of emotional communication and argue for the introduction of a new notion of 'positive emotional effect' to complement the existing notion of 'positive cognitive effect'. They also suggest that recent developments in relevance theory, specifically work on indeterminacy of meaning and on procedural meaning, make it uniquely capable of accommodating these vaguer aspects of communication.

In the final chapter of the volume, Anne Furlong demonstrates a new application of relevance theory through a discussion of how relevance is achieved when adapting a 'literary' work from one communicative medium into another (e.g. from written text into film). She argues that adaptations should be understood as communicative acts in their own right, so as falling under the presumption of optimal relevance like any other ostensive acts, and suggests that assumptions about the source texts can form part of the context in which that new communicative act is interpreted.

To conclude this summary of the contents of the volume, it just remains to emphasise that while these twenty chapters cover a multitude of different topics (linguistic, pragmatic, cognitive and aesthetic), they are bound together by their application of the principles and concepts of relevance theory. Collectively, they are testimony to the insights of that framework and its ongoing capacity to engage with and provide illuminating answers to a wide range of questions about human communication.

The primary motivation for us to call on the community of scholars working within relevance theory to contribute to this book was our wish to pay (long overdue) tribute to Deirdre Wilson. To this end, we also invited two of Deirdre's closest and longest-standing colleagues and friends, Dan Sperber and Neil Smith, to write short reflective prefaces to the volume. Dan reflects on the origins of Deirdre's and his work on relevance theory, its development over the decades and its future directions, while Neil reflects on the very significant impact of Deirdre's work and charismatic teaching in shaping the profile and reputation of the Linguistics department at University College London (UCL).

Although she officially retired from UCL in 2008, Deirdre has continued to work intensively within the field of pragmatics, both in the ongoing collaboration with Dan (as detailed in his reflective notes), and in developing other collaborative projects, two of which are especially noteworthy. In the first of these, she was a founding member of the Centre for the Study of Mind in Nature (CSMN), a ten-year centre of excellence (2007–2017) based at the University of Oslo, where she worked on the 'Linguistic Agency' project, focusing on the topic of metarepresentation (both mental and linguistic) and its role in communication. The second major collaboration was on the Balzan Project *Literature as an Object of Knowledge* (2010–2014), led by Terence Cave, at the University of Oxford, on which she was officially a senior consultant, but in the end much more than that. Deirdre collaborated with philosophers and linguists (at the CSMN) and with literary specialists (on the Balzan project).

At the CSMN, Deirdre considerably developed her body of work on the pragmatics of non-literal language use. This included new ideas about how the cognitive linguistics approach to metaphor might interact with the relevance-theoretic approach (Wilson 2011a), extensive work on the nature of irony, how children acquire the ability to produce and understand it (Wilson 2013) and how it differs from other (often co-occurring) figurative uses, such as hyperbole, jokes and banter (Wilson 2017), and a new take on the phenomenon of metonymy, which had not been much discussed before within relevance theory (Wilson & Falkum forthcoming). Another strand of work conducted at this time concerned the conceptual/procedural distinction, which was initiated within relevance theory in the 1980s by Diane Blakemore, with a particular focus on the meaning of discourse connectives such as *but*, *after all*, and *well* (e.g. Blakemore 1987, 2002). Deirdre has developed this distinction considerably, suggesting that many more linguistic expressions have a component of procedural meaning, which activates a cognitive inferential process rather than mapping to a conceptual representation. In her most recent papers on this topic, she has developed the intriguing idea that certain linguistic expressions might activate particular domain-specific procedures belonging to modules (or sub-modules) which play a significant role in linguistic communication, including those involved in mind-reading, emotion reading, social cognition, parsing, and epistemic vigilance (Wilson 2011b, 2016). In parallel with her work on these innovative areas of theoretical research, Deirdre has collaborated with colleagues who specialise in assessing the pragmatic capacities of clinical populations, in particular those with autism spectrum disorders (e.g. Chevallier et al. 2010, 2011).

The investigation with Terence Cave and other literary specialists on the Balzan project was a largely new direction, both for relevance theory and for literary studies, and Deirdre played a key role in driving forward the project's aim of developing a cognitively informed and cognitively inflected literary criticism: 'it [literature] invites a cognitive mode of criticism, one which asserts the priority of the individual literary work as a unique product of human cognition' (Cave 2016). This culminated in their co-edited book *Reading Beyond the Code: Literature and Relevance Theory*, in which literary theorists explore the applicability to literary texts of concepts, principles and distinctions from relevance theory, including the showing/telling distinction, the comprehension/interpretation continuum, 'weak implicature', 'ad hoc concepts', and 'echoic use', among others.

Deirdre's own chapter in that volume is called 'Relevance theory and literary interpretation', and in it she assesses the extent to which a pragmatic theory like relevance theory can shed light on the interpretation of literary utterances. She acknowledges that there are significant respects in which communication via a literary text differs from the kind of face-to-face communication that has been the main focus of pragmatic theory, while insisting that it must, nevertheless, draw on the same basic cognitive and communicative abilities employed in all ostensive communication and inferential interpretation. As she notes, a particular interest for literary scholars is the treatment of 'non-propositional' phenomena, including imagery, emotions and sensorimotor processes, which seem to play a heightened role in many literary works. Drawing on the many discussions of these phenomena that took place with colleagues on the Balzan project, she develops the idea that a new broader notion of pragmatic inference (see Sperber & Wilson 2015) may play a key role in providing a more unitary account of the full range of non-propositional effects.

A second important insight that Deirdre explores in the chapter concerns a distinction between the internal and external relevance of a literary text. The 'internal' relevance of a literary work concerns the way in which aspects of the fictional world created by the author guide and constrain the ongoing interpretation of the text, giving rise to cognitive implications and other effects that are contained within the fictional frame. The 'external' relevance of a text, on the other hand, concerns the cognitive effects it may have on beliefs and assumptions about the actual world that the reader has independently of the text. Developing an early idea in Sperber and Wilson (1987b: 751), Deirdre suggests that this duality of expectations of relevance and of cognitive effects achieved might be explained in terms of an author simultaneously performing ostensive acts on two levels: 'a lower-level act of describing a fictional world, and a higher-level act of *showing this world* to the reader as an example of what is possible, or conceivable' (Wilson 2018). The expectations of relevance raised by the lower-level act would be 'internal', while the higher-level act would create 'external' expectations of relevance. As with her very detailed work on irony, metaphor and metonymy, Deirdre's work on literary interpretation opens up new lines of thought for future investigation within the relevance theory framework.

We hope this collection of chapters by Deirdre's colleagues and former students[1] gives some indication of the powerful shaping effect of her ideas

---

[1] Deirdre Wilson has worked collaboratively with a great many colleagues, supervised scores of doctoral and postdoctoral students, and been a committed mentor to many other students and scholars across the world. Naturally, but regrettably, it was impossible for us to include all those who we know would have made valuable contributions to this volume.

and of her brilliance and clarity in communicating them. We offer it to her as a small token of our gratitude, respect and affection.

Acknowledgements

This volume has involved the cooperation and coordination of a great many people, all of whom have shown tremendous enthusiasm for the project. We would like to thank our authors, both for their individual chapters and for their excellent work in reviewing and commenting on each other's chapters. We are also grateful to Alison Hall, Larry Horn, Rebecca Jackson, Ira Noveck, Tim Pritchard, Agustin Vicente, Catherine Wearing and especially Nigel Fabb for their help with the reviewing process.

Reflections on the Development
of Relevance Theory

Personal Notes on a Shared Trajectory

Dan Sperber

The editors of the volume asked me to provide a broad overview of the beginnings of relevance theory back in the 1970s, how it has developed over the decades and where I see it moving in the future, reflecting in the process on the collective work that Deirdre Wilson and I initiated and that has been joined and considerably enriched by many others. Here are some personal notes to help address these questions.

Deirdre and I met at Oxford in the mid-sixties and started a long conversation about pop music, nihilism, and things. The works of Noam Chomsky and Paul Grice were evoked. Ten years later, Deirdre published her MIT doctoral dissertation, *Presuppositions and Non-Truth-Conditional Semantics*, and I published *Rethinking Symbolism*. Discussing our overlapping interests, we decided to write a joint paper exploring how to bridge semantics, pragmatics, and rhetoric. The paper became a book, *Relevance: Communication and Cognition* (published in 1986). And now, many years later, the conversation continues.

Our work started at a time when philosophy of mind, inspired by the emergence of cognitive psychology, was in the process of superseding philosophy of language as the main locus of challenging novel ideas (epitomised by Jerry Fodor's 1975 *The Language of Thought*). And the work of Chomsky was changing the way not just linguists but also philosophers would think of language and its relationship to mind. Exciting times.

Grice then was not a central figure. He had been developing his ideas independently of the cognitive and the Chomskyan revolutions. Still, his approach to meaning linked philosophy of language and philosophy of mind in a way that would appeal to cognitive psychologists: speaker's meaning, as he analysed it, was a higher-order psychological phenomenon; comprehension was, to an important extent, inferential. For a linguist working in semantics like Deirdre, Grice's idea led to novel insights on a variety of problems that had no easy solution in a grammatical or formal semantic framework. For a social scientist like myself, dissatisfied with semiotic approaches to communication and culture, Grice's work suggested novel ways of articulating the mental and the social.

In his 1967 William James Lectures (Grice 1989), Grice had outlined an account of how comprehension can be achieved even when semantic encoding and decoding do not by themselves fully do the job (which, we were soon to argue, they never do). This offered him a way to answer a philosophical question much debated at the time: to what extent does the meaning of connectives like *and*, *or*, and *if* in English correspond to that of their logical counterparts? Grice's sketch explained how these English words might have a simple unambiguous semantics identical to that of logical operators and, yet, be interpreted in conversation in many different ways.

Grice's outline (the Cooperative Principle, the maxims, the distinction between what is said and what is implicated, and so on) had implications, some of which he himself discussed, that went well beyond the semantics of connectives. Still, this was a philosophical sketch not intended to provide a ready-to-use battery of conceptual tools and hypotheses for an empirical science of pragmatics.

Grice himself underscored the vagueness of some of his notions, 'relevance' in particular. Nevertheless, over the past fifty years his sketch has often been discussed as if it were a full-fledged theory; his ideas have been accepted and sometimes challenged as dogma. In philosophy in particular, the adjective 'Gricean' is often used as if it referred to a definite range of facts and to a clear enough account. In substance: these cumbersome facts can be taken care of by means of the Gricean maxims, so let's ignore them and resume business as usual.

For our part, Deirdre and I saw Grice's ideas as a starting point for an exploration of poorly mapped or unmapped territories. We accepted the insight that what makes it possible for the hearer to infer the speaker's meaning from her utterance together with contextual information is the existence of definite expectations raised by the very act of communication. We didn't, however, take for granted or even as particularly plausible that these expectations were exactly captured by the Cooperative Principle and the ten maxims. Like all pragmaticists, we wanted empirically well-supported, fine-grained analyses of pragmatic phenomena rather than allusions to what a proper analysis would look like. Even more importantly, we wanted to contribute to a scientific understanding of the cognitive mechanisms that produce such interpretations. Not all pragmaticists shared this latter goal.

So, between our initial project of 1975 and the publication of *Relevance* in 1986, we worked on a series of issues, from presuppositional effects to ironical interpretations, from mechanisms of inference to the interpretation of moods and speech acts, and, in so doing, we went far beyond our initial hunches that all the Gricean maxims could be reduced to relevance and that metaphorical and ironical interpretations were neither triggered by a violation of a maxim of truthfulness nor guided by simple relationships of similarity or opposition. The issues, it turned out, were much more varied and intricate than we had realised and yet, we saw, they could be handled in a neatly integrated manner.

I have not re-read *Relevance* since Deirdre and I worked on the 1995 *Second Edition*. To prepare the present remarks, I have now looked at chunks of it and I am struck by how much, with the help of collaborators and also critics, we have moved, mostly ahead but also, in part, away from the 1986 version of the theory. While some aspects of the initial theory have been abandoned, some underdeveloped hunches in that early work have come to play a more important role.

For instance, much of the second chapter on 'Inference' has become quite obsolete. The way we would now think about mechanisms of inference is rooted in a modular view not just of peripheral but of all cognitive mechanisms. Still, the chapter provided a notion of contextual effects that was sufficiently explicit to help us develop two central claims: that cognition aims at maximising relevance and that comprehension is guided by precise expectations of relevance elicited by the very act of communication. In this same second chapter, we argued in passing that non-representational properties of mental representations (having to do, in particular, with the way they are neurally implemented) may contribute in important ways to the output of mental computations. This idea, which we then used just to introduce the notion of 'strength of assumptions', now plays a much more important role in our thinking about, for instance, competing inputs to cognitive processes or about the epistemic effects of saliency (as developed in our 2015 paper 'Beyond speaker's meaning').

Between the 1986 and the 1995 editions of *Relevance*, some twenty students of Deirdre defended their PhD and made a variety of important contributions to the theory. Diane Blakemore's work on procedural meaning (see Blakemore 1987) and Robyn Carston's work on the explicit–implicit distinction and the pragmatics of explicature (see Carston 2002), in particular, inspired much further research. Students, colleagues, and we ourselves did new work on many aspects of verbal comprehension, such as illocutionary force or figures of speech, and on implications of the theory beyond standard pragmatics, in philosophy of language, literary theory, and cognitive psychology. Collaboration with psychologists on experimental testing of relevance theory hypotheses took off.

The 'Postface' of the 1995 *Second Edition* shows what our attitude was at the time: the theory, we thought, needed minor revisions (in formulation more than in substantive content) but the main challenge was to take advantage of it to better explain a wider range of pragmatic phenomena than we had done so far. This is what the expanding community of relevance theorists did quite effectively in the following years.

How wide a range of phenomena is relevance theory in a position to better explain? Relevance theory has sometimes been criticised by pragmaticists favouring a sociolinguistic approach for being anchored in a narrow cognitive perspective, but as we argued in our 1997 'Remarks on relevance theory and the social sciences', there is no principled discontinuity between cognitive and social aspects of communication. On the contrary, a proper pragmatic approach should help bridge gaps that are caused more by the parochialism of academic disciplines and sub-disciplines than by thought-through theoretical disagreements. Relevance theory work has, over the years, thrown light on a variety of sociolinguistic phenomena, from advertising and propaganda to politeness and verbal aggression, but much more could and should be done.

Linguists interested in pragmatics but who view it as an extension or complement of grammar have focused on a much narrower range of issues than we did. In Grice's 'conventional implicatures' and 'generalised conversational implicatures', and in presuppositions, in particular, the role of the context can be minimised (or so it seems). This is convenient if you would rather use tools borrowed from, or at least inspired by, formal semantics, which are not adapted to model actual cognitive processes or to deal with the role of open-ended contexts in ordinary comprehension.

Attention to open-ended contexts has been at the centre of much work in relevance theory, in particular in lexical pragmatics. A variety of phenomena falling under quite different explanations in other approaches: approximation, ad hoc narrowing and/or broadening of meaning, 'scalar' interpretations, hyperbole, and metaphor have all been shown to result from one and the same comprehension procedure: follow a path of least effort in constructing an interpretation of an utterance and stop when your expectations of relevance (which can be revised up or down in the course of comprehension) have been met. The whole process involves a progressive mutual adjustment of explicatures and implicatures. The hypothesis that this is how comprehension proceeds is specific enough to be experimentally testable. To improve the testability, it would be useful now to work on proper cognitive modelling of the comprehension procedure. Most current work in formal pragmatics is irrelevant to such modelling. Bayesian approaches, however (which, up to now, have been mostly used to formalise quite shallow pragmatic hypotheses), might be more useful.

Pragmaticists working within a relevance theory perspective have done experimental work on the development of pragmatic abilities in children's use of language. But what about pragmatic development before language? Highly relevant work about this has been done from a different perspective. Developmental psychologists Gergely Csibra and Györgi Gergely and their collaborators at the Central European University in Budapest have produced rich experimental evidence in support of their natural pedagogy theory (e.g. Csibra & Gergely 2009), which gives a central role to ostensive communication in the teaching and acquisition of general knowledge. According to this theory, children are able, already well before they acquire language, to recognise ostensive signals and to interpret an adult's behaviour differently depending on whether it is presented to them ostensively or not. Research on natural pedagogy has given rich evidence that ostensive communication is already at work in infancy, extending the scope of relevance theory, not just in principle, but quite concretely, well beyond linguistic communication.

This is relevant not only to developmental but also to comparative psychology. Juan Carlos Gomez (e.g. Gomez 1996) had argued that ostension, or at least a simplified form of it, is already present in great apes' interactions. More recently, Josep Call, Michael Tomasello, and their collaborators at the Max Planck Institute in Leipzig (e.g. Bohn et al. 2015), in their studies of communication in great apes and in children, have thrown more light on the role of ostension in early human communication and on its possible role among humans' closest relatives. At this stage, the evidence concerning great apes is interesting enough to warrant more investigation but little more can be said with confidence. Let me, however, share a hunch. Progress in this direction will involve looking at possible precursors of ostensive communication not in the realm of animal signalling systems but in that of manipulation of attention.

There are many ways in which primates and other social animals influence the behaviour of conspecifics by manipulating their attention. This can be done without any mind-reading ability on either part. With some rudimentary mind-reading ability, however, the animal whose attention is being manipulated may recognise that such manipulation is intentional and this may enhance its expectation of relevance: a male chimpanzee is drawing a female's attention to his state of sexual arousal; she had noticed it by herself, but his drawing her attention to it may increase her willingness to mate with him. There is evidence that chimpanzees can influence the behaviour of others by manipulating their attention in such an overt way. Proto-ostension?

In 2015, Deirdre and I published an article, 'Beyond speaker's meaning', which is neither about evolution nor primate communication but which raises related issues. We revisit in particular the continuum of cases between meaning and showing. At the showing end of this continuum, optimally relevant information may be provided just by what is shown, and the fact that it is *ostensively* shown may add very little or nothing. Say Mary and Peter (who is distracted) are about to cross the street. She draws his attention to a fast-approaching car. Peter steps backward just as he would have if he had noticed the car by himself. Did ostension add anything over and above redirecting his attention? Not much, but still: it is now mutually manifest that she intended him to pay attention to the looming car and to warn him of the danger. There might be a weak implicature that he was being imprudent. He might be irritated by this, thinking he would have noticed the car anyhow, or he might be grateful. Or he might be oblivious of what Mary intended in directing his attention, in which case, communication will still have been effective, even if not wholly so, without any mind-reading on Peter's part.

In other words, when ostensive communication involves displaying some direct evidence for a relevant conclusion that the communicator intended to convey, the addressee may be able to reach this conclusion without attending to the intention of the communicator. In such cases, attention to, and interpretation of, the communicator's communicative intention may not be necessary for communication to be largely successful. Conversely, an individual may, without having a full-fledged communicative intention, overtly display relevant evidence for a conclusion she intends her audience to accept. This behaviour may be mistaken for an instance of regular ostensive communication. Such a mistake, however, need not create much of a misunderstanding either.

Taking a behaviour to be ostensive (in the full sense) when it is not, or not recognising a behaviour as ostensive when it is, may occur fairly commonly without much compromising communication. This happens, for instance, with babies or with dogs (we seeing more ostension than there is in their behaviour, they seeing less in ours). As I suggested, chimpanzees may communicate in a proto-ostensive way without having or attributing communicative intentions.

What I mean by 'proto-ostension' is, more precisely, a form of interaction where A draws B's attention to some state of affairs in a manifestly intentional way and this elicits in B the expectation that this state of affairs is relevant to him or her. There is no communicative intention on the part of A, no attribution by B to A of an informative intention, let alone of a communicative intention. I suggest we may have missed how much proto-ostensive communication takes place in ordinary human interaction.

In each other's presence, people tend to monitor each other's mental states, at least in a shallow way. By the same token, people tend to behave in a way that may lightly impinge on others' attention and influence their mental states (not randomly but in a way desirable to the attention-manipulating individual). For instance, in the presence of others, we may adopt a bodily posture that suggests social ease and competence. This may be done with a low level of awareness and interpreted with a low level of attention. Or we may go more ostensive: if we have reason to suspect that others have noticed us slumping, we may change posture in an ostensive way, conveying that we are in control after all. It takes very little to move from a non-ostensive informative behaviour to an ostensive and communicative one.

In relevance theory, we have often noted that full-fledged ostensive behaviour typically conveys further information in a non-ostensive way; for instance, a lecturer may non-ostensively convey that she has an attractive voice. Still, we may not have paid sufficient attention to (1) the degree to which non-ostensive, proto-ostensive, and ostensive forms of interaction fall under a more general category of action on others by means of manipulation of their attention, (2) the ease with which human interaction can take or lose in a fraction of a second an ostensive character, (3) the degree to which ostensive and non-ostensive communication co-occur in the same interactions, and (4) the fact that relevance theory provides useful tools to describe not only ostensive but also non-ostensive and proto-ostensive aspects of interaction and to explain what gets communicated to whom and how.

These points are relevant not only in an evolutionary, comparative, or developmental perspective, but also in studying ordinary human interaction. They may also be relevant in studying the role of both ostensive and non-ostensive forms of communication in arts such as music or literature.

A musical performer, for instance, is requesting her audience's attention to her performance as a whole in a manifestly intentional way. This overall ostension provides a frame within which the audience is encouraged to react throughout the performance in a personal way. To enjoy its emotional, aesthetic, and cognitive effects, listeners must pay attention to the music and to their own experience, but they need not pay attention at every juncture to the intentions of the performer – in fact, they should not. Still, there may be moments where the music (because of the score, the way it is performed, or both) is overtly requesting added attention to what is intended and, if this is recognised, produces extra effects.

So, the issue is not whether music is a form of ostensive or of non-ostensive communication. It is both. A better question is how a musical performance achieves its effects by hovering back and forth (to a different degree in different types of music and styles of performance) across a blurred zone, on one side of which the intentions of the performer (or of the composer) are irrelevant to appreciation, on the other side of which they are definitely relevant, while inside this zone, individual listeners may each differently optimise their experience by giving a greater or a lesser guiding role to what they sense of the intention of the performer.

Mutatis mutandis, similar suggestions could be made about dancing, painting, literature, and other art forms. With even more adjustment, such a perspective might help us think better about a variety of forms of social interaction, from clothing to flirting to ritual, many communicative aspects of which are neither wholly ostensive nor wholly non-ostensive.

When proto-ostension would be enough to achieve an intended effect in an addressee, why do we still so often resort to full-fledged ostension? Ostensive communication may involve a modicum of extra investment on the part of both the communicator and the addressee, but it carries extra benefits. To the extent that some information has been ostensively communicated, it is now mutually manifest (or 'common ground') and, therefore, can be taken for granted in future communication. Moreover, ostension makes it mutually manifest that the communicator intended the addressee to accept this information and hence that she takes responsibility for it. Ostensive communication carries a commitment to the truth of an assertion, the desirability of a request, and so on. Ostension, in other words, is, among other things, a means to overcome an audience's epistemic vigilance.

Proto-ostension (in essence, an encouragement to pay attention to some state of affairs and derive whatever conclusions one wishes from it on one's sole responsibility) may be appropriate when there are no epistemic vigilance concerns. A fiction writer draws the reader's attention to a narrator of her own making who is fictitiously engaging in ostensive communication with them. The fictitious communicative intentions of this fictitious narrator matter throughout: they determine the content of the narration. Still, there may be ways in which the writer gives occasional evidence of her own communicative intentions. This is likely to happen, for instance, if readers are encouraged not just to follow and enjoy the narrative but to derive some moral lesson from it, or at least to form some moral impression. There, ostension makes manifest the commitment of the writer and may sway or at least nudge a vigilant reader to the intended conclusion or in the intended direction.

In pure argumentation, we have a different articulation of ostension and proto-ostension. The addressee must pay attention to the speaker's meaning to properly understand the argument. Once understood, however, the argument is intended to stand on its own and convince the audience by its own force, and not because the arguer intended her audience to accept the conclusion of the argument, not, that is, through trust in the arguer. (Of course, pure argumentation is rare; more commonly, arguers use mixed means of persuasion.)

To conclude, many intriguing questions continue to emerge, both from the foundational ideas of relevance theory that Deirdre and I worked on together in the 1970s and 80s, and from its subsequent collective development to the present day. To answer these questions, we must of course borrow from other disciplines and traditions. Still, there are some underused tools in our own toolbox.

Acknowledgements

This work was supported by the European Research Council under the European Union's Seventh Framework Programme (FP7/2007-2013) / ERC grant agreement n° [609819], SOMICS.

The Source of Relevance

Neil Smith

The whole idea of being categorized repelled her.

(Wilson 1991:10)

This volume of chapters on topics in relevance theory has been assembled in honour of Deirdre Wilson, with all its chapters written by former students and/ or colleagues of hers. My aim is to describe the impact of Deirdre's presence on the linguistics scene in London and the significance of her work in establishing the new sub-discipline of pragmatics. This work shaped the development of our thinking (hence our research and teaching) on a range of linguistic issues, especially in the realm of meaning.

Relevance theory is, of course, the outcome of a long and very fruitful collaboration between Deirdre Wilson and Dan Sperber, and it is neither possible nor desirable to disentangle their respective contributions. Given the occasion of the present volume and my knowledge of the protagonists, I hope I will be forgiven for concentrating on Deirdre and her role with no intention of slighting Dan and his. I will begin with some personal reminiscences and continue with some remarks on relevance theory. The former is self-explanatory, the latter will attempt to add to the evidential base for one aspect of the theory and then suggest a surprisingly neglected area which could benefit from more attention.

I first met Deirdre in 1970 when she joined the small group of linguists at University College London (UCL), straight from her doctoral studies with Chomsky at MIT. I was employed (in the departments of Africa and of Linguistics) at the School of Oriental and African Studies (SOAS), where there was some hostility to generative linguistics and to linguistic theory more generally. In the hope of finding an intellectual ally, I hastened to arrange a meeting. I had hoped, even expected, to find an ally; I hadn't expected to find someone who would act as a mentor, an inspiration and a friend for the rest of my life. Deirdre rapidly became the third major intellectual influence on my life as a linguist, forming a 'natural class' with Noam Chomsky and Jerry Fodor. At MIT I had been captivated by Chomsky's 'Remarks on nominalization'

I am grateful to Robyn Carston for her perceptive and helpful comments on the first draft of this preface. She is not responsible for remaining infelicities and misapprehensions.

(Chomsky 1970); later I was convinced of the innate basis of language by Fodor's *Language of Thought* hypothesis (Fodor 1975). The third strand in my development was provided by Deirdre.

Most work on language use had been suspicious of, hostile to and incompatible with work in generative grammar. Deirdre's work with Dan Sperber had, as one of its many virtues, explicit compatibility with contemporary Chomskyan linguistic theory. I was a rapid convert as I could finally see how to achieve an overarching view of what later became known as 'FLB' – the faculty of language in the broad sense (Hauser et al. 2002). Not long after getting my first glimpse of what such an integrated position might look like, Deirdre and I began to collaborate on producing an introductory book on *Modern Linguistics* (Smith & Wilson 1979). The task of collaborating with Deirdre on writing this book was formidable. I would spend weeks drafting and redrafting (part of) a chapter and then pass it on to her as 'just a very rough first draft', hoping it wouldn't be dismissed or ignored. Rather, my offerings always came back annotated with constructive suggestions, clearer explanations, and more cogent examples (on both interpretations of that phrase).

Apart from learning a lot of pragmatics and logic – blank spots in my previous education – I was systematically tutored in semantics (cf. Wilson 1975), in aspects of syntax (cf. Pullum & Wilson 1977), and in the need to integrate disparate ideas into a coherent whole. It is not generally known that Deirdre's first (linguistics) article 'If that' (Wilson 1970) gave 'a partial syntactic characterization of ... largely semantic facts' but simultaneously gave hints of the need for pragmatic considerations to be taken into account, while showing sensitivity to the subtlest nuances of language use. This sensitivity manifests itself not only in her injunction to co-authors to pay attention to matters stylistic – in particular to eschew clichés (something I have tried hard to do ever since), but also in her own felicitous phrases. An example which springs to mind is the 'warm lifebelt of words' from her first novel (Wilson 1991: 12).

I was not the only one to come under Deirdre's influence. As she and Dan developed relevance theory throughout the 1980s, she circulated drafts of their work to staff and students at UCL for comment. At the same time, she was teaching an array of degree courses in semantics and pragmatics, drawing out key ideas from Grice's work on 'conversational logic' and comparing them with the emerging relevance-based pragmatic theory. Grounded in cognitive science and developing a definition of 'relevance' based on notions of 'processing effort' and 'contextual effects', relevance theory provided a new dawn for the discipline. Because of Deirdre's brilliance as a teacher and communicator, pragmatics rapidly became a core subject in the BA and the MA Linguistics programmes, one which attracted large numbers of students fascinated by the richness of its insights. It promised explanations for communication and miscommunication, for non-literal uses of language (such as irony, metaphor, and hyperbole), for strong and weak implicatures, and most importantly, for how linguistic communication sits within a wider picture of the human mind, interfacing with the language faculty, perceptual capacities, theory of mind, and memory. This aspect of the UCL Linguistics degrees made them unique in the UK (in fact, in the world) and distinguished the department, already strong in syntax and phonology, from all other Linguistics departments.

As more complete drafts of the chapters of what was to be *Relevance: Communication and Cognition* became available, we formed the 'Relevance reading group', attended by staff and postgraduate students, who pored over and discussed every word of every version. This weekly group met for the next twenty-five years, evolving from a total focus on Dan and Deirdre's 1986 book (and later their 1995 *Postface*) to a wider array of pragmatics papers, both relevance-theoretic and other, as the field grew ever more prolific. As a result of this increasingly visible activity, UCL Linguistics became *the* place to go for students who wanted to pursue a doctorate in pragmatics, with Deirdre as their supervisor. They came from all over the world: Australia, China, Germany, Greece, Italy, Japan, Korea, Mexico, New Zealand, Norway, Spain, and the USA, as well as the UK, and many have gone on to have significant academic and research careers of their own. The dissertation topics Deirdre has supervised range from specific issues, such as the meaning and effects of sentence-final particles and discourse connectives, and the distinction between conceptual and procedural meaning, to general issues such as the explicit–implicit distinction, the mechanisms of non-literal language use, the nature of different textual genres, and even to issues that go beyond the usual disciplinary bounds of linguistics, such as the role of rationality in pragmatics, the communicative nature of translation, the dynamics of dialogic interaction, and the way in which verbal humour works. This remarkable record – a unique output from a Linguistics department – is due to Deirdre's drive and imagination; in a word, to her passion.

All this was in a gentler era when people had time for lunch, which provided the environment for heated, but amicable, discussions on anything from the nature of presuppositions and the status of transformations (meaning-preserving or not) in a generative grammar, to the desirability of arming the police and how to solve the problem of death. Deirdre had a solution for almost all the issues we debated and is still working on the others.

Even though Deirdre is an accomplished novelist (Wilson 1991), the core of her achievement is relevance theory, which 'offers nothing less than the makings of a radically new theory of communication, the first since Aristotle' (Fowler 1989: 16). Despite the entanglement point alluded to at the beginning, it is intriguing to look at those articles in which Deirdre's name appears first – on the assumption that when the alphabet is overridden this is a sign of who contributed most. The list includes: 'On Grice's theory of conversation'

(1981), 'Pragmatics and modularity' (1986), 'Mood and the analysis of non-declarative sentences' (1988a), 'Representation and relevance' (1988b), 'On verbal irony' (1992), 'Linguistic form and relevance' (1993), 'Pragmatics and time' (1998), 'Truthfulness and relevance' (2002), and on. She has, of course, also published many other papers, as lead author, with her former students and other colleagues (see, for instance, the list in Wilson & Sperber 2012).

It is time to turn to specific issues as I promised some remarks on the theory. Consider the topic of metarepresentation, the understanding of which has been greatly increased by Dan and Deirdre's work (e.g. Sperber 2000; Wilson 2000). Implicit in their work is an intricate interaction among the metarepresentational, the metalinguistic, and the metacommunicative (that is, the speaker's metarepresentation of thoughts to be conveyed and the audience's metarepresentation of the communicator's intentions, where this 'ability is a specialisation of the more general mindreading ability' (Wilson 2000: 414)). These three categories suggest that we carve up the domain as in the 'meta'-space in Table 1.

If correct, this suggests some modification of my own previous work, and an extension to wider domains. Ianthi Tsimpli and I have previously exploited relevance theory to explain some of the striking behaviour of the polyglot *savant* Christopher. We had characterised him (Smith & Tsimpli 1995: 74) as having problems with the relevance-theoretic notion of 'interpretive use', implicitly with anything metarepresentational, so that he fails to understand not only irony and sarcasm but a variety of other phenomena: lying, jokes, the use–mention distinction, pretence, metalinguistic negation, metaphor, rhetorical questions, and so on. Assuming the partition in Table 1, this is not quite right. Providing an example of each of the eight categories (where possible) will simultaneously provide a revised account of Christopher's (dis)abilities and some novel directions to pursue.

(1) describes simple cases of irony and sarcasm (where someone's words are echoed back to them with a dissociative attitude); (2) is illustrated by Christopher's parroting of a complete dialogue with no communicative intent – he is communicatively indifferent and his recitation of a (Greek) conversation was 'a purely linguistic exercise without any social component' (Smith & Tsimpli 1995: 176); (3) and (7) are excluded because metacommunication entails metarepresentation; (4), which accounts, in my view, for the alternation in some speakers between *pavement* and *sidewalk* or *bonnet* and *hood*, is excluded by relevance theory (cf. Sperber 2000) because it is not a representation of content. The remaining categories (5) and (6) point in new directions: (5) could pertain to 'targeted' musical pastiche, as in Grieg's *Holberg Suite*, and (6), which one could think of as 'untargeted' caricature, would describe Leonardo da Vinci's studies of people with deformities. (8) is, in one sense, 'outside the meta-space' but could pertain to ordinary non-verbal communication.

Table 1 *The 'meta'-space*

1	2	3	4	5	6	7	8	
+	+	+	+	-	-	-	-	Metalinguistic
+	+	-	-	+	+	-	-	Metarepresentational
+	-	+	-	+	-	+	-	Metacommunicative

The chapters which follow give some indication of the wealth and variety of the research stimulated by Deirdre and Dan's work. However, as a linguist, I would like to make a plea for more collaboration and cross-fertilisation between pragmatics and syntax. In this age of specialisation it is hard to keep up with any single domain, let alone more than one, but I think it is a pity that syntax has been relatively neglected in recent work in relevance theory.

I would like to mention briefly one case where the significance of the syntax–pragmatics interaction is evident. This is the phenomenon of sequence of tense, where the tense of the matrix sentence typically restricts the morphosyntactic tense of the embedded clause. This phenomenon exhibits 'particular pragmatic effects' which raise interesting issues regarding the relation between syntax and pragmatics (for discussion, see Cormack & Smith, in prep). For instance, an utterance of *John said Mary was pregnant* gives rise to an ambiguity: the time of the pregnancy is either now or at the time of John's speaking. This sequencing of tense is the default option, and for some speakers it is the *only* option. For some other speakers, however, including me, this is not the case. If I wish to endorse the current validity of John's assertion, I may suspend sequence of tense and produce: *John said Mary is pregnant*, a form which is simply ungrammatical for 'strict' speakers, even though it simultaneously disambiguates the utterance. Evidence that the suspension of sequence of tense indicates my endorsement of the current validity of John's assertion comes from the fact that where endorsement is impossible or anomalous, sequence of tense cannot be suspended – as when I try to endorse myself: contrast *I thought I was allowed to smoke now I'm 10* with the impossible **I thought I'm allowed to smoke now I'm 10*. The literature on tense is replete with rival and inconclusive claims as to whether such phenomena necessitate a 'pragmatic' treatment of sequence of tense, a syntactic one, or some combination (see e.g. Reichenbach 1947; Comrie 1985, 1986; Hornstein 1990; Declerck 1991). Such claims are often made in the absence of any explicit pragmatic framework. It is clear that different speakers have different grammars, so a syntactic treatment is inevitable. But the choice of which form to use – for those who have such a choice – is pragmatically determined. How these domains fit together needs more collaboration between syntacticians and pragmaticists.

Deirdre has an amazing range of talents, but she will be remembered most in the academic world for her development of relevance theory with Dan. They have been the inspiration for what you are about to read: work across linguistics, pragmatics, philosophy and cognitive science, on a range of languages, by experts from around the world. No one working in pragmatics, be that on figurative language, on evidentiality, on (meta-)representation, on mood, on polysemy, on acquisition, or even on the emotions, can afford to ignore their work. Syntacticians shouldn't either, but they need a warmer welcome. No one reading this volume would want to ignore it, even though the going sometimes demands extremely hard work. But the rewards are rich. Theodore Zeldin (Deirdre's husband) once remarked that breakfast with Deirdre was like having a daily tutorial. We should all have such tutors.

Deirdre need have no worry about the truth – and relevance – of the epigraph to this preface. She is a fine teacher, researcher, writer, thinker, communicator, linguist, pragmaticist, and more – ultimately, she is simply not categorisable.

Part I

Relevance Theory and Cognitive
Communicative Issues

1 Scientific Tractability and Relevance Theory

Nicholas Allott

1.1 Introduction

There is a widespread view that communication and language use more generally are too complex to study systematically and scientifically[1] (e.g. Putnam 1978; Fodor 1983; Chomsky 1992a,b and perhaps Davidson 1986). Here I suggest that three distinct arguments have been given for the view. The first, due to Fodor (1983), is that utterance interpretation is unencapsulated and holistic: any information may be relevant to working out what a speaker meant. We have, Fodor claims, no good theories of unencapsulated cognitive processes, and the prospects of developing any are dim.

The second argument comes from Chomsky: language use is a mystery because it is a species of human intentional action. He claims that we cannot develop naturalistic theories of such phenomena. In his view, human action is free, in the strong sense that it is not causally determined, and it is a mystery how this is compatible with its evident coherence and appropriateness to circumstances (Chomsky 1991: 40–1). The third argument, which can be found in Putnam, Chomsky, and perhaps Davidson, is that because many or even all of our mental faculties are simultaneously involved in utterance interpretation, it is too complex to study scientifically. As the claim is sometimes hyperbolically put, a theory of language use and communication would require, *per impossibile*, 'study of everything' (Chomsky 1992b: 103).

This chapter aims to examine and defuse these arguments, at least insofar as they pertain to theories of utterance interpretation and production seen as cognitive abilities. Of these, the account developed within Sperber and Wilson's relevance theory is the most fully articulated. From the outset, relevance theory has been in dialogue with scepticism about pragmatics, particularly that of Chomsky and Fodor, thinkers with whom it shares key assumptions. It adopts from Chomsky the aim of providing a fully explicit account of a cognitive capacity (Sperber & Wilson 1986/1995: 94) and from Fodor the Computational/

---

[1] What is meant by 'systematically and scientifically' will, I hope, become clear enough for present purposes in the course of the chapter.

Representational Theory of Cognition (Sperber and Wilson 1986/1995: 71–2).[2] Sperber and Wilson have replied to Fodor's argument explicitly (in their 1986/ 1995 and 1996 work);[3] in addition, to the extent that relevance theory's account of communication is successful, it is a challenge to all sceptical worries about the possibility of pragmatics.

While my own inclination is to think that relevance theory provides the most promising account of communication currently available, I remain as neutral as possible about that here. The arguments under consideration are meant to tell against all cognitive accounts of utterance interpretation and production, and I try to provide general, in-principle responses to them. I devote most attention to the third argument, in part because the first two have received critical attention elsewhere: the first from Sperber and Wilson (1986/1995, 1996), Carston (2002: 1–3), Wilson (2004), and Allott (2008); the second from Kasher (1991) and Allott (2008: 198ff.).

In Section 1.2 of this chapter I set out the three arguments in more detail and discuss some connections between them. In Section 1.3, I briefly summarise responses to the first two arguments. In Section 1.4, I give a somewhat fuller response to the third, 'interaction effect' argument. I note, first, that it has been essential to scientific progress to abstract away from real complications in order to frame law-like generalisations. Some special reason would need to be given for thinking that this 'Galilean style' of theorising should not apply in pragmatics, but what little has been said on the topic is unconvincing. Both extant pragmatic theories and work on heuristics in cognition more generally suggest that fruitful generalisations are being found. An argument that there can be no modelling or prediction of a certain sphere of human activity is obviously in trouble if as a matter of fact such modelling and prediction is being successfully carried out. I briefly review evidence that has been accumulating in recent decades that bears out one key prediction of relevance-theoretic pragmatics, concerning the extreme context-sensitivity of even the most common pragmatic inferences, thus lending support to its assumptions, and to the general project of cognitive theories of utterance interpretation.

1.2   The Arguments against Pragmatics

In this section I set out in more detail the three arguments against the possibility of systematic study of language use and communication. All three

---

[2] Carston writes, 'The relevance-theoretic framework developed in the 1980s by Dan Sperber and Deirdre Wilson can be seen as a response to the challenge presented by these sceptics' (2002: 2) i.e. Chomsky, Davidson, and Fodor, *inter alia*.

[3] They write 'It seems, then, that our undertaking – and the whole pragmatic enterprise if our understanding of it is correct – should fall (and we use the word advisedly) under Fodor's First Law of the Nonexistence of Cognitive Science' (Sperber & Wilson 1986/1995: 66).

aim to show that pragmatics is intractable at present, and, most likely, in principle.[4]

1.2.1   Argument 1: Interpretation Is Unencapsulated

Fodor (1983) distinguishes between central and peripheral systems, where peripheral systems such as the visual system process information from sensory transducers in a rather fixed, reflex-like manner, uninfluenced by general beliefs (he calls this last property 'encapsulation'), while the hallmark of central cognition, which includes general reasoning and decision-making, is its ability to integrate information from many sources, including memory, the senses, and testimony.

Utterance interpretation appears to be a species of central belief fixation, and as such it falls under Fodor's First Law of the Non-Existence of Cognitive Science. That is, 'The more global ... a cognitive process is, the less anybody understands it' (Fodor 1983: 107). By 'global', Fodor means at least 'isotropic' and 'Quinean'. A process of reasoning is isotropic if information from any domain may be relevant to the conclusion, and Quinean if the metric for a good solution is global: e.g. in deciding whether to believe a proposition one should take into account its effect on the overall simplicity and coherence of one's whole belief system. Scientific theorising is taken as a paradigm case of central cognition (Fodor 1983: 104, 2005: 27). Its isotropy is demonstrated by such cases as the relevance of the rate of cooling of the sun to Darwin's theory of evolution (Carruthers 2003), or of rabbit designs on native American pots to the astrophysics of supernovae (Antony 2003).

The task of working out what someone meant on the basis of what noises/ gestures they made also seems to be isotropic. Just about any belief can affect the interpretation of an utterance. For example, whom one takes the speaker to be referring to with 'he' in an utterance of the sentence in (1.1) may depend on information about the prevalence of corruption in the local police force.[5]

(1.1)   A policeman arrested John yesterday; he had just taken a bribe.
         (cf. Recanati 2004: 32)

1.2.2   Argument 2: Intentional Action Is a Mystery

A second argument against the possibility of scientific study of language use and communication is less well known. Chomsky divides questions into

---

[4] A more careful treatment than I have space for here would more clearly distinguish claims about what is feasible now from the in-principle arguments.

[5] Or, more accurately, information about the speaker's beliefs (about the hearer's beliefs etc.) about such corruption.

problems – those which are currently amenable to systematic study – and mysteries, those which are not (Chomsky 1991; Smith & Allott 2016: 203, 368 n.18). He argues that language use is a mystery because it is a type of intentional action, and human intentional action is free in the strong sense that it is not causally determined. In his view, humans, unlike machines, are only 'incited and inclined' towards certain actions, not 'compelled' to perform them (Chomsky 1991: 40), and we will therefore never be able to develop theories of human action: 'theories of behaviour will always miss the crucial point: the person could have chosen to act otherwise' (Chomsky 1996: 17). This is reflected in scientists' current practice, he claims: 'issues of will and choice ... are not even on the agenda'; 'no one even raises the question of why this plan is executed rather than some other one, except for the very simplest organisms' (Chomsky 2002: 58).[6]

Recent work on attention provides an illustration of this point. People have some conscious control over attention: 'even without moving our eyes, we can focus our attention on different objects at will, resulting in very different perceptual experiences of the same visual field. The phrase "at will" points to an area beyond serious empirical inquiry' (Chomsky 2002: 58–9). That is, the effects of consciously shifting attention can be and have been studied (e.g. Beck & Lavie 2004), but such work does not aim to provide a theory of the choice of locus of attention. Rather, participants are typically asked to attend to one part of a screen, and the effects of their doing so are measured.

There *are* studies of the capture of attention, where the location of attention is for a period of time not under conscious control (e.g. Dalton & Lavie 2004; Lavie & De Fockert 2005). It is an aim of this work to discover the causes of attention capture. But this tends rather to make Chomsky's point than otherwise, since apparently it is only when attention is *not* under conscious control that scientists try to discover the factors that govern its location. The parallel with language use is that production of utterances is stimulus-independent: a speaker can choose to say anything or nothing (a commonplace of linguistics since Chomsky's famous [1959] review of Skinner).

1.2.3   Argument 3: Use of Language Is an Interaction Effect

The third argument is that the interpretation of utterances 'cannot be studied in practice' and 'is not a topic of empirical enquiry' (Chomsky 1992b: 120) because it involves many or even all the capacities of the mind and we cannot

---

[6] See also Chomsky (1975: 25).

(at present at least) study the mind as a totality. It is worth quoting Chomsky at length here:

There is ... a ... problem, which we can formulate in vague terms but which cannot be studied in practice: namely to construct an 'interpreter' which includes the parser as a component, along with all other capacities of the mind – whatever they may be – and accepts non-linguistic as well as linguistic input. The interpreter, presented with an utterance and a situation, assigns some interpretation to what is being said by a person in this situation. The study of communication in the actual world of experience is the study of the interpreter, but this is not a topic of empirical enquiry for the usual reasons: there is no such topic as the study of everything ... the proper conclusion is not that we must abandon concepts of language that can be productively studied, but that the topic of successful communication in the actual world of experience is far too complex and obscure to merit attention in empirical inquiry. (Chomsky 1992b: 120)

Similar views have been expressed by Putnam, and perhaps Davidson, as I explain below.

This argument is obviously related to Fodor's above, but is, I think, logically independent. That a process of belief fixation is or should be isotropic and Quinean does not entail that the majority (or predominant part) of one's mental faculties are involved in it. Nor does the involvement of the majority of one's mental faculties in some task entail that the task one is performing either is or should be isotropic or Quinean. Likewise (and more obviously), this third argument is logically independent of the claim that free will and mental causation are mysteries.

Hilary Putnam has also claimed that language use is not currently investigable because it involves human cognition as a whole. In his view, 'language speaking is [a] paradigm example' of a human ability that: 'may not be theoretically explicable in isolation. It is almost certainly impossible to "model" a language speaker without modelling full human functional organization. But the latter may well be unintelligible to humans when stated in any detail!' (Putnam 1978: 65).[7] The reason for this unintelligibility, according to Putnam, is the structured complexity of the mind: 'Human functional organization evolved over one to two million years. There is no reason it must have a description that would fit into one book, or even into the Bodleian Library' (Putnam 1978: 64).

---

[7] See also Chomsky's discussion of Putnam's views (Chomsky 1992a: 205ff.). While he endorses Putnam's general conclusion: that ' "language speaking" and other human abilities do not currently fall within naturalistic inquiry' he describes it as 'understated and not quite properly formulated' (Chomsky 1992a: 206), part of his complaint being that 'language speaking' and 'human being' are 'concepts of common-sense understanding', and scientific theories will not incorporate common-sense notions (Chomsky 1992a: 206).

1.2.4   Davidson's View

Davidson, in his famous paper on malapropisms (1986), appears to argue against the possibility of a systematic theory of utterance interpretation (as noted by Chomsky 1992b: 108–9 and Carston 2002: 1). However, his argument (if it is successful) establishes only that interpretation depends in general on world knowledge and general beliefs as well as stable word meanings and rules of grammar. This is hardly controversial among pragmatic theorists; further argumentation would be needed to establish the conclusion that interpretation cannot be studied.

Davidson points out that speakers and hearers can coordinate on meanings even when words are used idiosyncratically, e.g. *monogamy*, where 'monotony' was meant. His conclusion is that *if* we assume that knowing a language is sufficient for communication 'we have erased the boundary between knowing a language and knowing our way around in the world generally' (Davidson 1986: 265). He suggests giving up this conception of language.

Davidson's conclusion is common ground with pragmatic theorists, who view interpretation as inference informed (but by no means determined) by linguistic decoding (a view implied by Grice's work [1989] and explored in detail by relevance theory: [Sperber and Wilson 1986/1995: 2–15, 21–8, 1987a: 697–9]). One looks in vain in Davidson's paper for a further argument that studying such inference is impossible. He suggests the involvement in interpretation of 'wit, luck, and wisdom ... knowledge of the ways people get their point across, and rules of thumb for figuring out what deviations from the dictionary are most likely' and asserts that the process cannot be regularised, comparing it with 'the process of creating new theories to cope with new data in any field' (p. 265). Presumably, then, Davidson would endorse an argument like Fodor's, and there are also hints here of the third, 'interaction effect', argument, but he does not develop either.

1.2.5   Summary: What Can Be Studied?

What is regarded as a good domain for theory construction varies across the thinkers we have been considering. Putnam's view is the most sweeping: 'in practice and ... quite possibly in principle' we cannot study human beings 'the way we study hydrogen atoms' because phenomena of our thought and behaviour involve the whole mind and this is too complex to allow for prediction or explanation (Putnam 1978: 64).

Both Fodor and Chomsky are more optimistic, arguing that we can study some mental phenomena by 'isolat[ing] coherent systems that are amenable to naturalistic inquiry and that interact to yield some aspects of the full complexity' (Chomsky 1992a: 214). On Chomsky's influential view, progress in the study of language requires abstracting away from the bulk of *use* of language ('performance') to focus primarily on the underlying grammatical 'competence' and secondarily on certain tightly constrained performance systems that make use of it, such as the parser, i.e. the device that takes a transduced string of speech sounds as input and produces a structural representation of a sentence. Fodor's argument suggests that the performance systems that can be studied are those that are encapsulated. He takes these to be 'peripheral' systems including various perceptual and motor systems and the parser, on the assumption that their operation is independent of general knowledge. More subtly, if there are top-down influences on peripheral systems, those who are in general agreement with Fodor's argument might say that the systems can, nonetheless, be studied to the extent that one can abstract away from such influences.

1.3   Discussion of the First Two Arguments

1.3.1   Discussion of Fodor's Argument

Fodor's argument is certainly worth taking seriously, and it has been very influential. However, there is considerable consensus that it conflates normative and descriptive considerations.[8] It might be true that decision-making and belief fixation *ought* to be isotropic and Quinean, at least if we abstract away from limits of time and mental capacity.[9] But this does not at all establish whether human inferential processing in any given domain is in fact holistic, which is presumably an empirical question.

Sperber and Wilson point to two disanalogies between scientific confirmation and utterance interpretation which suggest that the latter is a great deal less open ended (Sperber & Wilson 1986/1995: 66–7, see also Sperber & Wilson 1996; Carston 2002: 1–3). First, utterance interpretation is fast, starting during the utterance and typically concluding a few hundred milliseconds after the utterance ends. This strongly suggests that a lot of information that *might* have been considered is not used at all.

---

[8] See, e.g., Wilson (2004).
[9] Sperber and Wilson (1996: 531) question this abstraction:

> By Fodor's criterion of rationality, since we fail to consider all the relevant evidence, we are … irrational … [W]ould you *want* to be rational in his sense? Do you want to consider all the (internally and externally) available evidence every time you fix a belief – which still would not guarantee that all your beliefs would be true, but would guarantee that you would fix much fewer of them? Fodor's rationality is a purely epistemic matter: the only utility is truth, and no price is too high to pay to increase the chances that your beliefs are true … A kind of rationality worth having is one based on sound accounting principles, where not only benefits, but also costs are weighed.

Second, the input is from a helpful source, a human being acting as a communicator – that is, someone who wants to be understood and will therefore devise her utterance so that it is a good clue to her intended meaning. Sperber and Wilson postulate that human beings have a comprehension heuristic, a fast and frugal mechanism which exploits this fact (Sperber & Wilson 1986/1995: 45, 2002; Wilson & Sperber 2004). It does not search for all potentially relevant information but treats the mental accessibility of information in a context as a (fallible) indication of its significance (Sperber 2000: 132).[10] The heuristic evaluates potential interpretations in order of accessibility, and 'locally', i.e. as a function of immediate consequences for the belief system, not in terms of the effect on overall coherence or simplicity. (For more detail, and discussion of Sperber and Wilson's arguments that this system is ecologically rational, see Allott 2013).

Note that, as a response to Fodor's argument, it does not matter whether or not the details of current relevance theory (or any other pragmatic theory) turn out to be correct. Fodor has to show that nothing of this kind could work, and that is a hard case to make, particularly given the ongoing successes of work on efficient heuristics (Gigerenzer & Todd 1999; Gigerenzer et al. 2011) and fast 'system 1' thought (Evans 2008; Kahneman 2011) in several domains of cognition.

1.3.2   Discussion of the Argument from Freedom of the Will

Chomsky appears to rest his argument about the impossibility of studying voluntary action on his controversial view that human actions are not causally determined. A more mainstream take on free will is that free acts must be rationally chosen and that this implies that all the relevant steps leading to the act are rationally caused. This entails some form of compatibilism, the view that the freedom of the will is compatible with causal determination of actions (Hobart 1934; Davidson 1970).[11]

A perhaps more compelling aspect of Chomsky's scepticism about theories of communicative acts is his claim that we lack understanding of how human action comes to be coherent and appropriate to circumstances across an indefinitely wide range of circumstances (Chomsky 1991: 40–1).[12] This

---

[10] In communication, this is justified by the speaker's interest in being understood, but Sperber and Wilson argue that in the areas for which human cognition is well adapted, true assumptions are more likely to seem relevant than false ones (Sperber & Wilson 1986/1995: 116–7, read in the light of their [1995: 263–6] redefinition of relevance), and that '[i]f that is so, then Fodor's suggestion that scientific thinking can be taken as typical of central thought processes is dead wrong' (Sperber & Wilson 1986/1995: 117).

[11] An anonymous reviewer points out that Chomsky's view that actions are not causally determined is compatible with compatibilism. This is correct, but I suspect that he adopted his view (in part, at least) because he takes free will to preclude mental causation.

[12] My thanks to John Collins (p.c.) for making this point clear to me.

claim could be developed into equivalents for human voluntary action of argument 1 or argument 3. Indeed Rey, commenting on Chomsky's view, suggests that a better explanation of difficulties in studying voluntary action might be something like the third argument: 'Voluntary action may be merely a complex *interaction* effect, like the *actual* activity of a machine, or the precise path of a leaf in a lake, about which, indeed, general systematic theorising or prediction may be quite idle' (Rey 2003: 130 n.16, his italics).

Even if Chomsky were right both that voluntary actions are not causally determined and that they are *therefore* beyond normal scientific explanation, it's not clear how much of a problem this would be for pragmatic theorising, for two reasons. First, most work in pragmatics concerns interpretation of utterances. The task is to explain how a hearer works out what the speaker meant by her utterance, drawing on linguistic ability, world knowledge, and beliefs about the context. Interpretation is obviously a different task from production of utterances, as Chomsky notes (1991: 40). It is not a voluntary action (and perhaps not an action at all): when you hear an utterance in a language that you understand, you generally cannot help interpreting it.[13]

One of Chomsky's arguments for his views about free will is the phenomenology of voluntary action: it is, he thinks, just obvious that one could do something other than what one actually does.[14] This at least doesn't apply to utterance interpretation, where the phenomenology is quite different. Chomsky's scepticism about theories of interpretation rests instead on the 'interaction effect' argument (1991: 40).

One might also think that the *production* of utterances could be factored into two conceptually (if not temporally) distinct components: first, choosing what to try to convey and second, selection of a means to do so. Insofar as voluntary action is mysterious, the mystery might be confined to the first of these elements. Pragmatic theorists interested in production could then study the second (Kasher 1991: 141).

1.4   Pragmatics and the Galilean Style

The third argument is that language use cannot be studied scientifically because it is a massive interaction effect, and so a theory of language use would need to be a 'theory of everything'. In this section I argue that this claim is in conflict with reasonable views about the role of abstraction in science.

---

[13] Sperber and Wilson take this to speak in favour of their view that there is an utterance-interpretation module, that is, a task-specific, autonomous mental unit whose action is triggered by stimuli that fall within its task domain (Sperber & Wilson 2002).

[14] In an interview he said, 'Free will is simply an obvious aspect of human experience. I know – as much as I know that you're in front of me right now – that I can take my watch and throw it out the window if I feel like it' (Chomsky 1983).

It has been crucial to the progress of science that scientists abstract away from most of the complications of actual phenomena in order to get at interesting regularities and laws. Insight into some phenomenon is prioritised over coverage of all. Ironically, some of the clearest and most trenchant statements of this view are due to Chomsky, who calls it 'the Galilean style' (following Weinberg 1976; Chomsky 1978a: 9–10, 1978b: 14, 1980: 218, 2002: 98–100),[15] for instance: 'The great successes of the modern natural sciences can be attributed to the pursuit of explanatory depth which is very frequently taken to outweigh empirical inadequacies. This is the real intellectual revolution of the seventeenth century' (Chomsky 1978a: 9–10).

So, for example, Galileo ignored air resistance in framing his laws of motion, and was right to do so. Any attempt at stating laws which tried to cover all the actual phenomena of the motion Galileo or anyone else observed would have been a hopeless mess. According to John Losee's historical survey of the philosophy of science: 'much of Galileo's success in physics may be attributed to his ability to bracket out various empirical complications in order to work with ideal concepts such as "free fall in a vacuum", "ideal pendulum", and the "frictionless motion of a ship through the ocean"' (Losee 1980: 59).[16] This kind of abstraction may well be essential to science. At the very least, we find it at the centre of a number of striking successes of modern science, from Galileo to the ideal gas law and Chomsky's work on grammatical competence. What Losee calls 'ideal concepts' are central: there is no requirement that we can ever see the law or regularity in operation in perfect isolation from the complications that we have abstracted away from. There are no ideal gases, and linguistic competence is not manifested in the absence of performance systems.[17]

The ontological status of the laws and other generalisations reached by abstraction is a matter of debate. Views range from Nancy Cartwright's famous claim that they are false (albeit often useful and interesting) (Cartwright 1983), to Chomsky's view that 'it is the abstract systems that you are constructing that are really the truth; the array of phenomena is some distortion of the truth because of too many factors' (Chomsky 2002: 99). Similarly, the physicist Steven Weinberg claims that physicists (presumably including himself) 'give a higher degree of reality [to] abstract mathematical models of the universe ... than they accord the ordinary world of sensation'.[18] Whatever the ontological

---

[15] Weinberg cites Husserl (Weinberg 1976: 28; Chomsky 2002: 98–9). See also Botha (1982).

[16] For discussion of idealisation in Galileo's work, see also McMullin (1985).

[17] Indeed, for all we presently know, 'the world [could be] interaction effects all the way down, maybe even in fundamental physics' (Georges Rey p.c.).

[18] For Weinberg and Chomsky, the Galilean style includes this metaphysical claim about levels of reality. I prefer to use the term more broadly as a label for ways of doing science that work on the assumption that abstraction is (often) essential to progress in science.

status of scientific laws, the argument that phenomena characterised by inter-action effects cannot be studied seems at odds with how science has been suc-cessfully practised. Science is both more opportunistic and more various than the argument seems to give it credit for.[19] Scientists fasten onto whatever scien-tific laws, generalisations, abstractions, and idealisations – of varying degrees of depth and generality – will do explanatory work.

Recall that the reason Putnam gives that 'language speaking … may not be theoretically explicable in isolation' is that '[i]t is almost certainly impossible to "model" a language speaker without modelling full human functional organ-ization' (Putnam 1978: 65). It is obviously crucial what he means by 'model' here, and this is not entirely clear. As noted above, the intended contrast is with the way that it is possible to model hydrogen atoms. But it's not clear why the demand should be to model a language *speaker* as a whole rather than to model some processes or system that underlie language use, or still less ambitiously, not to model them but simply to capture some regularities of their workings.

This issue is less clear in Chomsky's comments on pragmatics, but when he says that '[t]he study of communication in the actual world of experience is the study of the interpreter' (Chomsky 1992b: 120), he seems to define it in a way that precludes scientific abstraction as he conceives of it. Elsewhere in the same paper he argues that phenomena in the actual world are in general not the target of explanatory work because they are far too complex, even in the case of the motion of one body: 'it is no part of physics to determine exactly how a particular body moves under the influence of every particle or force in the universe, with possible human intervention, and so on. This is not a topic' (Chomsky 1992b: 102).

Perhaps there is a way to defend the 'interaction effect' argument against the charge that it neglects the role of abstraction, however. One could take the claim to be that some phenomena, including pragmatics, are not underpinned by any one system and that these, therefore, cannot be fruitfully studied. The idea would be that idealisation is required but here abstracting away from the complications will not reveal any underlying core that is simple and law-like. It would be a considerable stretch to construe Putnam's view this way, but it seems a more charitable way to take Chomsky's remarks about pragmatics, given his espousal of the Galilean style. It may also be a reasonable interpret-ation of Davidson's scepticism about theories of interpretation.

But this way of construing the objection to pragmatics recasts it not so much as an *argument* that the study of language use is hopeless, but as a *hunch* that it will turn out that way, on the basis that it will turn out to lack a law-like core. No doubt, hunches of this sort can be useful. Scientists are often productively

---

[19] On the heterogeneity of science (and the world), see Dupré (1993); Cartwright (1999).

guided in their activities by their gut feelings about which areas of investigation will be fruitful. But such hunches provide no objective basis to dismiss a field of study.

To summarise: I have suggested that there are two ways of construing the 'interaction effect' argument and that both run into problems. At base, the issue is that science is in the business of finding underlying regularities by abstracting away from complexity, and it's hard to make an a priori case that there are no interesting regularities to be found in a certain area. Scientists can follow their hunches, but they have to be prepared to be surprised by results.

No doubt cognition is complex and involves many interlinked systems, but the successes of work on fast and frugal heuristics and system 1 thought are relevant here (as they were to Fodor's argument). They are, as it were, proofs of concept: cases where simple principles have been successfully factored out of the messy totality of human cognition. As noted above, relevance theory claims that such a heuristic underlies utterance interpretation and postulates principles that govern its operation. Rival, neo-Gricean pragmatic theories also propose (other) principles and heuristics. Their concern with default pragmatic inferences and those connected to the use of particular linguistic items (Sperber & Wilson 2005: 471–2) is a different focus, but no less an abstraction.

1.4.1   Some Successful Predictions

In recent decades the field of experimental pragmatics has emerged (from theoretical pragmatics, psycholinguistics, and the psychology of reasoning, *inter alia*) and bloomed (Noveck & Sperber 2004; Breheny 2011; Phelan 2014). As in other areas of experimental psychology, predictions are made on the basis of theory and tested. Obviously its practitioners act on the basis that there are regularities in language use that can be studied.[20]

There has by now been far too much work to summarise here. I discuss only one high-level property of interpretation that has emerged from a number of studies: pragmatic inference is highly context sensitive in the sense that there are apparently no default implicatures.

Grice's ground-breaking work on conversation (Grice 1967[1989]) is agnostic about the order of processing. Prominent neo-Gricean accounts (e.g. Gazdar 1979; Atlas & Levinson 1981; Horn 1989) predict that there are 'default' implicatures which are generated in interpretation where a certain

[20] My focus here on evidence from experiments is not meant to imply that it is the only or the best evidence. There is no obvious limit on sources of evidence in science. As in other areas of linguistics, speaker intuitions have been important in pragmatics (Drożdżowicz 2015, 2016). (But see Breheny (2011: 562–3) for an argument that in pragmatics, experimental results are more reliable than intuitions.)

word or construction is used, even when they are not speaker-intended. Hearers have to generate them and then suppress them in such cases. For example, these accounts treat (1.2b) as a default implicature of (1.2a):

(1.2)   a. Some of these penguins have suitcases.
          b. Not all of these penguins have suitcases.

Sperber and Wilson's relevance theory makes opposite predictions: there are no strong defaults, and from the beginning of hearers' processing of utterances, it is sensitive to the intentions of the speaker. So, for example, in a context in which the speaker is known to have only partial knowledge, a hearer of an utterance of (1.2a) will not generate (1.2b).

Breheny, summarising a slew of work on the topic, argues that it shows that the strong defaultist view is untenable: 'even apparently common implicatures are not generated solely on the basis of linguistic context in on-line comprehension' (Breheny 2011: 566). Recent work has shown that 'at an earl[y] stage in processing, participants are sensitive to what the purpose of the utterance is and that they are aware of more informative alternatives' (Breheny 2011: 568). Of course, relevance theory is not the only possible or conceivable theory that would make these predictions. But actual rivals have either made no clear prediction or predicted the opposite.

In philosophy of science there is considerable agreement that predictive successes of a theory lend support to those of its theoretical posits that are essential to the predictions, although it is controversial what it takes for a theoretical posit to be essential.[21] There is no space here for discussion of which of the posits of relevance theory are supported by the experimental results mentioned above. What is crucial in the context of this chapter is that regardless of their implications for particular pragmatic theories, such predictive successes shift the burden against claims that systematic investigation of communicative language use is impossible.

Acknowledgements

It is an honour to be able to offer this chapter as a small indication of the great debt of gratitude that I owe to Deirdre Wilson for her inspiration, support, and encouragement over many years.

The content of the chapter has been considerably improved by comments from John Collins, Georges Rey, the audience at my talk at the CSMN closing conference in May 2017, an anonymous reviewer, and the editors of this volume: Robyn Carston, Billy Clark, and Kate Scott. My thanks to them all.

---

[21] Peters (2014) provides a useful recent review of the debate.

2   Language Processing, Relevance and Questions

Richard Breheny

2.1   Introduction

Sperber and Wilson (1986/1995) propose an account of concepts such as
focus and background in terms of on-line processing of linguistic structure.
The theory is that language processing systems anticipate how an utterance is
intended to be relevant and that stress placement can impact on such anticipatory processes. This *process-oriented* approach sheds light on the link between
the *Question–Answer congruence* constraint on focus, on the one hand, and the
Givenness constraint for post-focus material, on the other. The relation between
these phenomena is still a current issue in focus research (see Büring 2007,
2016). In Section 2.2, I will review why I think an approach which appeals to
anticipatory processes remains promising.

   In the 1980s, research on anticipation in language processing was still
inchoate and had been limited to anticipation of aspects of the form of
sentences uttered. Although much subsequent psycholinguistic research has
more extensively demonstrated the operation of anticipation in language
processes, it has extended the focus almost exclusively to anticipating
utterance content. Only relatively recently has psycholinguistic research
actually considered whether language processes anticipate the intended
source of relevance for the utterance – its intended context. In Section 2.3,
I review this recent work and argue that it points to an important role for
the very kind of processes Sperber and Wilson postulated. I will highlight
potential implications for research on negation processing and referential
processing. In Section 2.4, I turn to the question of what this new work says
about how the source of relevance is represented in utterance processing.
A currently popular idea is that discourse or conversation is structured
by Questions Under Discussion (QUDs) and that relevance is defined in
terms of QUDs (Roberts 1996/2012; van Kuppevelt 1996; Ginzburg 2012).
Alternatives to this view can be found in relevance theory and elsewhere
(see Carnap 1950; van Rooy 2003; Russell 2012). Although somewhat preliminary, our evidence speaks against a basic implementation of the idea that
representations of context take the form of questions. The chapter closes

with a brief discussion of what it might mean to describe utterance context in terms of a question.

2.2   A Link between Language Processing and Focus/Background

It is now a given in psycholinguistic research that utterance stimuli are processed incrementally for information about what the likely syntactic structure and semantic content will be (MacDonald et al. 1994; Levy 2008). It is also well established that not only linguistic information in the stimulus but also information from context affects parsing decision processes (Altmann & Steedman 1988). For example, the string *put the apple on* has a favoured parse according to which the preposition *on* forms part of the second, location, argument of the verb *put*. However, when there are two apples in the visual context, participants show a reversal of this default preference to a parse where the preposition forms part of a modificational structure (Tanenhaus et al. 1995). Although this is an impressive demonstration that contextual information can impact at different levels of the parse, this research focuses on how current input (*on*) fits into the sentence being uttered. Beyond such backward-looking processes, it has also been established that anticipatory inferences are generated given current evidence. For example, participants anticipate an edible object in a visual display after hearing *the boy will eat...* more than after *the boy will move...* (Altmann & Kamide 1999). Similarly, participants integrate background knowledge to anticipate a motorcycle rather than a carousel after *the man will ride...* and vice versa after *the girl will ride...* (Kamide et al. 2003 – see also van Berkum et al. 2005). The latter results demonstrate a virtuous interaction between input, context and anticipation: stimuli like *man* and *ride* activate contextual information (in this case, from encyclopaedic memory), which feeds into anticipation of likely referents, and so forth.

In their account of the focus–background distinction, Sperber and Wilson (1986/1995) postulate that comprehenders use linguistic form and activated contextual representations to anticipate how the speaker intends the utterance to be relevant. Their approach to how focal stress determines informational 'focus' is built around the idea that a focal scale is created in the course of processing a sentence. For example, parsing (2.1a) involves first encountering *Alice*, when some tentative hypotheses are generated about the syntactic and referential properties of this expression, as illustrated in (2.1b). Sperber and Wilson propose that this stimulus prompts some anticipatory hypotheses about the continuation of the syntactic structure and propositional content. The latter would take the form of assumption schemas. For example, in the absence of other information, parsing the first word of (2.1a) might give rise

to a hypothesis about the continuation in (2.1c), where *P* is a kind of conceptual variable:

(2.1)   a. Alice kissed Bruce$_F$.
        b. Syn: [$_{DP}$ Alice], Sem: *Alice Liddell*
        c. Syn: [$_{IP}$[$_{DP}$ Alice][$_{I'}$…]], Sem: *P(Alice Liddell)*
        d. Syn: [$_{IP}$[$_{DP}$ Alice][$_{I'}$[kissed][$_{DP}$…]]], Sem: *Q(λx.kissed'*
           (x)(Alice Liddell))

In Sperber and Wilson's relevance theory (RT), the input up until this point
will impact on activated contextual representations. Activated contextual
representations, in turn, serve as the likely source of relevance for the intended
explicature (input proposition). If, for the sake of convenience, we describe how
utterances achieve relevance in terms of what question they address, then the
assumption schema in (2.1c) corresponds to the question 'What about Alice?'

When we come to the second element of the string, *kissed*, we get hypotheses about the syntactic properties and intended interpretation of the verb, and
some anticipatory hypotheses, as in (2.1d). In this case, the assumption schema
corresponds to 'Who did Alice kiss?'. The final element of the string (marked
with subscript 'F' to indicate prosodic prominence – described in ToBI anno-
tation as H* or L+H*, followed by a boundary tone, %) comes as an answer to
this last question. When prosody has this somewhat canonical shape, Sperber
and Wilson observe that the so-called scope of focus could be narrow (the constituent *[Bruce]*) if only the final assumption achieves relevance in the activated
context. However, if Alice's potentially kissing someone is relevant, i.e. the
second assumption schema is itself relevant, then the perceived 'new' part of the
sentence is the verb phrase. The pairings of syntactic and semantic anticipatory
hypotheses outlined in (2.1c–d) constitute what Sperber and Wilson call a focal
scale for this sentence. In contrast to this *stress-based* account of focus, featural
accounts (e.g. Selkirk 1984) assume that a grammatical Focus feature may project to higher nodes in the tree. Where *kissing Bruce* is deemed new information
in the context, both the object DP and VP are marked with a focus feature.

Were intonational prominence to fall on the verb instead of the complement,
as in (2.2), intuition suggests that this better fits with a context where the relation between Alice and Bruce is in some way at issue in the context. Sperber
and Wilson's proposal is that sentence-medial focal stress can impact on sentence processing by altering the focal scale. Thus, while the decisions about the
category and reference of the subject given the input *Alice* remain the same,
(2.2b), the only anticipatory hypothesis for (2.2a) is as in (2.2c).

(2.2)   a. Alice kissed$_F$ Bruce
        b. Syn: [$_{DP}$ Alice], Sem: *Alice Liddell*
        c. Syn: [$_{IP}$[$_{DP}$ Alice][$_{I'}$V [$_{DP}$Bruce]]], Sem: *R(Bruce Berry)*
           (Alice Liddell)

As I observe in Breheny (1996, 1998), when this is the effect that focal stress has on the focal scale, the listener ought to be able to anticipate the source of relevance given the input prior to the focally stressed element. This means that an issue relating Alice to Bruce would be, in some sense, inferable at the mention of Alice. A further implication of this account is that it explains the observation that material following a single focally stressed element should be 'Given' (see Schwarzschild 1999; Büring 2007, 2016).

This kind of stress-based account has better coverage than grammatical-feature accounts in cases where medial focus information is complex. For example, (2.3 B) is used where *plotting to kiss* is intuitively 'new' information in the context of (2.3 A). The only options that a feature projection system allows are focus on [*kiss*], [*kiss him*] or [*plotting to kiss him*], none of which satisfy the Question–Answer congruence requirement (Büring 2007).[1]

(2.3)   A: What's the deal with Alice and Bruce?
          B: She is plotting to kiss$_F$ him.

A clear implication of this RT approach to focal stress is that one need not analyse it in linguistic-featural terms. But if not, then at what level of description does this account work? Or, where do these focal scales come from? To address this question, we can move forward in time to more recent work on intonation in the RT framework, which has explored the roots of intonational meaning (Wilson & Wharton 2006). In that work, focal stress intonation is seen as signalling a greater interest or effect when producing the stimulus. If we assume this account of the underlying meaning of focal stress, focal scales could be a by-product of the processing of this signal by probabilistic mechanisms that operate in the parser (see e.g. Levy 2008). That is, a typical or likely precondition for placing stress on an expression would be that it is the most 'informative'[2] among neighbouring words, and that would typically be because it completes a highly accessible assumption schema, or, as it were, answers an accessible question. Of course, being process-oriented, this approach implies there can be exceptions, as where two forms are stressed in a sentence (2.4), or where the element that is

---

[1] In Breheny (1998) I discuss how examples related to (2.3) also pose problems for Reinhart's (1995) stress-based account.

[2] In recent probabilistic approaches to language processing, 'informativity' is analysed in terms of surprisal, which is defined in terms of likelihood (see Levy 2008). It is unclear, however, whether all concepts in language processing should be reduced to probabilistic terms (see Jones & Love 2011). Informativity here could be analysed in terms of warranting greater attention. It is an open question whether attention (and related notions like, 'activation') can be analysed purely in information-theoretic terms.

stressed is clearly of great interest, despite the sentence meaning being 'all news', as in (2.5):

(2.4)   A: What's the deal with the Minister and her assistant?
          B: She's denying$_F$ she slept$_F$ with him.

(2.5)   Nixon$_F$ died.

2.3   Inferring Source of Relevance On-Line

As described above, the RT approach to phenomena like focus assumed that hypotheses about the source of relevance for an utterance are made in incremental processing. At the time of Sperber and Wilson (1986/1995), this assumption was necessarily speculative as no experimental research was available to support it. In this section, I will briefly review more recent research that does support this assumption. I will focus on work with negation and clefting, but also mention evidence taken from other domains.

A consistent finding from psycholinguistic research into negation is that negative sentences are somewhat more difficult or 'costly' than their positive counterparts. Negative sentences take longer to process or verify, and cause more errors (Wason 1961; Gough 1966; Clark & Chase 1972; Carpenter & Just 1975). One approach locates the cost of negation in terms of processes required to contextualise negative sentences (Wason 1965; Nieuwland & Kuperberg 2008), another argues that negative sentences require an extra step of processing, since the positive argument is necessarily represented in the course of negation comprehension. The latter view is supported by evidence suggesting that the positive argument is represented in the course of processing negative sentences (Clark & Chase 1972; Carpenter & Just 1975; Fischler et al. 1983; Kaup et al. 2007). To take one example, Kaup et al. (2007) ask participants to respond to visual probes after reading positive or negative sentences (*The bird is / is not in the air*). They find that shortly (250 ms) after reading a positive sentence, participants are faster to respond to an image of the topic (a bird) in the state described by the predicate (being in the air) than the topic in an opposite state (e.g. nesting). But for negative sentences, participants are faster to respond to the same image (a bird in the air) than an image consistent with the truth of the negative sentence (nesting). At longer time intervals (1200 ms), the effect is reversed for negative sentences, and participants are faster to respond to images consistent with the negative proposition expressed (nesting). Kaup et al.'s results, and others from sentence verification and event-related potential (ERP) studies, support two-stage views of negation processing and prove problematic for 'contextualist' accounts of the cost of negation. However, in Tian et al. (2010) we argue that these results could still be explained in contextualist terms if one adopts the suggestions in Sperber and Wilson (1986/1995) that elements of the linguistic form can provide cues to how the sentence being uttered is intended to be relevant. Tian et al. note that sentential negation is overwhelmingly used in contexts where the intended source of relevance for the utterance could be described in positive terms; typically as addressing the positive question, *Is the bird in the air?* or contradicting a salient claim or assumption.[3] In laboratory experiments which present negative sentences without context, participants will infer the most likely source of relevance for the sentence. Such a representation of positive context for negative sentences could be what explains Kaup et al.'s effect. Tian et al. note that if a negative sentence were processed where such cues were not available, then Kaup et al.'s effect should disappear. In fact, cleft sentences with negative predicates, e.g. *It was John who didn't cook the spaghetti*, are typically used when the context is congruent with the negative proposition expressed. That is, we assumed that clefting is associated with a specific focal scale, with the clefted element filling in the conceptual variable in the assumption schema, *someone did not cook the spaghetti*. Our proposal, then, is that different cues from sentence form will trigger the activation of different sources of relevance for simple negative and clefted negative sentences. In a study using the same procedure as that in Kaup et al. (2007), we replicated the effect for simple negative sentences (*John did not cook the spaghetti*) but found the reverse effect for cleft negative: in the cleft condition, participants were faster to respond to images consistent with the truth of the negative proposition (raw spaghetti) than the argument of negation (cooked spaghetti). These results supported our contextualist hypothesis and disconfirmed the long-standing idea that processing negative propositions necessarily involves representing the positive argument.

While Tian et al. (2010) support the thesis that information in the linguistic stimulus is used to infer the likely source of relevance, the effects we reported are from a probe that is presented after the sentence is read. In follow-up work (Tian et al. 2016), we demonstrate that inferring the source of relevance for a negative sentence and its content can occur incrementally and in the same time course. This visual-world eye-tracking study had a similar 'look and listen' procedure to Altmann and Kamide (1999 – mentioned above). Participants preview images consistent with the positive and negative state of affairs (an open and shut window), as well as two unrelated distractor images prior to hearing

---

[3] In Tian et al. (2010, 2016) we describe the typical context for a negative sentence simply in terms of the question, *whether the bird is in the air*. In those papers we wished to avoid the theoretical issue of what the source of relevance is, and how it is represented (as should be apparent in those texts). However, in retrospect, our use of *whether* S to describe context in those papers may seem to imply a commitment to the QUD theory (discussed below), even though we wished to remain neutral on that. I think the characterisation of the likely contexts for negative sentences given in this current chapter is a better, neutral, characterisation.

either positive or negative sentences. Consistent with previous eye-tracking work (Altmann & Kamide 1999; Kamide et al. 2003 among many others), when participants hear the positive sentence, *Bill has opened his brother's window*, they anticipate the target (open window) right from the verb, *opened*. However, for the simple negative sentence, *Bill has not opened his brother's window*, although gaze bias to the two window images increases significantly from the onset of the verb, *open*, that bias is split between the target closed-window image and the positive-consistent open-window image. This equal allocation of attention between positive and negative images continues for a relatively long time (until after participants hear *window*). We interpret this data to suggest that participants are entertaining representations of the positive and negative states of affairs, consistent with them representing both the likely context and the content of the sentence. For cleft items, *It is Bill who has / has not opened his brother's window*, participants' gaze bias forms to the correct target at the same rate in positive and negative sentences and significantly faster than in the simple negative condition. These results demonstrate yet again that when the intended source of relevance is congruent with the negative proposition, the delay in processing negative sentences (relative to positive) disappears.

Beyond the domain of negation research, there is some evidence that inferring the likely source of relevance impacts on sentence processing. For example, Clifton and Frazier (2012) manipulate whether a context sentence containing an existential modal, *could go to Paris*, would impact on parsing decisions downstream, compared to a control condition, *did go to Paris*. The idea is that the modal context makes discourse continuations that address the question of going to Paris relevant in a way that the control condition does not. Clifton and Frazier demonstrate that this aspect of discourse context does impact on syntactic parsing decisions. In a similar vein, but relevant to the form/context interaction, Kehler and Rohde (2016) provide evidence that aspects of sentence form (e.g. the gender of a subject pronoun) can affect how participants anticipate the intended source of relevance for the sentence that follows.

2.4   Representing the Source of Relevance and 'Question Under Discussion'

The research reviewed in the last section works with the idea that language processing is sensitive to the likely source(s) of relevance for an utterance. That research, including our own, is presented as being more or less neutral as to how we characterise relevance, or what would be a 'source of relevance'; or, at least, nothing in that research hangs too much on these issues. Yet all of the above research uses a handy manner of describing relevance in terms of the question an utterance addresses. Going back to Section 2.2, I also fell back on using questions as a means to characterise the impact of activated assumption schemas in context. Indeed, Sperber and Wilson themselves use this descriptive technique when they originally presented their ideas about prosody and context. It happens that many theoretical researchers work with a theory that utterances are related to conversational context by the questions they address (Ginzburg 1996, 2012; Roberts 1996/2012; van Kuppevelt 1996). In particular, Roberts (1996/2012) defines a Gricean notion of relevance in terms of contextually established Question(s) Under Discussion (QUDs). So, could it be the case that language users in fact represent questions as part of utterance interpretation? In this section I will make some very brief comments on some of the ways in which relevance has been approached, contrasting the QUD approach to Sperber and Wilson's. I will review some recent work of ours (Tian & Breheny 2015) which looks at how we process polar questions. That work, taken together with the results mentioned in Section 2.3, point to a conclusion that, at least when it comes to negative sentences, we do not actually represent polar questions as the intended source of relevance. I conclude with some observations about what it means to describe the source of relevance in terms of a question.

Roberts (1996/2012) outlines a pragmatic framework based on the idea that conversation is a joint inquiry, structured around raising and resolving questions. In this framework, an assertion must address the question that is currently prioritised in the common ground (i.e. is at the 'top of the stack'), and the assertion is relevant to that question iff (if and only if) it at least partially answers it. Thus, the source of relevance for an utterance in this framework is a question. In this context, a question should be thought of in the semantic sense outlined in Groenendijk and Stokhof (1984) and elsewhere. That is, a question is a partition of the space of logical possibilities, one that corresponds to the set of full answers to the question. Thus the polar question, ?p corresponds to a bi-partition of the space of logical possibilities, with one cell containing possibilities where p is true and the other with the possibilities where it is false. In this system, an assertion acts to eliminate at least some of the cells in the partition.

Although this QUD framework is presented in model-theoretic terms, and is somewhat neutral as to the nature of the psychological processes or representational states of a speaker and hearer when an assertion is made, we can nevertheless assume that it provides a description, at a computational level, of cognitive states. As such, the commitments of this framework regarding the role and status of questions (qua semantic objects) in cognition are somewhat different to those of, say, relevance theory.[4] In QUD theory, relevance is defined in terms of questions. By contrast, relevance is defined independently

---

[4] Here I contrast the QUD theory with Sperber and Wilson's relevance theory, but much of what I say would hold if the point of contrast were to other approaches to relevance, such as outlined in van Rooy (2003) and Russell (2012), the latter inspired by Carnap (1950).

of questions in RT. In fact, Sperber and Wilson (1986/1995) analyse the speech act of asking a question in terms of relevance – a person who asks a question typically presents herself as someone for whom true answers to the question would be relevant. Thus, when a theorist uses a question to describe a stimulus (like focal stress) in terms of how it signals a likely source of relevance, this has different significance in QUD theory and RT. In QUD theory, the specific question determined by focus must be 'at the top of the stack' in the current conversation. In RT, this mode of description merely implies that some specification of the assumption schema would be relevant in the context.

We can see a fairly clear difference between the two approaches if we consider polar questions. Logically, the polar question *Is the window open?* corresponds to a bi-partition of a space of possibilities. Eliminating a cell of this partition is how assertions would achieve relevance in the QUD theory.[5] In contrast, to use the question *Is the window open?* to describe a context in RT is to imply that the proposition that the window is open, if true, would be relevant to the listener. Typically, the latter would be the case if the listener actively entertains the assumption but holds it with a less than certain degree of confidence, or if the assumption could combine with others already activated, leading to further implications.

I turn now to a recent set of studies reported in Tian and Breheny (2015) which probe the representational state of participants as they process a polar question, e.g. *Has Bill shut his brother's window?*. In these studies, we use the same eye-tracking methods, visual stimuli and procedure as in Tian et al. (2016). All that is different is that we swap assertions (*Bill has / has not opened his brother's window*) for polar questions. Of the latter, there are three kinds: *Has Bill opened his brother's window? Hasn't Bill opened his brother's window? Has Bill not opened his brother's window?*. Participants preview a display with an image of an open window and one of a shut window, plus two distractor images, and then they hear the stimulus while the direction of their gaze is recorded. Recall that in the assertion study, gaze bias to the target formed from the onset of *opened* in the simple positive condition. In three studies using polar questions (each with small variation on procedures), Tian and Breheny (2015) find that the bias to the two window images increases but is split between both of the states for each type of question. This dividing of attention continues until the onset of the final word of the input (*window*). From that point, for positive questions, a significant bias to the positive image emerges and remains for some time past the end of the input. This gaze data suggests two things. That when processing a polar interrogative sentence,

---

[5] One issue for QUD theory that is noted in Büring (2003) and van Rooy (2003) is that a perfectly viable and apparently relevant answer to a polar question could be *Presumably*. However, such an answer does not serve to eliminate either cell in the bi-partition.

representations of both logical possibilities become active initially. However, for positive polar questions it seems that representations consistent with the positive state of affairs become more activated once the question is processed. Thus, it seems, representing the semantic interpretation of an interrogative form does involve activation of states consistent with the cells of the partition of logical space. However, the late bias to the positive image suggests some inference about the speaker's state of inquiry. Perhaps, this is a matter of hearers inferring the typical manner in which an answer would achieve relevance for the speaker. In RT terms, this would involve having activated representations of the positive assumption, either embedded under some description of its degree of certainty, or as part of assumption schemas that would make the positive relevant. Our results for the 'high'-negative condition (*Hasn't Bill opened his brother's window?*) provide good support to our interpretation of the positive condition. Here, as for the positive question, attention is split between both window images until late in the sentence. At this point, a bias to the positive image forms also. As is widely observed in the literature (see e.g. Ladd 1981; Romero & Han 2004), high-negative questions typically signal that the speaker has a prior belief or expectation for the positive state of affairs, although this belief is somewhat less than certain (typically due to some recently acquired piece of evidence). Thus, high-negative questions seem to suggest that relevance would be achieved by weakening the strength of the positive assumption about the current state of affairs based on prior expectation.

Our results for low-negative questions (*Has Bill not opened...?*) serve as a kind of control condition. These show no overall bias in this later time period and significantly lower bias than in the positive polar question. Again, this is consistent with observations in the literature that low-negative questions are ambiguous – in the sense that they are used either when the speaker presents the negative assumption as potentially relevant, or in similar contexts to high-negative questions, where they seem to seek disconfirmation of the positive assumption. Thus we gain support for the idea that a late positive bias in positive and high-negative question processing manifests hearers representing how relevance would be achieved for the speaker.

To sum up our polar-question research, comprehenders are liable to activate representations consistent with both logical possibilities when processing a polar question. However, as seems consistent with observations made in the literature on negative questions (Ladd 1981), question forms trigger inferences about the state of the speaker who asks the questions. In the case of positive polar questions, representations congruent with the positive state of affairs become more activated. This latter result is consistent with Sperber and Wilson's account of the speech act of asking a question.

Now we can return to our studies on processing negative assertions. Recall that we found that participants initially activate representations of the positive state of affairs when processing negative assertions, e.g. *John has not cooked the spaghetti* (Kaup et al. 2007; Tian et al. 2010). Our research strongly suggests this phenomenon is the by-product of participants representing the likely source of relevance for simple negatives. As mentioned above, likely contexts involve either a salient assumption of the positive proposition (being denied by the negative assertion), or the positive polar question having been raised.[6] In QUD theory, a negative sentence with focus on negation itself would only be congruent with the polar QUD at the top of the stack. Now, a perhaps simplistic implementation of the QUD theory of context would be to assume that the QUD that an assertion is intended to be relevant to is activated when processing that assertion. Given the results of our polar-question study, this would mean that a representation of both logical possibilities should become activated when a polar question serves as context for an assertion. Thus, this implementation of the QUD theory predicts no overall bias to either positive or negative image after a negative sentence is read, contrary to a much replicated finding.

When we consider the polar-question study results and the negative-assertion study results together, we can perhaps deconstruct what it means to describe the source of relevance for an utterance in terms of a question. As discussed, this is a practice that is widely adopted in pragmatics and in experimental research, including in theoretical discourse about focus (as instantiated in Section 2.2 of this chapter). Coming from the perspective of QUD theories, such a description implies an activated representation of the semantic interpretation of the corresponding interrogative sentence – a partition on the space of possibilities. The alternative is to understand the question in the theorist's description as that which the hearer might have asked, i.e. the speaker has formed their utterance in a way that would be consistent with the hearer having asked the question. Our results suggest that the latter understanding of this practice is the correct one.

Acknowledgements

The research reported here stems from my first research project as a PhD student, working with Deirdre Wilson. This work and all of my subsequent research has been guided by Deirdre's unswerving vision for a unified, psychologically plausible theory of human communication. I am deeply indebted to Deirdre for her inspiration and am forever grateful that I was lucky enough to work with her, first as a student and later as a colleague.

---

[6] Though negative assertions could address negative questions, Tian and Breheny (2015) report a corpus survey showing that questions are 94 per cent positive.

3   Quasi-Factives and Cognitive Efficiency

Axel Barceló Aspeitia and Robert J. Stainton

3.1   Introduction: Motivation and Game Plan

The term 'quasi-factive' is our own coinage, hence readers can be forgiven for not knowing what our topic is. To indicate that right off, it's best to start with examples:

(3.1)   It isn't widely known that Obama has been arrested

(3.2)   Please do not acknowledge at the press conference that
         Obama has been arrested

Both very strongly suggest something which is false, namely that Obama has been arrested. Yet the first sentence, a declarative, is strictly speaking true. And the second, an imperative, expresses an order that is wholly appropriate given the actual facts.

Such sentences are interesting for several reasons. They may seem to call for an analysis in terms of 'weak logico-semantic support': patently, there is less than full-on encoded entailment of the complement in (3.1), but maybe something less strict is at work. They raise the familiar issue of how much linguistic convention contributes to in-context meaning, versus how much is owed to general-purpose cognitive and pragmatic factors. For instance, does (3.1) have a composition-ally fixed standing linguistic content such that it is weakly logico-semantically implied that Obama has been arrested? Or is such an alleged 'reading' really just a pragmatic effect of a univocal sentence? In addition to these long-standing issues in philosophy of language and linguistic pragmatics, we are motivated by something social and ethical. The (seeming) mismatch between what such sentences mean in the language versus how they are standardly used can give rise to what Mitch Green [p.c.] has labelled 'verbal sleight of hand', wherein a hearer may be bamboozled into embracing a belief without explicit semantic endorsement by the speaker. That is, such sentences work a kind of magic. As in a magic trick – or, maybe better, a 'con job' – there is a distracter, namely the complex embedding structure. There is an illusion created, viz., that the speaker has logico-semantically committed himself to the truth of a claim. Finally, and to anticipate, in creating the illusion, the trickster exploits a natural psychological tendency in humans: their perfectly appropriate quest for cognitive efficiency.

So much for motivation. Our discussion will proceed as follows. Moving beyond examples, we offer a fuller description of the phenomenon: the salient characteristics of quasi-factives, and various sub-kinds. Then a sketch of a cognitive-pragmatic explanation of why we hear them as we do. We end with a major concern.

3.2   Description

A first crucial step is to sort out terminology. Recognising that usage varies widely, we will simply stipulate: a *factive verb* is one such that, in the right linguistic context, the complement of that verb is analytically entailed by the truth of the matrix sentence. 'Know' is the paradigm example, but other factive verbs include 'inform', 'recall', 'recognise', 'regret', etc. A *factive sentence*, on the other hand, is one in which the linguistic context *is* right, so that the complement of the factive verb actually is analytically entailed. Thus (3.3) and (3.4) both contain factive verbs and are factive sentences:

(3.3)   Juanito knows that Ottawa is the capital of Canada

(3.4)   Rifat informed her mother that Ottawa is the capital of Canada

Crucially, as we use the terminology, there can be non-factive sentences which contain factive verbs. (3.5) is not a factive sentence, nor is (3.6):

(3.5)   Juanito knows whether Regina is the capital of Canada

(3.6)   If Rifat purchases a house and a condo, she will regret buying a condo

Quasi-factives fall within this genus of cases. Our species is especially interesting because it is hard not to *hear* our sentences as factive.[1] Said out of the blue, (3.1) and (3.2) are understood as very strongly suggesting the truth of the complement. Indeed, the hearer might easily report the speaker of (3.1) and (3.2) as having 'said' that Obama has been arrested; relatedly, the truth of the complement may naturally be heard as 'main point'.[2] All of this presumably has something to do with the fact that suggesting the truth of the complement is part of the usual usage of (3.1) and (3.2) – as contrasted with one-off particularised conversational implicatures. A final and seminal feature of our

---

[1] Does the term 'quasi-factive' apply to a kind of sentence type or to (potential) utterances of a certain sort? Are quasi-factives, like factive sentences, united by a properly logico-semantic set of features, or are they a 'pragmatic kind'? In this introductory description, we leave such issues open, so as not to beg too many questions.

[2] In the earliest discussion of the facts that we are aware of, Hooper (1975: 97ff.) recognises, albeit using different terminology, that the complement of 'I'm not surprised that the dog bit the mailman' may easily be heard not only as 'said' but as 'main point' – with 'I'm not surprised that' being understood as merely parenthetical. For additional early discussion, see Green (1976). Simons (2007) addresses in compelling detail similar sorts of phenomena.

quasi-factives is this: *if one stops and pays attention*, one notices that (3.1) and (3.2) are not factive sentences in our sense. More than that, in the case of (3.1), the falsehood of the complement entails the truth of the whole. Thus, though it sounds humorous, there is no contradiction in saying:

(3.7)   It isn't widely known that Obama has been arrested, because
         he hasn't been arrested!

(3.8)   Please do not acknowledge at the press conference that Obama
         has been arrested, because he hasn't been arrested![3]

There are numerous sub-varieties of our quasi-factives (Barceló & Stainton 2016). The factive verbs may involve propositional attitudes or discourse. The propositional attitude verbs, in their turn, divide into cognitive/perceptual ones (such as 'forget', 'notice', 'know', 'recall', 'recognise', 'realise' and 'see') and emotional/evaluative ones (e.g., 'amuse', 'be proud', 'bother', 'care', 'excite' and 'find it odd/surprising/terrific/tragic/unacceptable/wonderful'). Examples of the discourse sub-variety, beyond 'acknowledge', include 'admit', 'confide', 'confirm' and 'reveal'. (Some speakers hear 'confess', 'note' and 'report' as discourse-reporting factive verbs too.)

There are also various syntactic configurations which yield quasi-factive sentences. The verbs can take clausal complements – including finite ones (as in our original examples), but also infinitival clauses and small clauses:

(3.9) I_1 can't recall [$_S$ e_1 being shot]

(3.10) I_1 don't regret [$_S$ e_1 leaving]

(3.11)   No one saw [$_{SC}$ him nude]

And the complements don't have to be clausal:

(3.12)   I didn't recognise [$_{NP}$ Clarice]

(3.13)   Have you been informed about [$_{NP}$ Carson's forced resignation]?

(3.14)   I am not pleased about [$_{NP}$ the recent imprisonment of the Governor]

Also, the cancelling negative environment need not be a plain-old negative particle, as in (3.1) and (3.2). Equally effective is a negative lexical entry or a negating quantifier phrase:

(3.15)   It's *seldom* reported that Queen Elizabeth was born in Germany

(3.16)   *No one* noticed the recent imprisonment of the Governor

(3.17)   I *refuse* to recognise that it doesn't bother you that Clarice is in jail

---

[3] See Carston (1998a) for a more developed argument supporting the claim that sentences like (3.7) and (3.8) are not contradictory.

More controversial as negating contexts are non-declarative moods as in (3.13) above and (3.18) and (3.19) below, and the antecedent of a hypothetical conditional, as in (3.20) and (3.21):[4]

(3.18)   Is it widely known that Obama has been arrested?

(3.19)   Did her husband express surprise that Clarice has been arrested?

(3.20)   If Chang realises that Bob has been arrested, he will cry.

(3.21)   I would be remiss if I neglected to thank Daniel for his feedback.

3.3   Our Cognitive-Pragmatic Explanation

We call our examples 'quasi-factives' precisely because they include factive verbs and are heard, in the usual case, as requiring (even as part of 'what is said' or the 'main point') the truth of the complement; yet, on the other hand, because of the negative environment, careful reflection establishes that there is no such entailment, and that cancellation is possible. These are sentences, then, which are not genuinely factive, but where some sort of 'quasi' is in play. We turn now to an explanation of how they work this magic. That explanation has a logical bit and a psychological bit.

With factive verbs, as a matter of analyticity, there is always the conjunctive claim that the agent stands in at least one relation to a proposition, and that said proposition (however expressed syntactically) is true.[5] For instance, and simplifying, 'Rob knows that Obama is in jail' entails the conjunction {[(Rob believes that Obama is in jail) & (Rob has good justification for believing that Obama is in jail) & (Rob's justification and belief about Obama being in jail are connected in the right way) & ...] & (Obama is in jail)}. As a result, a negative embedding environment induces the negation of an (implicitly) conjunctive claim. Let's put things schematically, and then work through an example. A factive sentence of the form $A\Phi(p)$ entails $\{[A\Phi_1(p) \& A\Phi_2(p) \& A\Phi_3(p) \& ...] \& p\}$. Hence $\sim A\Phi(p)$, a schema for our quasi-factives, entails $\sim\{[A\Phi_1(p) \& A\Phi_2(p) \& A\Phi_3(p) \& ...] \& p\}$. Now, the negation of a conjunction is logically equivalent

---

[4] The generalisation seems to be that negative contexts, in the sense at issue, are those which license negative polarity items (NPIs). We won't explore that observation here. As an interesting aside, notice that quasi-factives can embed within each other, as in (3.17). The effect of the complement seeming-to-be-said is retained even in such cases.

[5] We set aside in this brief chapter a complication noted by Karttunen (1971: 56*ff*), namely that the complement of the factive verb may consist of an open sentence, one bound by a quantifier higher up in the matrix sentence. His example is [Some₁ senators regret that [they₁ voted for the SST]]. In such cases, it isn't strictly the case that the complement *considered in isolation* is guaranteed to be true by the factive nature of the verb.

to a disjunction of negations: De Morgan's law states that $\sim(q\ \&\ r)$ is equivalent to $(\sim q\ \lor \sim r)$. Applying this, $\sim\{[A\Phi_1(p)\ \&\ A\Phi_2(p)\ \&\ A\Phi_3(p)\ \&\ ...]\ \&\ p\}$ is equivalent to $\{\sim[(A\Phi_1(p)\ \&\ A\Phi_2(p)\ \&\ A\Phi_3(p)\ \&\ ...]\ \lor \sim p\}$. Applying the law a second time, to the first complex disjunct, we get as the entailment of a quasi-factive:

(3.22) $[\sim A\Phi_1(p)\ \lor \sim A\Phi_2(p)\ \lor \sim A\Phi_3(p)\ \lor\ ...]\ \lor \sim p$

Applying this abstract machinery to an example, (3.23) below entails the negation of a conjunctive claim: $\sim\{[($Rob believes that Obama is in jail$)\ \&$ (Rob has good justification for believing that Obama is in jail) & (Rob's justification and belief about Obama being in jail are connected in the right way) & ...] & (Obama is in jail)$\}$.

(3.23)   Rob doesn't know that Obama is in jail

This is equivalent to $\{\sim[($Rob believes that Obama is in jail$)\ \&$ (Rob has good justification for believing that Obama is in jail) & (Rob's justification and belief about Obama being in jail are connected in the right way) & ...] $\lor \sim$(Obama is in jail)$\}$. And that, in turn, leaves us with two potential truth-makers for (3.23): [$\sim$(Rob believes that Obama is in jail) $\lor \sim$(Rob has good justification for believing that Obama is in jail) $\lor \sim$(Rob's justification and belief about Obama being in jail are connected in the right way) $\lor$ ...] on the one hand and $\sim$(Obama is in jail) on the other.[6]

The psychological bit is even more complex. We will therefore lay it out in two steps. Importantly, the two (major) negative disjuncts differ, and along two axes. In the cases that work most effectively, the complement p is surprising. This makes the negation, $\sim p$, *un*surprising: that the Queen was not born in Germany, e.g., is hardly newsworthy. In comparison, the negation of the relational bit, i.e., of the first (major) disjunct in (3.22), will be more noteworthy. Suppose Elizabeth the Second was born in Germany; it would be surprising if this curious and important fact were seldom reported. The first contrast between the two disjuncts, then, pertains to the amount of 'cognitive pay-off': there is little of it, if the complement p is being negated; but there is rather more if the relation-stating disjunct $[A\Phi_1(p)\ \&\ A\Phi_2(p)\ \&\ A\Phi_3(p)\ \&\ ...]$ is denied. A second

---

[6] A logico-metaphysical subtlety merits mentioning, one suggested by Soames' (1977: 276) criticism of Wilson (1975). Strictly speaking, there are *many* potential truth-makers for a sentence like (3.23): e.g., $\sim[($Obama is in jail$)\ \lor$ (Rob has good justification for believing that Obama is in jail)] would render the sentence true. We hold, however, that such logical combinations are not among the most psychologically accessible potential truth-makers – any more than $\sim[($Obama is in jail$)\ \lor (3^2=11)]$ is, though it too is sufficient for the truth of 'Rob doesn't know that Obama is in jail'. Thus, it is the psychological aspect of our story, not the logical bit, that leaves only two salient options.

difference is this. A quasi-factive $\sim\!A\Phi(p)$ is not a cost-effective choice in terms of conveying that the complement is false, since there is a far less cognitively taxing option: namely, saying $\sim\!p$. In contrast, there isn't a readily available alternative for phrasing $[\sim\!A\Phi_1(p) \text{ v } \sim\!A\Phi_2(p) \text{ v } \sim\!A\Phi_3(p) \text{ v } ...]$.

Returning to (3.23), that Obama is not in jail is unsurprising. Besides, there is a much more straightforward way of getting it across: saying 'Obama is not in jail'. In contrast, the relational bit is surprising: it would top all the headlines around the world if Obama were in jail, and thus Rob would be expected to know. And, as Gettier cases teach us, there is no straightforward way of getting across just the relational bit [$\sim$(Rob believes that Obama is in jail) v $\sim$(Rob has good justification for believing that Obama is in jail) v $\sim$(Rob's justification and belief about Obama being in jail are connected in the right way) v ...]. (Hence those final ellipses.) The upshot: it would be twice-over more cognitively efficient for the speaker to intend the negation-of-the-relations truth-maker. So, for pragmatic reasons, the hearer ignores the not-in-jail disjunct.[7]

A second step in our psychological story is required because our explanandum is that the complement p is heard as 'said' in quasi-factives. But the foregoing only explains why $\sim\!p$ is not conveyed. These are patently not the same: e.g., if someone utters 'It's raining', they will almost certainly not convey that the Queen was not born in Germany – yet they won't be heard as saying that she was.

We thus need to revisit a simplification. As the formulation in (3.22) actually makes clear, what we have sometimes referred to as *the* relational disjunct is actually disjunctive content-wise. Hence, as far as the logico-semantic content of a quasi-factive sentence goes, any of $\sim\!A\Phi_1(p)$, $\sim\!A\Phi_2(p)$, $\sim\!A\Phi_3(p)$, etc., could be intended. But none is very psychologically accessible, especially in the presence of a very manifest concept, namely $\sim\!\Phi(p)$. It is altogether natural, given that both negation and Φ are maximally salient, for a hearer of a quasi-factive sentence $\sim\!A\Phi(p)$ to therefore construe '*the* relational disjunct' as $A\!\sim\!\Phi(p)$. Finally, $[\sim\!A\Phi_1(p) \text{ v } \sim\!A\Phi_2(p) \text{ v } \sim\!A\Phi_3(p) \text{ v } ...]$ is not factive, nor are any of its disjuncts. However, given that the 'relational verb' Φ is factive, so is $\sim\!\Phi$. Hence the sentence which the hearer 'leaps to' as more psychologically accessible, $A\!\sim\!\Phi(p)$, is factive too. Thus, in terms of logico-semantic relations, $\sim\!A\Phi(p)$ does not entail $A\!\sim\!\Phi(p)$; nor is it even weakly logico-semantically supported. Nonetheless, the move from the former to the latter is explicable because of our natural inclination towards cognitive efficiency.

---

[7] In effect, this is the inverse phenomenon of what Grice (1981) called 'conversational tailoring': instead of ignoring the implicit conjuncts that are already part of the common ground, here we ignore the implicit disjuncts.

Let us continue with (3.23) as our worked example. Psychological step one explains why the proposition THAT OBAMA IS NOT IN JAIL gets ignored. But how does OBAMA IS IN JAIL get to be 'said'? 'Know' is an extremely complex verb. The quasi-factive sentence (3.23) will thus provide an extremely complex relational disjunct: [~(Rob believes that Obama is in jail) v ~(Rob has good justification for believing that Obama is in jail) v ~(Rob's justification and belief about Obama being in jail are connected in the right way) v ...]. Any negated disjunct (and, as per footnote 6, any subset of them), is a potential truth-maker for our sentence. And none is factive. However, these are not nearly as cognitively salient as the proposition ROB FAILS-TO-KNOW THAT OBAMA IS IN JAIL, because the verb 'know' has actually been *spoken*, as has a negating particle. Hence the most cognitively salient content, barring special contexts, will be this – and it may, in the right circumstances, be heard as 'said'.[8] Finally, 'fail-to-know' functions like a factive verb. Hence this recovered-content entails that Obama is in jail. And content which is entailed by the 'said' is often itself heard as 'said', and even as 'main point'. Voilà.

That is our positive explanation. We haven't space here to address alternative accounts, except to mention one competing syntactic approach. It is crucial to distinguish our position from it. We have no objection to the observation that quasi-factives are reminiscent of scope-of-negation ambiguities. It is perfectly appropriate, e.g., to describe the effect of (3.1) in terms of hearing it as expressing the proposition OBAMA HAS BEEN ARRESTED, BUT THAT ISN'T WIDELY KNOWN (or more exactly, albeit much less colloquially, as BUT IT IS WIDELY THE CASE THAT PEOPLE FAIL-TO-KNOW THAT OBAMA HAS BEEN ARRESTED), this contrasting with the wide-scope negation of the whole proposition, as in IT IS NOT THE CASE THAT IT IS WIDELY KNOWN THAT OBAMA HAS BEEN ARRESTED. It is a mistake, however, to move from this to the idea that one should explain the 'ambiguity of quasi-factives' in the same way one explains, e.g., the contrasting readings of 'Rifat doesn't like cats and dogs'. In particular, we reject the postulation of multiple trees underlying (3.1), such

---

[8] Speaking of 'special contexts', it may seem problematic for our account that there is a kind of case where the 'quasi-factive effect' does not show up. Karttunen (1971: 63) noted them in passing: he pointed out that 'John didn't regret that he had not told the truth' need not inevitably suggest the complement's veracity, e.g., when the issue of whether John regretted not telling the truth has been explicitly raised. In fact, far from posing an objection, we think such cases provide additional support for our account. It explains these exceptions quite nicely. If someone out-and-out asks 'Does Rob know that Obama is in jail?' then answering with (3.23) need not be heard as quasi-factive because the mental representation /rob knows that obama is in jail/ is already activated; the necessary cognitive processing has already taken place. So, a correction with the fully spelled-out sentence is no longer as unduly demanding, and the pay-off is higher because a salient issue has been wholly and explicitly addressed.

that the hearer is tricked by an equivocation between them. (For instance, some theorists might postulate an underlying tree where the complement clause has been fronted, and another in which it remains *in situ*; others might posit one tree which has [neg] being the sister of the verb, and another which has [neg] as the sister to the matrix sentence. In both cases, the former tree actually would be factive, while the latter would not – thence the verbal sleight of hand.) Our account agrees on how quasi-factive sentences are *heard* (i.e., as suggestive of a scope-of-negation ambiguity), but we do not explain the phenomenon in any such way. To phrase our proposal another way, the hearer accesses a *narrow-negation content* in processing the utterance, and for cognitive-pragmatic reasons. (Compare: the sentence [$_S$ That is not a bachelor] is surely not *syntactically* ambiguous among [[neg][$_A$ male]], [[neg][$_A$ adult]], [[neg][$_A$ human]] and [[neg][$_A$ unmarried]]].)

3.4   Connection to Deirdre Wilson's Work

In this section, we underscore three points of contact with Deirdre Wilson's ground-breaking work. This should clarify still further our view, and it will afford an opportunity to hark back to the initial triad of issues in philosophy of language.

Wilson (1975) was a pioneer in her treatment of presupposition. She criticised the then-dominant view that it involved some sort of weak logico-semantic supporting relation. To explain, in (3.3) and (3.4) we encountered genuine entailment: both sentences logically require that Ottawa be the capital of Canada. Similarly, the truth of (3.24) logico-semantically guarantees the truth of (3.26):

(3.24)   Jane has stopped smoking

(3.25)   If Jane has stopped smoking, Mauricio will be thrilled

(3.26)   Jane has smoked at some time in the past

But something less potent seems to be present in the relationship between (3.25) and (3.26): the former seems to merely provide weak, defeasible, logico-semantic support; there seems to exist merely an encoded *suggestion* of the truth of (3.26). Such appearances notwithstanding, Wilson rejected this whole picture: 'presuppositional analysis has no place in semantics' (Wilson 1975: xii). This isn't to deny that there is some 'suggesting' going on in a use of (3.25), but it is the speaker who suggests that Jane once smoked; and she does so by means of Grice-style pragmatics. Here we find a first connection with our treatment of quasi-factives. By definition, quasi-factive sentences do not entail the complement. One might suppose, however, that they 'weakly logically support it'. With Wilson, we think to the contrary that a *speaker* of a quasi-factive sentence will 'suggest things' – but these do not follow logically, not even 'weakly', from the sentence she uses. We would equally echo two of her arguments for this approach. First, the class of quasi-factive constructions is heterogeneous in terms of grammatical structure. Along with Wilson, we think that's because what they really have in common is something about which of their potential truth-makers are pragmatically appropriate – rather than anything about shared syntactic form. Second, our mutual pragmatics-oriented approach explains why the 'support' we find in quasi-factives is so weak that it allows for cancellation: it's because there isn't logico-semantic support after all. Cancellation is just what one expects from a pragmatic phenomenon: the hearer draws a non-monotonic inference based on available evidence; the speaker then provides additional evidence, explicitly ruling out the inference's conclusion via cancellation; what had seemed the most plausible hypothesis about speaker meaning thereby gets rejected.

Closely related is Wilson's Grice-inspired position on the role of conventional linguistic meaning in fixing what people naturally 'hear' as the meaning. In many cases, people 'hear' as part of sentence-meaning what is actually supplied pragmatically. Our view on quasi-factives dovetails with her stance. We do not believe that a *sentence* like (3.1) has, as a matter of its standing linguistic meaning, a 'reading' on which it (weakly) requires the truth of the proposition OBAMA HAS BEEN ARRESTED. Syntax and compositional semantics do not yield any such encoded 'reading'. Instead, cognitive-pragmatic factors make it such that people tend to interpret typical utterances this way. Connecting even more directly, Wilson noticed forty years ago that (3.27), a paradigm example of a quasi-factive sentence, does not logically entail (3.28):

(3.27) Mary doesn't regret that her grandmother was trampled by an antelope

(3.28) Mary's grandmother was trampled by an antelope

She held that the first sentence is logically equivalent to:

(3.29) Either the grandmother was trampled and Mary doesn't regret it, or the grandmother wasn't trampled.

Hence (3.27), she says, is simply true if no trampling occurred. This, of course, represents the heart of our view.[9]

---

[9] In fact, what Wilson is implicitly proposing here differs slightly. The way that she phrases example (3.29) suggests that she takes the logical equivalent of the quasi-factive sentence $\sim\!A\Phi(p)$ to be $\{[(p\ \&\ (\sim\!A\Phi_1(p)\ \text{v}\ \sim\!A\Phi_2(p)\ \text{v}\ \sim\!A\Phi_3(p)\ \text{v}\ \ldots)]\ \text{v}\ \sim\!p\}$. This contrasts with our present account because p appears as a conjunct within the first (major) disjunct. In this respect, the view seems closer to a position we pursued in Barceló and Stainton (2016: 73ff.). An advantage of this approach is that it explains directly why p is heard as said, once the second (major) disjunct has been set aside by the hearer on the grounds of cognitive inefficiency. There is then no need for our 'second psychological step'.

A final point of contact pertains to Wilson's later work. In order to keep our ideas accessible to non-specialists, we haven't spelled them out using the rich resources of relevance theory proper. However, the psychological story we tell about quasi-factives co-opts its notion of a cognitive cost–benefit analysis. Specifically, the reason why one of the logical options is typically ignored, according to us, has to do with (i) the comparative improvement of the cognitive environment given the processing cost of the complex linguistic stimulus and (ii) the much higher manifestness of the 'wrong' factive relational verb (in bold), $A\sim\Phi(p)$, as opposed to the actually-entailed non-factive $[\sim A\Phi_1(p) \lor \sim A\Phi_2(p) \lor \sim A\Phi_3(p) \lor \ldots]$.

3.5   A Major Challenge

Both our description of the phenomenon and our explanation of it are incomplete and rough and ready, and hence open to a range of objections. This is inevitable in such a brief treatment. There is, regardless, one major challenge that is too important to postpone till a future paper. It arises because of phenomena which look very similar to quasi-factives in terms of surface effects, but where our logico-psychological mechanisms seemingly don't apply.

In the first class of cases, including (3.30)–(3.37) below, the structure and elements of the sentences are similar to quasi-factives: there is a propositional attitude or discourse verb, and some kind of negative environment. And the sentence is typically heard as factive.

(3.30)   Don't tell anyone that Kathy has been arrested

(3.31)   No one is denying that Rob is a serial killer

(3.32)   Has it been announced that Mick Jagger was elected President of the United States?

(3.33)   Was Clarke ever questioned about Jenna's murder?

(3.34)   It's very hard to believe that Obama is dead

(3.35)   No one imagined that Pluto was inhabited

(3.36)   Rogelio had no idea that Pluto was larger than the Earth

(3.37)   Who would have suspected that Trump was born in Russia?

However, none of these sentences contains a factive verb: 'announce', 'deny', 'question' and 'tell' are discourse verbs, but not factive ones; 'believe', 'have an idea that', 'imagine' and 'suspect' are propositional-attitude verbs, but not factive ones. Indeed, some of these verbs suggest that their complement is *false*: e.g., 'deny that', 'have an idea that' and 'imagine that'.

There is, then, seemingly no complex conjunction analytically entailed in the corresponding positive sentences; hence the negative-environment versions do not entail a pair of negative disjuncts, either of which would render the whole negated sentence true (with one of these disjuncts being ignored for psychological reasons). In Barceló and Stainton (2016), we addressed this by suggesting, tentatively, that our logico-psychological account could be extended to such cases. One might speculate, e.g., that 'No one imagined' in (3.35) is naturally heard as 'No one even imagined'. The latter, in its turn, (sort of?) entails that no one knew... And then our story would apply. Or again, because of a principle of charity, or because of human's automatic trust in testimony, maybe 'Don't tell anyone that p' is heard as strongly suggesting that p... And then, once again, the negation-of-a-conjunction mechanism applies. (So implicitly committed were we to this strategy that we applied the label 'quasi-factive' to cases like (3.30)–(3.37) when explaining the phenomenon.) At this point, we are even less sanguine about assimilating such examples to our logico-psychological apparatus. There are issues about the plausibility of the specific stories: e.g., how does 'even' get read into (3.35), and why is the negative (3.30) heard as making the arrest more believable than the positive 'Tell someone that Kathy was arrested'? But even if such minutiae could be dealt with, there's a larger worry, namely that both (3.1)–(3.2)/(3.9)–(3.21)/(3.23)/(3.27) on the one hand and (3.30)–(3.37) on the other seem to belong to a still larger family of cases. And there's simply no hope of applying our exact mechanism to that overarching family. There is no negation in (3.38) and (3.39), and no discourse or propositional-attitude verb in (3.40). And yet, the 'verbal sleight of hand' clearly arises.

(3.38)   Axel hopes to return to space

(3.39)   I'm delighted to say that Paul Simon has been elected President of the United States!

(3.40)   If Neil Young were healthy, he would be touring

Happily, we can at least gesture at two avenues of escape consistent with our overarching linguistico-philosophical commitments. Possibly, there simply is no genuine underlying kind at work hereabouts, in terms of mechanism – not even one that underlies both (3.1)–(3.2)/(3.9)–(3.21)/(3.23)/(3.27) on the one hand, i.e., genuine quasi-factives, and (3.30)–(3.37) on the other. There are merely shared superficial effects. If this is correct, quasi-factives per se would remain a proper explanatory kind, characterised by the specific logico-psychological mechanisms we have proposed. (To give an analogy, just as the existence of sea creatures which swim and feed in superficially similar ways is no threat to cartilaginous fish being a unique and interesting kind, it is no threat to the reality and specialness of quasi-factives that there are other similar means to 'con' hearers.) The other avenue, the one we presently incline towards, is that all these cases are united by more than the superficial similarities: there is something shared at the level of psychological processing. Specifically, the general cognitive efficiency story can be told in all cases – it's only the specifics of the logical bit which will vary. (Again, see Barceló & Stainton 2016.)

3.6   Concluding Remarks

We conclude by reiterating what we have and have not done.

We described a sub-class of non-factive sentences containing factive verbs. What's peculiar about them is that they are, as it were, heard as factive – and hence lend themselves to 'verbal sleight of hand'. We then offered a positive account of how this surprising effect is achieved. Logically speaking, the sentences analytically entail a pair of negative disjuncts – one about the relation (e.g., Rob not believing, not having justification, etc.) and one about the propositional relatum (e.g., THAT OBAMA ISN'T IN JAIL). Psychologically, the latter disjunct would violate a requirement of cognitive efficiency; hence something *maximally salient and intimately connected conceptually to the former* is seized upon. But this latched-upon content (here, the content FAILS-TO-KNOW) entails the truth of the embedded proposition: if Rob fails-to-know p, then p is true. (Compare the English 'misperceive', the French 'ignore' and the Spanish 'desconoce'.) In many contextual circumstances, then, the complement may be heard as 'said' and even as 'main point' – though as a matter of linguistic convention it isn't in fact entailed, nor is it even 'weakly logico-semantically supported'.

We haven't attempted to explore alternative explanations, and we haven't filled in the details of our description and explanation (e.g., how the varied negating contexts apply in the sub-cases). Nor have we offered anything like a full response to the major concern about generality. Nonetheless, we hope our discussion will contribute to progress on the three philosophical issues mentioned at the outset.

Acknowledgements

Drafts of this chapter were presented at: the Mutual Belief in Pragmatics Conference, Shan'xi University; Linguistic Talks at Western, in London, Ontario; a philosophy of language discussion group at Universidad de los Andes; and the Faculty of Linguistics, Philology and Phonetics at the University of Oxford. We are grateful to the organisers and to all those present. We must especially single out Santiago Amaya, Ash Asudeh, Tomás Barrero, Lesley

Brown, Mitch Green, Mandy Simons and Elizabeth Allyn Smith for very fruitful suggestions. Thanks also to Adam Sennet, for encouragement and tutorials on presupposition; to David Bourget, Robyn Carston, Angela Mendelovici and Chris Viger for detailed comments on the penultimate draft; and to the editors and an anonymous referee for helpful feedback. Special thanks are owed to our dear friend and philosophical co-conspirator Ángeles Eraña Lagos, to whom we dedicate our work on this project. The research behind this chapter was partially funded by DGAPA Project 'Términos numéricos e implicatura escalar' IN401115 and by a grant from the Social Sciences and Humanities Research Council of Canada.

Our many and varied debts to Deirdre Wilson, *sine qua non*, go without saying; but they are implied throughout.

4 Evidential Explicatures and Mismatch Resolution

Victoria Escandell-Vidal

4.1 Introduction

Among the many contributions made by Deirdre Wilson to pragmatics, the notion of 'explicature' developed within the framework of relevance theory (Sperber & Wilson 1986/1995; Wilson & Sperber 1988a, 1993; Wilson 2000, 2005, 2011b; Carston 2002) occupies a central place. In Sperber and Wilson's approach, explicitly communicated content is not merely the result of a mechanical process of decoding, but 'a combination of linguistically encoded and contextually inferred conceptual features' (Sperber & Wilson 1986/ 1995: 182). Explicatures vary in their degree of explicitness and complexity, from basic developments of a logical form to more complex representations where the propositional content can be embedded under various layers of higher-level assumptions and metarepresentations related to illocutionary force, propositional-attitude and degree of commitment, among others.

The notion of explicature represents a radical departure from the common understanding of the relations between the explicit and the implicit, on the one hand, and decoding and inference, on the other; it also offers a novel way to establish the division of labour between semantics and pragmatics. The research space thus created is particularly suited for dealing with cases where both decoding and inference seem to play a role in determining the explicit content of an utterance. Among such cases, those in which certain interpretations arise in a systematic way without being directly stipulated by grammar have a privileged status. This is precisely the kind of phenomenon I want to discuss here.

Knowing the grounds on which an assertion is made (whether on direct perception, inference or hearsay) can be highly relevant in interaction. To avoid being misinformed, we humans are endowed with mechanisms for 'epistemic vigilance' (Sperber et al. 2010). In fact, languages can have 'evidentials', specialised grammatical devices to indicate the speaker's source of knowledge (Chafe & Nichols 1986; Ifantidou 2001; Aikhenvald 2004, 2014; Speas 2008). Quechua (Faller 2002) and Tibetan (Garrett 2001), for instance, have a closed class of dedicated grammatical markers; other languages – including Germanic and Romance languages – resort to describing the information source by lexical means, such as adverbials, parenthetical and embedding constructions, modal verbs, etc. (Dendale & Tasmowski 2001).

Contrary to what one would expect, in Spanish we can find utterances in which an evidential commitment seems to arise without any overt grammatical or lexical evidential indicator. Compare the examples in (4.1) and (4.2):

(4.1)   a. *María es joven.*
             María be(*ser*).PRS.3SG young.
             'Maria is young.'
        b. *Juan viene mañana.*
             Juan come.PRS.3SG tomorrow.
             'Juan is coming tomorrow.'

(4.2)   a. *María está joven.*
             María be(*estar*).PRS.3SG young.
             'Maria looks young. [>I saw her.]'
        b. *Juan venía mañana.*
             Juan come.IMPF.3SG tomorrow.
             'Juan was coming tomorrow. [>I was told.]'

The basic predications expressed are roughly the same for each pair, but the examples in (4.2) carry additional evidential information: (4.2a) commits the speaker to being the direct source for the assertion (experiential interpretation, +EXP); the information asserted in (4.2b) is presented as second-hand, a case of covert quotation in which the information conveyed is presented as attributed to a different speaker (reportative interpretation, +REP; Wilson 2000). Most significantly, these enriched interpretations are obligatory without situating the utterances in any particular context.

These facts demand a principled explanation, for which I will address the following questions:

• What is the status of the extra evidential content in (4.2)?
• Where does it come from?
• What are the implications of this phenomenon for linguistic theory?

4.2   Encoded Meaning? Conversational Implicature?

A most remarkable property about the evidential entailments in (4.2) is their systematicity. It could seem, then, natural to suppose that the evidential commitment is encoded by the items that happen to be different with respect to (4.1), namely the copula *estar*, 'be' – instead of *ser*, 'be' – and the 'imperfecto' (an imperfective past) instead of present tense.

For the copula, some scholars (Querido 1976; see also Roby 2007) have suggested that the meaning of *estar* includes an 'immediate experience requirement' as a lexical feature, as happens in English with verbs like *look*, *seem*, *taste*, *feel* or *smell* (Stephenson 2007; Pearson 2013). However, this cannot be the right explanation for Spanish, since many occurrences of *estar* – in fact, most of them – do not carry any systematic evidential entailment, as illustrated in (4.3):

(4.3)   a.   María está enferma/cansada
             'Maria is ill/tired.' [-EXP]
        b.   Las tiendas están cerradas.
             'Shops are closed.' [-EXP]

If the evidential indication was indeed encoded, the discourse segment in (4.4) should be unacceptable, but it is not; in fact, the second sentence provides a totally plausible explanation as to why the speaker has not seen Maria recently, which is also compatible with the overt indication of second-hand information:

(4.4)   Hace tiempo que no he visto a María. <u>Está enferma</u>. Me lo
        ha dicho su hermana.
        'I've not seen Maria for quite a while now. She is ill [-EXP].
        Her sister told me.'

As for the 'imperfecto', it is an imperfective past that focalises the inner part of a situation while blurring its limits (de Swart 1998; Cipria & Roberts 2000; García Fernández & Camus Bergareche 2004; De Saussure & Sthioul 2005). It does not encode that the information is reported, and so it is compatible with indications of direct perception, as in (4.5):

(4.5)   Vi que Juan <u>hablaba</u> por teléfono.
        'I saw that Juan was talking on the phone.' [-REP]

If the evidential commitment in (4.2) is not part of the encoded meaning, one might suppose that it is a conversational implicature. However, this does not seem to be the case either. Conversational implicatures are highly context-dependent, so they can vary from context to context. However, there is no set of contextual assumptions that can modify or cancel the evidential commitments found in (4.2). Adding an explicit indication that the speaker had direct access to a certain state of affairs is perfectly compatible with the experiential interpretation of *estar* but does not strengthen it in any significant way:

(4.6)   Acabo de ver a María. Está muy joven.
        'I've just met Maria. She looks very young.' [+EXP]

Contextual assumptions cannot weaken or cancel the evidential entailment either. If the context makes it manifest that the speaker could not have obtained the information through direct experience, the evidential commitment will not be affected, resulting in a blatant contradiction:

(4.7)   #Hace tiempo que no veo a María. Está muy joven.
         #'I haven't seen Maria for quite a while now. She looks very young [+EXP].'

Similarly, the speaker of (4.2b) can provide further information about her source, but cannot identify herself as the origin without incurring any contradictory commitments:

(4.8)   #Juan <u>venía</u> mañana. Lo decidí yo misma.
         #'Juan was coming tomorrow [+REP]. I decided it.'

The question still remains: What then is the status of these commitments? Before giving an answer, I want to address other crucial questions, namely, when and why the evidential commitments in (4.2) arise.

4.3   Feature Mismatch

Let's begin with the evidential uses of *estar* by considering a further set of examples:

(4.9)   Juan está muy joven/alto/guapo
         'Juan is(*estar*) very young/tall/handsome.' [+EXP]

(4.10)   Juan es muy joven/alto/guapo.
         'Juan is(*ser*) very young/tall/handsome.' [-EXP]

The examples in (4.9)–(4.10) show that, even with the same predicates, the evidential commitment appears in (4.9) with *estar*, but not in (4.10) with *ser*. This strongly suggests that the evidential entailment is not carried by the copula or by the predicate alone, but by the combination of *estar* with certain adjectives, such as *joven* 'young', *alto* 'tall' and *guapo* 'handsome', but not *enfermo* 'ill', *cansado* 'tired' and *cerrado* 'closed' (cf. (4.3)). To account for this distribution, some brief considerations about the semantics of the copulas and the adjectives are in order.

As for the copulas, I assume that the semantics of *ser* and *estar* is the same, except for the fact that *estar* includes an additional meaning component: the requirement to link the predication to a specific topic situation. According to Maienborn (2005), *estar* carries the additional presupposition that the referential argument z is related (via a free variable R) to a specific discourse situation s_i:

(4.11)   *ser*: $\lambda P \, \lambda x \, \lambda z \, [z \approx [P(x)]]$
         estar: $\lambda P \, \lambda x \, \lambda z \, [z \approx [P(x)] \, / \, [s_i \mid R \, (z, s_i)]]$ (Maienborn 2005: 168)

Thus, while *estar* needs a spatiotemporal anchor, *ser* does not include such a requirement (cf. Brucart 2012; Escandell-Vidal 2018a,b).

As for the adjectives, I adopt the distinction between 'individual level predicates' (ILPs) and 'stage level predicates' (SLPs) (Milsark 1974; Carlson 1977; Kratzer 1988, 1995). According to Carlson (1977), ILPs express properties of individuals (i.e., of objects and kinds), while SLPs are predicated of stages (i.e., spatiotemporal 'slices' of individuals). SLPs require the property they denote to be linked with an external situation. Kratzer (1995) refines the original distinction and argues that ILPs and SLPs differ in argument structure: SLPs have an extra argument position for events or spatiotemporal locations (Davidsonian argument), whereas ILPs lack this position.

The ILP/SLP distinction has proven useful in accounting for a wide range of apparently unrelated grammatical phenomena, such as the possibility of *there*-insertion in copular sentences in English (Milsark 1974), the interpretation of bare plural subjects (Carlson 1977) and the compatibility with modifying adverbials (Kratzer 1995). Only SLPs seem natural in perception reports, as depictive secondary predicates and in absolute constructions. The ILP/SLP distinction has been invoked to account for copula choice in Spanish. Thus, it is assumed that *ser* combines naturally with ILPs such as *altruista* 'altruistic', *inteligente* 'intelligent', *astuto* 'clever' and *japonés* 'Japanese', whereas *estar* goes with SLPs such as *disponible* 'available', *descalzo* 'barefoot' and *roto* 'broken' (for discussion, see Leonetti 1994; Marín 2004, 2010, 2015; Camacho 2012; Pérez Jiménez et al. 2015).

With these ideas in mind, a generalisation easily emerges: the evidential commitment occurs only when *estar* is combined with an ILP. Crucially, this is a situation in which the requirements imposed by the copula are not satisfied within its local domain. *Estar* requires a spatiotemporal anchor, but the ILP lacks spatiotemporal properties. Then, the features of the copula and those of the predicate do not match (Escandell-Vidal 2018a,b).

Let's turn now to the case of the 'imperfecto'. Imagine that Ana asks *¿Qué sabes de María?* 'What do you know about María?'. The examples in (4.12)–(4.13) are all possible answers. Only those in (4.12) carry an entailment of second-hand information:

(4.12) a. Se examinaba del carnet de conducir uno de estos días.
            'She was doing her driving test one of these days.' [+REP]
        b. Salía de cuentas la semana pasada.
            'The baby was due last week.' [+REP]

(4.13) a. Estudiaba derecho.
            'She was studying law.' [-REP]
        b. Salía con un chico italiano de la facultad.
            She was going out with an Italian boy from college.' [-REP]

The question is again how to account for the distribution of the reportative interpretations.

As has been acknowledged in the literature (de Swart 1998; Berthonneau & Kleiber 1993; Cipria & Roberts 2000; Leonetti 2004; De Saussure & Sthioul 2005), the semantics of the Romance 'imperfecto' contains two requirements: first, as an imperfective tense, it selects atelic, homogeneous situations (i.e., states and activities, in Vendler's (1957) terms); second, being a non-autonomous tense, a temporal reference point in the past has to be identified.

The reportative examples in (4.12) fail to meet the two semantic requirements of the 'imperfecto' (Leonetti & Escandell-Vidal 2003; Escandell-Vidal & Leonetti 2011). First, the atelicity requirement is not satisfied by the *Aktionsart* of the lexical predicate: the predicates in (4.12) are telic (accomplishments and achievements). Second, the requirement to identify a reference point in the past is not satisfied either.

The examples under consideration, then, share a significant property: they contain a mismatch, a conflict between the requirements of a head and the features of its arguments (Pustejovsky 1993, 2011; de Swart 1998, 2011; Francis & Michaelis 2003; Carlson 2006). Both *estar* and the 'imperfecto' require a spatiotemporal anchor, but crucially in the relevant examples this semantic requirement is not fulfilled by the items with which they combine. Rather than resulting in bare ungrammaticality (as would happen if the features involved were active for syntactic computation only), mismatches involving interpretable features trigger inferential processes to satisfy the encoded requirements (Escandell-Vidal & Leonetti 2011; Escandell-Vidal 2018a,b). The process of mismatch resolution is carried out by adding new assumptions at the interpretive level. The result is a systematically enriched interpretation in which some meaning components cannot be explained in terms of strict compositionality.

4.4   Mismatch Resolution and Evidentiality

The evidential commitment found in examples like those in (4.2) is, thus, a result of the inferences made to resolve a feature mismatch. In the case of *estar*+ILP, this requires anchoring the predication to a spatiotemporal situation; in the case of the double mismatch with the 'imperfecto', this requires finding a past reference point and representing an atelic situation. In this section I will argue that the evidential interpretations are the optimal way to achieve these goals.

To understand how my proposal works, a closer look at evidential indications is in order. Following Nikolaeva (1999), Speas (2010) and Kalsang et al. (2013), I assume that evidential systems do not actually encode information about the knowledge source, but rather about more abstract relations between three situations:

  i. 'Evaluation Situation' (ES), the minimal situation of which the propositional content *p* is true.
 ii. 'Information Situation' (IS), the minimal situation in which the speaker came to know that *p*.
iii. 'Discourse Situation' (DS), the one in which the sentence is uttered.

There are two possible relations: inclusion ($\subset$) and accessibility ($>$). Evidential systems encode relations of inclusion and accessibility among ES, IS and DS. Each language grammaticalises a specific subset of such distinctions. A direct evidential indicates that the ES (in which *p* obtains) is included in the IS (in which the speaker came to know that *p*), and both ES and IS are accessible from the DS (the discourse situation). A hearsay evidential encodes that the IS is accessible from the DS, and the ES is accessible from the IS.

(4.14)   Direct evidence: ES $\subset$ IS; ES>DS; IS>DS
         Reportative evidence: IS>DS; ES>DS

This account is clearly reminiscent of Reichenbach's (1947) account for tense and temporal relations, which also considers three temporal points (event time, reference time, discourse time) and two relations (simultaneity and precedence).

My proposal, then, is that the evidential commitment that appears in (4.2) is the result of inferring the existence of a specific IS and establishing relations among ES, IS and DS that are of the same sort as those found in evidential systems – the obvious difference being that in mismatch resolution the relations are inferred, not encoded.

Take first *estar*+ILP structures. ILPs lack a spatiotemporal anchor for the predication. Inferring the existence of a situation in which the information has been directly acquired is a way of providing the copula with the spatiotemporal anchor it requires. The idea is as follows. Witnessing an event, or experiencing a situation, entails at least three things: first, that a perceptible event has taken place; second, that this happened within the witness's deictic sphere; third, that the time interval in which the state of affairs obtained is contained within, or overlaps with, the interval of the witnessing experience. Thus, any perceivable state of affairs necessarily entails the existence of a perception situation. So, when no other anchor is available, invoking the IS is always a readily accessible option to bind a predication.

This is, in fact, what happens in *estar*+ILP combinations. The assertion in (4.2a) is felicitous only if the situation that is at the basis of the assertion of *p* is contained in the situation where the speaker acquired her knowledge. The missing anchoring requirement of *estar* is satisfied by inferring an IS that contains the ES. Linking the predication to the situation in which the information has been acquired is a way of providing the predication with the spatiotemporal anchoring that the copula requires.

This abstract relation among situations is all that we need to account for the phenomenon under discussion and to explain a number of related phenomena. For example, it is usual to take for granted that *estar* predications are transitory, whilst permanent states are expressed by means of *ser*. One could imagine, then, that *estar*+ILP constructions always convey transitory states. It is possible indeed to obtain a variety of temporary readings with *estar*+ILP, in which the time span of the attributed property (ES) is limited to the IS:

(4.15)   Juan estuvo muy amable.
           'Juan was(*estar*) very friendly.' [≈Juan was not friendly
           before or after the IS]

Similarly, (4.9a) is compatible with the assumption that Juan was not that tall before the IS – though he will presumably be tall also after the IS.

However, nothing prevents *estar*+ILP constructions from expressing permanent properties, as long as they can be observed:

(4.16)   Estuvo muy amable, como siempre.
           'He was(*estar*) very kind [+EXP], as usual'

Here, the ES overlaps with the IS and is true also before and after the IS. So, what is crucial is that the speaker presents her assessment as a result of direct perception, not the length of the time span for which the state of affairs holds.

As for the 'imperfecto', the reportative interpretation arises when a double mismatch occurs. This double mismatch has to be solved by adding a past reference point and by obtaining an atelic interpretation. Inferring the existence of a past situation where the speaker has acquired the information (IS) provides the 'imperfecto' with the past reference point needed for its interpretation. In this case, the acquisition situation cannot be one of direct experience, because it would entail that the event encoded has already taken place, which would be incompatible with the imperfective nature of the 'imperfecto'. Inferring a non-asserted event preserves imperfectivity. The result is an interpretation where the speaker reports the information she received in the past (IS) about an event (ES) taking place in the future with respect to this acquisition situation in the past, with no claim about the direct accessibility of the reported event (ES) from the discourse situation (DS), but only from the information situation (IS).

This is exactly what hearsay evidentials indicate: that the ES is accessible from the IS, and the IS is accessible from the DS (Speas 2010). Thus, by inferring a past hearsay event both the requirements of the 'imperfecto' are satisfied: a past reference point is added and an imperfective event is thus represented.

This explains various significant facts about the examples under discussion, such as the co-occurrence of a past tense with future reference deictic adverbials (*mañana* 'tomorrow' in (4.2b)): this is possible because the past reference point is related to the IS (not to the ES), whereas the deictic adverbial indicates the expected event time (ES) without implying that the event has actually taken place. This is so even when the adverbial has past reference, as *la semana pasada* 'last week' in (4.12b).

The existence of two situations also makes it possible to explain why sentences like (4.17) can contain two deictic adverbials, each pointing in a different direction, without creating incompatibility:

(4.17)   Ayer venía mañana.
         'Yesterday he was coming tomorrow.' [+REP]

The first adverbial, with past reference, identifies the time in which the (inferred) IS took place; the second one, with future reference, indicates when the ES is supposed to take place. The sentence in (4.17) thus means that, according to the information the speaker received the day before, someone was supposed to come tomorrow.

Mismatch resolution is an inferential process that follows the same principles as other inferential processes, particularly consideration of relevance on the basis of accessibility and effort/effects balance. Crucially, mismatch resolution does not involve any kind of aspectual shift of the predicate's grammatical class. Thus, in experiential interpretation of *estar*+ILP, the ILPs are not changed into SLPs: in (4.2) and (4.9) the predicates still make classificatory assessments – the difference being that the assertions are relativised to an experiencer. Similarly, reportative readings do not change the aspectual class of the predicate either: telic predicates are not turned into atelic predicates; rather, it is the whole predication that is interpreted in a way that makes it possible to satisfy the requirements of the verbal tense. The inferential processes do not modify the procedures encoded.

The need for an experiencer is also the key to understanding why some structures can sound more marked than others. Predicates of personal taste, which already include an experiencer role in their argument structure, such as *rico* 'tasty' and *divertido* 'funny' (Ninan 2014; Pearson 2013) illustrate the less marked cases. Evaluative adjectives follow, together with moral and aesthetic predicates, since their application crucially depends on the appraisal of a judging individual, who decides on the applicability of adjectives such as *simpatico* 'friendly', *torpe* 'clumsy' and *inteligente* 'intelligent', not on an objective state of affairs:

(4.18)   El Rey estuvo simpático con los periodistas. (Europa Press, 1 June 2011)
         'The King was friendly with the media.' [+EXP]

(4.19)   Bruselas estuvo torpe y ciega (F. Ónega)
         'Brussels was (=behaved) clumsy and blind.' [+EXP]

(4.20)   La Real estuvo inteligente y caritativa (El País, 16 September 1998)
          'The Real [Sociedad de San Sebastián, a football team] was intelligent and charitable.' [+EXP]

Relational adjectives, such as *democrático* 'democratic' and *británico* 'British' give rise to the most marked cases, since the ES and the role of the experiencer can be a priori more difficult to infer:

(4.21)   a.   La cinta ha estado democrática. (Australian Open 2017;
                Federer vs Nadal match)
                'The tape has been democratic.' [+EXP]
          b.   Juan está muy británico.
                'Juan is being very British.' [+EXP]

In (4.21a) the sports commentator wanted to communicate that the net has favoured both players equally. By using *estar* he indicates that his assessment is a result of having watched the match. In (4.21b), the speaker communicates that, according to her experience, Juan is doing things in a way she finds stereotypically British. In both cases, the extra processing effort is balanced by extra interpretive effects (Escandell-Vidal 2018a,b).

Other phenomena can be accounted for along the lines suggested here. Interestingly, experiential interpretations are not merely an oddity found in languages with two copular verbs. The effect of direct perception can be obtained also in languages without copula alternation, provided that the adequate conditions are met. According to Fernald (1999), English copular constructions with ILPs, when explicitly delimited by adverbials encoding spatiotemporal restrictions (such as *sometimes*, *often*, *rarely*), carry a systematic entailment of observability:

(4.22)   Max is sometimes intelligent. [+EXP]

Example (4.22) is interpreted as conveying the additional assumption that on certain occasions Max behaves in an intelligent way, so the speaker has been able to witness the event upon which her assertion is grounded. The adverbial requires identifying a spatiotemporally bound situation – exactly the same requirement as *estar* in Spanish. It is not surprising, then, that the anchor needed for the adverbial is linked to the IS in which the direct evidence for the assertion has been acquired. Similar cases have been described for French by Martin (2008).

Feature mismatch could also be the basis of some readings of the English progressive described as conveying direct evidence or experiential involvement. If we assume that the present progressive indicates a non-delimited event instantiating the property denoted by the predicate (Žegarac 1990), the prediction is that the progressive will select eventive predicates. But if the progressive is combined with a stative verb, this requirement will not be met. A mismatch arises and a repair strategy is triggered whereby a perceptible event is inferred – again, typically, a form of behaviour – which provides observable evidence for the asserted property:

(4.23)   Peter is being a good baby. [+EXP]

Finally, it is worth noticing that the suggested solution can, *mutatis mutandis*, account for similar uses of the past progressive in English, such as those in (4.24), which happen to have exactly the same reportative entailments as the corresponding Spanish examples:

(4.24)   a. John was coming tomorrow.
          b. Yesterday John was coming tomorrow.

According to Lyons (1977: 814), (4.24a) has roughly the same meaning as *John said that he was coming tomorrow*, *John intended coming tomorrow*, and *I was told that John was coming tomorrow* (cf. also Palmer 1974: 38). Since the mismatch involved in the English sentences involves the same features as the one found in Spanish – a past imperfective progressive in need of a past reference point – it is no surprise that the repairing inferences follow the same path and give rise to the same reportative interpretation.

4.5   Higher-Level Explicatures

In the previous sections I have argued that evidential commitment arises when certain grammatical conditions are met, namely when a feature mismatch occurs between the requirements of a head and the features of the items with which it combines. It is the linguistic form – not the context – that triggers the inferential process that adds the evidential commitment. In this section I will return to the question of the status of these entailments.

In all the cases under discussion, an IS is added to the propositional schema to provide the anchor required by a selecting head. The outcome is a metarepresentation of the form 'The speaker has direct evidence for *p*' and 'The speaker has hearsay evidence for *p*', respectively. The resulting representations fall squarely under the relevance-theoretic notion of 'higher-level explicature', a development of a logical form where the proposition expressed 'is embedded in a range of different sorts of higher-level descriptions including (weak) speech act and propositional-attitude descriptions' (Carston 2002: 119). Evidential indications are included among inferential developments of the logical form of a proposition contributing to explicatures (Ifantidou 2001). Higher-level explicatures include the propositional content as a proper subpart and are formally and functionally different from implicatures. They are explicit, can give rise to entailments and raise new questions under discussion, but are not asserted. This explains why they escape truth-conditional operators, such as negation:

(4.25)   a.   María no está guapa.
              'Maria doesn't look pretty.' [+EXP]
         b.   Juan no venía mañana.
              'Juan was not coming tomorrow.' [+REP]

In (4.25) the negation affects only the basic predication, not the evidential explicature. Thus, (4.25a) cannot mean 'Maria looks pretty, but you don't have direct experience of it'. Similarly, (4.25b) cannot mean that the speaker does not have hearsay evidence for John's coming tomorrow. Again, this behaviour reproduces that of the sentences with grammatical evidentials (Faller 2002; Garrett 2001).

Evidential explicatures contribute metarepresentations related to epistemic vigilance (cf. Wilson 2000, 2011b; Sperber et al. 2010; Unger 2012). In copular constructions, the experiential explicature 'The speaker has direct evidence for *p*' expresses a relation between a particular mental state of the speaker and the thought *p*. The speaker presents herself as asserting something for which she claims to have direct evidence. This is particularly important when, as in the present case, the predication is evaluative, and hence it is ultimately a matter of individual taste, thus giving give rise to 'faultless disagreement' (Kölbel 2003). Hearsay interpretations are representations of attributed utterances: the speaker reproduces a representation that resembles someone else's utterance, while explicitly conveying that she is not the direct source of the content represented. Thus, both experiential and reportative indications provide specific cues for accurate appraisal and representation of assumptions, which goes hand in hand with accurate tracking of speakers' reliability.

4.6   Concluding Remarks

In this chapter an account of the evidential interpretations that arise in some Spanish constructions with *estar* and the 'imperfecto' has been offered in terms of inferential mismatch resolution. This process is triggered by the properties of the linguistic form: the context plays no role in determining either the kind of evidence expressed or its strength. The evidential assumptions do not affect truth conditions; they are 'higher-level explicatures' (Sperber & Wilson 1986/1995), which provide relevant input for mechanisms of epistemic vigilance.

My proposal suggests a general hypothesis about how mismatches involving spatiotemporal anchoring will be repaired by inferring situations of information acquisition that give rise to evidential commitments:

• Experiential interpretations are obtained when the (unsatisfied) head does not require a disjoint reference point (absolute interpretations). This is consistent with related cases of evidential interpretations in copular constructions in languages without copula alternation (Fernald 1999 for English; Martin 2008 for French).

- Reportative interpretations are obtained when the (unsatisfied) head requires a disjoint reference point (relative interpretations). This is also consistent with related cases in English (Lyons 1977).

The existence of mismatches such as those discussed here, and the effects they have, supports a particular view on the interaction between grammar and pragmatics. Linguistic items have formal attributes (including requirements to combine with specific categories or specific semantic features) that are relevant for syntactic computation (Escandell-Vidal 2018a,b). When syntactic requirements are not fulfilled, the derivation crashes; in contrast, if a semantic requirement is not met, the derivation can proceed, but the mismatch has to be solved and an inferential process is activated to satisfy the otherwise unfulfilled requirements.

The predictability and systematicity of the evidential entailments analysed here is a consequence of the existence of a mismatch and the abstract nature of the features in conflict, which have to be satisfied at any cost (Escandell-Vidal & Leonetti 2011; Carston 2016a). Since these features are not accessible to consciousness, the process of mismatch resolution takes place at a subconscious level.

A number of familiar phenomena can be accounted for along the lines suggested here, including mass/count shifts, metonymy and deferred reference, aspectual clashes, non-temporal uses of verbal tenses and evidential interpretations of tensed sentences. It is thus possible to avoid pervasive polysemy and maintain well-established grammatical distinctions, while allowing for flexible and controlled ways of developing the explicit content of an utterance. The fact that we can find similar mismatches that trigger similar inferential processes with similar results in different languages provides additional support to the idea that these processes are systematic because they are subject to general cognitive principles.

Modelling evidentiality in terms of a limited set of relations among situations provides an economical and powerful framework for mismatch resolution. It also suggests an interesting cognitive generalisation by restricting the kind of relations among situations that the human mind can process and can find it useful to encode.

My proposal also offers a natural explanation for the solid intuition that sentences containing mismatches can be more or less marked, so they can require extra processing effort. This seems in fact to be the case, as psycholinguistic experimental research has shown by means of self-paced reading tests, eye-tracking and magnetoencephalography (Piñango et al. 1999; McElree et al. 2006; Pickering et al. 2006; Brennan & Pylkkänen 2008). As predicted by relevance theory, this extra processing cost legitimates the expectation of extra interpretive effects.

The inferential process of mismatch resolution originates at the level of the encoded meaning and is constrained by the features of the encoded meaning, but it is not encoded by linguistic expressions. It might be the origin of grammaticalisation, but until that takes place, it is only guided by expectations of relevance.

Acknowledgements

This research has benefited from a grant from the Spanish Ministerio de Economia y Competitividad to the project SPIRIM, FFI2015-63497-P. Various topics included here have been presented at different conferences. I am grateful to the audiences for suggestions and criticism. Thanks also to the anonymous reviewer for useful comments and to the volume editors for their help and advice. Needless to say, any remaining shortcomings are my own.

5 Representation and Metarepresentation in Negation

Jacques Moeschler

5.1 Introduction

Metarepresentation has been the subject of many philosophical and psychological discussions (see Sperber 2000 for an overview) and there have been a few studies of its role in pragmatics (e.g. Noh 2000; Wilson 2000; Allott 2017). Topics such as reported speech, various kinds of negation and irony have been explored in some detail, as has the role of evidential and discourse markers in indicating the presence of metarepresentation. However, several issues concerning the relation between negation and metarepresentation remain unsettled (Horn 1985, 1989; Carston 1996, 2002; Moeschler 2010), including the following.

First, when negation is applied to scalar predicates, it gives rise to different interpretations and inferences. However, no formal or cognitive account has yet explained what the cognitive effects of descriptive and metalinguistic uses of negation are.

Second, the category of metalinguistic negation is generally associated with presuppositional denial (see Ducrot 1984 as a classic example) or with uses of negation scoping on a linguistic form. In this contribution, negation will be associated with two metalinguistic uses, an upward entailing one with scalar predicates, and a presuppositional one. Taking into account these two observations, I will defend a pragmatic approach to negation distinguishing three main uses: a descriptive one and two metalinguistic ones.

Third, whereas standardly only descriptive uses of negation are said to be truth conditional, I will defend here a general truth-conditional approach to negation by illustrating the representational effects of descriptive and metalinguistic uses of negation. In a nutshell, I will argue that those three uses have propositional effects: the descriptive use aims at erasing some old information that has been present in the context, whereas metalinguistic negation, in its upward entailing use, aims at strengthening the positive counterpart (POS) of the negative utterance (NEG). As for presuppositional negation, it erases both the explicature and the presupposition of POS. In other words, the three main uses of negation advocated in this chapter will be described not just at the semantic level (scope and entailment), but mainly at the level of their cognitive effects.

Fourth, the main criterion for distinguishing between these three uses of negation is based on the semantic and pragmatic effects of the corrective clause (COR) following the NEG. It will be argued that COR is mainly responsible for the semantic and pragmatic differences between these three uses of negation. With descriptive negation (DN), COR entails NEG, whereas with the upward entailing negation, COR entails POS. When COR follows a presuppositional negation, it entails the negation of the POS (NEG) and its presupposition. Moreover, as far as pragmatic effects are concerned, DN has as a main effect the elimination of POS from the context, upward negation the strengthening of POS, and presuppositional negation the elimination of both POS and its presupposition from the context.

This chapter is organised as follows. Section 5.2 is devoted to metarepresentation and negation. Section 5.3 discusses the entailment and scope properties of the three uses of negation advocated in this chapter. Section 5.4 presents the pragmatic arguments linked to cognitive effects and Section 5.5 discusses the prediction our approach makes about the processing of descriptive and metalinguistic negation, and its implications for further research. Finally, Section 5.6 sketches the main consequences of the proposed analysis.

5.2   Metarepresentation and Negation

Let us start with Deirdre Wilson's definition (2000: 411) of what a metarepresentation is: 'A metarepresentation is a representation of a representation: a higher-order representation with a lower representation embedded within it.' For Wilson, embedded representations can be (i) utterances (public representations), (ii) thoughts (mental representations) or (iii) sentences or propositions (abstract representations). As examples, Wilson gives cases of direct, indirect and free indirect quotations, hearsay adverbs, echoic utterances adopting a questioning or dissociating attitude to the thought metarepresented, pragmatic markers, tag questions, and metalinguistic negation (MN). However, all the examples of MN that are given are about the form of the utterance, as in (5.1) to (5.3):

(5.1)   Around here we don't eat tom[eiDouz] and we don't get stressed out. We eat tom[a:touz] and we get a little tense now and then.

(5.2)   Mozart's sonatas weren't for violin and piano, they were for piano and violin.

(5.3)   I didn't manage to trap two mongeese: I managed to trap two mongooses.

All these examples are clear cases of metalinguistic uses of negation, where the speaker rejects (i) the American pronunciation of 'tomatoes' and the expression 'stressed out', (ii) the description of Mozart's sonatas and (iii) the inappropriate plural form of 'mongoose' in English.

The view of MN reflected in the uses in (5.1) to (5.3) is consistent with the definition of metarepresentation, but is not generally acknowledged, since 'linguists generally define denial as involving the rejection of an attributed utterance' (Wilson 2000). In other words, these uses of metalinguistic negation tend to be interpreted as cases of 'regular negation', because the 'rejections of attributed thoughts [are treated] as cases of regular negation' (Wilson 2000: 252). In contrast, a relevance-theoretical account of MN would treat all these cases as echoic (Sperber & Wilson 1986/1995; Wilson 2000; Wilson & Sperber 2004).

A second step in the definition of MN has been made by Horn, whose examples are not merely rejections of forms or expressions, but rejections of implicatures, that is, non-truth-conditional contents. To illustrate, in examples (5.4) and (5.5), negation scopes over a scalar implicature (Horn 1989: 384), for instance 'he does not have more than three children' in (5.4) and 'you didn't eat all of the cookies' in (5.5):

(5.4)   He doesn't have three children, he has four.

(5.5)   You didn't eat some of the cookies, you ate all of them.

Horn gives three diagnostics distinguishing metalinguistic from descriptive negation (Horn 1989: 392–413). First, metalinguistic negation is not incorporated:

(5.6)   It is {*impossible, not possible} for you to leave, it's necessary.

Second, metalinguistic negation is incompatible with negative polarity items (NPIs):

(5.7)   Chris didn't manage to solve {some, *any} of the problems – he managed to solve all of them.

The last test is the *mais* test, based on Anscombre and Ducrot's (1977) analysis of *mais* ('but'): Horn hypothesises that metalinguistic negation is marked by $mais_{SN}$, whereas descriptive negation is marked by $mais_{PA}$. $Mais_{PA}$ (*aber* in German, *pero* in Spanish) is argumentative, and implies the realisation of two speech acts, whereas $mais_{SN}$ (*sondern* in German, *sino* in Spanish) is the realisation of one single speech act. Moreover, $mais_{SN}$ is syntactically incompatible with a complete corrective clause:

(5.8)   Descriptive negation
         Il n'est pas grand,   'He is not tall'
         a. $mais_{PA}$ petit   'but small'

       b. il est petit   'he is small'

       c. $mais_{PA}$ il est petit   'but he is small'

(5.9)   Metalinguistic negation

       Il n'est pas grand   'He is not tall'

       a. $mais_{SN}$ très grand   'but very tall'

       b. il est très grand   'he is very tall'

       c. *$mais_{SN}$ il est très grand   'but he is very tall'

In other words, the *mais* test claims that descriptive negation is paired with $mais_{PA}$, whereas metalinguistic negation is followed by $mais_{SN}$, because $mais_{SN}$, contrary to $mais_{PA}$ (5.8c), is incompatible with a full corrective clause (5.9c).

All these tests are useful, but they do not apply to all cases. First, the incorporation of negation is restricted to lexical contrasts that are expressed morphologically. Antonymy, for instance, is out of the scope of this test (e.g. *beautiful/ugly*, *warm/cold*), because the negative opposite is not morphologically overt, but lexically covert.[1] Second, the NPI test concerns only the downward vs. upward entailing negation, but not the presuppositional negation. Third, the *mais* test is not convincing. On the one hand, it cannot be applied to presuppositional negation, as (5.10) shows:

(5.10)   I have not stopped smoking, *SN I never smoked.

In effect, blocking presupposition projection requires a justification, that is a reason why it is not projected. The simplest way is to give COR a contradictory content to the presupposition. Therefore, this contradiction relation cannot be made explicit with a contrastive connective such as SN, because the contradiction occurs in the argumentative use of *mais* between implicatures, as shown in (5.11):

(5.11)   Il est paresseux, mais intelligent.

       'He is lazy, but smart.'

       a. he is lazy +> we cannot hire him as a TA

       b. he is smart +> we can hire him as a TA

On the other hand, it has been shown that the syntactic argument, according to which SN is not compatible with the complete corrective clause whereas PA is, cannot suffice because it is not descriptively adequate. German examples

---

[1] Another argument can be given: the morphological vs. syntactic negation is, at least as regards epistemic adjectives, distributed in a complementary way: true modals such as 'possible' and 'necessary' prefer a negation marker over a morphological prefix, as opposed to epistemic adjectives such as 'likely', 'avoidable', 'inevitable', 'desirable', 'certain', 'believable' (Casartelli 2017).

show that descriptive negation is followed by *sondern* (SN) as well as metalinguistic negation, but when the contrast is argumentative, descriptive negation is followed by *aber* (PA):

(5.12)   Mein Haus ist nicht schön, {sondern, *aber} gewöhnlich.
          'My house is not beautiful, but ordinary.'

(5.13)   Mein Haus ist nicht schön, sondern wunderbar.
          'My house is not beautiful, but extraordinary.'

(5.14)   Mein Haus ist nicht schön, aber bequem.
          'My house is not beautiful, but comfortable.'

Finally, if we use another criterion by Anscombre and Ducrot (1977) defining the difference between SN and PA, it reveals that upward negation is more acceptable with *en revanche* ('on the other hand'), a connective strengthening PA, rather than with *au contraire* ('on the contrary'), a connective strengthening SN. (5.15) and (5.16) are good illustrations:

(5.15)   a. Ma maison n'est pas belle, SN au contraire quelconque.
             'My house is not beautiful, SN on the contrary ordinary.'
          b. # Ma maison n'est pas belle, SN en revanche quelconque.
             'My house is not beautiful, SN on the other hand ordinary.'

(5.16)   a. # Ma maison n'est pas belle, PA au contraire extraordinaire.
             'My house is not beautiful, PA on the contrary gorgeous.'
          b. Ma maison n'est pas belle, PA en revanche extraordinaire.
             'My house is not beautiful, PA on the other hand gorgeous.'

As it stands, no clear formal, i.e. morphosyntactic, criteria are sufficient to differentiate descriptive vs. metalinguistic negation. We assume that the differences between descriptive and metalinguistic negation mainly lie at the semantic and pragmatic levels. This is the reason why we do not include in our analysis of MN cases like (5.1) to (5.3), which are clearly echoic and correcting the form of a previous utterance. We suspect, as mentioned in Zuo (2017) for Chinese, that these cases have more non-representational, that is, emotional, effects than representational ones.

5.3   Entailment and Scope of Negation

In what follows, I differentiate three uses of negation: one descriptive use (DN), and two metalinguistic ones (MN): MN1 is the negation of a scalar (conversational) implicature, whereas MN2 is the negation of a presupposition. To make these three uses straightforward at the descriptive level, I will differentiate three types of content: NEG is the negative content of the negative proposition (i.e. *not* P); POS is the positive content of the negated proposition (i.e. P); COR is the content of the corrective proposition following NEG. Examples (5.17) to (5.19) are examples of these three uses:

(5.17)   Izuki is not beautiful, he is ordinary.

(5.18)   Izuki is not beautiful, he is fantastic.

(5.19)   I don't regret having failed, since I passed.

The difference between these three types of negation can be made explicit at the semantic level where the following entailments hold:

(5.20)   DN   COR → NEG

(5.21)   MN1   COR → POS

(5.22)   MN2   COR → ¬POS ∧ ¬PP$_{POS}$

In others words, within descriptive negation, the corrective clause entails the negative one, whereas its positive counterpart is entailed by metalinguistic negation 1 (MN1). As regards MN2, both the assertion (POS) and its presupposition (PP$_{POS}$) are under the scope of negation. Examples (5.23) to (5.25) make these relations explicit:

(5.23)   Izuki is ordinary → Izuki is not beautiful.

(5.24)   Izuki is gorgeous → Izuki is beautiful.

(5.25)   I passed → not (I regret having failed) ∧ not (I failed).

An important question is what triggers these entailments. Let us take NEG without COR, as in (5.26) and (5.27):

(5.26)   Izuki is not beautiful.

(5.27)   I don't regret having failed.

What are the entailments of these utterances? (5.26) has a downward-oriented meaning 'less than beautiful', which does not imply that the 'less-than' meaning equals one of the antonyms of 'beautiful' (see Moeschler 2018 for a development). On the other hand, in (5.27), the presupposition 'I failed' is projected. We assume indeed that negation is semantically downward entailing and preserves presupposition. Contrastively, when a corrective clause (COR) is added to NEG, the scalar orientation of negation can be upward entailing, and the presupposition cancelled, as shown in (5.18) and (5.19).

Now, this is a description, but not an explanation. So, what could be the explanation? For instance, why is negation not ambiguous between its downward and upward orientation, as well as between preserving and cancelling presuppositions? As proposed by Horn (1985, 1989), we assume that negation is not semantically ambiguous – there are not two negation operators with two different semantics – but has different pragmatic uses (cf. Section 5.5).

The non-ambiguity stance supports the thesis that negation is semantically downward entailing and presupposition preserving. But how to explain that negation is downward entailing regarding its semantics? The explanation goes as follows: negation is downward entailing without COR, because the targeted zone of the scale by negation is identical to the propositions compatible with NEG (Moeschler 2013). For instance, (5.29a) and (5.29b) are propositions that follow from (5.28), whereas in (5.30), COR ('she has four') entails (5.31):

(5.28)   Anne does not have three children.

(5.29)   a. Anne has two children.
          b. Anne has one child.

(5.30)   Anne does not have three children, she has four.

(5.31)   a. Anne has four children.
          b. Anne has three children.
          c. Anne has two children.
          d. Anne has one child.

So, what is the function of COR? As the entailments in (5.31) show, (5.30) entails that Anne has three children. In that case, how can it be possible that (5.30) entails POS and asserts NEG? In other words, how can it be that (5.30) is not contradictory? (5.30) is indeed not contradictory, because negation scopes over the scalar implicature of POS, i.e. (5.32), but not over POS itself:

(5.32)   Anne does not have more than three children.

So, COR entails Anne has four, three, two and one child(ren), and negation scopes over the scalar implicature of POS. This answers two questions: (i) why is (5.30) not contradictory? Because negation scopes over the implicature of POS, and not over POS itself; (ii) why is COR required to make these entailments explicit? Because without COR, the preferred reading would be downward.

Unfortunately, this answer is not sufficient. Why does negation not scope over the implicature of POS in the absence of COR? That is, why does (5.33) not implicate the negation of the implicature of POS, i.e. (5.34)?

(5.33)   Anne does not have three children.

(5.34)   It is not the case that Anne does not have more than three children.

Logically, the entailment of (5.33) (Anne has two children) is compatible with (5.34), but only partially. (5.34) entails that Anne has three children, which entails Anne has two children, but (5.33)'s entailment is contradictory with Anne has three children, i.e. POS. In other words, COR entails POS, but POS is contradictory with NEG, and therefore, the entailments of (5.33) cannot be compatible with the negation of the implicature of POS. So, the conclusion is straightforward: in (5.33), NEG cannot target the implicature of POS.

The upshot is that we now have a semantic argument for distinguishing downward and upward entailing negation. The same type of argument can be used for distinguishing the two types of metalinguistic negation. With MN2, both POS and its presupposition are under the scope of negation. So, whereas MN1 entails both COR and POS, MN2 defeats both POS and its presupposition. Table 2 summarises the semantic and pragmatic differences between the three types of negation, where P corresponds to the content of POS and Q to its implicated or presupposed content.

5.4   Cognitive Effects of Negation

However, Table 2 does not clearly state how these three uses of negation yield different cognitive effects. Recall that in relevance theory (Sperber & Wilson 1986/1995; Wilson & Sperber 2004) there are three types of cognitive effects: the addition of a new assumption, the strengthening of an old assumption, and the eradication of an old assumption. We will see that the main contextual effects of negation are the eradication and the strengthening of old assumptions. As we understand these effects, it means that the main function of negative utterances is a modification of the previous context or, in other words, the restructuring of the common ground.

Let us start with DN: its main cognitive effect is the eradication of POS from the common ground. COR has the function of strengthening NEG, as the entailment relation between COR and NEG shows (COR → NEG). The inferential schema is given in (5.35), and the full deductive demonstration in (5.36):

(5.35) a. Contextual assumption   POS
        b. Utterance explicature   NEG ∧ COR
        c. Contextual effect   ~~POS~~

(5.36) Demonstration of (5.35)
        a. POS   Contextual assumption
        b. NEG ∧ COR   Utterance explicature
        c. COR   ∧-elimination rule (from b)
        d. COR → NEG   COR entailment
        e. NEG   Modus ponens (c–d)
        f. NEG → ¬POS   Negation
        g. ¬POS   Modus ponens (e–f)

Table 2 *Semantic and pragmatic properties of three types of negation (the crossed variables mean that propositions Q and ¬Q are defeated by negation)*

	Assertion	Entailment	Presupposition	Implicature
DN	¬P		Q	
MN1	¬P	P ∧ Q		~~¬Q~~
MN2	¬P	¬P ∧ ¬Q	~~Q~~	

As (5.36) shows, under POS hypothesis (contextual assumption), ¬POS is inferred. So, what COR contributes to the interpretative process is the eradication of POS from the context.

What about MN1, that is, upward entailing negation? As Table 2 shows, the main effect of MN1 is the strengthening of POS (POS+), since POS is entailed by COR. (5.37) gives the general template, whereas (5.38) gives the demonstration of (5.37):

(5.37)   a. Contextual assumption   POS
         b. Utterance explicature   NEG ∧ COR
         c. Contextual effect   POS+

(5.38)   a. POS   Contextual assumption
         b. NEG ∧ COR   Utterance explicature
         c. COR   ∧-elimination rule
         d. COR → POS   COR entailment
         e. POS   Modus ponens

POS is already an assumption. So, starting from other premises to obtain as a conclusion the same proposition POS leads to its strengthening (notated as POS+), that is, POS is further confirmed as the conclusion of a distinct non-demonstrative inference.

As far as presuppositional negation is concerned, things are paradoxically easier. NEG simply erases POS and its presupposition.[2]

---

[2] An alternative context is possible, when the context is negative. Then NEG confirms in a first step what is in the context, and in a second step, defeats its presuppositions. This situation is exemplified in the following example:

   A: I saw Abi. Apparently, she does not regret having failed.
   B: Indeed, she does not regret having failed, because she passed.

Table 3 *Semantic and pragmatic properties of negation*

	Entailments	Utterance explicatures	Contextual assumptions	Contextual effects
DN	$COR \rightarrow NEG$	$NEG \wedge COR$	POS	~~POS~~
MN1	$COR \rightarrow POS$	$NEG \wedge COR$	POS	POS+
MN2	$COR \rightarrow \neg POS \wedge \neg PP_{POS}$	$NEG \wedge COR$	POS	~~POS~~ $\wedge PP_{POS}$

(5.39) a. Contextual assumption $POS \wedge PP_{POS}$
    b. Utterance explicature $\underline{NEG \wedge COR}$
    c. Contextual effect   ~~POS~~ $\wedge$ ~~PP~~$_{POS}$

The contextual effect is obtained through the following demonstration:

(5.40) a. POS   Contextual assumption
    b. $POS \rightarrow PP_{POS}$ Presupposition
    c. PP_{POS} Modus ponens (a–b)
    d. $NEG \wedge COR$ Utterance explicature
    e. COR $\wedge$-elimination (d)
    f. $COR \rightarrow \neg PP_{POS}$ COR entailment
    g. $\neg PP_{POS}$ Modus ponens (e–f)
    h. $\neg PP_{POS} \rightarrow \neg POS$ Presupposition cancellation entailment
    i. $\neg POS$ Modus ponens (h–i)
    j. $\neg PP_{POS}$ Reiteration of (g)
    k. $\neg POS \wedge \neg PP_{POS}$ $\wedge$-introduction (j, k)

In other words, in a context in which POS implies its presupposition PP, COR entails the negation of PP_{POS} and the presupposition cancellation entails the negation of POS, both POS and its presupposition are defeated (k).

Table 3 summarises the contextual effects and the semantic and pragmatic effects.

We now have good reasons for distinguishing between three uses of negation. The question is how we can explain that MN, whatever its scope (presupposition or implicature), can have representational effects.

5.5   Consequences

At the beginning of the chapter, we referred to Deirdre Wilson's definition of metarepresentation. Now, the question is: do metalinguistic uses of negation satisfy her description of what a metarepresentation is? For instance, do descriptive and metalinguistic uses of negation, which have the same logical form (5.41), have different explicatures, at the pragmatic level, as represented in (5.42)?

(5.41)   ¬P

(5.42)   a. Descriptive negation: It is not the case [that P]
          b. Metalinguistic negation: It is not the case that
             [X can utter/think [that P]]

If the semantics is the same, the pragmatics is not the same, and some contextual effects, as shown in Section 5.4, are different. However, these contextual effects are all about truth-conditional properties of both descriptive and metalinguistic negation. In other words, these effects are truth conditional, that is, representational. In other words, metalinguistic uses of negation have representational properties, exactly as descriptive uses have.

As an illustration of this claim, let us come back to the propositional effects of both uses of metalinguistic negation: in upward entailing negation, the strengthening of POS is accompanied by the cancellation of an implicature, whereas in its presuppositional use, negation cancels both the assertion and its presupposition. These contextual effects are propositional, hence truth conditional. Indeed, cancelling an implicature corresponds to the elimination of the contextual effect of the positive counterpart of NEG, whereas cancelling an assertion and its presupposition is equal to eliminating these contents from the context.

However, two more points must be made here. First, it must be stressed that the cancellation of both an implicature and a presupposition is not trivially predictable: as we have shown earlier, the cancellation of the implicature of a positive utterance can only be triggered by a metalinguistic use of negation, and is only detectable through the presence of COR or a strong contextual clue. For instance, in a recent set of experiments, Blochowiak and Grisot (2018) have shown that a matching context with MN1 gives the right prediction: in other words, MN is context sensitive, just as DN is.

Second, the cancellation of a presupposition cannot be obtained without a corrective clause giving a reason for cancelling the presupposition. From a purely cognitive point of view, this is a demanding process that can be pointed out only with unusual ways of speaking, or even aggressive or crude expressions such as 'what the fuck!', or von Fintel's (2001) HWAM test ('hey, wait a minute'). Moreover, when a connective such as 'because' or 'since' is used, it does not express a Correction (DN) or a Contrast (MN1) discourse relation, but an Explanation one (Moeschler 2018):

(5.43)   The king of France is not bald, {because, since} there is no
          king of France.

Finally, one consequence of using negation is its effect on the current context. Up to now, we have given a simple description of the contextual effects of the three uses of negation. But what are their effects on the current context?

If context is defined as (a part of) the common ground (CG), it means that each negative utterance implies that CG has properties which match its usages and will be consequently modified. These effects are described as follows:

i.   With DN, POS is removed from the CG and substituted by an alternative proposition. When COR is present, COR replaces POS. When COR is absent, no substitution is obtained, and only NEG is proposed.

ii. With MN1, scoping over the implicature of POS, COR adds a new proposition to the CG and POS is strengthened, whereas NEG is not at issue. Again, as COR is necessary to trigger an upward entailing reading, COR positively contributes to the contextual effects of NEG.

iii. With MN2 (presupposition cancellation), both POS and PP_{POS} are removed from the CG and replaced by an alternative proposition, that is, COR. As COR can be introduced by a factive connective such as 'since' or 'because' (Moeschler 2011, 2016), COR strongly contributes to the restructuring of the CG.

5.6   Conclusion

In this chapter, we have proposed an account of three uses of negation, one descriptive, and two metalinguistic, each with contextual and semantic effects whose nature is propositional. One prediction of this analysis is that metalinguistic negation should not be costlier in cognitive effort than descriptive negation. As reported in Blochowiak and Grisot (2018), experimental results support a contextual approach to negation: if the relevant context is given, no differences in processing between descriptive and metalinguistic readings are observed in French, thus supporting parallel experimental results obtained with eye-tracking techniques in Korean (Noh et al. 2013).

The experimental finding is crucial, because it confirms the pragmatic-contextual approach advocated in this chapter. But, of course, some questions remain unanswered. First, do metalinguistic uses of negation have, as well as propositional effects, non-propositional ones, such as, for instance, an ironic attitude or an indication of aggressive feeling? This is descriptively confirmed for Chinese, as reported in Zuo (2017). Second, what are the consequences of the contextualist approach to MN? We predict that MN is interpreted in a one-step process, like DN. The exception, that is, a two-step process to MN, is cases of deliberate humour, as predicted in the semantic and pragmatic ambiguity approaches (see, respectively, Burton-Roberts 1989; Horn 1989). We predict that this is not how MN is ordinarily processed, but only when specific conditions are in place so that the addressee is garden-pathed by the speaker's negative utterance. One typical example is Pierre Desproges' famous statement about Marguerite Duras:

(5.44)   Marguerite Duras n'a pas seulement écrit que des conneries. Elle en a aussi filmées.
'Marguerite Duras has not only written bullshit. She has filmed it, too.'

In effect, in this example, the predicted set of alternatives to *conneries* ('bullshit') includes, for instance, *chef d'oeuvre* ('masterpieces'), whereas COR introduces an alternative belonging to a different set, the alternatives to *écrire* ('write').

Third, how does processing the cancellation of a presupposition work? Can we predict that the same type of contextual approach applies as with upward entailing negation? In other words, is a negative utterance interpreted directly as having wide scope because the context matches the contextual effects of negation? This is an open question that can only be answered through an experimental approach.

Acknowledgements

For about thirty years, Deirdre Wilson has been an intellectual inspiration and support to me. Her fidelity, friendship and care have been more than inspiring, simply human. We met at UCLA in 1983, and since then, my scientific life has changed, for the best.

This chapter has benefited from the support of the Swiss National Scientific Foundation (project LogPrag n° 100012_146093) and the Thematic Network: Language & Communication (project ComplexVar, University of Geneva). Many thanks to Joanna Blochowiak, Cristina Grisot and Karoliina Lohiniva for their help and comments, and Stephanie Durrlemann for her English double-check. A special acknowledgement to the editors (especially Robyn Carston) and to the reviewers for their support, questions, challenges and comments.

6 Pronouns in Free Indirect Discourse: A Relevance-Theoretic Account

Anne Reboul

6.1 Introduction

This chapter is dedicated to an issue that has been, to my knowledge, ignored in relevance theory (RT): the interpretation of indexicals, and specifically of pronouns, in free indirect discourse (FID). While FID has been discussed in RT (see, e.g., Blakemore 2009, 2010, 2013a; Blakemore & Gallai 2014; Wilson 2000), this specific question, one which looms large in the semantic literature on FID, has not been investigated in relevance-theoretic terms.

The major description of FID was given by Banfield (1982) and highlighted the fact that it was somewhat intermediate between direct discourse and indirect discourse. Where direct discourse presents itself as a faithful quotation (e.g., *John said/thought: 'Damn. It is raining and I've forgotten my umbrella.'*), and where indirect discourse uses embedding, is subject to sequence of tenses and sequence of pronouns, and prohibits interrogative and exclamative forms, as well as interjections, etc. (*John said/thought that it was raining and he had forgotten his umbrella*), FID, while subject to sequence of tenses and pronouns, welcomes interjections, interrogative and exclamative forms, etc. and prohibits embedding (*Damn, it was raining and he had forgotten his umbrella, said/thought John*).

The main source of the semantic discussion about the interpretation of indexicals in FID is Schlenker (2004). He noted that, while the semantic view regarding the interpretation of indexicals in a given sentence is that they are interpreted relative to a Kaplanian context (a list of indexes for the speaker, the hearer, the location and the time when the sentence is uttered; see Kaplan 1989), this cannot be the case for indexicals in FID.

To see why, let us compare (6.1) and (6.2):

(6.1) I am here today. Where will I be tomorrow to say that it was yesterday?

(6.2) Tomorrow was Monday. Monday, the beginning of another school week. (…) She had had enough. (Lawrence 1971/1920: 181)

In (6.1), all indexicals (i.e., pronouns, spatial and temporal indexicals, such as *here* and *now*, as well as tenses) are interpreted relative to a Kaplanian context based on the situation of utterance, where the *Speaker* is myself, the *Time* is the 22nd September 2017, the *Location* is Cluny and the hearer is my daughter Abigaël. Regarding (6.2), a standard example of FID, however, the situation is rather different. Here we have three indexicals of interest: *she*, *tomorrow* and the past tense (*was*). Let us suppose that the Kaplanian context for (6.2) is made of a *Speaker* (Lawrence), a *Time* (20th January 2019), a *Location* (London) and an (anonymous) *Hearer*. *She* is interpreted, not problematically, as the person the *Speaker* refers to. Let us suppose that we interpret *tomorrow* as the day after *Time*, i.e., as the 21st January. We then must interpret the past tense as before *Time*. But, clearly, this leads to a contradiction: *tomorrow* cannot be interpreted as both before and after *Time*. Schlenker's solution for this problem is to propose that in FID, indexicals are not resolved relative to a single Kaplanian context, but relative to two different Kaplanian contexts: the Context of Utterance, which is constituted relative to the situation in which the narrator produces the utterance (identical with what was described above); and the Context of Thought, which is constituted relative to the situation in which the character whose utterance or thought is reproduced in FID (the thinker, hereafter) produced the utterance or thought in question.

As is the trend in current formal semantics, Schlenker takes these two Kaplanian contexts to correspond to possible worlds. On his approach, the Context of Utterance is the 'real' context (corresponding to what occurred – is true – in the story), and this is the context relative to which tenses and pronouns are interpreted. However, all other indexicals are interpreted relative to the Context of Thought. Given that the Context of Utterance is the 'real' context, this means that pronouns and tenses are used *de re*, or transparently. On the other hand, all other indexicals are used *de dicto*, in an opaque way, which is why they are resolved relative to the thinker's mental states as represented by the Context of Thought.[1]

It is important to note that this repartition of indexicals in FID is not arbitrary. It is motivated by the fact that in FID (at least in most European languages, and certainly in French and English), the pronouns and tenses are subject to sequence of pronouns and sequence of tenses: in other words, the 1st-person is replaced by a 3rd-person pronoun, the present by a past tense, and so on and so forth. Thus, it makes perfect sense to divide the indexicals in FID according to whether they are or are not subject to the sequences just mentioned. However,

---

[1] In Schlenker's terminology, all indexicals apart from tenses and pronouns shift from the Context of Utterance (the real context) to the Context of Thought.

this elegant analysis has a weak point: it can only be maintained if pronouns and tenses are indeed used only transparently in FID.

Regarding pronouns, it seems clear that this is not always the case. In some cases, at least, the thinker's state of mind must be taken into account in the resolution of the pronoun, which means that the pronoun should be interpreted relative to the Context of Thought, and not relative to the Context of Utterance. Yet, while the thinker might be mistaken as to the properties of the individual concerned, unless she is hallucinating, she is referring to an individual that exists in the Context of Utterance. Here there are two different possibilities and we will turn to some examples.

The first sort of problem is the case where the referring expression comes with a presupposition that cannot be satisfied in the Context of Utterance (even though the referent exists in the Context of Utterance). Doron (1991) gave the following example: Mary, whose thought is being reported in FID, wrongly believes that Robin is male, while Robin is in fact female. In such a case, the masculine seems to be mandatory in FID:

(6.3)   Where was *he/#she* this morning, for instance? (Mary wondered).

The problem here is that the use of the masculine comes with a presupposition that the referent is a male. But the referent in the Context of Utterance is a female, not a male, and thus the presupposition is not satisfied. Schlenker has suggested that the use of the masculine in (6.3) might be due to the use of a 'pronoun of laziness', but this seems an ad hoc solution in view of other examples that show that referential expressions in FID are not, on the whole, used transparently. This is the case for definite descriptions used referentially, as in (6.4), in a case where Sandra believes of the referent that he is holding a glass of Martini when he is in fact holding a glass of water:

(6.4)   The man with the glass of Martini/#The man with the glass of
         water was nice, Mary said/thought.

In (6.4), the definite description also comes with a presupposition (that the referent is a man with a Martini) that, again, is not satisfied in the Context of Utterance. This makes the 'pronoun of laziness' account of (6.3) less than convincing. It is also the case for proper names: if the character is in error as to the name of the referent, it is the erroneous name and not the correct one that should appear in an FID report, as shown by (6.5) in a context in which Peter believes erroneously that Orcutt's name is 'Jones':

(6.5)   Jones/#Orcutt was a spy, Peter thought.

In (6.5), the presupposition is that the referent bears the name Jones, and, again, the Context of Utterance does not satisfy the presupposition. In other words, it seems that, in FID, referential expressions are not, or are not always, used transparently.

The second type of counterexample is not at the level of reference, but concerns the properties attributed to the referent in, e.g., the predicate. Here are a few examples (borrowed from Reboul et al. 2016). The first comes from Flaubert's *L'Education sentimentale*:

> (6.6)   He [Frédéric] displayed the utmost gaiety on the occasion. Madame
>   Arnoux was now with her mother at Chartres. But *he* would soon
>   come across her again, and would end by being her lover. (Flaubert
>   2013, loc. 30142, also quoted in Banfield 1982)

In (6.6), the pronoun *he* in the second sentence refers to Frédéric in the Context of Utterance according to Schlenker. But the Frédéric it refers to succeeds in becoming Madame Arnoux's lover, something that Frédéric fails to do in the novel. This only occurs in the Context of Thought, reflecting Frédéric's (erroneous) belief, not in the Context of Utterance. In other words, *he* in the second utterance does not so much refer to Frédéric in the Context of Utterance, as it in fact represents the way Frédéric refers to himself in thought (with the third person, because of the grammatical constraints due to sequence of pronouns). While resolving the pronoun strictly on the Context of Utterance preserves reference, it seems to miss something important for the interpretation of the utterance in this case.

This, by the way, is not something that only occurs with 3rd-person pronouns. It also occurs with 1st-person pronouns. Here is an example, taken from *Great Expectations* by Dickens:

> (6.7)   My dream was out; my wild fancy was surpassed by sober reality;
>   Miss Havisham was going to make *my* fortune on a grand scale.
>   (Dickens 2011, loc. 194670. Also quoted in Banfield 1982)

While someone is making Pip's fortune, it is not the mad but respectable Miss Havisham, but the escaped convict Magwitch, whom Pip detests.

So, while in some cases of FID, Schlenker's semantic solution, according to which pronouns and tenses are interpreted relative to the Context of Utterance and all other indexicals relative to the Context of Thought, seems perfectly satisfactory, his account comes to grief in two other types of cases. The first type of case is due to the fact that referential expressions in FID are not used transparently. When the thinker is in error as to the gender of the referent, the gender presupposition attached to the pronouns is not satisfied in the Context of Utterance. In the second type of case, the referent can be identified in the Context of Utterance (as the presupposition associated with the pronoun is satisfied in it), but the properties which are attributed to it are properties that it has in the Context of Thought, but not in the Context of Utterance.

In what follows, I will propose a pragmatic account of how pronouns are interpreted in FID. To do so, I will use the relevance-theoretic notion of enrichment, applying it to the singular concepts corresponding to the referents, using the mental files framework proposed by Recanati (2012).

6.2   A Pragmatic Approach to the Use of Pronouns in Free Indirect Discourse

Before turning to the pragmatic account I intend to propose here, I would like to reject an apparent semantic solution. As noted above, it is not only pronouns but referential expressions in general that are used *de dicto* (or opaquely) in FID (see (6.3)–(6.5)). One obvious solution would be to propose that, if this is the case, all indexicals (and indeed all referring expressions) in FID (with the possible exception of tenses) are resolved against the Context of Thought. This would not only solve the problem raised by (6.3)–(6.5), it would also solve the problem raised by (6.6)–(6.7). But this would be problematic for three reasons: first, it fails to account for the sequence of pronouns that is a central grammatical feature of FID; second, the referring expressions do have referents in the Context of Utterance as well as in the Context of Thought; third, it fails to account for the fact, often important in the story, that the character's beliefs about the referent are erroneous. Thus, this simple solution would not be satisfactory.

Let us now turn to the pragmatic solution. The most obvious solution to the three issues just described is that the referring expressions in FID should be resolved on both the Context of Utterance and the Context of Thought: this would allow a solution for both sequence of pronouns and keeping track of the discrepancy between Context of Utterance and Context of Thought.

Sperber and Wilson (1986/1995) proposed a distinction between the *logical form* of an utterance (obtained through purely linguistic processes) and its *propositional form*. The propositional form is such that it can be (in principle) evaluated for truth value, while the logical form cannot. To go from the logical form of the utterance to its fully propositional form, pragmatic inferential processes of enrichment, reference resolution and disambiguation are necessary. In recent years, the proposal has materialised as lexical pragmatics (see, e.g., Carston 2002), in which a concept in the logical form is enriched, giving rise to a so-called ad hoc concept, leading to a fully propositional form. This suggests that such a process might be at play in FID regarding referential expressions. A first idea would be that pronouns in FID are indeed first resolved on the Context of Utterance (as advocated by Schlenker) and then enriched on the Context of Thought.

A prima facie objection is that pronouns do not correspond to concepts and, hence, no process of conceptual enrichment is possible for pronouns.

However, the situation is not desperate, given the possibility of 'singular concepts', concepts corresponding to referents. A recent and convincing proposal to that effect is the theory of mental files (see Recanati 2012). Recanati proposes that, corresponding to referents, there are mental files, each such file corresponding to a referent with which the subject is in a relation allowing her to gather information about it. For reasons of space, I will ignore the question of what happens when the subject mistakenly thinks that a single referent corresponds to two different individuals (so-called Paderewski cases), or that two referents correspond to one individual (inverse Paderewski cases). What is more relevant for FID is the account Recanati proposes for cases in which a speaker attributes an erroneous belief regarding a referent to someone else. In such a case, the speaker has a file for the referent, but she cannot simply add the belief that she knows to be erroneous to the content of that file. Rather, the speaker adds a second file, indexed to the believer, and linked vertically to the first one. The notion of a vertical link is designed both to establish the fact that the indexed file corresponds to the same referent as the first one and to quarantine the contents of the first file (the information that the speaker has about the referent) from those of the indexed file (the erroneous belief). The interpretation process is parallel: the hearer builds a file indexed to the individual whose belief is represented, and links this indexed file vertically to the regular file corresponding to the referent. Additionally, Recanati proposes a distinction between *semantic reference* and *speaker reference*. The distinction is based on the notion of presupposition introduced above. When the presupposition is satisfied by the file the hearer already has, the reference is *semantic*. When the presupposition is not satisfied, the referential expression resorts to *speaker reference*. While in both cases, reference is assigned through pragmatic processes (following the relevant procedures in the case of pronouns), with speaker reference, the hearer must build an indexed file vertically linked to the original one, with the erroneous characterisation as its content. While Recanati does not discuss FID, a similar proposal would seem adequate for the cases discussed above.

This, however, is not the only case in which the hearer will have to build an indexed file. The same will happen when the thinker is being reported as predicating an erroneous property of the referent (which may or may not be herself), even when the reference is semantic. In such a case, just as in cases of speaker reference, the hearer must enrich the reference assignation by building an indexed file vertically linked to the original one, with, again, the erroneous characterisation as its content.

So, to sum up, the enrichment process only occurs when it is necessary for the interpretation to reach the hearer's expectations of relevance. This will obviously happen in cases of speaker reference, such as (6.3)–(6.5) above. It will also occur in cases where the reference is semantic, but the thinker predicates an erroneous property of the referent, as in (6.6)–(6.7). Enrichment in such a case is not the construction of an ad hoc concept through strengthening or weakening. Rather, the enrichment lies in the construction of an indexed file vertically linked to the original one. It is this indexed file, and not the regular file it is vertically linked to, that will appear in the propositional form of the utterance.

6.3   Back to Examples

Let us begin with examples (6.3)–(6.5). In all cases, the presupposition carried by the referential expression is not satisfied: Robin is not a man, the nice man is not holding a Martini and Orcutt is not named Jones. Hence, in all three cases, the reference is speaker reference and not semantic reference. This is not detrimental to reference assignment, given that reference assignment is a pragmatic process, depending on the thinker's referential intention and not on her erroneous beliefs. So, the correct file can be identified. However, the discrepancy between the thinker's belief and the file contents is a problem. This is solved by creating an indexed file vertically linked to the initial one. In (6.3), *he* will be assigned to the ROBIN file, but given that this file contains the information that Robin is a woman, a second file will be created, indexed to Mary as the thinker of (6.3), ROBIN$_{MARY}$, containing the information that Robin is a man, and vertically linked to the file ROBIN to secure reference. For (6.4), *The man with the glass of Martini* will be assigned to the SMITH file, but given that this file contains the information that Smith is holding a glass of water, a second file, SMITH$_{SANDRA}$, will be created, containing the information that Smith is holding a glass of Martini, and vertically linked to the file SMITH. For (6.5), *Jones* will be assigned file ORCUTT, but given the name discrepancy, a file ORCUTT$_{PETER}$ will contain the information *named Jones* and will be vertically linked to ORCUTT. And, in all cases, it is the indexical file that enters the propositional form of the utterance.

In cases (6.6)–(6.7), the reference is semantic (i.e., there is no discrepancy between the presupposition carried by the referential expression and the contents of the file), but the problem arises with the predicate that attributes to the referent a property it does not have. The solution is like that just proposed for (6.6). For (6.6), the hearer, having assigned the file FREDERIC to the 3rd-person pronoun, builds a file FREDERIC$_{FREDERIC}$, with the information that Frédéric becomes Madame Arnoux's lover, which is vertically linked to the initial file FREDERIC to secure reference. For (6.7), having assigned file PIP to the 1st-person pronoun, the hearer builds a file PIP$_{PIP}$, containing the information that Pip's benefactor is Miss Havisham, which is vertically linked to PIP to secure reference. Again, it is the indexed files that will appear in the propositional forms.

The main difference between, respectively, (6.3)–(6.5) and (6.6)–(6.7) is that, whereas in (6.3)–(6.5), the information in the indexed file comes from the presupposition of the referential expression, in (6.6)–(6.7), it comes from the properties assigned to the referent outside of the referring expression. Thus, in all of these cases, the reference assignation process does not exhaust the pragmatic interpretation process. It is followed by an enrichment process, which consists, once a regular file has been assigned to the referential expression, in constructing a file indexed to the thinker, vertically linked to the initial file to secure reference, and containing the information discrepant with the contents of the original file. This enrichment process does not systematically occur for FID, it only occurs when expectations of relevance make it necessary.

There is an additional reason to advocate a pragmatic account of FID. One important thing to note about FID is that not all FID utterances wear their FID status on their sleeve, so to speak. Side by side with utterances such as *Tomorrow was Monday* (from (6.2)), where the co-occurrence of the past tense and *tomorrow* is a clear cue that the utterance does not represent the narrator's perspective, there are a lot of utterances where no indexicals apart from pronouns and tenses arise, which are, given sequence of tenses and sequence of pronouns, ambiguous between an FID reading and a purely narrative reading. This is the case with *She had had enough* (also from (6.2)), which may be either the narrator reporting the character's state of mind from his own perspective, or reporting it from her own perspective, i.e., reproducing in FID the character's thought: 'I have had enough'. Given that this utterance occurs in a context which is clearly FID, it will presumably be interpreted as FID. In the case of (6.3), the interrogative form makes an FID interpretation very plausible. In cases (6.4)–(6.5), the very discrepancy between the presuppositions linked to the referential expressions and the existing files also naturally leads to an FID interpretation. But things are less simple for (6.6)–(6.7).

In (6.6), *But he would soon come across her again, and would end by being her lover* might be a prediction of the narrator rather than the expression of Frédéric's hubris. And in (6.7), *Miss Havisham was going to make my fortune on a grand scale* might again be Pip the narrator's (true) prediction as to what will happen rather than Pip the character's erroneous past belief. At the point at which the utterance occurs in each novel, the reader is in no position to know, respectively, that Frédéric will never become Madame Arnoux's lover or that Miss Havisham is not Pip's benefactor. Neither does either utterance occur in a context that would force an FID reading. Rather, the context offers subtle hints that these utterances represent the characters' states of mind rather than the narrators' sober predictions: in both cases, the FID utterance is preceded by utterances relative to the character's emotions, gaiety in Frédéric's case, elation in Pip's. The FID utterance is thus plausibly interpreted as an FID representation of the character's state of mind, explaining his emotion, as described in the previous utterances. Clearly, a narrator's predictions could not play such an explanatory role. In addition, all of Blakemore's publications on FID (2009, 2010, 2013a; Blakemore & Gallai 2014) are also relevant here, as audience-directed expressions, voice and discourse markers can be expected to play a role in the disambiguation process. Thus, FID, in addition to potential discrepancies in information leading to a pragmatic process of enrichment, is also often the object of a disambiguation process between a narrative reading and an FID reading.

6.4   Conclusion

Thus, while most mainstream treatments of FID have been syntactic and semantic (see, e.g., Banfield 1982; Schlenker 2004), it clearly needs a pragmatic approach. For one thing, it seems that referential expressions in FID, including pronouns, are not used transparently, leading to major difficulties for purely semantic accounts. With a pragmatic account, cases where such transparent uses of referential expressions lead to a semantic conflict can be solved by a pragmatic enrichment, leading to the construction of files indexed to the thinker, but preserving reference through vertical links to regular files. These regular files can be seen as on a par with Schlenker's Context of Utterance, while the indexed files can be seen as on a par with his Context of Thought. It is the indexed files that enter the propositional forms in such cases. The same mechanism can account for the cases in which the thinker erroneously attributes properties to referents that they do not have.

Finally, the pragmatic approach can take in its stride the ambiguity of many FID utterances through context-dependent disambiguation processes. For all those reasons, a relevance-theoretic pragmatic account of FID should be preferred to a semantic account *à la* Schlenker.

7   The Development of Pragmatic Abilities

Myrto Grigoroglou and Anna Papafragou

7.1   Introduction

It is widely assumed that human communication in adults relies on a complex species of mind-reading that involves inferentially reconstructing the meaning that the speaker had in mind and wanted to convey (Grice 1975; Sperber & Wilson 1986/1995). Children's pragmatic abilities, however, present a paradox. Experimental work has shown that remarkable competence in important preconditions for pragmatic reasoning is present from infancy (see Baillargeon et al. 2016 for a recent review); nevertheless, research on a variety of linguistic phenomena (e.g., reference, implicature, metaphor, irony) has demonstrated that children's pragmatic abilities are fragile and task-dependent even until late in childhood (e.g., Waggoner & Palermo 1989; Noveck 2001; Bucciarelli et al. 2003; Filippova & Astington 2008).

Sometimes, the paradox surfaces even within the realm of a single phenomenon. For instance, in the domain of referential communication, some experimental evidence shows that even 2-year-old children can successfully integrate another person's perspective in both their comprehension and production of referring expressions (O'Neill 1996; Nadig & Sedivy 2002; Morisseau et al. 2013), yet other evidence shows that children frequently ignore their interlocutor's perspective as late as age 8 or 9 (e.g., Deutsch & Pechmann 1982; Epley et al. 2004). For other phenomena, there is debate in the developmental literature about whether they truly rely on rich pragmatic computations about others' intentions or might involve non-pragmatic mechanisms. In word learning, for instance, some commentators treat mutual exclusivity (i.e., the bias to assume that a label applies only to one object) as the result of a pragmatic process that assesses the speaker's referential intentions (Woodward & Markman 1998; Diesendruck & Markson 2001) and others consider it a lexical constraint that does not involve intention recognition (Preissler & Carey 2005; Regier 2005; de Marchena et al. 2011). Together these conflicting patterns and perspectives raise two interrelated questions: What accounts for the complex pattern of results in children's pragmatic development? And how do children become adult-like, competent communicators?

In this chapter, we focus on scalar implicature as a paradigmatic case of children's pragmatic development and start to sketch a framework for answering these questions. In recent years, scalar implicature has been the topic of very active experimental investigation, mainly because it displays an easily testable division between semantic and pragmatic meanings. After briefly introducing scalar implicature (Section 7.2), we review experimental evidence that reveals a complex pattern of successes and failures in implicature derivation in children (Section 7.3). We next examine different accounts that have been put forth to explain children's performance and sketch a proposal that provides a new explanation of the child data (Section 7.4). Finally, we discuss new directions in the study of scalar implicature that have important implications for theoretical accounts of pragmatics (Section 7.5) and conclude by connecting the phenomenon of scalar implicature to a broader picture of the nature and scope of children's early pragmatic abilities (Section 7.6).

7.2   Scalar Implicature

Implicatures are components of speaker meaning that are communicated without being explicitly stated. Scalar implicatures are a type of conversational implicature that arises when the speaker uses a weaker scalar item from a scale of items organised in terms of semantic strength. Such scales may be lexically defined (e.g., <all, most, ..., some>, <and, or >, <n, ..., three, two, one>, <must, should, might>, see Horn 1972, 1984; Levinson 1983, for additional examples) or contextually defined (see Hirshberg 1985, for a discussion on contextual ad hoc scales). Sentences (7.1)–(7.5) are examples of scalar implicature, where (a) can be used to imply (b); in (7.1)–(7.3), the scales are lexically defined, but in (7.4)–(7.5) they are contextually constructed:

(7.1)   a. The professor graded some of the exams.
        b. The professor did not grade all of the exams.

(7.2)   a. We'll order pizza or sushi tonight.
        b. We will not order both pizza and sushi tonight.

(7.3)   a. He owns three cars.
        b. He does not own more than three cars.

(7.4)   a. Max and Alicia are engaged.
        b. Max and Alicia are not married.

(7.5)   a. Mary liked the crust.
        b. Mary did not like the filling.

On contextualist accounts, including Grice's (1975) framework and relevance theory (Sperber & Wilson 1986/1995; Carston 1995, 1998b; Noveck & Sperber 2007; see also Sauerland 2004, 2012; Geurts 2010), scalar implicatures (as well as other types of pragmatic inference) arise as a result of a rich computation which takes into account the speaker's conversational purpose and his/her knowledge of background facts. On a Gricean (1975) account, scalar implicatures in (7.1b)–(7.5b) arise because the hearer realises that the speaker did not use a stronger, more informative, term that would have been relevant (thus violating the Maxim of Quantity). On a relevance-theoretic account (Sperber & Wilson 1986/1995; Carston 1995, 1998b; Noveck & Sperber 2007), scalar implicatures arise when a weak scalar term fails to satisfy the hearer's expectations of relevance. The scalar inferences (7.1b)–(7.5b) are drawn by the hearer in an attempt to make the utterances satisfy this expectation with the least amount of processing effort. On both accounts, the fact that the speaker in (7.1a)–(7.4a) opted for a weaker scalar item gives the hearer reason to think that the stronger scalar alternative does not hold.[1]

7.3   Experimental Evidence on Scalar Implicature

Although adults compute scalar inferences when these are warranted by context (Bott & Noveck 2004; Breheny et al. 2006; Grodner et al. 2010; Degen & Tanenhaus 2015), children often fail to derive scalar implicatures until fairly late in development. In an early demonstration, Noveck (2001) found that French-speaking 5-, 7- and 9-year-old children were very likely to accept sentences like 'There might be a parrot in the box' when it was clear from context that there 'had to be a parrot in the box', while adults tended to reject them. Similarly, in the same study, 8- and 10-year-old children did not object to logically true but pragmatically infelicitous sentences like 'Some giraffes have long necks', while adults were equivocal. Relatedly, Chierchia and colleagues (2001) found that 5-year-old children often accepted pragmatically infelicitous statements with disjunction (e.g., 'Every boy chose a skateboard or a bike', when every boy chose both a skateboard and a bike), while adults readily rejected them. These findings were taken to suggest that although children can calculate logical, semantic meaning, they have difficulties computing pragmatic meanings. Later work further confirmed these early findings (e.g., Guasti et al. 2005; Papafragou 2006; Huang & Snedeker 2009; Foppolo et al. 2012).

---

[1] On other, grammatical/lexicalist accounts, the scalar implicatures in (7.1b)–(7.3b) are mediated by linguistic-level representations and arise by default, and thus differ from the context-driven inferences in (7.4b)–(7.5b) (see Levinson 1995, 2000; Chierchia 2004; Chierchia et al. 2009). We will not be discussing these accounts here (but see Section 7.5 for experimental evidence against these accounts).

Despite children's difficulties, there is now robust evidence showing that, under certain conditions, children can be sensitive to the pragmatic reasoning required for scalar implicature generation. For instance, Papafragou and Musolino (2003) showed that 5-year-old children failed to reject logically true but pragmatically infelicitous sentences such as 'Some of the horses jumped over the fence' in a story in which all of the horses had jumped over the fence; however, the children's performance improved after they received training on how to treat under-informative sentences and were presented with supporting context (see also Guasti et al. 2005; Foppolo et al. 2012).

Other studies have shown that the type of response and other task characteristics affect children's success in scalar implicature tasks. In Katsos and Bishop (2011), 5-year-old children who readily accepted true but infelicitous *some*-statements in a binary judgement task demonstrated clear signs of sensitivity to implicature when they were asked to use a 3-point scale to evaluate the same statements. Specifically, when children were asked to use one of three strawberries (small, medium, large) to reward a speaker based on how well he answered questions about a story, children – just like adults – rewarded the speaker with a small strawberry for false responses, a large strawberry for true and felicitous responses and, critically, a medium-size strawberry for true but pragmatically infelicitous *some*-responses. Similarly, in Pouscoulous et al. (2007), methodological changes improved performance. Specifically, in this study, French-speaking 4-, 5- and 7-year-old children who were asked to perform an action-based task (i.e., remove tokens from boxes or add tokens to boxes to make them conform to statements such as 'Some of the turtles are in the boxes') were highly successful in deriving scalar inferences; nevertheless, children as old as 9 who were asked to evaluate the same sentences in a binary judgement task that additionally differed in other design features (e.g., adding distractors in the stimuli, using a less frequent quantifier) largely failed to derive the implicatures.

Even though most of the above studies involved lexical (quantifier) scales, other paradigms have shown similar findings with contextual scales. For example, in Papafragou and Tantalou (2004), Greek-speaking 5-year-olds were shown scenarios in which an animal had to perform an action off-stage (e.g., colour four stars). The animal was asked a question about whether it had performed the action (e.g., 'Did you colour the stars?'). In critical trials the animal responded with a weak scalar term (e.g., 'I coloured some'). Children were asked to give a prize to the animals who had successfully completed the task. Children were remarkably successful in deriving scalar inferences (i.e., withholding the prize from the animals that used *some*). Furthermore, they succeeded with both lexical scales (such as <*all, some*>) and contextual scales ('Did you eat the sandwich?' – 'I ate the cheese'). A more recent study that used a referential communication paradigm showed successful derivation of scalar implicature from context-based scales in even younger children (Stiller et al. 2015). In this study, children were asked to select a target referent from a display of three closely matched alternatives. For example, the experimenter said 'My friend has glasses' when one 'friend' did not wear glasses (irrelevant referent), one friend wore glasses only (pragmatically felicitous referent), and one friend wore glasses and a hat (logically compatible but pragmatically infelicitous referent). Children, often younger than 4, correctly picked the pragmatically felicitous referent, thus showing signs of successful implicature derivation.

In sum, experimental findings from almost two decades of research have demonstrated that children are, in fact, capable of the reasoning processes required for scalar inference, at least from the age of 4 (see also Eiteljoerge et al. 2016 for corpus evidence that children produce utterances with the weak scalar quantifier *some* in ways that suggest an awareness of the contrast between *some* and *all*). Nevertheless, the conditions under which children are more likely to put these reasoning processes to use are very heterogeneous, leaving several possibilities open about the nature of children's difficulties.

7.4   The Nature of Children's Pragmatic Difficulties

Several theoretical possibilities have been proposed in the literature to explain children's mixed performance with scalar implicature. According to a first possibility, children often fail to compute a scalar inference because, unlike adults, they lack the necessary processing resources (Chierchia et al. 2001; Reinhart 2004; cf. Pouscoulous et al. 2007). This account posits that acceptability judgement tasks (on which children typically fail) have high metalinguistic demands and predicts that, in simpler pragmatic tasks, children will be more successful in deriving scalar implicatures. Although this prediction is reasonable, there is currently no concrete evidence that children's particular difficulty with scalar inference relates to processing limitations such as working memory or attention deficits.

According to a second possibility, children fail to reject logically true but pragmatically infelicitous statements in binary judgement tasks not because they are insensitive to violations of informativeness but rather because they are more tolerant of such violations than adults (Katsos & Bishop 2011). According to this view, a mechanism for pragmatic reasoning is in place from an early age but is masked by the typical experimental methods used. This proposal successfully explains children's failures in standard binary acceptability judgement tasks. However, this account cannot explain why children have difficulties with scalar inferences in eye-tracking tasks that simply involved following spoken instructions (e.g., Huang & Snedeker 2009) or why children successfully derived scalar inferences in certain studies that used binary judgements (e.g., Skordos & Papafragou 2016).

According to a third possibility, children fail to derive scalar inferences across many different tasks because they have problems generating the stronger scalar alternative (e.g., they cannot access *all* when hearing *some*; Chierchia et al. 2001; Barner & Bachrach 2010; Barner et al. 2011). Evidence for this possibility comes from the fact that, even though children fail to reject pragmatically infelicitous sentences with a weak scalar term in a binary task, they correctly choose the stronger, more felicitous statement if presented with both the strong and the weak alternative (Chierchia et al. 2001; see also Ozturk & Papafragou 2015). Thus, children are not oblivious to the relative informativeness of the two scalar terms but cannot spontaneously recover the stronger scalar alternative when needed for a scalar inference. Further evidence for this possibility comes from the fact that children have difficulties with generating the stronger alternative from lexical scales (e.g., < *all, some* >) in tasks that do not involve scalar implicature computation, but they do not have problems deriving alternatives related to contextual scales, presumably because the latter do not rely on establishing a stored relation between lexical items (Barner et al. 2011). Nevertheless, this explanation fails to account for children's failure to compute scalar implicatures from sentences containing *some* in tasks where the stronger alternative (i.e., *all*) was present in other experimental sentences and was thus, in principle, accessible (e.g., Noveck 2001).

An alternative, much broader, theoretical possibility is that the main source of children's pragmatic difficulty with scalar implicature lies not so much with recognising that particular terms are members of a scale or accessing the stronger alternative but rather with spontaneously estimating that stronger scalar terms constitute *relevant* alternatives in a given exchange (Papafragou & Skordos 2016; Skordos & Papafragou 2016; cf. Bott & Noveck 2004; Noveck & Sperber 2007; Pouscoulous et al. 2007). Recent evidence provides a clear demonstration of how the saliency of alternatives combined with the transparency of relevance expectations contribute to children's successful implicature computation. Skordos and Papafragou (2016) found that 5-year-old children, in a binary judgement task, rejected pragmatically infelicitous sentences with a weak scalar term (*some*) only when the stronger alternative (*all*) was made both accessible and relevant to the goals of the conversation. By contrast, when the stronger alternative was salient but irrelevant to the goal of the task, children were unlikely to compute an implicature. Crucially, scalar implicature computation from the quantifier *some* was also facilitated by the presence of a quantifier such as *none* that did not constitute a stronger alternative and was not even a member of the <*some,... all*> scale: as Skordos and Papafragou (2016) proposed, *none* could not have given access to the quantifier scale itself but encouraged children to consider the broader domain of relevant alternatives (i.e., quantifiers). These results show that a major problem for children when computing implicatures (and potentially other types of pragmatic inference) is their inability to spontaneously reconstruct expectations of relevance if these expectations are not sufficiently clear in the context.

This theoretical proposal offers a coherent framework for explaining the conflicting results in prior literature. First, it is in accordance with findings showing that children have no difficulty calculating implicatures in tasks that provide a sufficiently supportive context (e.g., Papafragou & Musolino 2003; Papafragou & Tantalou 2004; Guasti et al. 2005; Foppolo et al. 2012). Typically, in these tasks, the stronger alternative was made both salient and relevant by the experimental manipulations. Relatedly, this proposal can also explain children's successes with context-based scales, in which the stronger alternative was both (visually) accessible and relevant to the computation of an implicature (e.g., Papafragou & Tantalou 2004; Barner et al. 2011; Stiller et al. 2015).

Second, this proposal can also account for children's inability to calculate implicatures in tasks where the stronger alternative was present in the experimental stimuli and thus accessible for the purposes of implicature computation (Noveck 2001; Foppolo et al. 2012). For instance, recall that in Noveck (2001), young children failed to detect under-informative *some*-sentences ('Some giraffes have long necks') when asked to evaluate different types of *all* and *some* statements. Notice that, in this task, the strong and weak scalar statements described completely different states of affairs (an example of a strong statement would be 'All elephants have trunks'). Therefore, although the stronger scalar term *all* was present in various statements throughout the task, it was not clear that it was a relevant alternative to the weaker scalar term *some*. Interestingly, this explanation may also account for adults' relatively high rates of non-pragmatic responses in this task.

Finally, a relevance-based account of scalar implicature computation can explain why alternative methods for evaluating pragmatically infelicitous statements (i.e., non-truth-value judgement tasks) typically show successful implicature computation in children (e.g., Papafragou & Tantalou 2004; Pouscoulous et al. 2007; Katsos & Bishop 2011). For instance, in Katsos and Bishop (2011), children may have been more likely to show signs of implicature computation given a 3-point Likert scale compared to a binary judgement task because the possibility of a gradient response made children realise that the goal of the task was not to evaluate truth conditions but rather the felicity of pragmatic meanings. Thus, the presence of a scale encouraged children to evaluate the 'goodness' (and not the truth) of an under-informative statement in relation to other potential alternatives.

7.5   New Directions in the Study of Scalar Implicature

A key component of contextualist approaches is the assumption that the derivation of scalar implicature (in case the literal, semantic meaning does not satisfy
expectations of relevance) engages a rich computational process that integrates
the speaker's epistemic state (see Grice 1975; Sperber & Wilson 1986/1995;
Carston 1995, 1998b; Sauerland 2004, 2012; Noveck & Sperber 2007; Geurts
2010; cf. Levinson 2000; Chierchia 2004; Chierchia et al. 2009, for an alternative view). On these approaches, the hearer typically reasons that the use of an
informationally weaker statement means that the speaker either does not know
that the stronger scalar statement is true or knows that the stronger statement is
not true (Horn 1972, 1989; Sauerland 2004; van Rooij & Schulz 2004; Spector
2006; Noveck & Sperber 2007; Geurts 2010; Franke 2011). However, in early
experimental work on scalar implicature, the role of speaker knowledge remained
unexplored.

Recent experimental evidence from adults provides support to contextualise
models of scalar implicature derivation in which information about speaker
knowledge is integrated at early stages of the pragmatic computation (Bergen
& Grodner 2012; Breheny et al. 2013). For example, Bergen and Grodner
(2012) used a reading-time paradigm, where participants read scenarios told
from a first-person perspective. Introductory sentences established whether
the speaker had full or partial knowledge of an issue (e.g., 'At my client's
request, I meticulously compiled the investment report / At my client's request,
I skimmed the investment report'), followed by critical sentences that included
the weak quantifier *some* (e.g., 'Some of the real estate investments lost money')
and continuations that referred to the complement of the set mentioned in the
critical sentence ('The rest were successful despite the recent economic down-
turn'). Results showed that participants took longer to read sentences with
some when it was established that the speaker had full – compared to partial – knowledge of the issue (presumably because the speaker generated the
implicature *not all* in the full-knowledge condition). Furthermore, participants
in the full-knowledge condition were faster to read the continuation sentence
compared to participants in the partial-knowledge condition (presumably
because the generated implicature had already evoked the complement set).
Similarly, Breheny et al. (2013), using a visual world paradigm, demonstrated
that the speaker's epistemic state (i.e., whether he had witnessed the whole
event or parts of an event) affected the derivation of ad hoc scalar implicatures
at early stages of pragmatic processing.

More recent work with children has shown some success in integrating
speaker knowledge in scalar implicature computation but also some developmental limitations (Hochstein et al. 2014; Papafragou et al. 2017b). For
instance, in Papafragou et al. (2017b), 4- and 5-year-old children watched two

videos, where two almost identical agents ('twins') performed the same action (e.g., colour a star). In one video, an observer witnessed the whole event; in the other video, the observer fell asleep halfway through the action and only watched part of the event. At the end, children heard either a strong or a weak statement (e.g., 'The girl coloured all/some of the star') and had to attribute it either to the fully knowledgeable or to the partially knowledgeable observer. Results showed that 5-year-olds were able to attribute informationally strong statements to knowledgeable observers and informationally weak statements to partially informed observers, but 4-year-olds could not reliably link the observer's (i.e., speaker's) epistemic state to the informational strength of different statements.

These findings have important implications for theoretical debates about the nature of children's pragmatic abilities more generally. The fact that 5-year-olds at least were able to consult the speaker's epistemic state when computing an implicature provides evidence in favour of the view that children have the ability to integrate information about other people's perspectives in pragmatic reasoning. These results are consistent with a growing body of experimental work on other domains of pragmatics where children were found sensitive to others' mental states from a very young age. These domains include word learning (e.g., Sabbagh & Baldwin 2001; Southgate et al. 2010; Papafragou et al. 2017a) and perspective taking (e.g., O'Neill 1996; O'Neill & Topolovec 2001; Nadig & Sedivy 2002; Morisseau et al. 2013).

These findings from Hochstein et al. (2014) and Papafragou et al. (2017a) raise the possibility that simpler experimental tasks might reveal that children younger than 5 can reason epistemically when computing implicatures. In direct support of this possibility, a new study using context-based scales and a very simple task inspired by the literature on referential communication has shown that 4-year-old children are very successful in integrating speaker knowledge when computing scalar implicatures (Kampa & Papafragou 2017). In this study, participants saw two nearly identical pictures side by side. In the first picture, a girl was sitting across a table facing forward towards the participant. Midway across the table was a tall cardboard box split into two vertical, see-through compartments. Each compartment contained an object and both objects (e.g., a spoon and a bowl) were clearly visible both from the girl's and from the participant's perspective. The second picture was identical to the first but one of the compartments was blocked, such that the girl in the picture could only see one of the two objects in the box (e.g., the spoon but not the bowl). Participants heard either a strong statement (e.g., 'I can see a spoon and a bowl') or a weak statement (e.g., 'I can see a spoon') and had to pick the box that the girl was talking about. Four-year-old children performed above chance in matching weak statements to displays where the girl had limited knowledge of the contents of the box, although their performance was still not adult-like.

7.6   Conclusion

In this chapter, we examined the development of children's pragmatic abilities with a focus on scalar implicature, a well-studied case of pragmatic inferential process in children. The current state of the art suggests that children have the ability to compute scalar implicature from a young age but have problems estimating what constitutes a relevant alternative, if relevance expectations are not made sufficiently clear by the experimental context. The present approach goes some way towards resolving a paradox in the domain of pragmatic development, whereby children appear to have underlying pragmatic abilities but may not be able to implement them consistently in all contexts.

It remains an open question how to draw more precise connections between developmental data and specific theoretical proposals about the nature of pragmatic processing. Beyond broad points of agreement, contextualist accounts diverge in their underlying principles. For present purposes, this has implications for terms such as 'relevance'. Within relevance theory, relevance is a trade-off between processing costs and expected cognitive gains (Sperber & Wilson 1986/1995). Under this account, the listener's expectations of relevance determine whether an implicature will be calculated or not; the favoured interpretation is the one that satisfies these expectations with the least cognitive effort. Within the Gricean framework, relevance is defined with respect to the conversational goals, for instance, the 'Question under Discussion' (QUD; Roberts 1996/2012; Krifka 1999; cf. Stalnaker 1979). Under this view, implicatures are generated only if they are triggered by an answer to the QUD. Existing developmental work has not attempted to adjudicate between contextualist accounts but this remains a ripe opportunity for further research.

A further important direction for future work would be to uncover the mechanisms that underlie pragmatic development across a range of phenomena such as word learning, referential communication, implicature, presupposition, metaphor, etc. At present, connections between these domains have not been explicitly drawn, although it is clear that the same pragmatic considerations underlie many of these phenomena. The computation of different types of implicature is a case in point. Developmental evidence from relevance implicatures is consistent with the conclusion from the study of scalar implicatures that children have difficulties evaluating speaker intentions when they have to reconstruct relevance for themselves. There is evidence that children under the age of 6 are generally unable to generate novel, non-conventional relevance inferences (Bucciarelli et al. 2003; Loukusa et al. 2007; de Villiers et al. 2009; Verbuk & Shultz 2010). For instance, de Villiers et al. (2009) presented children with short dialogues (e.g., 'Dad: What happened to the ham?', 'Boy: The dog looks happy!') and were asked to explain what a speaker meant (e.g., 'What did the boy mean? Why did he say that?'). Children under the age of 6 were unable to offer an explanation that invoked a relevance implicature (e.g., 'The dog ate the ham'). In contexts where relevance computations were simpler, however, even 3-year-olds appeared to draw these inferences (Tribushinina 2012; Schulze et al. 2013; see Grigoroglou & Papafragou 2016 for discussion). By integrating findings from a variety of linguistic phenomena, future work can provide a broader account of the developmental trajectory of children's pragmatic abilities.

Acknowledgements

Deirdre Wilson introduced one of us (Anna) to the world of pragmatics, and her wisdom, insight and support have ever since been invaluable. She has been a constant source of inspiration. Preparation of this chapter was supported in part by grant #1632849 from the National Science Foundation.

Part II

Pragmatics and Linguistic Issues

8   Mood and the Analysis of Imperative Sentences

Mark Jary and Mikhail Kissine

8.1   Introduction

Wilson and Sperber's 'Mood and the analysis of non-declarative sentences' (1988a) is an important and influential contribution to the literature on the semantics of imperative and interrogative sentences, not least because it highlights non-directive uses of the imperative, such as audienceless cases like (8.1) and predetermined cases like (8.2):

(8.1)   Please don't rain.

(8.2)   Please be out (muttered by a child sent to apologise to someone).

Wilson and Sperber's account of imperative semantics seeks to accommodate such uses by positing that the encoded meaning of imperative sentences presents the proposition expressed as potential and desirable, without specifying to whom the desirability applies. This enables Wilson and Sperber to account for cases where directive force is evident as instances where the proposition expressed is desirable to the speaker, but without thereby postulating directive force as the encoded meaning of the imperative.[1] It also enables them to deal with uses of the imperative to give advice (8.3) and permission (8.4) as cases where the state of affairs described by the utterance is desirable to the hearer rather than to the speaker, hence avoiding the problems faced by theories that treat the imperative as necessarily entailing the expression of the speaker's desire (see e.g. Harnish 1994).

(8.3)   Take paracetamol.

(8.4)   Go ahead. Marry her. But you'll regret it.

But what does it mean, in speech-act terms, to present a proposition as desirable and potential? In answering this question, Wilson and Sperber introduce the generic speech-act descriptor 'telling to': to tell somebody to P is to present

---

[1] There are a number of reasons for not building directive force into the imperative's semantics. See Jary and Kissine (2014), and references therein, for discussion.

P as both desirable to someone and potential.[2] An interpretation of an utterance of an imperative sentence is thus a higher-order explicature that has the structure given in (8.5), as exemplified by (8.6). The move from (8.6) to the more precise (8.7) is a result of pragmatically resolving, in favour of the hearer, the underspecification of to whom the proposition expressed is desirable. In the case of a command such as (8.8), the desirability would be attributed to the speaker.

(8.5)   S is telling H to P.

(8.6)   The speaker is telling the hearer to take paracetamol.

(8.7)   The speaker is advising the hearer to take paracetamol.

(8.8)   Stand up!

But while this approach has many merits, it is not without problems. A desideratum of any account of the semantics of the imperative sentence type is that it explain why the imperative cannot be used to make assertions. Wilson and Sperber's account, however, offers no explanation of why an utterance of an imperative is not open to interpretation as a *claim* that the state of affairs described is desirable and potential (see Jary 2011: 269–70). Another desideratum is that an account of imperative semantics should explain the strong preference of imperatives for agentive interpretations. For example, (8.9) cannot be uttered as a good wish, i.e. as merely presenting winning the lottery as potential and desirable, but must be interpreted as telling the addressee to take some action that ensures that he win the lottery:

(8.9)   Win the lottery.

The root of these problems, we contend, is that Wilson and Sperber posit only one format of mental representation: factual representations that can serve as premises and conclusions in inference (see Sperber & Wilson 1986/1995: 73–5). To entertain, unembedded, such a representation is to adopt its content as a belief. The trouble with this one-format approach is that it does not allow thought to lead to action: beliefs can only beget further beliefs. In order to model thought processes aimed at instigating and directing action, it is necessary posit an additional format of representation whose tokening results in action (by means of an association with motor representations). Relating such a format with the interpretation of imperative

---

[2] Wilson and Sperber's (1988a) treatment of the semantics of mood appears somewhat different from that in Sperber and Wilson (1986/1995). How the two approaches should be identified is explained by Wilson (1998–9). See Jary (2010: 124–6) for discussion.

sentences, we will show, results in an account of imperative semantics that treats this sentence type as encoding potentiality, but that also explains the imperative's strong preference for agentive predicates and its absolute aversion to assertoric use. Furthermore, the nature of this format of mental representation requires that we differentiate between how imperatives are interpreted by an addressee and how they are interpreted by an audience. The latter, we will see, is broadly in line with the higher-order explicature approach advocated by Wilson and Sperber (1988a; Sperber & Wilson 1986/ 1995). However, it is the former that underlies the idiosyncratic semantic characteristics of the imperative.[3]

8.2   Two Types of Mental Representation

As noted above, Sperber and Wilson (1986/1995: 73–5) posit just one type of mental representation: assumptions. An assumption is a propositional form of a type whose tokening amounts to adopting the attitude of belief towards that proposition. Assumptions can be embedded within other assumptions, but an unembedded assumption is a 'factual assumption': to entertain such a representation is to believe its content. Assumptions serve as premises and conclusions in inference. In this paper we will call representations of this type 'doxastic representations', and contrast them with action representations. An action representation is of a type whose tokening is capable of causing action through an association with motor representations. Such a format of representation must be posited if we are to model how thought can result in action: doxastic representations alone allow us to model the move from belief that P to the belief that Q, but not from the belief that Q to the intention to bring about R.[4]

Of interest here is the nature of action representations. Due to their role in the psychology and behaviour of the individual, such representations will have a number of essential characteristics not necessarily shared by doxastic representations. These result from the fact that an action representation with a particular content can only be entertained by the individual for whom it serves as a representation. This is in contrast to a doxastic representation: any number of individuals may hold doxastic representations with the same content.

---

[3] Due to space limitations, in this paper, we discuss only 2nd-person imperatives, termed 'canonical imperatives' by Aikhenvald (2010). However, we believe that an advantage of our proposal is that it can explain in a uniform manner 1st- and 3rd-person imperatives. We plan to explore this in future work. For guidelines on how to distinguish non-2nd-person imperatives from hortatives and the like, see Jary and Kissine (2016).

[4] This point is argued by Millikan (2004: ch.16), though it has its roots in the Sellarsian notion of a language-exit rule (Sellars 1953, 1954).

To see why this asymmetry exists, consider a situation in which you stand before a closed door. You form the intention to open the door. In the terms we are using, you have a doxastic representation with the content THE DOOR IS CLOSED and an action representation with the content I OPEN THE DOOR. Now imagine that a doppelganger of you is created and stands at your side. Both you and your doppelganger have a doxastic representation with the same content: THE DOOR IS CLOSED. However, the content of your respective action representations cannot be the same: your action representation is satisfied only if you open the door, while your doppelganger's action representation is satisfied only if she does. To borrow some terms from philosophy, the 'I' in the action representation is an essential indexical (Perry 1979); in other words, that representation is *de se* (Lewis 1979).

Now, of course, doxastic representations can also be *de se*: both you and your doppelganger will have a doxastic representation with the content THERE IS A CLOSED DOOR IN FRONT OF *ME*. For this thought to locate the holder's location in front of the door *from the holder's perspective*, it must be read as *de se*, that is, as essentially indexical. Note that what makes such a thought *de se* is not simply that it is about the holder, but that it is *about the holder and used by her to locate herself in the world*. This is what the notion of essential indexicality aims to capture. For current concerns, the key point is that while doxastic representations *may* be *de se*, action representations are *necessarily de se*. As a consequence, while it is possible that a doxastic representation has the same satisfaction conditions as an action representation (such as if you intend to open the door and I believe that you will open the door), it is not possible that two action representations have the same satisfaction conditions: each action representation is only satisfied if it itself causes the state of affairs denoted to be brought about (by the individual for whom it serves as a representation).

Besides their *de se* nature and their association with motor representations, action representations are notable in that they do not require that the agent of the act denoted be explicitly represented. Simply by virtue of the fact that they serve as action representations for an individual, that individual will be the agent. In other words, what makes you the agent of an action representation of yours is just that it is an action representation entertained by you. There need be no constituent of the representation that stands for you: the nature of this type of representation means that the tokener will necessarily be the agent of the act denoted.

Finally, action representations will be restricted to representing states of affairs that are neither ruled in nor ruled out by the doxastic representations of the individual. This follows from the basic requirement that a rational agent is unable to set itself goals that cannot be, or have already been, fulfilled. Consequently, action representations, under normal circumstances, will represent potential states of affairs.

8.3   Imperatives and Their Interface with Action Representations

Our claim is that imperative sentences are uniquely specified for interface with action representations. This is motivated by a number of considerations. First and foremost, the prototypical use of imperatives is to perform directive speech acts (Jary & Kissine 2016), and we define directives as speech acts which present the hearer with (what the speaker sees as) a reason to act (Kissine 2013: 104–6), so it is reasonable to assume that imperatives interface with a format of mental representation whose function is to trigger action. In addition, there are syntactic considerations that support this hypothesis.

First, there is the well-established fact that imperatives tend, cross-linguistically, not to require an overt subject. This is the case even in languages such as English, which normally do require overt subjects (see Jary & Kissine 2014: 101–3 and references therein for discussion of the extent of this tendency). Furthermore, a number of syntacticians have argued that the role of overt subjects in imperatives such as (8.10), (8.11) and (8.12) is not to form a predication with the verb but to identify the addressee (Platzack & Rosengren 1997; Zanuttini 2008; Alcázar & Saltarelli 2014).

(8.10)   You be good!

(8.11)   Someone help him.

(8.12)   The boy at the back sit down.

In particular, the role of overt 2nd-person subject pronouns in imperatives differs from that in declaratives: in a 2nd-person declarative utterance, it is taken for granted who the addressee is, and this fact is exploited to specify the subject of a predication; by contrast, an overt imperative subject (2nd-person pronoun or otherwise) serves to identify the addressee, and hence is only present when context alone is insufficient for this purpose. These subject considerations further motivate the claim that the imperative is specified for interface with action representations. Recall that we noted that such representations require no constituent that stands for the agent of the act denoted, this being implicitly specified by the functional role of the representation. Consequently, it would be unsurprising to find that a linguistic form specified for interface with representations of this type does not require a predication.

Interface with action representations also accounts for the lack of assertoric potential that imperatives display. Assertions are a means of sharing information; sharing information requires that representations of the same content be entertained by different individuals. As we saw above, action representations with a given content can only be entertained by the individual for whom they serve as such. The assumption that imperatives are specified for interface with action representations thus precludes their assertoric use, for their content cannot be shared. Furthermore, given that a function of truth judgements is to signal acceptance of a proposition, we would not expect imperatives to be amenable to truth judgements, as they cannot be used to put forward a proposition for sharing. And this is, of course, borne out by the data: imperatives have been widely noted not to be open to judgements of truth and falsity.

The strong preference of imperatives for action predicates is also to be expected on the current account, according to which interpreting an imperative entails interface with a representation whose function is to provoke action in the holder. On such a hypothesis, one would expect non-agentive predicates to be coerced into agentive readings, and this is what is found. In both (8.13) and (8.14), an interpretation is required in which the addressee acts in some way to bring about the state of affairs required.

(8.13)   Be the best in the class.

(8.14)   Have some self-respect.

Such coercion, however, will only be expected in cases where there is an addressee who seeks to interpret the imperative by means of interface with an action representation. In cases where the specified addressee manifestly cannot interpret the utterance, or where there is no specified addressee, the strong preference for agentive interpretations should not apply. As we will see in the next section, when we introduce the notion of consuming an utterance, this is exactly the pattern that is observed in the data, most notably in the audienceless cases highlighted by Wilson and Sperber (1988a), and in advertising imperatives.

A final observation that supports the hypothesis that imperatives are specified for interface with action representations is that, like these, imperatives are restricted to denoting potential states of affairs. This, of course, plays a central role in Wilson and Sperber's account of imperative semantics, but is also advocated by Davies (1986). Our view is that it is the only semantic feature of imperative sentences that counts as encoded by this form, for, as we will see, it constrains all interpretations of the imperative. This is in contrast to agency, for example, which, as we have noted and will go on to discuss in more detail, is absent in some uses of the imperative.

8.4   Consumers and Other Interpreters

The proposal we make, then, is that imperatives are specified for interface with action representations, and that characteristics that arise from the function of these representations explain a number of constraints on the interpretation of imperative sentences. In particular, the *de se* nature of action representations means that an utterance of an imperative can only properly be interpreted by the addressee. But what do we mean by 'properly interpreted' and how do we respond to the observation that people other than the addressee interpret imperative utterances? In particular, how do we account for the fact that utterances of imperatives update the conversational record, so that the action of the speaker and the obligations that may thereby be placed upon the addressee can become manifest to all observers of the speech event?

We do this by distinguishing between consumers and interpreters of an utterance.[5] Consumption is a type of interpretation, but not all interpretation is consumption. To consume an utterance is to interpret it by tokening a mental representation, of the type specified by the linguistic form, such that the utterance and the mental representation it triggers share the same satisfaction conditions.

As has been noted in the literature (see e.g. Schmerling 1982; Boisvert & Ludwig 2006) imperatives are satisfied only if the state of affairs denoted is brought about by the addressee. We have claimed that imperatives are specified for interface with action representations. Due to the *de se* nature of such representations, it follows that only the addressee can token a representation (of the type specified by the imperative morphosyntax) that has the same satisfaction conditions as the utterance. In other words, only the addressee can *consume* an utterance of an imperative. Declaratives, by contrast, are not restricted in their consumption: there is no constraint on who can token a doxastic representation with the same satisfaction conditions as the utterance. So, an action representation with the satisfaction conditions of (8.15) can only be tokened by John: the utterance can only be consumed by John. To be sure, other observers of the utterance can token a doxastic representation with the content 'John will open the door', but to do so is not to *consume* the utterance, because the representation tokened is not of the type specified by the linguistic form of the utterance.[6] This is in contrast to an utterance of (8.16): there is no restriction on who can token a doxastic representation with the same satisfaction (i.e. truth) conditions as the utterance, thereby consuming the utterance. Hence we can say that declaratives are for general consumption, but imperatives are not.[7]

---

[5] Other authors (Clark & Carlson 1982; Levinson 1988; McCawley 1999) have also advocated noting the distinction between addressees and other observers of the speech acts, be they participants in the speech event or otherwise. However, none of these authors draws the distinction, crucial to our analysis, between an interpretation with the same satisfaction conditions as the utterance (i.e. 'consumption') and other interpretations.

[6] Moreover, (8.15) on its own does not in itself provide a reason to form the belief that John will open the door: additional considerations are required.

[7] That imperatives can only be consumed by addressees, whereas declaratives can be consumed by non-addressees, is one reason we do not identify the role of addressee with being a consumer. Also, an utterance of an imperative can have a manifest addressee but no consumer. This is the case with examples (8.1), (8.2) and (8.17).

(8.15)   Open the door, John.

(8.16)   Mary closed the door.

So, while an addressee and a non-addressee can both consume an utterance of a declarative, only an addressee can consume an imperative. How, then, do non-addressees interpret utterances of imperatives? Our answer is that they do so very much along the lines suggested by Wilson and Sperber: by representing the utterance in speech-act terms. In other words, non-addressees interpret the utterance by tokening a doxastic representation of the speech event, with the schematic structure given in (8.5). This is not a consumption of the utterance, because the satisfaction conditions of the interpretation do not match those of the utterance: the interpretation is a description of a state of affairs in which the speaker does something, but there is no representation of the speaker in the utterance (*pace* Alcázar & Saltarelli 2014).

In our view, however, 'telling to' should not be glossed as 'presenting as potential and desirable', but rather as giving the addressee reason to bring about the state of affairs denoted by the utterance (i.e. as 'directing', in the sense of Kissine 2013: 104–6). The grounds for the utterance to stand as a reason will vary from utterance to utterance, and these grounds will determine its precise illocutionary force. If it stands as a reason because it is an expression of the speaker's desire, then it will count as a request; if the utterance denotes an act that falls within the scope of the authority that the speaker has over the hearer, then it will count as an order; if it is manifest that the speaker believes that the act denoted is of benefit to the hearer, then it will count as advice; and so on. At the generic level, the fact that the linguistic form employed is designed for interface with an action representation indicates that the addressee is being presented with a reason to act, and that, in turn, warrants classifying the speech act as a case of 'telling to'. The notion of desire only needs to be brought in, in certain cases, to specify the precise illocutionary force of the utterance.

8.5   Imperatives without Addressees

On our account, the strong preference that imperatives have for action predicates is due to the interface with action representations that results when they are consumed. Imperatives can only be consumed by addressees. Our account therefore predicts that the action constraint on imperatives should not apply when there is manifestly no intention that the utterance of an imperative be consumed. This will happen in two types of circumstance: when the utterance denotes an addressee but it is manifest that speaker does not intend the addressee to interpret the utterance; and when no addressee is specified by the utterance. The first type of case is exemplified by the examples from Wilson and Sperber (1988a) cited above and repeated below:

(8.1)   Please don't rain.

(8.2)   Please be out (muttered by a child sent to apologise to someone).

In (8.2), the child speaks as if he were addressing the person he has been sent to apologise to, but he has no intention that the utterance be interpreted by that person. In (8.1), the 'addressee' is the sky or the ominous dark clouds on the horizon: these are not the sort of things that can normally interpret an utterance. Another example is that of Dominicy and Franken (2002), spoken by an excited archaeologist to a recently discovered mummy that, if it turns out to be of the required age, will prove a theory of hers. Again, the 'addressee' is specified by the utterance, but there is no intention that the utterance be interpreted by that addressee.

(8.17)   Please, be born before 4000 BC!

In each of these cases, a non-agentive predicate is acceptable, and there is no coercion to an agentive interpretation. This is because, we argue, the utterance has no consumer and hence there is no requirement that it interface with an action representation. It is worth noting, however, that in each case the state of affairs is potential, relative to a background information set. In the case of (8.17), this is the knowledge state of the speaker, who is as yet ignorant of the age of the mummy. If she knew the mummy to date after 4000 BC, then she could not utter (8.17) to express a counterfactual desire. Consequently, we do not see potentiality as resulting from interface considerations, and we agree with Wilson and Sperber and with Davies (1986) that the imperative mood encodes potentiality as a constraint on its interpretation.

The second type of case in which we would expect the agency constraint on imperative interpretation not to hold is that in which no addressee is specified by the utterance. Advertising imperatives such as (8.18) and (8.19) are a clear example: in such cases, there is no addressee specified, and nobody is intended to interpret the utterance by tokening an action representation whose satisfaction conditions match those of the utterance. Indeed, it is hard to specify the satisfaction conditions of such uses: who is to be the envy of all her friends? And such cases cannot be described as instances of telling to.[8]

---

[8] It might be objected that advertising cases such as (8.18) and (8.19) have 'generic addressees' (cf. Sperber & Wilson 1986/1995: 158). While we do not want to get into terminological disputes, we are certain that there is a sense in which adverts and other broadcasts do not have an addressee in the strictest sense. The notion of telling someone that/to assume (a non-generic) addressee. Consequently, A's response in (i) is pragmatically odd, even if the BBC is her source of information.

(8.18)   Be the envy of all your friends.

(8.19)   Win up to £100 in this week's competition! (Davies 1986: 43)

Rather, the goal of the producer of the utterance is to get interpreters to buy a product (an action not specified by the utterance). It is not easy to describe an advertising imperative in illocutionary-act terms. A perlocutionary description is the best one can do:

(8.20)   The advertiser seeks to persuade A to bring about P (i.e. A's buying the product advertised) by presenting Q (i.e. the content of the imperative) as a desirable outcome of A bringing about P.

Whatever the correct analysis of such uses of the imperative, the crucial point for current concerns is that these cases do not specify an addressee. Hence, on our account, they cannot be consumed, only otherwise interpreted. As the agency constraint on imperatives is, we argue, a result of their consumption, our account predicts that this should not apply in such cases. And this is what we find: in neither (8.18) nor (8.19) is the stative predicate coerced to an agentive interpretation.

In our terms, advertising imperatives are cases where there is no consumer of the imperative because, due to the absence of an addressee, there is none specified by the situation in which the utterance is produced. By contrast, there are also cases in which one can be the consumer of an imperative without being the addressee. Signs and instruction-manual directions written in the imperative mood are a good example of this. When following a recipe, for example, one is seeking direction and thus tokens action plans as a result of interpreting sentences such as 'Add salt and stir'. However, the situation is not one that can be described as a context in which the interpreter is the addressee without stretching unreasonably the notion of participants to a conversation. Thus recipes and the like are produced in the absence of an addressee while nevertheless being translated into action representations by the interpreter.[9] The difference between the two cases is that in the latter the interpreter is

(i)   A: The Prime Minister has resigned.
        B: How do you know?
        A: ?The BBC told me.

By this token, advertising imperatives such as (8.18) and (8.19) are addressee-less: they have interpreters but not addressees, despite being grammatically 2nd-person. This is not to deny that broadcasters can choose linguistic forms that indicate the kind of interpreter they are aiming at. The choice of *tu* rather than *vous* in a French advertising imperative, for example, may indicate that the advertisement is aimed at younger people.

[9] Interestingly, in French and Spanish, the only circumstances in which infinitives can be used to give directions are cases such as those discussed where the producer of the utterance has no addressee in mind but proffers direction for whoever seeks it. (It is certainly the only use condoned by the Real Academia Española. See: www.rae.es/consultas/infinitivo-por-imperativo.) Thus we find infinitives used to give directions in published recipes and on signs,

seeking a course of action, and thus looking for properties to consume in the production of action representations. In the advertising case, by contrast, the interpreter is not seeking direction.

By distinguishing between consumers and (mere) interpreters of utterances, we are able to correctly predict the conditions under which imperatives will impose an agency constraint on their interpretation. When an addressee is both specified by and manifestly intended to interpret the utterance, there will be an agency constraint on its interpretation. This is a result of the addressee being required to consume the utterance by tokening a mental representation of the type specified by the linguistic form: an action representation. We know of only one possible counterexample to this claim: good wishes (also discussed by Wilson & Sperber 1988a). Cases such as (8.21) and (8.22) are directed at and expected to be interpreted by an addressee. However, in English, the use of imperatives in good wishes is highly unproductive: (8.9), for example, cannot be uttered as a good wish. More generally, languages differ greatly in how accepting they are of imperatives as good wishes (Jary & Kissine 2014: 65–9). As a result, we would rather treat such cases as peripheral to imperative semantics, requiring a special treatment that perhaps sheds light on cross-linguistic variation in imperative semantics and usage.

(8.21)   Get well soon.

(8.22)   Have a nice day.

(8.9)   Win the lottery.

8.6   Conclusion

On the analysis we have presented, there are two possible ways an utterance of an imperative can be interpreted: by means of a higher-order representation of the utterance (or of the attitude it expresses) or by tokening an action representation with the same satisfaction conditions as the imperative. The latter option is open only to addressees, while the former is open to both addressees and non-addressees. The higher-order interpretations are doxastic in nature, 'assumptions' in the RT framework, so how they can achieve relevance is well documented in the literature. But what about action representations? These

---

for example, but the giving of directions using infinitives in conversation is not acceptable. We conjecture that the acceptable situation for infinitive directions are those in which consumers are self-selecting, and thus no addressee need be specified by the utterance. In such a case, all that is required for interface with an action representation is an unsaturated agentive property, which an infinitive may encode.

cannot serve as premises, so cannot lead to contextual effects. What sort of positive cognitive effects can they have?

Humans are clearly capable of foreseeing some of the outcomes of their actions. So, if the foreseeable outcomes of a course of action constitute, or help towards, the achievement of a goal, or if they are beneficial to the individual in some other way, then the cognitive effect will be positive and justify the effort expended in interpreting the utterance. There thus seems to be no reason, in principle, why an imperative consumed by an addressee could not achieve relevance. However, the relevance theory model of cognition needs to include action representations in its ontology if it is to treat interpreters as agents rather than as mere cognisers. And once the need for this format of representation has been acknowledged, then the account of imperatives that we propose offers a straightforward explanation of a range of data.

Acknowledgements

We would each like to thank Deirdre Wilson for the support, encouragement and guidance she has given us over the years. We thank two reviewers for useful feedback on an earlier draft.

9   The Korean Sentence-Final Suffix *ci* as a Metarepresentational Marker

Eun-Ju Noh

9.1   Introduction

This chapter examines the meaning of Korean sentence-final suffix *ci*. Traditional accounts claim that the suffix *ci* is an epistemic marker which indicates the speaker's attitude towards the proposition expressed by the utterance. Although these epistemic accounts can address some instances of them, there are other cases that those accounts cannot handle. I suggest that the suffix *ci* marks a metarepresentation of the speaker's pre-existing thought. The term 'metarepresentation' as understood in relevance theory is shown to play an important role in explaining the various *ci* sentences.

The Korean language has various sentence-final suffixes. Some indicate the type of sentence, such as declarative, interrogative or imperative. Others are classified as epistemic markers that indicate the speaker's attitude towards the proposition expressed by the utterance. Evidential markers are included in epistemic markers.

The sentence-final suffix *ci* can be used for all basic speech acts, such as a statement, question or order/request. The *ci* sentence can be interpreted as communicating the speaker's belief in the proposition expressed (statement), asking for the listener's confirmation of what the speaker believes (question), or conveying the speaker's suggestion of carrying out the action described in the sentence (order/request). Thus, the suffix *ci* has been classified as an epistemic marker of the speaker's belief in the truth of the proposition. It has been referred to as a speaker's attitude marker (K. Lee 1993), a suppositive marker (Sohn 1999), or a committal marker (H. Lee 1991, 1999).

Consider the *ci* sentences in (9.1):[1]

(9.1) a. ku   salam   ttal-un   tayhakkyo-ey tani-**ci**.
           the   person   daughter-TOP   college-to   go-ci
           'His daughter goes to college.'
       b. ku hay   kyewul-un   emcheng   chwuw-ess-**ci**.
           that year   winter-TOP   very   cold-PST-ci
           'The winter that year was very cold.'

(9.2) a. ku   salam   ttal-un   tayhakkyo-ey tani-n-ta.
           the   person   daughter-TOP   college-to   go-IND-DC
           'His daughter goes to college.'
       b. ku hay   kyewul-un   emcheng   chwuw-ess-ta.
           that year   winter-TOP   very   cold-PST-DC
           'The winter that year was very cold.'

In (9.1), both sentences can be interpreted as conveying the speaker's belief in the proposition expressed. Similar sentences with a declarative sentence-type suffix, such as those in (9.2), can also be interpreted as conveying the speaker's belief. It seems that the difference between *ci* sentences interpreted as statements and ordinary declarative sentences is not clear.

With appropriate intonation or a question mark, the sentences in (9.1) can also be interpreted as questions about the truth of the proposition, suggesting that the speaker believes in the truth of the proposition and expects that the listener will agree with him. It seems that the traditional epistemic accounts can handle the *ci* sentences used in statements and questions.

However, the suffix *ci* can also be used to give an order or make a request, as in (9.3):

(9.3) a. ilccik   kkutnay-**ci**.
           early   finish-ci
           'Finish (it) early.'
       b. sey   si-ey   o-**ci**.
           3   o'clock-at   come-ci
           'Come at 3 o'clock.'

In (9.3), the verbs are base forms, and the sentences are interpreted as orders/requests. The traditional epistemic accounts extend their 'epistemic markers' or 'the speaker's attitude' to the *ci* sentences in a(n) order/request: K. Lee (1993) claims that in a(n) order/request, the speaker uses *ci* when she assumes that the listener will accept her suggestion. H. Lee (1999) claims that in a(n) order/request, *ci* indicates the speaker's belief in the value of the suggested action. Sohn (1999) states that *ci* sentences can be used for casual suggestions. Yet these accounts do not explain how the suffix *ci* acquires a different meaning in a(n) order/request from that of *ci* sentences used in a statement or question.[2]

Moreover, *ci* sentences can be negated. Consider (9.4), in which the negative expression *an-h* [not-do] 'do not' embeds the sentences from (9.1):

(9.4) a. [ku   salam   ttal-un   tayhakkyo-ey tani-**ci**] an-h-nun-ta.
           [the   person daughter-TOP   college-to   go-ci]   not-do-IND-DC
           'His daughter does not go to college.'
       b. [ku   hay   kyewul-un   chwup-**ci**] an-h-ass-ta.
           [that   year   winter-TOP   cold-ci]   not-do-PST-DC
           'The winter that year was not cold.'

In (9.4a), the embedded clause is identical to the sentence in (9.1a). In (9.4b), the embedded clause is almost identical to the sentence in (9.1b), except that the past-tense particle is moved into the matrix clause. The tense of the embedded clause depends on the tense of the matrix clause in Korean grammar.[3]

In the above epistemic accounts, the suffix *ci* used in (9.4) is classified as the same epistemic marker as in (9.1) and (9.3).[4] K. Lee (1993: 326) states, 'The function of "ci" in negation is not different from the speech-act marker "ci". The speaker uses the post-verbal negation (with *ci*) when he believes in the information and at the same time assumes that the listener is aware of the information (propositional content) and that the listener is likely to be committed to its truth.' H. Lee (1999: 272) states, 'In sum, "-ci" that occurs in construction of negation, i.e., the long form of negation "-ci anh-" and its contracted form "-cyanh-," has the same meaning as the sentence terminal suffix "-ci." Namely, it makes an explicit reference to and thus emphasizes the speaker's belief about the conveyed message.' In these quotations, the phrases 'the information' and 'the conveyed message' refer to the target of the negation. Considering that the speaker is denying the target, it is not consistent to say that the speaker indicates her belief in the target expressed by the *ci* sentence.

---

[2] Strictly speaking, an epistemic marker indicates the speaker's attitude towards the truth of the proposition. According to Hyland (1998: 45), epistemic modality 'expresses the speaker's opinion or belief concerning the truth of what is said.' Lyons (1977: 797) also comments that '[a]ny utterance in which the speaker explicitly qualifies his commitment to the truth of the proposition expressed by the sentence he utters … is an epistemically modal, or modalised, utterance.'

[3] In this chapter, I base my account on Kuno (1980), where long-form negation is referred to as sentence negation. Further discussion of the structure of long-form negation is beyond the scope of this chapter.

[4] Some scholars suggest that the *ci* used in negation – as in (9.4) and (9.5) – is a nominaliser of the verb, different from the sentence-final suffix *ci* used in (9.1) and (9.3). In this chapter, I refer to the other accounts claiming that they are the same suffix, such as K. Lee (1993) and H. Lee (1991, 1999).

Moreover, a *ci* sentence can be embedded within a negative imperative clause. In (9.5), the sentences in (9.3) are embedded within the negative imperative *mal-la* [do not-IMP] 'do not' and a contracted form *ma* 'don't,' respectively:

(9.5) a. [ilccik   kkutnay-**ci**] mal-la.
           [early   finish-ci]   do not-IMP
           'Don't finish (it) early.'
       b. [sey   si-ey   o-**ci**]   ma.
           [3   o'clock-at   come-ci]   do not: IMP
           'Don't come at 3 o'clock.'

In (9.5), the embedded clauses in square brackets are identical to the sentences in (9.3). Yet unlike (9.3), the embedded clause with *ci* cannot be what the speaker wants the listener to do. The speaker neither believes in the value of the suggested action, nor does she expect that the listener will accept the proposal. The epistemic accounts mentioned above cannot address the suffix *ci* in negative imperatives, as in (9.5).

So far, we have seen various uses of *ci* sentences. Although the traditional epistemic accounts show deep understanding of *ci* sentences, there are some cases that those accounts cannot deal with. I suggest that the suffix *ci* marks a metarepresentation of the speaker's pre-existing thought. Since a *ci* sentence represents her previous beliefs, the speaker can approve of it or question it, as in (9.1), or deny it, as in (9.4). The propositional form with a base verb form may express the speaker's thought about a potential state of affairs, which can be interpreted as a(n) order/request as in (9.3), or a negative imperative, as in (9.5).

9.2   The Suffix *ci* as a Metarepresentational Marker of the Speaker's Representation

9.2.1   *Metarepresentation in Relevance Theory*

Relevance theory distinguishes representation and metarepresentation. We represent a state of affairs in our thoughts privately or in our utterances publicly. We also represent the representation of a state of affairs privately or publicly. Thus, our utterance can be a representation of a state of affairs or a metarepresentation of another representation. (Since metarepresentation is also a kind of representation, we will denote a representation of a state of affairs as 'a description' instead of 'a representation' in order to distinguish it from 'a metarepresentation.') Consider (9.6) and (9.7):

(9.6)   I came back to school this semester.

(9.7)   a. Mary said, 'I came back to school this semester.'
         b. Mary$_i$ said that she$_i$ came back to school this semester.

If a speaker utters (9.6), she is describing the state of affairs in which she came back to school that semester. By contrast, if she utters either (9.7a) or (9.7b), she is metarepresenting Mary's utterance about her coming back to school.

In relevance theory, a metarepresentation resembles the original representation, and the degree of resemblance is determined by considerations of optimal relevance. The metarepresentation can be identical to the original, or it may only share some features with the original. If the metarepresentation resembles the form of the original, as in (9.7a), it is referred to as metalinguistic. If it resembles the concept of the original, as in (9.7b), it is referred to as interpretive. In this chapter, I do not distinguish between metalinguistic and interpretive use, and use the term 'metarepresentational use'. (For further explanations of metarepresentation, see Sperber & Wilson 1986/1995: ch. 4; Noh 2000; Wilson 2000; Carston 2002.)

Although it is true that every utterance may represent the speaker's thoughts, this will not be considered here. We interpret thoughts and utterances conveying these thoughts at the same level of representation. For example, if Mary utters a declarative sentence, as in (9.6), it is considered as a description of her coming back to school rather than a metarepresentation of her thought. Thus, a metarepresentational marker indicates that the utterance is not describing a state of affairs, but rather is representing another representation that exists at the time of the utterance.

9.2.2   The Suffix ci *as a Metarepresentational Marker*

I suggest that the suffix *ci* marks a metarepresentation of the speaker's thought that existed before producing the utterance. Compared with the epistemic accounts in which the suffix *ci* is an epistemic marker of the speaker's belief in the proposition, my metarepresentational account allows various speaker attitudes towards the proposition. For example, the speaker does not necessarily believe in the truth of the proposition expressed by a *ci* sentence. She can question it, given that it is her prior thought. Since the propositional content is indicated as a metarepresentation of the speaker's pre-existing thought, the question is likely to be interpreted as asking for confirmation. Thus, the metarepresentational analysis accounts for the fact that a sentence modified by *ci* can serve as a statement or question. The speaker can deny the thought metarepresented with *ci* in a negative sentence because it is not her current belief. In addition, the speaker's thought can relate to a potential state of affairs, as well as a real state of affairs. The thought about a potential state of affairs is represented with a base verb form, and the utterance is interpreted as a(n) order/request. In contrast to ordinary imperative sentences, the *ci* sentence does not directly describe a potential state of affairs, but rather metarepresents the speaker's thought about a potential state of affairs. Thus, it is not a direct order or request, but only a suggestion. Compare an ordinary imperative sentence in (9.8) and a *ci* sentence with a base verb form in (9.9):

(9.8) *ney   pang   chengso   com   cal   ha-ela.*
       your   room   cleaning   please   well   do-IMP
       'Clean your room well.'

(9.9) *ney   pang   chengso   com   cal   ha-**ci**.*
       your   room   cleaning   please   well   do-*ci*
       '(I think you should) Clean your room well.'

The imperative sentence in (9.8) is used to tell the listener to clean his room well. In contrast, the *ci* sentence in (9.9) is understood as metarepresenting the speaker's own thought about a potential state of affairs in which the listener cleans his room. That is why *ci* sentences with a base verb form are more likely to be interpreted as suggestions than as direct orders or requests.

What is to be noted further is that the *ci* sentence in (9.9) can be used when the speaker regrets that the potential state of affairs is not realised, meaning 'You should have cleaned your room well.' The intonation will be different from that of a suggestion. The original representation relates to a state of affairs that was potential in the past. Sentences with the imperative sentence-type suffix *la,* as in (9.8), cannot be interpreted as such. In this case, the desirable state of affairs can be realised only in the future because the speaker describes a potential state of affairs as she utters the sentence.

On the other hand, the potential state of affairs can be realised even by the speaker, when the *ci* sentence is interpreted as a promise, threat, or decision (see also H. Lee 1999: 260–1). The *ci* sentence in (9.10) can be interpreted as any of (a), (b) or (c):

(9.10) ku-ka han   sikan   ilha-yss-tamyen,   20 dale-lul   cwu-**ci**.
        he-NOM one   hour   work-PST-if   20 dollar-AC   give-ci
        literally: if he worked one hour, () give 20 dollars.

        a. 'If he worked one hour, (I suggest that you) give him 20 dollars.'
        b. 'If he worked one hour, you should have given him 20 dollars.'
        c. 'If he worked one hour, I will give him 20 dollars.'

As shown in (9.10), the *ci* sentences used with a base verb form are very different from regular imperative sentences because the latter cannot be interpreted as anything like (9.10b) or (9.10c).

Finally, a *ci* clause in long-form negation can also be explained as a metarepresentation of the speaker's representation. Consider (9.11), repeated from (9.4):

(9.11) a. [ku   salam   ttal-un   tayhakkyo-ey tani-**ci**] an-h-nun-ta.
       [the   person daughter-TOP college-to   go-ci]   not-do-IND-DC
       'His daughter does not go to college.'
    b. [ku   hay   kyewul-un   chwup-**ci**]   an-h-ass-ta.
       [that year   winter-TOP   cold-ci]   not-do-PST-DC
       'The winter that year was not cold.'

The embedded clause ending with *ci* is a metarepresentation of the speaker's previous representation. She may have believed it or simply represented it as relevant information if it turns out to be true.

As mentioned in Section 9.1, the epistemic accounts classify the suffix *ci* in long-form negation as the same epistemic marker as the sentence-final *ci* (K. Lee 1993; H. Lee 1999). Then, it will not be consistent to say that the speaker believes in the content of the embedded clause and simultaneously denies it. According to my understanding of *ci*, the embedded clause with *ci* metarepresents the speaker's prior representation of a state of affairs, which she denies in long-form negation.

The clause modified with the suffix *ci* in long-form negation may also represent the speaker's thought about a potential state of affairs, as in (9.12):

(9.12)   [ku-eykey   20 dale-lul   cwu-**ci**]   ma.
         [he-to   20 dollar-AC   give-ci]   do not-IMP
         'Don't give him 20 dollars.'

The sentence in (9.12) tells the addressee not to make real the potential state of affairs which is represented in the embedded clause.

Ci sentences are very often used for self-addressed questions. Compare *ci* sentences with a *wh*-word in (9.13) and ordinary interrogative sentences in (9.14):

(9.13) a. *yelsoy-lul   eti   twu-ess-**ci**?*
           key-AC   where   put-PST-*ci*
           'Where did (I/you/he/...) put the key?'
       b. *yeki-lul   encey   o-ass-ess-**ci**?*
           here-AC   when   come-PST-PST-*ci*
           'When did (I/you/he/...) come here?'

(9.14) a. *yelsoy-lul   eti   twu-ess-ni?*
           key-AC   where   put-PST-Q
           'Where did (I/you/he/...) put the key?'
       b. *yeki-lul   encey   o-ass-ess-ni?*
           here-AC   when   come-PST-PST-Q
           'When did (I/you/he/...) come here?'

The *ci* sentences in (9.13) can be addressed to the speaker herself, as well as to the addressee. In (9.13a), the sentence metarepresents the speaker's previous thought imperfectly with a *wh*-word for the missing part, perhaps because she cannot remember it properly. The speaker addresses the question to herself, trying to recover the missing part. The same holds for (9.13b). In contrast, the interrogative sentences in (9.14) are metarepresentations of relevant thoughts, which are desirable if the missing parts are completed, and are used only to the addressee other than the speaker (see Wilson & Sperber 1988a).

Finally, it should be noted that metarepresentational use is not always overtly indicated. It is the speaker's pragmatic choice whether the metarepresentation is overtly indicated or not. She can use other types of negation that do not use *ci*, and she can use a regular sentence-type suffix instead of *ci*.

9.3   Restrictions of *ci* Sentences

In this section, we look at some restrictions on the suffix *ci* that support the metarepresentational account. First, the suffix *ci* is not used to convey new information, even when the speaker believes that it is true. Consider (9.15):

(9.15)   [Looking out of the window]
        a.   *pi-ka*   *o-[n-ta/e/ney]*.
           rain-NOM   come-[IND-DC/ES/ES].
           'It's raining.'
        b.   ? *pi-ka*   *o-**ci***.
           rain-NOM   come-*ci*
           '? It's raining.'

In (9.15), when the speaker finds that it is raining, a declarative sentence-final suffix *ta* or other epistemic suffixes such as *e* and *ney* are acceptable, while *ci* is not.

If we define *ci* as a metarepresentational marker of the speaker's pre-existing thought, we can explain the restriction in the following way. The fact that it is raining outside is new information. Her utterance is more likely to describe the state of affairs beyond the window. Hence, *ci* is not appropriate. The speaker must not have represented this state of affairs prior to the visual stimulus triggering the utterance of (9.15b).

On the other hand, if the speaker had said that it was raining and the listener had not agreed, (9.15b) could be used as a confirmation question, meaning 'I was right, wasn't I?' In this case, the speaker is metarepresenting her previous thought that it was raining. The traditional accounts of *ci* as an epistemic marker fail to explain why new information cannot be used with *ci* even though the speaker believes it to be true.

A *ci* sentence is not used as a surprise question. Consider (9.16):

(9.16)   BOY [SHOWING HIS REPORT CARD TO MOTHER]: Mom, I got all As.
          MOM: Did you? Well done.

In (9.16), *Did you?* can be translated as *Kulay-ss-e?* ('You did so?') or *Kulay-ss-ni?* ('Did you so?'), but not as *Kulay-ss-ci?* ('You did so?'). The content of a surprise question is new to the speaker, so it cannot be a metarepresentation of the speaker's pre-existing thought. In such a case, *ci* is not allowed.

Finally, a *ci* sentence cannot be used when the speaker expresses her feeling about a state of affairs:

(9.17)   a. ?nuckey   wa-se   mianha-**ci**.
              late   come-because   sorry-ci
              '? I am sorry for coming late.' (as apology)
          b. ?ney-ka   hapkyekha-yse   kippu-**ci**.
              you-NOM   passed-because   happy-ci
              '? I am happy that you passed.' (as congratulation)

In (9.17), if the utterances are used for apologising and congratulating, respectively, the suffix *ci* is not acceptable. In apologies and congratulations, the utterance needs to convey what the speaker feels about what has happened, rather than metarepresent the speaker's pre-existing thoughts about her feelings. In contrast, a declarative sentence-type suffix *ta* or other epistemic markers *ney* or *e* are appropriate.

Yet *ci* can be used as an answer to a question regarding the speaker's feeling, as in (9.18):

(9.18)   A: Ne-nun   mianhacito   an-h-ni?
             You-TOP   feel sorry   not-do-Q
             'Don't you feel sorry?'
          B: mianha-**ci**.   Haciman   ettehkey   hay?
             feel sorry-ci.   But   how   do
             '(Of course) I feel sorry. But what can I do?'

In (9.18 B), *mianha-ci* '(I am) sorry' is a response to the question regarding the speaker's feeling. The speaker metarepresents her thought about her feeling in order to express her attitude of approval towards the thought.

9.4   Conclusion

Previous accounts have classified the Korean sentence-final suffix *ci* as an epistemic marker that indicates the speaker's belief in the truth of the proposition expressed by the utterance. These accounts can explain the *ci* used in statements and questions, but they cannot handle *ci* in orders/requests because such sentences lack propositions that the speaker can believe. They cannot deal with the *ci* used as the target of long-form negation either, because the speaker denies (does not believe) the target at the time of the utterance.

In this chapter, I suggest that the suffix *ci* is a metarepresentational marker of the speaker's own representation before producing the utterance. A *ci* sentence with a tensed verb involves a real state of affairs. In statements, the speaker approves of her previous thought, and in questions, the speaker questions whether her thought is correct. She wants her thought to be confirmed, in *yes–no* questions, or to be completed, in *wh*-questions. *Ci* sentences with the base form of the verb metarepresent the speaker's thought about a desirable or potential state of affairs. They are used in suggestions for doing something in the future, or for expressing regrets about an unrealised state of affairs in the past. In long-form negation, they are used with a proposition that the speaker has thought to be true or relevant if true.

In all of these cases, what is represented in a *ci* sentence is not a state of affairs, but the speaker's pre-existing thought about a state of affairs. This metarepresentational account can explain why *ci* sentences are interpreted as conveying the speaker's belief in statements, as the speaker's request for confirmation in questions, and as the speaker's suggestion in orders/requests. It can also explain why *ci* is not used with new information, in a surprise question, or with a performative sentence relating to the speaker's feeling about a state of affairs. The account of *ci* as a metarepresentational marker can explain many more cases of *ci* than the account of *ci* as an epistemic marker. I conclude that the distinction between representation (description) and metarepresentation, as well as differences in sentence types and epistemic degrees, can play an important role in the explanation of Korean sentence-final suffixes.

Acknowledgements

The idea of this chapter was first presented in 'The Korean sentence-final suffix *-ci*: An epistemic marker vs. a metarepresentational marker.' *Korean Journal of Linguistics* 41(2): 267–87, in 2016 (in Korean).

I owe a great debt of gratitude to Deirdre Wilson, who has been a teacher, a supervisor, and an example for my life. I believe that I may not be able to reciprocate what she has done for me in any way. I am very grateful to Robyn Carston, Billy Clark and Kate Scott for their efforts in this volume. I am also very grateful to anonymous referees for their invaluable comments. All of the remaining errors are mine.

10 Expressive Epithets and Expressive Small Clauses

Diane Blakemore

10.1 Introduction

This chapter focuses on the sort of expressions which occur in expressive DP epithets (e.g. 'the idiot') and expressive small clauses of the form *You-PredP* (e.g. 'you sweetie'). Expressive epithets are generally distinguished from ordinary descriptive DPs by the fact that they contain a predicate expression which contributes an affective or expressive meaning (Aoun & Choueiri 2000; Corazza 2005). As Potts and Roeper (2006) have shown, such expressions may also occupy the *PredP* position in expressive small clauses such as the ones in (10.5)–(10.6). While the emphasis has usually been on the negative or derogatory force of structures containing these expressions, they actually express a range of emotions ranging from anger, contempt and (feigned) annoyance (e.g. (10.1)–(10.3)) to affection, sympathy and admiration (e.g. (10.4)–(10.6)). Moreover, their expressive import may vary from context to context so that *bastard*, for example, can be used to convey a range of emotions and attitudes – including endearment.[1]

(10.1)   I've just been to see Darren. *The bastard* is going to fire 10 members of staff.

(10.2)   A: God! What was he doing?
         B: No idea. I thought *the weirdo* was going to kiss me at one point.

(10.3)   Come on *you old miser*, it's your turn to buy the drinks.

(10.4)   [the speaker and hearer are admiring a baby]
         Oh look, *the little poppet*'s smiling at me.

(10.5)   A: OK, you win. I'm going to tell her she can go.
         B: I knew you would, *you big softy*

(10.6)   A: I've done all the shopping.
         B: *You hero.*

---

[1] Hence my decision to refer to these epithets as *expressive epithets* rather than *pejorative epithets* (cf. Anderson and Lepore (2013a)).

The term 'expressive' or 'pejorative epithet' is not restricted to the expressions illustrated in (10.1)–(10.3), but is also used for highly offensive expressions known as *slurs* – for example, the racial slurs in (10.7)–(10.8) and the homophobic one in (10.8):[2]

(10.7)   We came from the UK for work, mainly. The old man was breaking his back for nothing, just about. Too many Pakis and Poles in the UK now. (www.kiwibiker.co.nz/forums/showthread.php/138141-Why-so-many-Poms-in-NZ)

(10.8)   I'll bet you they hire a nigger and a dyke before they're willing to even consider a white guy. (cited by Camp 2013)

However, in contrast with the expressions in (10.1)–(10.3), slurs are generally understood to target descriptive features which are considered to be associated with a particular nationality, race or class of people, and these descriptive features can play a role in reference assignment in the same way as the descriptive content of non-pejorative racial epithets. Speaker B in (10.9) may answer A's question with either the racially offensive utterance in (a) or with the angry but racially inoffensive utterance in (b):

(10.9)   A: Who's annoyed you now?
         B: (a) The pakis. They've won the cricket again.
              (b) The bloody Indian cricket team. They've won
                   again.   (example from Blakemore 2015)

In contrast, expressions such as *bastard*, *shit* or *scumbag* cannot be used as a means of identifying a referent. B's response in (10.10) is odd:

(10.10) A: Who's annoyed you now?
         B:?? The bastards/shits/scumbags. They've won the cricket again.

Croom (2014a: 232) argues that expressions such as *bastard* work primarily to indicate the emotional state of the speaker – an analysis which could be said to be consistent with the observation made by a number of linguists that certain expressive DP epithets contrast with other DPs in that they do not have any conceptual content which plays a role in the recovery of a reference and hence function more like anaphors (cf. Jackendoff 1972; Lasnik 1989; Aoun & Choueiri 2000; Huang 2000; Bosch 2001; Corazza 2005). Thus Bosch (2001: 3) points out that expressions like *bastard* or *scumbag* are no more

---

[2] There is a growing literature on slurs. See, for instance, Hornsby (2001); Croom (2008, 2011, 2014a,b); Hom (2008); Williamson (2009); Hedger (2012, 2013); Anderson and Lepore (2013a,b); Camp (2013); Jeshion (2013); Bach (2018). For my own account of the way slurs work, see Blakemore (2015).

useful for the purposes of reference assignment than apparently vacuous uses of terms such as *the guy* or *the chap*.[3]

This idea that the expressions used in expressive epithets have no descriptive content is also found in Potts' work on expressives (see Potts 2005, 2007a, 2012, and Potts & Roeper 2006). Potts and Roeper argue that expressions such as *bastard*, *softy* and *fool* can be found either in utterances in which they are 'wrapped' in descriptive meaning or in small clause (*You-PredP*) utterances in which the interpretation is purely expressive. They argue that while the utterance in (10.1) has both a descriptive meaning (e.g. DARREN IS GOING TO FIRE 10 MEMBERS OF STAFF), and an expressive meaning (e.g. whatever is expressed by *bastard*), the utterance in (10.11) is '*purely expressive*':

(10.11)   [to someone who has just admitted he has fired 3 members of staff]
          You bastard.

The present chapter aims to re-examine the claim that the expressions illustrated in (10.1)–(10.6) have no descriptive meaning, looking at the question from the perspective of Sperber and Wilson's (1986/1995) relevance-theoretic pragmatics. I argue that while the utterances containing these expressions are expressive in the sense that their relevance lies in the information they communicate about the speaker's attitude or emotional state, the hearer recovers this interpretation on the basis of the *conceptual* content which is taken to be communicated by the predicate expressions they contain. As we shall see, in contrast with the descriptive content of expressions used as slurs, the content derived from expressions used in expressive epithets is not the sort of content which can play a role in reference assignment. In the uses illustrated in (10.1)–(10.2), the role of the descriptive content of *bastard* and *weirdo* lies in the part it plays in the identification of the attitude the speaker holds towards an individual whose identity is established independently. Some expressions convey more specific evidence for the attitude communicated than others: the attitudes we hold towards a cheat or a fool are attitudes to someone who has exhibited a fairly specific range of behaviours, while the term *bastard* might be used for anyone who has annoyed or angered the speaker – including cheats and fools. However, the point is that in contrast with slurs which identify an

---

[3]   (i) Clearly, there are contexts in which *chap* does play a role in reference assignment. Consider, for example, a case in which A asks the question 'Who took your CDs?' in a context in which the answer has one of two candidates – a woman and a man.

(ii) Bach (2006) disputes the claim being made here, pointing out that utterances such as the following (due to Larry Horn) are acceptable:

I wouldn't hire that shyster.
That scumbag never returned my CDs.

However, neither Bach nor Horn acknowledge that in these examples it is the demonstrative together with the context which is doing all the referential work.

individual as a member of a particular social/racial group and communicate a pejorative attitude towards any member of that group, none of these expressions can be said to offend anyone other than the person understood to be the target of the epithet on that occasion.

It might be claimed that the question of whether an expression is a slur is a matter of linguistic convention to the extent that part of what we know about a word such as *paki* is that it is dedicated for offence towards a particular racial group.[4] Similarly, it might seem that the question of whether an NP could be part of an expressive epithet is a linguistic matter. Thus, certain expressions, e.g. *darling, sweetheart, poppet, bastard, scumbag*, could be said to be dedicated for expressive use, while other expressions, e.g. *pilot, gardener, author*, could never be used purely expressively. And, indeed, whereas the use of *darling, poppet* and *bastard* in the small clause structures highlighted by Potts and Roeper (2006) is entirely acceptable, the use of *pilot, gardener* and *author* in such expressions would be odd.

However, expressions such as *sweetheart* and *bastard* can be used as regular content words in utterances where they do not share the properties which, according to Potts (2005, 2007a, 2012), characterise expressives. In (10.12)–(10.13) they do not have the property of *non-displaceability* since they can be used to report both attitudes held in the past and attitudes attributed to other people:

(10.12) I used to think that Darren was a bit of a bastard, but I'm not
         so sure now.

(10.13) Mavis might look like a sweetheart, but in fact she's tough
         as old boots.

This would suggest that even the prototypical expressives which Potts and Roeper discuss have expressive interpretations (in Potts and Roeper's sense) in some contexts but not in others.

Indeed, as we shall see, there is a whole range of expressions which can be used in the *You-PredP* structures, but which would seem to be uncontroversially conceptual. The following are just a small selection of expressions which can appear both in the small clause structures in (a) and the regular descriptive utterances in (b), where they clearly can be used to report on past events, attitudes or emotions, or attitudes attributed to others:

(10.14) (a) You saint!
         (b) I used to think Maud was a saint, but it turns out that she's not
             as perfect as she looks.

---

[4] In view of the phenomenon of reappropriation, it might be more accurate to say 'sociolinguistic convention' (cf. Jacobs 2002; Hom 2008; Rahman 2012; Bianchi 2014; Croom 2014a,b).

(10.15) (a) You hero!
        (b) I thought he was a real hero when he offered to do the dishes,
            but it turned out he just wanted to get out of playing Monopoly.

(10.16) (a) You shark!
        (b) I used to think all lawyers were sharks until I met you.

(10.17) (a) You wizard!
        (b) I thought she would be a real wizard when it comes to computers,
            but apparently she's no better at trouble shooting than I am.

(10.18) (a) You racist!
        (b) Everyone thinks that Neville is a racist, but he's always been
            nice to me.

In Section 10.3, I shall argue that we can accommodate all these examples if we analyse them as communicating conceptual content which may play a role in the identification of the attitude the speaker holds towards an individual. In some contexts, the main relevance of the utterance will be understood to lie *entirely* in the information about this attitude, and we would say that the utterance has an expressive interpretation. In a framework which assumes that the form of an utterance is constrained by the speaker's goal of producing an optimally relevant utterance, the small clause (*You-PredP*) structure (and, in particular the absence of the copula), together with prosodic clues, can be seen as a means of guiding the hearer towards this expressive sort of interpretation rather than to one where the relevance lies in what Potts calls the 'at issue' content of the utterance. If this is right, then *contra* Potts, we do not need to say that certain expressions are semantically classified as expressives, or that an utterance has an expressive interpretation if it contains an expression or structure which is linguistically coded as expressive.

10.2   Relevance-Theoretic Semantics and the Meaning of Expressive NPs

According to Potts (2005, 2007a, 2012), one of the main properties which distinguishes expressives is their descriptive ineffability. In this sense, he argues, expressives can be compared with certain discourse particles (cf. Blakemore 2002). Just as a native speaker of English finds it difficult, if not impossible, to provide the meaning of discourse-initial *well* or *so* in descriptive terms, they will similarly 'hem and haw' when asked to provide a propositional paraphrase for the meaning of *damn* or *bastard*. In particular, he reports that only one of all the people he has interviewed about expressives has told him that *bastard* means 'vile, contemptible person' (Potts 2007a).

In a critical commentary on Potts' work, Geurts (2007) has argued that Potts is wrong to argue that the descriptive ineffability of expletives requires a different sort of analysis, since there are many words whose interpretations cannot be fixed independently of their use in a particular context, and which cannot always be given propositional paraphrases: his examples include *languid, green, pretty*. Within the relevance-theoretic framework of this chapter, Geurts' examples can be treated as words whose communicated content is underdetermined by their linguistically encoded content (cf. Carston 2002). For instance, the concept which is linguistically encoded by *languid* is a very general, abstract concept LANGUID which must be distinguished from the concept communicated by its use in a particular context (LANGUID*). On this account, then, *languid* is non-paraphrasable in the sense that it is not possible to pin down the concept which it communicates independently of the context in which it is used.

As I have indicated, this chapter argues that the expressive interpretation recovered from the use of epithets such as *the bastard, the weirdo, the poppet*, or *the big softy* is derived via the conceptual content they are taken to communicate on a given occasion. The point is that the concept communicated by each of these expressions will vary from context to context: it is recovered by the same sort of pragmatic enrichment processes that are involved in the interpretation of *languid*. This means that the attitude the hearer takes the speaker to be communicating will vary accordingly. Consider the interpretation of *bastard*, first, in (10.19a–b), where it is produced in the context of a tennis match between two friends, and, second, in (10.20a–b) where it is produced following a news report about a particularly heinous crime:

(10.19) (a) You're a lucky bastard.
         (b) You lucky bastard.

(10.20) (a) My god, how can they be such bastards?
         (b) The fucking bastards.

Whereas in the second context, *bastard* will be interpreted as communicating a concept (BASTARD*) which plays a role in the derivation of assumptions containing such concepts as ODIOUS, EVIL, MONSTROUS, LOATHSOME, VILLAINOUS, the use of the same word in (10.19) will not lead to any such assumptions, but communicates a concept BASTARD** which triggers assumptions that the speaker is experiencing considerably milder emotions, such as exasperation or annoyance.

While the concepts communicated by *bastard* and *idiot* may vary from context to context, this variation is all within a conceptual domain which is continuous with the domain of the linguistically encoded concept. In each case, the concept recovered is broader than the linguistically encoded concept, but in each case it is broader in a different way, and in each case gives rise to different assumptions about the emotional attitude of the speaker.

However, it seems that expressive epithets and the small clause structures discussed by Potts and Roeper (2006) may also feature expressions which communicate concepts which are *not* continuous with their linguistically encoded meanings. For example, (10.14a) and (10.15a) (repeated below) might be uttered on finding that the hearer has washed up an enormous pile of dishes:[5]

(10.14) a.   You saint!

(10.15) a.   You hero!

Such examples are acceptable *only* if *saint* and *hero* are understood figuratively. Thus it seems while it is appropriate to *describe* the Falklands War soldier, Simon Weston, as a hero, it would be inappropriate to produce the utterance in (10.15a) on meeting him, since it would convey some sort of hyperbolic, and hence insincere, intent.

According to Carston (2002, 2010) and Wilson and Carston (2008), the figurative interpretation of a word such as *saint* is recovered by pragmatically adjusting its semantically encoded meaning as part of the search for optimal relevance. To this extent, we might say that the interpretation of *saint* in (10.14) involves the same sort of interpretation process as the interpretation of *bastard*, *idiot*, *weirdo*. However, Carston and Wearing (2011) have argued that as they are used in examples such as (10.14a) and (10.15a), words such as *saint* are understood to communicate a concept which is discontinuous from the lexically encoded concept in the sense that they involve a domain shift. In its literal sense, the word *saint* would only be applied to people who have been canonised by the relevant religious authority (the Catholic Church), a property which clearly does not apply in the washing-up scenario described above. In this sense, the interpretation of *saint* involves narrowing of the lexicalised concept, resulting in a pragmatically derived concept SAINT*, which does not include properties such as the ones in (10.21a) but does include properties such as the ones in (10.21b):

(10.21) a. HAS BEEN CANONISED BY THE CATHOLIC CHURCH, IS HOLY, IS
              DEAD, IS IN HEAVEN, IS SUPERNATURAL
         b. IS KIND, IS THOUGHTFUL

In this sense, they argue, *saint* in (10.14a) is metaphorical. However, they also argue that as it is used in (10.14a), *saint* is hyperbolic, and hence involves

---

[5] As Camp (2013) and Carston and Wearing (2011) have pointed out, hyperbole and metaphor seem to be particularly effective means of expressing our emotional attitudes.

concept broadening. That is, while it is kind to do the dishes, this kindness is clearly not of the same order that characterises the kindness of saints (such as Mother Teresa of Calcutta). In this way, the example is simultaneously metaphorical and hyperbolic.

A similar analysis can be given for (10.15a). On the one hand, its interpretation involves narrowing the lexical concept to exclude people who have been prepared to sacrifice their lives for others and have demonstrated remarkable bravery, in the recovery of a concept which can be applied to someone who has carried out an unpleasant task and hence is worthy of praise. On the other hand, it involves broadening the properties which fall under the narrowed concept: doing the dishes is unpleasant and praiseworthy, but not *that* unpleasant and praiseworthy.

While it is relatively easy to make a list of the sort of expressions which might be used in a similar way (Carston and Wearing themselves provide a number of examples), it cannot be said that an expression can be *semantically* classified as expressive or non-expressive. For example, at first sight, the predicate *professor* might seem to be an unlikely candidate for use in the communication of a speaker's attitudes towards an individual, and that it could never be used in a *You-PredP* structure. However, there are contexts in which *professor* can in fact be understood to communicate a concept that is both narrower and broader than the one that it encodes and is acceptable in the sort of utterances under discussion. Thus when Barack Obama was described as 'professorial' in the first of his debates with Mitt Romney in the run-up to the 2012 US presidential election, the writer's intention was to draw attention to the fact that his responses were rambling, absurdly intellectual and out of touch with ordinary people (see Beth Hong, www.vancouverobserver.com/blogs/politicaljunkie). This may be unfair to university professors, perhaps, but it is exactly this sort of concept that would play a role in the interpretation of utterances such as (10.22):

(10.22)   Come on, you old professor, when I asked you to explain how to get my camera to work, I wasn't expecting a lecture on optics.

At the same time, none of the expressions discussed in this section are used exclusively in expressive epithets or in the non-descriptive *You-PredP* utterances discussed by Potts and Roeper (2006). Recall the (b) examples in (10.14)–(10.16). This means the difference between the verbless *You-PredP* utterances and the ones just listed cannot lie in the sort of expression which is used in the predicate phrase. Nor can it lie in the way this expression is interpreted – the same pragmatic narrowing and broadening processes are involved in both sorts of case. This leaves us with the question of what really does underlie the distinction that theorists have drawn between expressive and descriptive predicates.

10.3   Expressive Small Clauses

According to Potts and Roeper, whereas the second segment of the sequence in (10.1) (repeated below) has both a descriptive meaning (DARREN IS GOING TO FIRE AT LEAST TEN MEMBERS OF STAFF) and an expressive meaning (whatever is communicated by *bastard*), the small clauses illustrated in (10.23)–(10.25) are 'purely expressive' (Potts & Roeper 2006):

(10.1)   I've just been to see Darren. The bastard is going to fire 10 members of staff.

(10.23)   You bastard!

(10.24)   You idiot!

(10.25)   You cheat!

At first sight, it may seem that there are sentential constituents which look like these *You-PredP* structures – namely, the nominals in utterances such as (10.26)–(10.27):

(10.26)   You fools should read more carefully (example from Caroline Heycock, cited by Potts & Roeper)

(10.27)   We linguists should stick together.

However, as Potts and Roeper point out, since the *You-PredP* structures allow a singular pronoun form, they cannot be treated as nominals, which require the plural form of the pronoun (this point is due to Caroline Heycock):

(10.28)   * You fool should read more carefully.

Moreover, as Bob Borsley (p. c.) has pointed out, when the target of a *You-PredP* utterance is a single individual, the repetition of *you* is appropriate at the right edge of the sentence:

(10.29)   You bastard, you!

Potts and Roeper suggest that the nominals in (10.26)–(10.27) must be treated as a type of 'integrated appositive', and can thus be seen as examples of what Potts (2005) called 'multidimensional' meaning, in which the meaning is composed from an expressive meaning (determined by *fool*) and the regular type meaning determined by the expressive's argument (*you*). In contrast, they argue, the *You-PredP* utterances are examples of one-dimensional meaning. Thus, they propose that the domain of expressives divides into two sub-domains: the kind that determines multidimensional meanings and the kind that determines one-dimensional meanings (like those that appear in expressive small clauses).

According to Potts and Roeper, the interpretation of the small clauses in (10.23)–(10.25) depends, first, on the fact that they contain predicates semantically typed as *expressive*, and, second, on the absence of the copular verb, where this is explained in terms of the following principle:

(10.30) No verb meaning is expressive (Potts & Roeper 2006: 193)

According to their analysis, when a copular verb is combined with a predicate which is semantically typed as an expressive, as in (10.31), the result is undefined and the clause is blocked:

(10.31) *You are fool.

The assumption here is that the small clauses in (10.23)–(10.25) are 'purely expressive' to the extent that these structures have been used as a testing ground for expressivity. Thus, it was assumed that, in contrast with *sweetheart* or *fool*, a word such as *gardener* cannot have an expressive interpretation and for this reason is unacceptable in a 'purely expressive' small clause. However, as we have seen, it is not clear that the assumption that the predicates in these structures must be *semantically* typed as expressives can be maintained. The examples used by Potts and Roeper can be used in utterances in which they do not have the properties which, they assume, distinguish expressive meaning from descriptive meaning. Moreover, while it seems unlikely that *gardener* could have the sort of hyperbolic and/or metaphorical interpretation which would give the hearer access to the emotions and attitudes which would make its use acceptable in a *You-PredP* utterance, given the role of the context in the recovery of such an interpretation, I would be reluctant to completely rule out the possibility of an interpretation of *gardener* that would make its use appropriate for expressive purposes. At the same time, as it stands, the principle in (10.30) would appear to be an entirely arbitrary stipulation.

I suggest that we approach the interpretation of the small clauses in (10.23)–(10.25) by contrasting them with fragmentary utterances such as (10.32)–(10.33):

(10.32) Idiot.

(10.33) Cheat.

In particular, I would like to compare two possible types of interpretation for the utterances in (10.32)–(10.33), and show that only one of these is available for the small clause utterances in (10.23)–(10.25). Consider first, a situation in which you and I are watching a game of poker and I whisper (10.33) in your ear having directed my gaze towards a particular player. In such a situation, it will be mutually manifest that the relevance of my utterance lies in the assumption that the individual I have indicated (x) has the property of being a cheat. That is, it will be mutually manifest that I intend you to pragmatically enrich the linguistically encoded meaning for the recovery of a thought of the form X IS A CHEAT*. Clearly, the knowledge that someone is a cheat may cause you to adopt a particular sort of attitude towards him – an attitude of outrage, for example. However, this is not necessarily the only reason for wanting you to know that the individual is a cheat: the information may be relevant as an explanation of the fact that this individual has won the last few games; or it may be relevant as a warning not to play cards with this person; or, if we are officials in the casino, it may be relevant as an injunction to move in on the game and remove the individual from the casino. The point is that, whatever contextual effects I intend you to recover, you will recover them only from the pragmatically enriched descriptive assumption X IS A CHEAT*.

Now consider a situation in which it is mutually manifest to the speaker and a given individual x that there is evidence that x has cheated, and that some-time after the incident in which x is unmasked as a cheat the speaker happens to meet him and produces the utterance in (10.33). Clearly, in such a case, the utterance will have very different prosodic properties than the utterance produced in the previous scenario: it would likely be produced with a con-temptuous, aggressive tone of voice. However, the point is that produced in this sort of situation, the utterance is not relevant in virtue of communicating the assumption X IS A CHEAT*, since it is already mutually manifest to speaker and hearer that x is a cheat. In this context, the relevance of the utterance lies in the feelings and attitudes which cheats typically engender – feelings and attitudes which the hearer derives on the basis of the concept which the word *cheat* is taken to communicate. In contrast with the first type of case, where the concept communicated by *cheat* (CHEAT*) is understood to be a constituent of a pragmatically derived propositional representation, the hearer of the utterance in the second scenario is not intended to derive a propositional representation which has CHEAT* as a constituent: all he needs to do is to derive the relevant concept CHEAT* which, along with the prosodic clues provided by the utterance and accompanying facial expressions, will give him access to the attitudes and emotions which the speaker intends to communicate. For it is here that the relevance of the utterance lies. And it is in this sense that the interpretation recovered from (10.33) is an expressive interpretation which contrasts with the descriptive interpretation recovered in the first scenario. Clearly, we could draw a similar distinction between two different interpretations of (10.32).

Let us return to the *You-PredP* utterances and in particular to the utterance in (10.25):

(10.25) You cheat!

In contrast with (10.33), this utterance is not a sentence fragment, but is a com-plete syntactic structure. As we have seen, it is not the sort of structure which can be developed into a larger structure containing a copula. Thus we must distinguish the small clause structure in (10.34) from the structure in (10.35) where *you cheats* is a (plural) nominal functioning as the subject of a declarative sentence:

(10.34) You cheats!

(10.35) You cheats are going to be punished.

The point here is not that no verb meaning is expressive (as Potts and Roeper claim), but rather that the *You-PredP* structure is not a constituent of a clause, and is syntactically complete in itself. Since the *You-PredP* structure is syntactically complete, its use can be taken as evidence that the sort of pragmatically enriched descriptive interpretation which is recovered from the fragment in (10.33) in the first of the two scenarios is not an option, and that an optimally relevant interpretation can be obtained simply on the basis of the interpretation of the predicate (and the pronoun *you*, which identifies the hearer as a target). As I have suggested, this interpretation is based on the identification of the emotions or attitudes directed towards the audience[6] – emotions and attitudes which are identified on the basis of the concept recovered from the *PredP* in the given context. As in the first interpretation of (10.33), the speaker's tone of voice and facial expressions will contribute towards the identification of the attitude that is being communicated. However, the point is that the form of the utterance, and, in particular, the small clause structure, will play a role in guiding the hearer towards an expressive interpretation in which the relevance of the utterance will be understood to lie in the attitudes and emotions that are identified on the basis of the concept which the predicate expression (*cheat*) is taken to communicate in that context.

10.4   Conclusion

I have shown that the expressive import of utterances such as (10.25) *You cheat!* does not depend on them containing a predicate expression which is semantically typed as 'expressive'. Rather, such utterances have expressive import in the sense that their relevance lies in the emotions and attitudes which they communicate – emotions and attitudes which are recovered via the concept which is taken to be communicated by the predicate in a particular context. The *You-PredP* structure plays a particular role in guiding the hearer towards an expressive interpretation by blocking the sort of pragmatic enrichment processes which would lead to a descriptive interpretation. The structure indicates that those processes are not necessary for the recovery of an

---

[6] As Potts and Roeper (2006) show, in self-addressed utterances this may be the speaker herself.

optimally relevant interpretation and that the hearer is expected to find the relevance of the utterance in the attitudes and emotions which can be identified on the basis of the concept communicated by the predicate in the given context.

Acknowledgements

This chapter was written as a token of my everlasting gratitude for everything that Deirdre Wilson has given me over the years – support, friendship and inspiration.

Some of the research reported in this chapter was supported by the Leverhulme Trust. I am grateful to Robyn Carston for her help in getting the chapter into a form that allowed it to appear in this volume. Thanks also to an anonymous referee for constructive feedback.

11   Ad Hoc Concepts, Polysemy and the Lexicon

Robyn Carston

11.1   Introduction

According to the relevance-theoretic (RT) approach to lexical pragmatics, the interpretation in context of substantive words (nouns, verbs, adjectives) often involves the construction of an *ad hoc concept* or occasion-specific sense, based on interaction among encoded lexical concepts, contextual information and expectations of relevance (Carston 2002; Wilson & Carston 2007). This approach captures the flexibility of word meaning, its pragmatic responsiveness to the specificity of contexts of utterance, and the variability in familiarity and frequency of word senses across different individuals whom we, nevertheless, think of as speaking the 'same language'.

In this short chapter, I focus on the implications of this approach for (a) an account of the phenomenon of polysemy, understood as the case of a single word which has several established interrelated senses, and (b) the appropriate construal of the substantive (open-class) lexicon,[1] that is, the list of sound–meaning pairings that are stored in an individual's mind, enabling direct selection of a word meaning in utterance interpretation rather than an inferential pragmatic construction process.

The chapter is structured as follows: in Section 11.2, examples of polysemy are given and some of the issues they raise are outlined; in Section 11.3, the RT lexical pragmatic account is presented and the development of 'families' of related senses is described; in Section 11.4, some views on the mental lexicon and the representation of polysemy within it are discussed, concluding that two distinct and complementary construals are essential (the linguistic lexicon and the communicational lexicon). Section 11.5 is a brief summing up.

---

[1] The contrast here is with the 'functional lexicon', which consists of linguistic items that do not correspond to concepts denoting things in the world, but to grammatical objects (e.g. determiners, quantifiers, pronouns). These tend to be quite rigid in their uses, seldom polysemous, and generally closed to new items.

11.2   Polysemy – Pragmatics and/or Semantics?

Consider the following instances of the noun 'mouth' (rough paraphrases are given in brackets):

(11.1) a. The whale has a huge mouth.
       b. The mouth of the cave/tunnel is visible from here. (an aperture)
       c. The water at the mouth looks green. (part of a river that enters into an ocean)
       d. I have four mouths to feed. (whole body/person)
       e. He is a big mouth ('Mack the mouth'). (someone who talks too much)
       f. Stop putting words in my mouth.

(examples adapted from Vicente 2018)

Assuming for the moment that there is a single word 'mouth' here, it can clearly be used to express a multiplicity of distinct (but related) senses. If we take the physical mouth of animals/humans as the basic sense, most of the others are fairly transparently related to it (and each other), whether through a metonymic process (e.g. (11.1d), where the word for a body part is used for the whole body), or metaphorical extension (e.g. (11.1b), where the relation is one of perceived resemblance between animal mouths and entrances to caves), or some other kind of process (see Section 11.3). The lexical form 'mouth' may also be used as a verb, again with multiple senses:

(11.2) a. He mouthed obscenities at us. (mouth movement without sound)
       b. They're just mouthing empty slogans (saying something without belief in its content)
       c. She's mouthing off again.
       d. The new-born puppies mouthed each other's faces.

The cross-categorial nature of polysemy in English is widespread:

(11.3) a. He has a bad pain in his *back*.
       b. I'll *back* the car into the drive.
       c. Her *back* garden is tiny.

And each of these three words (noun, verb, adjective), all from the same root √back, can be used to express a range of distinct (but related) senses, as the following uses of the verb indicate:

(11.4) a. I backed the car into the drive.
       b. She backed the prints with cardboard.
       c. He backed Clinton for president.

Examples could be proliferated indefinitely, but the point should be clear enough: polysemy is ubiquitous. Every substantive word is polysemous, at least potentially so – if not now, then it's only a matter of time. Consider, for instance, the case of the noun 'laser', which was originally coined as an acronym, from the initial letter of each of the content words in the phrase 'light amplification by stimulated emission of radiation'. At that time (1957), 'laser' had a single concrete meaning. However, as noted by Panagiotidis (2014a), who discusses the example, a quick online search turns up expressions that could 'lexify', as he puts it (Panagiotidis 2014a: 294), in the near future:

(11.5)   a. 'get one's tattoos lasered' (verbal form)
         b. 'a laser stare', i.e. a persistent and piercing stare (adjectival use)
         c. 'throw a laser', i.e. a straight strong shot in football (a new sense of the noun)

The claim I ultimately want to defend is that the exigencies of human communication make it virtually inevitable that a word will become polysemous; these examples provide some initial support for this claim.

The question arises whether polysemy is a semantic or a pragmatic phenomenon. The fact that the various senses/concepts expressed by the few lexical forms discussed above vary greatly in how established (conventionalised) they are indicates that there is no simple across-the-board answer to this question. What does seem clear is that many of the senses of a polysemy cluster originate from pragmatic processes,[2] that is, a speaker uses a word with an established sense to express a different concept/sense and relies on the addressee's knowledge of the established word sense together with his capacity for relevance-driven meaning modulation to infer the new (ad hoc) concept/sense; how this works is outlined in the next section. In this respect, polysemy is a pragmatic phenomenon (it is the output of on-line pragmatic inferences). However, some ad hoc senses become frequently used and may eventually be fully conventionalised, hence 'semantic' in that they can be retrieved directly from the lexicon (decoded, in RT's terms) and so are potentially input to pragmatic processes of meaning modulation. There are differences across individual speakers with regard to how well-established specific senses of a polysemous word are, even though these speakers can all be said to 'know' the word involved. As noted in Wilson and Carston (2007: 241), an important function of pragmatic inference is to bridge lexical differences among members of a speech community, so that individuals who vary in their established senses for a word can end up with the same

---

[2] Linguists discuss another kind of verb polysemy, which arises from the array of distinct argument structures verbs may enter into, e.g. 'open' can be transitive ('John opened the door') or intransitive ('The door opened'). See Marantz (2013).

interpretation of an utterance containing that word, albeit via different routes (linguistic decoding and/or pragmatic inferencing).

Polysemy is often contrasted with homonymy, in that the senses of a polysemous word are interrelated (and recognised as such by native speakers), while homonymy involves several distinct words that happen (through some sort of historical accident) to have the same phonological form although their meanings are unrelated (e.g. bank/bank; race/race). Etymology, however intriguing, is not the point here, so it is quite possible that what is a case of polysemy for one person (e.g. the senses of 'mouth' in (11.1a) and (11.1c)) is homonymy for another person (i.e. the inferential connection between an animal mouth and a river mouth is unavailable to that individual), in which case, again, we would expect some differences in the processing of the lexical form 'mouth' across these individuals. More generally, for any case of homonymy, e.g. 'bank', each of the distinct words sharing a lexical form is itself almost bound to be polysemous (Carston 2013). It is worth noting here that one could take the stance that polysemy is a *pragmatic* phenomenon, *tout court*, so once a derived sense is fully conventionalised, it enters the lexicon as a distinct word (e.g. 'mouth' as applied to a river) and thus as a homonym. This is in some ways an appealing idea, but for now I am assuming that there are cases of word senses that are fully conventionalised and whose relatedness to other conventionalised senses of that one word remains psychologically real to the individual language user and so must be registered in some way in his mental lexicon. As discussed in the next section, this is the case of a single lexical entry whose meaning component is a 'polysemy complex', i.e. a bundle or cluster of conventionalised interrelated senses.

11.3   Ad hoc Concepts and Lexical Innovation

A central assumption of this chapter is that many cases of conventionalised polysemy have their origins in pragmatic processes of lexical meaning modulation. Here is a brief reminder of the relevance-theoretic account of word meaning modulation during utterance interpretation, using the two examples in (11.6) (and assuming that the Boris referred to is a forty-year-old man):

(11.6)   a. Boris is a bachelor.
          b. Boris is a child.

For (11.6a), uttered in an appropriate context, the lexically encoded concept BACHELOR may be narrowed to BACHELOR* (denoting a certain sort of unmarried man: perhaps one who is eligible for marriage or, on the contrary, one who values his independence and eschews committed relationships). For (11.6b), the encoded concept CHILD will be broadened to an ad hoc concept CHILD* whose denotation includes adults who behave in certain childlike ways.

Focusing on (11.6b), the pragmatic process is as follows: the atomic (unstructured) lexical concept CHILD gives access to an 'encyclopaedic entry' of general knowledge/beliefs about children, including the following:

(11.7)   a. They are young, need to be nurtured and looked after by adults
         b. They are still developing physically and psychologically
         c. They cannot take full responsibility for their own decisions and behaviour, etc.

Some elements of encyclopaedic information will be more accessible (more highly activated) than others, e.g. the information in (11.7c) in the case of (11.6b). These are used as contextual assumptions/premises in deriving contextual implications (e.g. Boris behaves irresponsibly), which, in turn, via a mechanism of 'mutual parallel adjustment' of explicit content (explicature), contextual assumptions and implications (implicatures), can modulate the concept expressed by a word, e.g. CHILD*. This inferential process stops when the specific expectations of relevance (formed on the basis of the presumption of 'optimal relevance' conveyed by all utterances) are satisfied.[3]

The result of such pragmatic processes of on-line lexical meaning adjustment may be a one-off ephemeral ad hoc concept/sense, or the word may come to be regularly used to express that concept/sense and, eventually, it might become an established sense of the word (hence 'semantic' polysemy). For instance, the narrowed sense of 'bachelor' as 'unmarried man who is eligible for marriage' is very well established and may be used more often than the pure definitional sense, in which case it is part of the stored polysemy complex for the word 'bachelor'. It seems less likely that this is the case for the broadened sense of 'child' understood as 'irresponsible dependent person'.

Consider now a second kind of on-line lexical creativity, that of *cross-categorial* modulations of meaning/sense (i.e. motivated coinings of new words). Clark and Clark (1979) discuss a large range of cases of established nouns that subsequently became used as verbs, such as the following:

(11.8)   a. The factory *sirened* midday and everyone broke for lunch.
         b. The police car *sirened* the Porsche to a stop.
         c. The police car *sirened* the daylights out of me.
         d. The boy *porched* the newspaper.
         e. Max tried to *teapot* a policeman.

(Clark & Clark 1979: 786)

---

[3] For more detailed accounts, see Wilson and Sperber (2004), Wilson and Carston (2007), Falkum (2015).

The opposite phenomenon occurs too (established verbs may be employed as nouns):

(11.9)   a. That was a great *get* by the tennis champion.
          b. James was an *embed* for two years in Afghanistan.

We can think of these as 'ad hoc words', that is, new on-the-spot coinages, which may or may not become established words of the language. With each of them comes the ad hoc concept it is used to express: SIREN*, PORCH*, EMBED*, etc.

Focusing on (11.8a)–(11.8c), each of the concepts expressed here is distinct, albeit clearly related, that is, the new verb 'siren' is polysemous, the senses roughly paraphrasable as follows:

(11.10)   a. SIREN*   'use the sound of a siren to signal a time'
          b. SIREN**   'use the sound of a siren to signal a request/order'
          c. SIREN***   'scare by means of the sound produced by a siren'

Clark and Clark (1979: 803) say: 'The interpretation of an innovative verb is strongly constrained by its syntactic environment … But these constraints do not work in a vacuum. To distinguish the interpretation of "siren midday" and "siren the Porsche to a stop", one must know the difference between factory and police sirens, and how they are used.' In other words, the addressee must employ his encyclopaedic knowledge about sirens and how they are used in different environments in order to pragmatically infer the concept of a particular kind of action being performed with a siren.

The result of the pragmatic process here is interestingly different from that of the cases discussed earlier in that the concept constructed is clearly not a narrowing or a broadening of the concept encoded by the noun from which it is derived, as its denotation belongs to a different class altogether, the class of actions rather than entities.[4] Nevertheless, the process involved is very similar to that above: following the relevance-based comprehension heuristic, the addressee infers the intended concept/sense, using the clues the speaker has provided, including syntactic constraints and the concept encoded by the noun 'siren', which is activated by the utterance, together with its most accessible encyclopaedic information, which in turn is partially determined by activation spreading from other concepts encoded by the utterance. The inferential process stops once the hypothesised interpretation satisfies expectations of relevance.

---

[4] It is similar to a part-for-whole metonymy in as much as the object (the siren) plays a part in the activity (the sirening). Wilson and Falkum (2015) make interesting suggestions about the relation between metonymy and the motivated coining of new words from existing ones.

Another set of cases discussed by Clark and Clark is the use of proper names as verbs, such as the following:

(11.11)   Max *houdinied* his way out of the prison cell.
            = Max managed to make an incredible escape from his prison cell.

This verb is probably quite well established now, although not as conventionalised as cases like 'boycott', 'lynch', and 'sandwich', which most speakers don't associate with any proper name, despite their etymology. More often than not, these creative uses of proper names as verbs are short-lived, as in (11.12), where 'Jarvis-Gann' was the name of a Californian tax-cut initiative that led to the axing of many jobs (Clark & Clark 1979: 785):

(11.12)   She was *jarvis-ganned* out of her teaching job.

Once a new word becomes relatively established, the sense with which it was coined becomes a source for further innovative uses:

(11.13)   The president cunningly houdinied out of the corruption allegations.

This kind of flexible on-line pragmatic construction of new senses for words, taking existing senses and their associated encyclopaedic information as input, is the origin of much polysemy. The senses that make up what I call a 'polysemy complex' are interrelated via chains of often very context-sensitive inference, and can differ from one another in arbitrarily many ways, their derivation depending on a wide array of different kinds of ordinary world knowledge, often unpredictable in advance of the utterance. They are not constrained by any semantic core or set of central properties of the originating concept/sense, or by any predetermined set of parameters to be contextually filled, but only by whatever encyclopaedic premises are most accessible and relevant on the particular occasion of use. Hence it is appropriate to talk of polysemy as involving 'families' of related senses.

To conclude this section, the components of an adequate treatment of polysemy include at least the following: (a) an account of how we generate and grasp new word senses in on-line communication, and (b) an account of how we mentally register and represent those related senses/concepts that become established and stably associated with a word. I believe that the relevance-theoretic account outlined in this section goes some way towards providing the first of these components. In the next section, I tackle the second one. A main point will be that the kind of lexicon which records the semantic polysemy of words must be quite distinct from the kind of lexicon that provides the basic input to the grammar. In developing this point, it emerges that another component of a full account of polysemy, namely, the common root in cases of cross-categorial polysemy, can be accommodated, albeit at a different level of explanation from that of the set of senses of a polysemous word.

11.4   The Communicational Lexicon and the Linguistic Lexicon

There is a striking difference between the way in which language is construed by many philosophers of language, on the one hand, and by linguists (in the generative grammar tradition), on the other hand. For many philosophers, language is a social competence and any particular language consists of a set of shared conventions,[5] which includes the established senses of words as well as various socio-cultural norms of language use (e.g. how to make a polite request). A particularly strong version of this position is taken by Lepore and Stone (2015), who maintain that all linguistic knowledge is a matter of conventions and who provide many examples of single words with multiple sense conventions (that is, cases of polysemy). For generative linguists, on the other hand, language is an individual's internal system of recursive computational operations, which effect mappings between sounds/gestures and meanings. There is, of course, no incompatibility here, but rather a difference of focus. As Hauser et al. (2002: 1569) say, language is not monolithic, and fruitful investigation requires carving up the broad folk notion of language into tractable domains of study, separating out questions concerning language as a communicative system and questions concerning the computations underlying this system. Hauser et al.'s focus is on the latter, the narrow I-language (syntax and its perceptual/cognitive interfaces), while most philosophers focus on language as a public communication system.

I suggest that, corresponding to each of these construals of language, there are distinct construals of 'the' lexicon, which can be characterised as follows: (a) a communicational lexicon (C-lexicon), which is a set of reasonably stable associations of particular formal elements (syntactically categorised phonetic/gestural objects) and senses/concepts, tacitly agreed on across a community of speakers (i.e. a set of conventions) and used by them as devices of communication; (b) a linguistic lexicon (L-lexicon), which is a component of the computational I-language system, and whose listed elements are the basic input to the system of combinatorial principles that generate the formal structures of the language. At this level it makes little sense to talk of public meaning conventions, and the elements of 'lexical meaning' here, if there are any, directly interact with, perhaps constrain, syntactic operations.

If this distinction is right, it seems clear that the lexicon of primary interest in the account of polysemy as outlined so far is the C-lexicon. This is the set of stored communicative units which both provides input to the pragmatic processes of relevance-based comprehension on any given occasion of

---

[5] The appropriate notion of convention for lexical senses is that of an 'enabling' convention (rather than a 'lawlike' convention) and is based on the weight of successful precedents (see Geurts 2018).

utterance and is itself, over time, shaped by those pragmatic processes as they give rise to new words and new senses for existing words. Nevertheless, the L-lexicon must also play a part in the bigger picture, with its listed elements connected in some way to those of the C-lexicon, a connection I will try to make at the end of this section.

We find something like this C-lexicon/L-lexicon distinction latent in a disagreement between two prominent linguists over the nature of 'the' mental lexicon. Jackendoff (1997) equates the lexicon with the 'store of *memorized elements* of language', as distinct from those aspects of language which are generated afresh on each use by combinatorial rules (syntax). On this construal, the lexicon contains not only words (with their various stored senses), but also larger multi-word items:

(11.14)   a. to spill the beans; to bury the hatchet
          b. the cat's got NP's tongue
          c. by and large; in cahoots with; kith and kin
          d. may the force be with you

Marantz (2001) finds this view of the lexicon excessively expansive:

Jackendoff argues that the 'lexicon' should be extended to include units larger than words/phrases. But doesn't [his] corpus rather argue against the correlation between 'memorized' and 'special linguistic properties'? We know we've encountered ['May the force be with you'] just as we know we've encountered 'nationalization' … That means we've stored these items – in some way or other. But does 'storage' necessarily imply 'storage in a special linguistic Lexicon'?

Marantz's question here points to a distinction between two kinds of stored language units: those that comprise a narrowly linguistic lexicon (L-lexicon) and a different kind of usage-based store of established communicational units, which seems to be what Jackendoff is discussing (the C-lexicon).

Let's look a bit more closely at the properties of these two lexicons, starting with the C-lexicon. The key claim is that it is not part of the narrow I-language faculty but falls outside it, within what generative grammarians calls the 'conceptual–intentional' interface systems (Chomsky 1995: 168). There is strong evidence to support this. First, there is a marked difference between the acquisition of syntax and the learning of (substantive) words. A native speaker's grammar (including the full panoply of embedded structures and long-distance dependencies) reaches a steady state relatively early in her lifespan, at around 5–6 years of age, from which point on her syntax is highly stable (Lust 2006). In contrast, the acquisition of new words and new senses for existing words goes on throughout our lifetime, and is responsive to new developments in our social-cultural environments, e.g. the relatively recent new words 'microwave', 'google', 'vape', 'photobomb', 'staycation', and new senses for existing words, such as 'transformation', 'binding' (in generative grammar), 'deflation', 'credit', 'derivative' (in economics), 'spin', 'surgery', 'snowflake' (in politics). Of course, young children do acquire words at a rapid rate, requiring very few exposures to any new word (a process known as 'fast mapping'), but this ability does not seem to involve a dedicated cognitive system in the way that the acquisition of syntax does (Markson & Bloom 1997). Rather, the ability involved also applies to domains other than language, specifically, to the learning of new facts about the world:

Children who heard a novel object described, in passing, as 'a koba' remembered which object the word referred to when tested a month later. However, children who heard a novel object described, in passing, as 'the one that my uncle gave me' were equally good at remembering which object the fact referred to. (Bloom & Markson 2001: 89)

Children are learning new words and new facts at an equally rapid rate and retaining them, so it seems reasonable to conclude that word learning for children, as for adults, is a function of more general cognitive systems (of learning and intentional inferencing) rather than of a dedicated language faculty.[6]

A second piece of evidence in support of a C-lexicon which is separate from the faculty of I-language comes from the fascinating phenomenon of Homesign (Goldin-Meadow 2005). It seems that deaf children who are not exposed to a conventional sign language (so get essentially no linguistic input), nevertheless, develop a large set of words and idioms, consisting of discrete gestures paired with concepts/senses. Although linguistically isolated, these children are socially active and integrated. Their signs are negotiated and (re)calibrated in the process of ostensive communicative interactions and many subsequently stabilise into lexical meaning conventions. Thus, the process is very much akin to the relevance-based account of lexical innovation discussed above, except that these children are creating words (or communication units) from the ground up, without the benefit of an established public lexicon to build on (Begby 2017).

The contents of the C-lexicon, then, are communication units of varying sizes and syntactic complexity: words (nouns, verbs, adjectives), phrasal idioms, frozen or frequent collocations, and even memorised sentences (see the list from Jackendoff in (11.14)). Crucially for the concerns of this chapter, a word is stored with its 'polysemy complex', an evolving set of interrelated senses/concepts, which are conventionalised to some appreciable degree. These are probably atomic concepts, in Fodor's sense (I see no reason to suppose otherwise), and will have associated encyclopaedic entries, as envisaged in

---

[6] Note that this doesn't mean that there are not some constraints on word learning that distinguish it from fact learning; children know the difference between words and facts, and will extend 'koba' to new items of the 'same category', but won't extend the learned fact in the same way.

the standard RT view of concepts (Sperber & Wilson 1986/1995). They are input to the pragmatic processes that form ad hoc concepts (occasion-specific senses), some of which may themselves subsequently become established and enter the C-lexicon.

The question now is what figures in the L-lexicon, the stored input elements of grammar or I-language (and how that lexicon connects with the C-lexicon). This is a hotly debated issue in current generative linguistics and I will do no more here than gesture at the position that seems most congenial to the account of polysemy I am developing, one which is being actively promoted by some within the minimalist grammar framework (see, in particular, Acquaviva 2014; Panagiotidis 2014a, 2014b). The claim is that it is categoryless roots which are the components of the substantive lexicon within I-language, that is, elements such as √mouth, √back, √siren, √houdini, which are available to be made into nouns, verbs or adjectives, and which must be, in order to be usable in thought and communication. (On this view, lexical structure is part of syntax, and what we think of as simple monomorphemic words are, in fact, phrasal structures made up of a root plus a syntactic categorising head, e.g. [√back + n], [√back + v].) The most contentious part of this proposal concerns the meaning of these roots, and there are currently two main positions on this: (a) a root has an underspecified schematic core meaning, which is common to all those lexicalisations based on it (Arad 2005); (b) a root has no semantic content or meaning at all, but is simply a 'distinguishing index or address', e.g. √4170, say, for the root that is common to all of the noun 'back', the verb 'back', the adjective 'back' (and morphological derivatives, such as 'backer', 'backing', 'half-back', etc.) (Panagiotidis 2014a).[7]

Whichever answer to the question of the meaning of roots turns out to be correct, we have here the basis for capturing cross-categorial polysemy (e.g. 'back', 'siren'). As Acquaviva (2014: 283) says:

> [this account] … may model the distinction between polysemy and homonymy in formal terms, letting only polysemous words share the very same syntactic root. Interpretations that are related as different senses of the same lexeme, e.g. *sad* as 'in a state of sadness' and 'inspiring sadness' could be associated with the very same syntactic object, including the root; this would distinguish senses which are variants of one core lexical interpretation, often derived through general cognitive mechanisms [pragmatics (RC)], from interpretations that instead belong to distinct lexemes (with distinct if homonymous roots), e.g. *race*, as 'running contest' and as 'genetically identified population'.

Thus, although the three words 'back' are stored separately in the C-lexicon, each with its polysemy complex, they are connected via the root √back in the L-lexicon.

---

[7] A significant point here is that the meaningless index/address account of roots is the only approach which can reconcile conceptual atomism (Fodor 1998) with lexical-syntactic decomposition (Acquaviva 2014; Panagiotidis 2014a).

Finally, the two lexicons register different properties of the language units they store and are thus subject to different constraints. Two such properties or constraints that have been discussed are compositionality and frequency. Fodor (2002) insists that the key constraint on each component of a lexical entry, including the meaning component, is that it contains 'nothing ... except what that item contributes to the grammatical representation of its hosts' (Fodor 2002: 76), thereby conforming to a strict principle of compositionality. Among the many properties ruled out by this constraint is that of the frequency of a word sense, because 'the relative frequency of the constituents of a lexical item doesn't predict the relative frequency of its hosts and vice versa' (Fodor 2002: 80), e.g. while both the financial sense of 'bank' and the colour sense of 'blue' are highly frequent uses of those words, that property is not inherited by the host phrase 'blue bank'. However, as is well known in psycholinguistics, frequency effects do impact on the production and comprehension of utterances in a range of ways (see, e.g., Lucas 1987; Weinberg 2002), so relative frequencies must be registered somewhere somehow in the mind of the language user. I suggest that word and sense frequencies are registered in the communicational lexicon, which is thus a component of what Fodor calls 'performance theory' (along with the effects of relevance, plausibility and context).

We might then ask whether semantic compositionality, Fodor's cherished requirement, is met by the entries in the L-lexicon. Strictly speaking, the answer is 'no', because it is not roots themselves but *categorised* roots (nouns, verbs, adjectives) which are the first domain of idiosyncratic content and, therefore, the basic input to the compositional meaning of their hosts (Panagiotidis 2014a). However, although roots do not strictly meet Fodor's constraint at the semantic level, they do not violate it either: since they are semantically empty or underspecified, they simply cannot feed the function that yields compositional interpretations. Roots are, of course, the basic atoms of *syntactic composition* (along with categorisers), and the output of the first phase of syntactic composition (that is, the syntactic categorisation of roots) provides the basic atoms of semantic composition.[8]

11.5   Summing Up

The main points made in this chapter are the following:

(a) Much polysemy originates in the process of communication: speakers use existing words to express new senses and coin new words, and hearers are able to pragmatically infer the ad hoc senses and words intended.

---

[8] There are many further issues raised by these two lexicons, including how the often non-compositional (idiosyncratic) meanings of communication units in the C-lexicon are

(b) Languages consist of a generative computational core and a system of communicative conventions, and there is a distinct lexicon or list of basic units corresponding to each of these components.

(c) Words (nouns, verbs, adjectives, etc.), which are listed in the communicational lexicon, are typically polysemous, that is, are associated with a cluster of interrelated senses, while categoryless roots, the items listed in the linguistic lexicon, have at most an underspecified schematic meaning[9] (and possibly no meaning at all).

(d) The senses of a polysemy complex comprise the meaning component of a single word (e.g. the noun 'back'), while the senses of a homonymous lexical form belong to distinct words (e.g. the two nouns 'bank'). Cross-categorial polysemy is associated with a single root (e.g. √back for the related noun, verb and adjective), while homonymous words have distinct roots (e.g. √bank-1 and √bank-2).

Acknowledgements

It is a pleasure to contribute to this volume in honour of Deirdre Wilson. My debt to Deirdre is incalculable, both intellectually and personally, as teacher, colleague, and friend.

I would like to thank Tim Pritchard, Agustin Vicente and Catherine Wearing for their helpful comments on an earlier version of this chapter, and also my co-editors, Billy Clark and Kate Scott, for a productive and enjoyable working relationship.

---

incorporated into the compositional structure delivered by I-language, an issue I hope to pursue in future work (see Acquaviva 2014 and Panagiotidis 2014b for relevant discussion).

[9] A similar view about the nature of the 'standing' meaning of a *word* has its advocates, that is, the idea that the core meaning of a word is not a sense (or concept) but a semantically underspecified schema, which constrains the senses/concepts that the word can be used to express. I review this and other views on word meaning in Carston (2012) and assess them more fully in Carston (forthcoming).

12   The Polysemy of a Norwegian Modal Adverb

Thorstein Fretheim

12.1   Introduction

What appears to be polysemy at the lexical level is often analysed in terms of ad hoc concepts derived by inferential modulation, i.e. lexical narrowing and broadening, as opposed to lexically stored polysemy. However, words that do not belong to one of the open lexical classes are not normally subject to pragmatic modulation. This chapter presents a semantic and pragmatic analysis of a Norwegian modal adverb, *gjerne*, whose polysemy is argued to be of the lexically stored sort.

The dual lexical meaning of *gjerne* is of a procedural, as opposed to conceptual, sort (e.g. Blakemore 1987, 2002; Wilson & Sperber 1993; Escandell-Vidal et al. 2011; Nicolle 2015; Fretheim 2016, 2017), despite the fact that this word has, on the one hand, a desiderative meaning that can sometimes be glossed as 'preferably', and, on the other hand, a consent or permission meaning that may be glossed variably as 'gladly', 'willingly', 'without reservation'.[1]

Gjerne gives the addressee a choice between two types of pragmatic procedure. Its two disjunctive meanings share the notion that future fulfilment of the eventuality described by the speaker is supposed to benefit someone. They differ in that the desiderative procedure relates to the speaker's own interest or what the speaker metarepresents as someone else's wish, while the consent or permission procedure concerns what the speaker judges to be in the hearer's, or some contextually determinable third person's, interest. Context-dependent activation of one of the procedures causes the hearer to seek an interpretation consistent with the assumption that it will be in the speaker's interest, alternatively in the hearer's interest, that the potential state of affairs becomes factual.

The study of polysemy, inside or outside of relevance theory, has been limited almost entirely to polysemy in substantive words, i.e. to semantic multiplicity in members of open lexical classes. Recent research on lexical pragmatics has demonstrated that words are frequently used with speaker meanings that depart

---

[1] An attempt to translate *gjerne* by seeking an adequate English gloss for it will often be less successful than a translation based on a freer paraphrase of the Norwegian sentence.

from their encoded meanings and are radically underdetermined by them, because they involve the construction of ad hoc, occasion-specific concepts (e.g. Wilson 2003; Wilson & Carston 2007; Falkum 2011, 2015; Kolaiti & Wilson 2014; Wilson & Kolaiti 2017). The speaker meaning of a function word like *gjerne* cannot be said to depart from its encoded meaning in a comparable way. Rather, what is encoded is a constraint on the direction of the hearer's inferential path, a constraint that causes the hearer to engage in further inferential processing that will make the stimulus sufficiently relevant.

The data to be presented in this chapter should not be analysed in terms of traditional lexical ambiguity, nor in terms of ad hoc modulation of a unitary lexical meaning. An account of the semantics and pragmatic implications of *gjerne* requires an approach that is consistent with relevance-theoretic reasoning about the relationship between encoded meaning and occasion-specific meaning but at the same time somewhat different from what is found in mainstream relevance-theoretic studies of lexical polysemy. *Gjerne* has no univocal meaning[2] and its meaning is not contextually enrichable in the received sense. Contextual information serves as input to mental activation of one of the two disjunctive lexical procedures. I side with those who claim that 'encoded word meanings are no more than a clue to the speaker's meaning' (Wilson & Kolaiti 2017: 149). That applies not just to words with a conceptual semantics, it applies equally to a modal modifier like *gjerne*. Activation of the thought that the eventuality described accords with the speaker's interest, alternatively with what the speaker believes to be in the hearer's interest, puts the hearer on the right track in the inferential phase of utterance interpretation.

The lexical duality of *gjerne* can be likened to the 'ambiguity' of English *please* (e.g. Wichmann 2004). In its utterance-initial position before an imperative, *please* licenses an interpretation of the speech act as either an act of granting permission or a request prompted by the speaker's own desire. *Gjerne* serves a similar function, but its range of uses differs from that of *please*, as I am going to show.

Section 12.2 of this chapter examines the interaction of *gjerne* with certain linguistic parameters that constrain its contribution to stimulus relevance,

---

[2] The belief that polysemy is always the result of ad hoc pragmatic modulation of a univocal encoded meaning has recently been questioned by Carston. What Carston (2016b) calls the 'too meagre' position on the polysemy of substantive lexical items involves what would ideally be a univocal schematic meaning, something abstract that needs to be modified by the hearer in a pragmatic process of occasion-specific conceptual narrowing or broadening (Wilson & Carston 2007). No convincing concrete proposal of this type of radically underspecified lexical meaning has ever been proposed, so an approach that ties lexical polysemy exclusively to the pragmatic output of the hearer's inferential processing is hardly viable. Some conceptually polysemous words are polysemous at the level of lexical semantics, not just polysemous at the level of pragmatic output.

including the predicate of the sentence, the two Norwegian modal auxiliaries *vil* ('will') and *kan* ('can') which frequently co-occur with *gjerne*, and the distinction between a 1st-person, 2nd-person and 3rd-person grammatical subject.

Sections 12.3 and 12.4 offer evidence that the polysemy of *gjerne* should be defined at the lexical level. An analysis that postulates a univocal lexical procedure is weakened by data demonstrating native speakers' and hearers' sensitivity to the difference between expression of the speaker's preference and expression of what the speaker believes to be someone else's preference. In Section 12.3, a tendency marker *gjerne* that is the outcome of a grammaticalisation process (e.g. Hopper & Traugott 1993; Traugott & Dasher 2005; Eckardt 2006) is argued to derive from the procedural meaning associated with the speaker's desire, occasionally the metarepresented desire of a third person. The consent/permission alternative was left untouched by this diachronic process. German *gerne* (or *gern*), Danish *gerne*, and Swedish *gärna*, all cognates of Norwegian *gjerne*, have gone through similar historical developments (Fretheim 2015a). Section 12.4 presents empirical evidence for the conclusion that the elliptical response *gjerne* causes the hearer to activate the desiderative procedure, while the elliptical response *gjerne for meg* (... for me) directs the hearer to the consent/permission procedure. A note on analogous uses of elliptical expressions that contain German *gern(e)* is added.

Section 12.5 contains my definition of the procedural semantics of *gjerne* based on the story told in previous sections. Section 12.6 concludes the chapter.

12.2   The Interaction of *gjerne* with Other Linguistic Constraints on Relevance

When the subject referent is the speaker, the Norwegian modal auxiliary *vil* ('will') in (12.1) has a desiderative meaning, while the modal auxiliary *kan* ('can') in (12.2) is indicative of the speaker's acquiescence or benevolence. *Gjerne* may therefore be regarded as a redundant sign of the speaker's wish to sit on the floor in (12.1) and her willingness to do so in (12.2).

(12.1) Jeg   vil   gjerne   sitte   på   gulvet.
        I   will   *gjerne* sit   on   floor-DEF
        'I want to sit on the floor, if that's fine with you.'

(12.2) Jeg   kan   gjerne   sitte   på   gulvet.
        I   can   *gjerne* sit   on   floor-DEF
        'I can sit on the floor, it's no problem.'

As (12.1) without *gjerne* would have sounded like an unmitigated expression of the speaker's will, the modal modifier is a politeness marker there, and in (12.2) it blocks the ability reading of *kan*.

When no other modal modifier is present, *gjerne* has the preference/desiderative reading of (12.3a) or the consent reading of (12.3b), depending on context.

(12.3)   Jeg   sitter   gjerne   på   gulvet.
         I   sit   *gjerne*   on   floor-DEF
         a. 'I would like to sit on the floor.'
         b. 'I am willing to sit on the floor.'

Gjerne indicates that present-tense *sitter* in (12.3) is used as a futurate, i.e. an expression of future time without future tense-marking. (12.3) without *gjerne* would be a statement in the indicative mood ('I'm sitting on the floor'). *Gjerne* shows that the state of affairs described is potential, not factual. In (12.1)–(12.2) and (12.3) alike, it directs the hearer to a higher-level explicature (Blakemore 1992; Wilson & Sperber 1993), notably to a communicated positive attitude to the speaker's coming to sit on the floor, either because the subject referent wants it or because the speaker has a reason to believe that someone else, most frequently the addressee, wants it.

A 3rd-person human subject in a sentence modified by *gjerne* expresses what the speaker metarepresents (e.g. Noh 2000; Wilson 2000; Allott 2017) as the subject referent's wish if the sentence includes the modal auxiliary *vil*, and the subject referent's intention to oblige someone if it includes the modal auxiliary *kan*. When a sentence modified by *gjerne* contains no modal auxiliary, a 3rd-person subject opens for either interpretation, like sentence (12.3) with its 1st-person subject.

My Norwegian informants' unanimous judgement is that *gjerne* sounds odd in a declarative or interrogative with a 2nd-person subject, but it occurs freely in imperatives with a 2nd-person null subject. (12.4) is a metarepresentation of what the speaker interprets as the hearer's wish. The speaker is granting the hearer permission to sit on the floor.

(12.4)   Sitt   gjerne   på   gulvet.
         sit   *gjerne*   on   floor-DEF
         'Do sit on the floor, if you feel like it.'

Observe that the import of *gjerne* in (12.4) cannot be rendered in an adequate way by any English *-ly* adverb whose stem is an adjective with a conceptual meaning, like *preferably* or *gladly*.

(12.5) is a note accompanying the item 'Today's fish' in the internet menu of a restaurant in Trondheim.

(12.5)   Ring   oss   gjerne   for å høre   hva   vi   serverer   i dag.
         ring   us   *gjerne*   for to hear   what   we   serve   today
         'Feel free to call us to find out what we're serving today.'

Gjerne prompts activation of the thought that the restaurant is offering a service for the benefit of potential customers, but at the same time one may presume that it is equally in the restaurant's own interest to receive phone calls enquiring about their menu. However, *gjerne* in an imperative cannot co-occur with the polite request marker *vennligst*, as in the ill-formed imperative **Vennligst betal gjerne med kort* (please pay *gjerne* with card).[3] At the explicit level, (12.5) is about a service that is meant to benefit potential guests. The communicator's own preference is nevertheless communicated as an implicature in the conventional expression *betal gjerne med kort* (pay *gjerne* with card): you are permitted to use a card – in fact, it is recommended.

What you do when you ask someone to bring an umbrella in case it rains is to recommend such action. An utterance of (12.6) expresses advice that the hearer is free to ignore or to heed. It is not a polite request similar to a *please*-modified English imperative.

(12.6) Ta   gjerne   med   deg   en   paraply.
        take   *gjerne*   with   you   an   umbrella
        'I'd advise you to bring an umbrella.'

No compositional semantics can account for the contribution of *gjerne* in imperatives like (12.4)–(12.5) on the one hand and (12.6) on the other. I have thus far linked the so-called consent or permission reading of *gjerne* to the speaker's willingness to act in the interest of the hearer or willingness to grant the hearer the freedom to act in a specified way, but this is not what (12.6) is about. You do not normally permit someone to bring an umbrella, but you can tell them that it is in their own interest to do so. What giving permission and offering advice have in common is the fact that the speaker believes fulfilment of the future state or event described to be in the hearer's interest. *Gjerne* does not by itself enable the hearer to interpret (12.4) as an act of permitting the hearer to sit on the floor and (12.6) as an act of advising the hearer to bring an umbrella. What is instrumental to the hearer's comprehension is the interaction of imperative mood, the procedural meaning of *gjerne* and the conceptual semantics of the predicate and its complement.

As labels like 'desiderative', 'permissive', 'compliant' and the like do not capture the polysemy of *gjerne* in an optimal way, the procedural meaning that activates the assumption that the potential state of affairs described is advantageous to the hearer will henceforth be termed the word's ALTER-interest meaning, and I shall use the label EGO-interest for the desiderative alternative.

---

[3] *Vennligst* – literally 'friendliest' – has a more restricted range of uses than *please*. It indicates that the speech act is a polite request. Unlike *please*, it rules out the hearer as beneficiary, exemplified by *Please help yourself to some more!*

In a sentence like (12.7), there is no animate subject referent, or inanimate one for that matter. Sentence-initial *det* is a formal subject.

(12.7) Det kunne gjerne ha   vært tannpirkere på bordet.
        it   could *gjerne* have been toothpicks   on table-DEF
        'I would have liked to see toothpicks on the table.'

The verbal complex *kunne ha vært* ('could have been') expresses counterfactivity, so *gjerne* activates the thought that the speaker, the only accessible agent, expresses a counterfactive wish by uttering (12.7). The absence of a service that includes free toothpicks for customers/guests contrasts with what the speaker views as desirable. An interpretation based on selection of the ALTER-interest procedure is blocked by the expressed counterfactivity.

To sum up, *gjerne* constrains the hearer's inference leading to recognition of a higher-level explicature related to the speaker's preference (EGO-interest) or to a preference that the speaker attributes to the hearer (ALTER-interest). The hearer's choice of one semantic variant at the expense of the other is typically just a first step in the pragmatic handling of a stimulus in need of further inferential processing. We have seen that one predicate can cause the addressee of an imperative modified by *gjerne* to interpret the utterance as an act of giving the hearer permission to act in a particular way, while a different predicate makes it more natural to associate the utterance with a piece of advice. Both interpretations depend on selection of the ALTER-interest procedure, but the conceptual semantics of the predicate helps the hearer identify the intended higher-level explicature.

12.3   First Argument for Stored Polysemy

Gjerne descends from Old Norse *gjarna(n)* (Heggstad 1963), which basically meant that the subject referent has a positive attitude to the eventuality described. An English cognate is the verb *yearn* (Barnhart 1988), whose semantics is on the conceptual side of the conceptual–procedural divide.

The desiderative meaning of *gjerne* is the historical basis for a grammaticalisation process whose end product is a phonologically identical marker of habituality or tendency. German and the rest of the Scandinavian languages underwent a similar drift.

This other word *gjerne* expresses a general proposition, in contrast to the singular proposition expressed by an utterance that contains the modal adverb. *Gjerne* as tendency marker has the ability to impact on the semantics of an utterance that denotes something in the past, whereas the modal adverb always points to a future state or event, either relative to the time of utterance or relative to a reference point in the past.

Whatever is desirable to you is presumably something you would like to see happen whenever there is an opportunity to bring it about. It makes sense, therefore, that the EGO-interest meaning was the starting point of a diachronic development that led to the emergence of the tendency marker *gjerne* as well as its counterparts in the other Scandinavian languages and German, a free form that serves a function similar to that of a bound morpheme in some other languages.

While the historical source of the tendency marker is the EGO-interest meaning of the polysemous adverb *gjerne*, the original desirability component is bleached over time and is eventually lost altogether in the emerging tendency marker, with the consequence that the tendency marker *gjerne* occurs freely in present-day Norwegian sentences that are meant to denote something inconvenient or unfortunate.

I conclude that, since there is a semantic link between the tendency marker *gjerne* and the EGO-interest meaning of the modal adverb, but none between the tendency marker and the ALTER-interest option, an account of the relation between EGO-interest and ALTER-interest in terms of a binary semantic choice at the lexical level is preferable to an account in terms of polysemy as the result of ad hoc relevance-driven inference.

12.4   Second Argument for Stored Polysemy

We have a strengthened case for lexically stored polysemy if there exists evidence that *gjerne* occurs in certain expressions whose dedicated function is to direct the hearer's attention to one of the two procedures, EGO-interest or ALTER-interest. I decided to look at three different elliptical responses in Norwegian whose sole form or central expression is *gjerne*. Twenty Norwegians were asked if they considered the three disjunctive fragmentary answers of B_1, B_2 and B_3 in (12.8) and (12.9) to be normal responses to A's question, or if they judged them to be marked or even unacceptable in the context of A's question. B_2 *gjerne det!* (… that) was acceptable to everyone in either talk exchange. In contrast, thirteen out of twenty felt that the answer B_3 *gjerne for meg!* (… for me) was not acceptable in (12.8). Three participants added spontaneously that B_3 was more relevant in (12.9) than in (12.8), because speaker B is complying with a request in (12.9), but not in (12.8). B_1 *Gjerne!* was unanimously judged to be acceptable in (12.8), but eight out of twenty said that B_1 sounded odd in (12.9).

(12.8)   A: Skal vi bytte plass?   (an offer)
              shall we change seats
              'Would you prefer to change seats with me?'

B_1: Gjerne!
'Yes, please!'

B_2: Gjerne det!
    gjerne that
    'Yes, please!'

B_3: #Gjerne for meg!
    gjerne for me
    #'No problem!'

(12.9) A: Kan vi bytte plass?   (a request)
          can we change seats
          'Could we change seats, please?'

        B_1: (#)Gjerne!
            'Yes, please!'

        B_2: Gjerne det!
            'No problem!'

        B_3: Gjerne for meg!
            'No problem!'

My informants' reactions indicate that *gjerne det* is used indiscriminately for expression of EGO-interest and ALTER-interest. B_1 *Gjerne* directs the hearer to the EGO-interest procedure. B_3 *Gjerne for meg* shows B's willingness to satisfy A's request, consonant with ALTER-interest. While all informants accepted B_3 in (12.9), less than half of the informants judged B_1 in (12.9) to be deviant. The reason for this fairly modest number of rejections of (12.9) B_1 may be that, even if it is in A's interest to change seats with B, it is not unlikely that B judges the swap to benefit B as well.

I then asked the same group of people how they evaluated (12.10) B_1, B_2 and B_3 as alternative responses to A's offer.

(12.10) A: Vil du ha litt mer ost?
           will you have some more cheese
           'Do you want some more cheese?'

        B_1: Gjerne!
            'Yes, please!'

        B_2: Gjerne det!
            'Yes, please!'

        B_3: #Gjerne for meg!
            #'If you like.'

Now twenty out of twenty accepted B_1–B_2 and rejected B_3. Some said B_3 was a rude reaction that sounded as if B couldn't care less.

My informants' distribution of responses to the data in (12.8)–(12.10) shows that they were sensitive to some conventional differences in meaning between the three elliptical answers *gjerne*, *gjerne det* and *gjerne for meg*. B_1 and B_3 offer mutually exclusive clues to determination of how the word *gjerne* contributes to relevance. For a majority of participants, the sentence fragment *gjerne* accompanied by no complement gave rise to a cognitive effect dependent upon mental activation of EGO-interest as an inherent property of that response, whilst *gjerne for meg* supported activation of the ALTER-interest alternative.

It might be suggested (as it was by one reviewer of this chapter) that my conclusions based on the distribution of responses are weakened by the fact that the respondents did not come close to agreeing. However, it does seem significant that the participants' unanimous acceptance of B_3 given in response to A's request in (12.9) contrasts with their unanimous rejection of B_3 produced in response to A's offer in (12.10). Moreover, some participants may have interpreted (12.8) A as an indirect request in spite of speaker A's modal auxiliary *skal*, which would justify their acceptance of (12.8) B_3, *gjerne for meg*.

At this juncture it may be informative to turn to German. There are (at least) three German elliptical responses with *gerne*: *Gerne*, *Meinetwegen gerne* ('As far as I'm concerned, go ahead!') and *aber gerne* ('But sure!'). The response *gerne* is apparently neutral with respect to EGO-interest vs. ALTER-interest, like the Norwegian fragment *gjerne det*. According to my German informants, *Meinetwegen gerne* and *aber gerne* both express ALTER-interest, like Norwegian *gjerne for meg*, but it would be wrong to equate the meanings of *Meinetwegen gerne* and *aber gerne* just because both express a willingness to fulfil the hearer's wish. The former stresses the fact that the speaker is not objecting to what the hearer has asked for (though other people might object); the latter stresses the speaker's readiness to please the hearer. The ALTER-interest procedure encoded by *gjerne for meg* does not discriminate between a possibly indifferent response that implies 'I have no objection' and a service-minded response believed to gratify the hearer. Either interpretation is consistent with ALTER-interest, so *gjerne for meg* is in need of further contextual input in order to be interpreted in the same way as *Meinetwegen gerne* or in the same way as *aber gerne*. While German has two semantically distinct sentence fragments that share the ALTER-interest component, Norwegian has a single fragment *gjerne for meg* that conventionally expresses ALTER-interest but gives no more exact information about the speaker's emotional attitude. *Meinetwegen gerne* conventionally constrains the hearer's pragmatic interpretation more than *gjerne for meg*.

My conclusion is that, by virtue of their procedural semantics, the elliptical response types *gjerne*, *gjerne det* and *gjerne for meg* differ in regard to their ability to activate either the EGO-interest procedure or the ALTER-interest procedure. I do grant sceptics the right to question an analysis that makes *gjerne for meg* a syntactic idiom, because I cannot disprove that the PrepP *for meg* has a conceptual meaning similar to that of English *for my part*. Nevertheless, the two fragment responses *Gjerne* and *Gjerne for meg* have different consequences for the hearer's pragmatic processing. That supports my analysis of *gjerne* as a lexical item that causes the addressee to make a contextually informed choice between two lexical alternatives, one directing the hearer's attention to an inferential path that yields a pragmatic output prompted by the EGO-interest procedure, the other prompted by ALTER-interest. The German distinction between the elliptical responses *gerne*, *Meinetwegen gerne* and *aber gerne* points to a similar conclusion about a binary lexical choice that constrains, but does not by itself determine, the hearer's pragmatic processing.

12.5   The Procedural Meaning of *gjerne*

My present take on the procedural meaning of *gjerne* is expressed in (12.11).

(12.11)   i. EGO-interest: Fulfilment of the eventuality described is in the interest of the speaker (or a 3rd-person referent whose thought is reported by the speaker).
          ii. ALTER-interest: Fulfilment of the eventuality described is understood by the speaker (or a 3rd person whose thought is reported by the speaker) to be in the interest of the hearer or a discourse-activated 3rd-person referent.

12.6   Conclusion

The lexical meaning of *gjerne* is procedural. Its contribution to relevance cannot be fully accounted for in terms of the principle of compositionality and it is not possible to enrich it in context.[4] Rather, its communicative function is to signal that the hearer should either process the speaker's utterance as a message intended to serve the speaker's own interest or as a message intended to serve someone else's interest.

---

[4] It is traditionally believed that the adverb *gjerne* has a suppletive comparative form, *heller* ('rather'). Unlike *gjerne*, this form often appears in sentences in which the preferred or right alternative is overtly expressed but the dispreferred or wrong alternative to which it is compared has to be derived by means of enrichment. The explicature of an utterance of a sentence like *Jeg vil heller sitte på gulvet* ('I would rather sit on the floor') must be enriched in such a way that some alternative to sitting on the floor is present in the pragmatically derived explicature of the utterance. Does this reveal the existence of a counterargument to my procedural semantics solution for *gjerne*? Not necessarily. I question the validity of grouping *gjerne* and *heller* together in the same gradation paradigm. *Heller* has a desiderative meaning and cannot be used in acts of granting permission.

My conclusion that an analysis in terms of ad hoc modulation of a uni-vocal encoded meaning would be a wrong tack for the modal adverb *gjerne* rests mainly upon two defended claims: (i) the tendency marker *gjerne* is the result of grammaticalisation of the EGO-interest meaning, and this is true of its cognates in other Germanic languages as well; (ii) the elliptical expressions *gjerne* and *gjerne for meg* direct the hearer to the disjunctive EGO-interest and ALTER-interest procedures, respectively. A group of respondents were found to be sensitive to the difference in meaning between the two utterance types *Gjerne* and *Gjerne for meg*, the former causing them to activate an EGO-interest strategy as part of their pragmatic processing, the latter directing them to an interpretation based on activation of the ALTER-interest alternative.

Which procedure, EGO-interest or ALTER-interest, is selected by the hearer in a given instance depends on several interacting parameters, notably the lin-guistic meanings of predicates (and arguments or adjuncts when applicable), the reference of animate subject nominals, the co-occurrence of *gjerne* with other procedural indicators, and purely contextual premises that constrain utterance comprehension.

Since I have examined a single word in a single language, one may legit-imately ask: how typical is the kind of polysemy I have postulated for *gjerne*? This is no unique phenomenon. *Da* (literally 'then') is a Norwegian poly-semous right-detached discourse particle with two lexically stored procedural meanings (Fretheim 2014, 2015b). One of its two semantic variants causes the hearer to relate the proposition expressed in the host sentence to the speaker's own belief, and to construe the speech act as a request for confirmation of the propositional content of the preceding host sentence; the other variant is meant to trigger the inference that the speaker is metarepresenting a propos-ition believed by the hearer to be true but by the speaker to be dubious or down-right false. The form *'a* (*da* without the onset consonant), typical of south-east Norwegian speech, has only the latter metarepresentational meaning of *da* that signals a conflict of opinion between speaker and hearer, arguably a sign that the two lexically encoded meanings assigned to the particle *da* in Fretheim (2015b) are kept apart in the minds of users of the colloquial variant *'a*.

Acknowledgements

I want to express my gratitude to an eminent linguistic scholar and great source of inspiration: Deirdre Wilson.

I am indebted to the following people for their support and feedback: Patrick Grosz, Christoph Unger, Jeanette Gundel, Wim van Dommelen, Regina Tödter, Maj-Britt Mosegaard Hansen, Elizabeth Closs Traugott. I would also like to thank two anonymous reviewers. Finally, I want to thank Robyn Carston, Billy Clark and Kate Scott for their admirable editorial work.

13 Noun-Noun Compounds from the Perspective of Relevance Theory

Anne Bezuidenhout

13.1 Introduction

N-N compounds, such as 'city boy', 'dog bed', or 'wart pill', cannot be explained by 'Fregean composition'. That is, the meaning of such compounds cannot be recovered solely from the meanings of their constituents plus the way they are syntactically combined. See Jackendoff (2010: 417) and Bauer (1983: 80, 1978: sections 3.4, 3.5). Instead, they display openness in the way they are interpreted.

In Section 13.2, I lay out some assumptions about the nature of N-N compounds. In Section 13.3, I describe Lieber's (2011) attempt to provide a semantic explanation of N-N combination, which I argue is unable to provide an adequate account of the productive mechanisms used to interpret novel N-N compounds of the sort I am interested in. In Section 13.4, I turn to a psychological account of concept combination proposed by Wisniewski and Gentner (1991). I argue that it leaves questions unanswered and has shortcomings because it is based on data from the interpretation of N-N compounds presented out of context. In Section 13.5, I review corpus-based studies by Lapata (2002) and Maguire et al. (2010). The latter suggest that, along with basic semantic category information about words, people exploit the frequency-based information concerning the co-occurrence of words that is stored in their mental lexicons to interpret novel N-N compounds. While there is evidence that we rely on statistical information, it seems that, especially in the comprehension of novel N-N compounds, other information plays a role too. In Section 13.6, I offer a pragmatic account based on ideas from relevance theory that I suggest can address all these worries. My overall conclusion is that we need such a pragmatic account, which is based on situated language use, in order to reveal and explain the productive mechanisms involved in N-N combination.

13.2 Some Basic Facts about N-N Combination

There has been an extensive debate as to what distinguishes compounds from phrases. Various tests for phrases versus compounds are discussed by

Haspelmath and Sims (2013: 190–5). However, I will not discuss this issue further in this chapter and will assume that the examples used below can be shown to meet any reasonable set of criteria for compoundhood.

Lieber (2011) classifies nominal compounds into six types. I use her classification scheme but restrict my attention to N-N compounds, as opposed to the many other sorts of nominal compounds that are possible in English (e.g., Adj-N compounds such as 'long bow', V-N compounds such as 'attack dog'). See Jackendoff (2010: 424) for additional types of nominal compounds and examples. Below are examples of basic N-N compounds in Lieber's six categories:

1. Coordinate endocentric (e.g., 'student-athlete')
2. Coordinate exocentric (e.g., 'mother-child' as a way of referring to the pair)
3. Subordinate endocentric (e.g., 'city employee')
4. Subordinate exocentric (e.g., 'dogleg' – as in a sharp bend in a road)
5. Attributive endocentric (e.g., 'dog bed')
6. Attributive exocentric (e.g., 'ponytail')

I also accept that more elaborate N-N compounds can be formed by recursive and conjunctive processes, as in the following example, where the square bracketing indicates how the complex is built up recursively: [[baseball [helmet and glove]] manufacturer]. However, in this chapter I will be narrowly focused on basic N-N compounds of Lieber's attributive endocentric variety.

An endocentric N-N compound is one whose second noun serves as both its syntactic and semantic head. That is, the second noun carries any inflectional affixes (the plural of 'dog bed' is 'dog beds', not 'dogs bed') and it specifies the semantic type of the compound (a dog bed is a type of bed). I will refer to the two nouns making up a basic attributive endocentric N-N compound as the modifying and the head noun respectively. In contrast to endocentric compounds, exocentric compounds are not semantically right-headed; a ponytail is not a type of tail, but rather a type of hairstyle that resembles the tail of a pony. Coordinate endocentric cases also do not have a semantic head, as both nouns apply equally to their intended referent. For example, a student-athlete is someone who is both a student and an athlete. Although they are not my focus in this chapter, I will make some brief contrastive remarks in Sections 13.3 and 13.5 about coordinate and subordinate endocentric compounds.

When faced with an attributive endocentric N-N compound, simply knowing which is the head noun does not help one to interpret it, as there are an unlimited variety of meaning relations that can hold between the concepts expressed by the two constituent nouns. Jackendoff (2010: 416) lists seven examples with 'cake' as the head noun, along with glosses that show the relation is different in each case. Two of his examples are 'birthday cake' and 'marble cake'. Moreover, even if the glosses he suggests for his seven examples are the ones

Table 4 *Sadock's (1998) classification scheme for noun-noun compounds*

Relation	Example compound	Meaning gloss
Part-whole	'mountain top'	Top part of a mountain
Material composition	'wood house'	House made from wood
Location of entity	'city boy'	Boy who lives in the city
Modification	'skinhead brothers'	Brothers who are skinheads
Purpose-instrument	'sound card'	Card that controls sound
Other	'alibi witness'	Witness who can provide an alibi for the accused

that come most easily to mind when these compounds are presented out of context, and even if some of these meanings have become lexicalised, these are not the only possible interpretations for these compounds. For example, 'coffee cake', which Jackendoff glosses as 'cake to eat along with coffee', may in some contexts mean *cake made with coffee as an ingredient* or even *iced vanilla cake whose decorations represent coffee.*

Sadock (1998) claims that the semantic relations holding between the modifying and head nouns in endocentric attributive N-N compounds belong to a fairly restricted range of types. Table 4 shows the classification scheme for the types of relations that he proposes.

Others who have proposed similar classification schemes include Downing (1977), who lists twelve relations, and Gagné and Shoben (1997), who offer a list of sixteen basic relations.

The fact that Sadock has an 'Other' category already signals that there is some unruliness here. Moreover, it is not clear how we decide in context what the intended relation between the modifying and head noun is. Consider Sadock's example 'city boy', in which he assumes the noun 'city' has the function of locating the boy. However, someone can be called a city boy even if he was neither raised in nor lives in a city. I might say 'Peter is a city boy at heart' if Peter was born and lives in the countryside but has tastes and manners that are citified. And in some cases, 'city' could signal a social organisation rather than a physical location, as in 'city hall'.

Can we make some better progress on trying to understand and systematise the seemingly limitless ways in which N-N compounds can be understood? In many instances, our understanding seems to be generative rather than to consist in some rote memorisation of the meanings of these forms. In the following three sections I examine semantic, psychological (schema-based), and statistical accounts of nominal combination, respectively.

13.3   A Semantic Account of N-N Combination

Lieber (2011) uses an extended metaphor to describe her aims in her essay. She talks of the syntactic structure of compounds as their skeleton, of their semantic structure as their musculature, and of their pragmatic features as their fat. As Jackendoff (2010: 424) notes, the syntactic structure of endocentric N-N compounds is rather minimal. They are syntactically right-headed and nominal combination allows for the sort of recursion illustrated above. Lieber's focus in her essay is on the 'musculature' of such compounds. Her aim is to see how much of the interpretation of nominal compounds can be attributed to their semantic structures rather than their pragmatic 'fat'.

Lieber proposes that the lexemes (lexical bases and affixes) of each language are defined semantically in terms of some subset of a finite stock of universal features. Some of these semantic features may be syntactically active, while others will be merely semantically but not syntactically active. Lieber proposes that English has seven syntactically active semantic features. These features are associated with functions that take arguments. In English, nouns designate things/substances/essences that 'are characterized by at least the feature [material] and possibly also the feature [dynamic], if they are processual in nature' (Lieber 2011: 81). So for example, the noun 'dog' will be associated with the one-place function [+ material ([])] and the noun 'mother' with the two-place function [+ material, + dynamic ([], [])]. Verbs, adjectives, etc. will be associated with other such function-argument structures. Since my concern is with N-N compounds, I will confine my attention to Lieber's characterisation of the semantics of nominal expressions.

In addition to these functional meanings, nouns may also be associated with features that are merely semantically active. So, for example, the noun 'dog' may be associated with the features <+animate>, <–human>, and the noun 'mother' with the features <+animate>, <+female>. Finally, there will be encyclopaedic information associated with these nouns. Dogs may be classified as four-legged creatures, as being disposed to wag their tails, etc. A mother may be thought of as nurturing and protective towards her offspring, etc. This encyclopaedic information is the pragmatic 'fat' in Lieber's extended metaphor.

Lieber explains how the meaning of a N-N compound arises by positing a process whereby we align the function-argument structures associated with the component nouns. She systematically examines compounds from each of her six types and describes the sorts of alignment processes involved in each. I will discuss only her treatment of endocentric attributive compounds.

In an attributive complex such as 'dog bed', Lieber proposes an explanation in terms of a Principle of Co-Indexation. The nouns 'dog' and 'bed' are both associated with a one-place meaning function of the form [+material ([])]. Since their associated functions have only one argument place each, these argument places are co-indexed and we assume that we have just a single referent for the complex nominal, whose type is determined by the semantic head noun 'bed'. However, we must also consider the further semantic information encoded by these nouns. The noun 'dog' is associated with the features

<+animate>, <–human>. On the other hand, the noun 'bed' is associated with features such as <–animate>, <+artefact>. Clearly these features are semantically incompatible, which rules out the possibility of a coordinate meaning (such as may be possible for 'student-athlete'). Moreover, we don't have the possibility of a subordinate meaning either (such as may be possible for 'city employee', where the function-argument structure of 'employee' contains a second embedded argument position that can be co-indexed with the argument position in the function associated with 'city', leading to the construal of the city as the employer).

Lieber acknowledges that, in the 'dog bed' case, the interpretation 'is free to be fixed by context' (2011: 98), although she also thinks that we operate with certain pragmatic biases that favour one interpretation over another. These are likely to lead us to the interpretation that a dog bed is a bed for a dog to sleep in rather than a bed made from dogs. I agree that we have such pragmatic biases. Our encyclopaedic knowledge is not completely unstructured, and we undoubtedly rely on past observations of regularities when engaging in categorisations. See Levin et al. (2014) for a corpus study that reveals some of our categorisation biases. The important point for my purposes is that the semantic structure of endocentric attributive compounds is not sufficient to deliver a productive interpretation mechanism. The interpretation of such compounds is not fixed by semantic rules, and at best merely constrained by such rules.

13.4   Schema-Based Models of N-N Combination

Can we make progress on understanding the productive processes used in the interpretation of N-N compounds by considering psychological, schema-based models of concept combination? Wisniewski and Gentner (1991) explore the Concept Specialisation Model (CSM), a model of concept combination proposed by Murphy (1988). According to the CSM, concept combination is a two-stage process. First, the modifying concept is used to fill a slot in the head concept. Then, in a second phase, encyclopaedic knowledge is used to refine and/or augment the combination concept to accommodate the imported concept.

To illustrate this two-stage process, suppose we are asked to interpret 'elephant box', where the concept *box* is assumed to have a slot that lists its possible contents. The first step will be to fill this slot with the information that the box contains (or is designed to contain) an elephant. This will now induce a second stage of processing, in which the values associated with the dimension and material composition slots in the *box* concept are refined. We are likely to assume that an elephant box's dimensions are large – at least large enough to contain an average-sized adult elephant – and that it is composed of sturdy material, or else it won't be effective at containing the elephant. In this case, it is the head concept that is specialised in order to accommodate the modi-fying concept. But, in other cases, it could be the modifying concept that is specialised in order to accommodate the head concept.

Matters are not as straightforward as this example suggests. For one thing, it is not always going to be the containment slot in the *box* concept that is filled when the concepts are combined. The modifying concept may instead target the slot for intended users of the box, as in 'bankers box', or for typical uses of the box, as in 'flower box', or the material composition of the box, as in 'ivory box', or the exterior appearance of the box, as in 'elephant box' construed to mean *box shaped like an elephant* or *box decorated with pictures of elephants*.

Even though CSM is silent on how we decide what slot in the head concept is to be filled, it may seem that the CSM has reasonably adequate resources to explain N-N compounding, since it is still slot filling we are doing, what-ever the slot that is filled. However, when Wisniewski and Gentner (1991) conducted a series of experiments using novel N-N compounds, they found that only 40 per cent of the interpretations provided by their participants for their 400 novel N-N compounds could be explained along the lines of the 'ele-phant box' example already discussed. They conclude that there are additional processes at work in concept combination, which they call 'property mapping' and 'structure mapping'.

An example from their data to illustrate property mapping is 'robin snake', which was interpreted by one of their participants to mean a red snake. In this case, instead of the entire concept *robin* being merged as a slot filler in the con-cept *snake*, only one salient property of a robin, its red colour, is transferred and fills the colour slot in the *snake* concept, replacing the default colour value. Wisniewski and Gentner call this process 'property mapping' because we align the two concepts by filling their colour slots with the same colour value (red in this case).

The process that Wisniewski and Gentner call 'structure mapping' requires something more than slot filling. This can be illustrated with an example from their data, 'pony chair', which was interpreted by one of their participants as a small chair. As they note, this cannot be a case of property mapping, where the default value for pony size fills the size slot in the concept *chair*, because a chair the size of a pony would not be small. Rather, a pony is type of horse that is small relative to other horses, and by analogy, 'pony chair' was interpreted as a type of chair that is small relative to other chairs. In other words, the novel concept *pony chair* and its hypernym *chair* are put into relation to the concept *pony* and its hypernym *horse*.

The elaborated CSM that includes processes of property and structure mapping faces similar problems to those faced by the simple CSM. It is silent on how we decide which processes to use in particular cases. Do we use full-concept-slot-filling (as in the case of 'elephant box'), or do we use property mapping (as in the case of 'robin snake'), or do we use structure mapping (as in the case of 'pony chair')? And if we opt for slot filling, how do we decide which slot in the head concept gets filled? After the fact, as Wisniewski and Gentner did with their experimental results, we can analyse people's paraphrases and surmise that one or another of these concept combination strategies was used. But how do we, as interpreters faced with a speaker's utterance of one of these novel compounds, decide how to combine the two concepts?

13.5   A Statistical/Corpus Approach

Statistical approaches suggest that, along with basic semantic category information of words, people exploit frequency-based information concerning the co-occurrence of words that is stored in their mental lexicons to interpret novel N-N compounds. If the constituent nouns of a novel compound express concepts similar to those that the nouns that constitute known compounds express, then the way in which the new combination is used is likely to be similar to the way in which the known combinations are typically (frequently) used. See, for example, Maguire et al. (2010: 53). So, if N-N compounds of the substance-artefact form (such as 'clay pot' and 'plastic chair') are typically used to express the idea that the artefact is made from the substance, then a newly encountered N-N complex of this form, say 'sand chair', will be understood to mean a chair made from sand.

One problem is that frequency information can lead one to ignore a more plausible interpretation of 'sand chair', namely as a chair designed to be used on sandy beaches. Moreover, even if comprehension of novel N-N compounds relies on such statistical reasoning, this is likely to result in the retrieval of conceptual relations that are too coarse-grained. Thus, pragmatic specialisation will be needed in addition, in order to retrieve the intended meanings.

Let us assume that the following nominal compounds with head noun 'pill' are stored in an interpreter's mental lexicon:

(a) Headache pill
(b) Fertility pill
(c) Birth control pill
(d) Lettuce pill
(e) Calcium pill

If we assume that the basic semantic category for the constituents in the compounds (a)–(c) is something like <bodily condition> for the modifiers and <medicinal substance> for the head noun 'pill', then we get something like 'medicinal substance FOR bodily condition' as a frequently occurring relation for such compounds. However, this would be an underspecified meaning, as in each of the lexically stored cases there is additional information available, such as that headache pills relieve pain that is already present but that fertility pills help increase something that is lacking in a female's reproductive system in order to enhance her fertility. And so on for the other nuanced meanings. The compounds (d)–(e) presumably manifest a different pattern, something like 'medicinal substance CONTAINS element'. Let us suppose that the FOR relation out-ranks the CONTAINS relation in terms of frequency in this person's lexicon.

Suppose the interpreter now encounters the novel (for him) complex 'wart pill'. Relying on the semantic categorisation of the modifying and head nouns and the available frequency information, the person predicts that this means 'a pill FOR warts'. But this is a semantically underdetermined result. Do these pills cure warts or do they encourage their growth? Encyclopaedic information has to be brought to bear, to the effect that (at least in our beauty-obsessed culture) warts are unsightly things. They are not things people would want to encourage to grow. A wart pill is thus likely a pill that gets rid of warts. There is also a chance that it is the CONTAINS relation that is the correct one in this case, even though this is a less frequently encountered relation for this interpreter. It could be that a wart pill contains ground up warts and is sold as a folk remedy for some type of ailment.

Thus, in the best-case scenario, frequency information will help you narrow down the intended relation but will not fully resolve it. Pragmatic processing is needed to supplement the results of the frequency-based processing. In less favourable cases, the frequency information could even result in an interpretation that is incorrect, so that pragmatically available information will then be needed to access the intended meaning, as in the hypothetical 'wart pill' example described above.

Such disruptions in processing have in fact been found in experimental studies. For example, Gagné and Shoben (1997) found that people were slower to interpret 'plastic crisis' (= a crisis ABOUT plastic) than 'plastic furniture' (= furniture MADE FROM plastic), presumably because 'plastic' in the modifier role is more frequently associated with the MADE FROM relation than other potential relations and thus the frequency information interfered with and delayed recovery of the correct interpretation.

Computational linguists have also tested statistical models on corpus data and compared the performance of these models to human performance on the same task. Lapata (2002) describes several variants of a probabilistic algorithm built to predict whether the modifying noun of a N-N complex with a de-verbal head is the object (as in 'car lover') or the subject (as in 'child behaviour') of the head noun. One of her models was successful 86.1 per cent of the time in classifying the modifier noun as either the subject or object of the head noun. This was only 3.6 per cent lower than the intersubjective agreement rating of 89.7 per cent that was obtained using two human judges who performed the same classification task. These cases with de-verbal heads belong to Lieber's (2011) subordinate endocentric type. Since they are not the focus of my chapter, I will say no more about Lapata's findings other than to note that subordinate endocentric N-N compounds are more constrained in their interpretations than N-N compounds of the attributive endocentric type. Lapata is beginning with the easiest cases to set a lower bound that statistical models must meet, whereas I am focused on the most unconstrained cases to demonstrate the important role that pragmatics plays.

13.6   A Relevance Theory Account of Novel N-N Compounds

Novel N-N compounds require what Jackendoff (2010: 417) calls 'enriched composition' for their interpretation. The idea of pragmatic processing at the sub-propositional level is built into the heart of Sperber and Wilson's (1986/1995) relevance theory (RT). According to RT, local pragmatic processes of narrowing and/or broadening operate at the lexical level to create ad hoc concepts, which are the input to compositional processes at the level of the sentence. Thus, RT promises to be helpful in accounting for the interpretation of N-N compounds, which also involve sub-propositional processes of (complex) concept construction. Note that the enriched composition involved in understanding N-N compounds concerns the pragmatic process of putting concepts together with a contextually appropriate meaning relation. This is different from the process of narrowing or broadening of a single concept, which is usually what is meant by ad hoc concept construction within RT. However, these processes are not unconnected. In the process of uncovering the intended conceptual relation underlying a N-N compound, the meanings of one or both of the constituent nouns may undergo processes of narrowing or broadening. This should become clearer when I discuss some examples below.

The Communicative Principle of Relevance states that every utterance conveys a presumption of its own optimal relevance, which means that the audience to whom it is addressed can expect that the utterance will be worth their effort to process because this processing will yield positive cognitive effects for no gratuitous processing effort. (The audience's expectations for the degree of relevance will be tempered by knowledge of the speaker's own particular set of abilities and preferences.) N-N compounds are compact forms for packaging information. When a speaker uses a N-N compound, the audience can assume that there is easily accessible contextual information that will help them unpack the specialised meaning relation that the speaker intends to convey. The audience is therefore warranted in using contextual information in order of its accessibility to derive cognitive effects and they should stop processing once their expectations of relevance are satisfied (or abandoned).

In RT, it is often claimed that explicature and implicature construction are parallel processes. However, even at the level of explicature construction, there are multiple processes operating in parallel. Bottom-up processes (e.g., lexical and phonological ones) and top-down processes (e.g., the accessing of schema-based knowledge) act in tandem to aid in the construction of ad hoc concepts and to put these concepts together with appropriate meaning relations. This yields higher-level chunks of meaning that (ultimately) contribute to the explicature. This is what I claim happens in understanding N-N compounds.

The lexical processes I have in mind are ones that access bigram frequency information based on the semantic categories of the head and modifying nouns. See Maguire et al. (2010). Phonological information concerns stress patterns, which can be helpful, given that fronted stress is often a cue for the existence of a compound as opposed to a phrase. Schema-based information is triggered by assumptions in the mutual cognitive environment (CE) of the interlocutors. The information in the mutual CE will be structured, with some information foregrounded and some backgrounded. Hence assumptions will be more or less accessible, depending on their information structural features. Moreover, the information in the mutual CE will be of different kinds, including linguistic (what has just been said), perceptual (what can be immediately sensed), social (what the social status of the interlocutors is), and encyclopaedic (what is known about the world). In other words, the RT account I am advocating for the interpretation of novel N-N compounds combines aspects of both the schema-based and statistical approaches discussed in Sections 13.4 and 13.5 respectively.

Most experimental studies of N-N compounds have presented participants with out-of-context compounds. Experimental tasks generally require participants to make some sort of judgement, such as whether or not the N-N combination makes sense. Frequency information does seem to play a role in performance on such tasks, as was discussed in Section 13.5. However, the interpretations that result are likely to be too coarse-grained. Hence, empirical investigations using contextualised novel N-N compounds are needed in order to explore the relevance-driven comprehension procedures that I am postulating.

Let us consider some examples of contextualised N-N compounds. The following is taken from an article titled 'Going Clean' in *New Scientist*, 8 October 2016, p. 28:

(13.1)   Scarred landscapes, billowing smoke, seabirds writhing in liquorice gloop: there's no denying fossil fuels have an image problem.

When reading this passage (which is the opening salvo of the article), one is primed by the article's title ('Going Clean') and by the talk of blighted landscapes and billowing smoke to think of the bad effects of oil. By the time one begins to process 'seabirds writhing' one readily conjures up an image of gulls covered in viscous, tarry oil. Therefore, the only contextually sensible interpretation of the 'liquorice gloop' that covers the birds is that it is viscous oil that resembles liquorice in being sticky and black. The interpretation 'gloop MADE FROM liquorice' is never (consciously) considered, and if seriously considered, would lead to a deviant interpretation. Only someone who went back to think of the N-N complex 'liquorice gloop' as a complex in its own right would even consider this a possible interpretation. However, since the RT comprehension procedure instructs interpreters to stop processing as soon as their expectations of relevance have been met, only the 'gloop RESEMBLING liquorice' interpretation will be considered, as it does indeed lead to adequate cognitive effects for no gratuitous processing effort.

In contrast to this, consider the following (constructed) example:

(13.2)   Jonny loves cars, so his mother made him a birthday cake beautifully decorated with a car made from coloured icing. It had little *liquorice wheels* and cranberries for headlights.

Here we are primed by the prior mention of birthday cake decorations to access the 'X MADE FROM liquorice' interpretation for 'liquorice wheels'. The complication here is that the plural noun 'wheels' is being used metonymically; it stands not for actual wheels but wheel representations (just as 'stone lion' would be understood to refer to a stone representation of a lion). In other words, this is a case in which a pragmatic process of broadening operates on the meaning of 'wheel', coerced by the meaning relation that is accessed and by the fact that it is already established that we are talking about cake decorations. Thus, the final interpretation of this N-N compound will be 'wheel-representation MADE FROM liquorice'. Again, the RT comprehension process terminates with this interpretation and we need not consider other possibilities, such as 'wheel RESEMBLING liquorice'.

I said above in relation to example (13.1) that the interpretation 'gloop MADE FROM liquorice' is never *consciously* considered. Critics are likely to say that it is nevertheless *subconsciously* entertained, on the assumption that 'X MADE FROM liquorice' is the most frequently occurring relation in people's mental lexicons involving 'liquorice' as a modifier. The idea would be that the interpretation 'X MADE FROM liquorice' is activated but that it loses the 'race' to reach conscious awareness because the competing interpretation 'X RESEMBLING liquorice' gets a boost in its activation level from information available in the discourse context that is consonant with it. On the other hand, arguably the RT comprehension procedure works in such a way that the irrelevant interpretation is never considered at all, even subconsciously, as the first information to be accessed in context already yields a satisfactory interpretation. This hypothesis remains to be experimentally investigated.

Am I claiming that in the RT comprehension process, frequency information never plays a role? No. Other things being equal, frequency-based information will yield the most accessible assumptions – the ones that will be considered first, as per the RT comprehension procedure. I agree with Gagné and Shoben (1997) that interpretations based on frequency information are default interpretations, ones we fall back on when nothing else in the context jumps out at us.

In this chapter, I have discussed N-N compounds that refer to categories of things. However, there are many one-off combinations of nouns that are used to refer to individuals. Jackendoff (2010) gives an example of 'bike girl' used to refer to a girl who brought her bike into the lobby of his apartment building. Downing (1977) argues that cases like this are not true N-N compounds but rather one-off referential devices. I would argue that the same pragmatic mechanisms of concept combination are involved in both sorts of cases, although space considerations prevent me from elaborating on this issue here. Moreover, it is likely that the processing of N-N compounds such as 'bike girl' will be similar to the referential processing involved in metonymies such as 'The ham sandwich wants the bill', where 'the ham sandwich' refers to the person who ordered the ham sandwich, or to cases of metaphorical reference resolution, as in 'That festering sore needs to be dealt with soon', where the demonstrative refers to a derelict house that is used by drug pushers and addicts.

13.7   Conclusions

I have argued that accounts of the comprehension of novel attributive endocentric N-N compounds that rely only on the semantic properties of the constituent nouns, or on the semantic categories of the constituent nouns coupled with information about their bigram frequencies, offer only partial insights into these comprehension processes. These accounts must be supplemented with one that appeals to local pragmatic processes of ad hoc concept construction, which are guided by the relevance-driven comprehension procedure. The concepts associated with N-N compounds are larger chunks of meaning than the ad hoc concepts that have been discussed in the RT literature in terms of concept narrowing or broadening. However, since the constituent concepts of a compound concept may need to undergo broadening or narrowing in the process of concept combination, the local pragmatic processes of complex concept construction are intertwined with the processes of concept narrowing and broadening, as my example involving the interpretation of 'liquorice wheels' was intended to show. My overall conclusion is that we need something like this RT-based pragmatic account, which is based on situated language use, in order to reveal and explain the productive mechanisms involved in understanding novel attributive endocentric N-N compounds.

Acknowledgements

I am honoured to be contributing to this volume celebrating Deirdre Wilson's career. She has been a role model for me ever since I first encountered her work. I thank the editors and an anonymous referee for their insightful feedback on an earlier version of this chapter.

14 Procedural Syntax

Eleni Gregoromichelaki and Ruth Kempson

14.1 Introduction

Within psychological linguistic theories, relevance theory (RT, Sperber & Wilson 1986/1995), with its focus on explaining how communication works, early on directed attention to general cognitive processes, notably an efficiency-driven processor striving to balance cognitive goals against processing effort. In this chapter, we will argue that taking such a goal-directed processing approach can be extended much deeper so that fundamental natural language (NL) properties, namely, the structuring of NL signals, can be explicated. We are going to introduce a grammar framework, Dynamic Syntax, which, in conceptualising NLs as procedures for (inter)action, directly provides an alternative 'knowing-how' motivation of NL structure. The top-down predictive articulation of DS can be seen as a radical extension of the concept of *procedure* widely adopted in RT (Blakemore 1987, 2002; Wilson, 2000, 2011b). Under this extension, procedures are not some add-on to an otherwise standard form–meaning encoding but a total replacement of the code-based model. We believe that this approach, despite its novelty, is compatible with Wilson (2016), where the notion of 'procedure' is cashed out in non-representational dispositional terms following Bezuidenhout (2004). However, a challenge that then arises is how to account for the reification of such procedures as exemplified in apparent metarepresentational practices like quotation, reporting, citation etc. We will argue that even such phenomena can receive adequate and natural explanations through a grammar that allows for the dynamic ad hoc creation of occasion-specific content through self-referential mechanisms.

14.2 Split Utterances: The Challenge of Incrementality

A ubiquitous feature of informal conversations is how little exchanges rely on the formulation of the complete, well-formed sentences/thoughts that standard grammars take as their remit (see e.g. Miller & Weinert 1998). Instead, people opportunistically rely on the linguistic and non-linguistic context for what to say and understand, coordinating verbal and non-verbal actions, and handling efficiently what have been considered elsewhere as 'degenerate' inputs (Radford 2004; Chomsky 2006):

(14.1)   [Context: Friends of the Earth club meeting]
    A: So what is that? Is that er… booklet or something?
    B: It's a book
    C: Book
    B: Just … talking about al you know alternative
    D: On erm… renewable yeah
    B: energy really I think……
    A: Yeah
                     [British National Corpus (BNC)]

Thus, linguistic behaviour in dialogue undermines basic theoretical notions like the abstract concepts of 'sentence' and 'syntactic constituency': interlocutors can take over from each other at any point in a clausal sequence across all syntactic and semantic dependencies, change or abandon strings while incomplete, and still manage to coordinate successfully. Stainton (2006) presents evidence that standard syntactic/semantic accounts cannot deal with various types of 'fragments' in conversation through ellipsis analyses and, instead, an RT-type pragmatic account is required:

(14.2)   A: Covent Garden?
    B: Right at the lights. Then straight on up.

However, the phenomenon is much more extended and problematic. Firstly, contra Stainton, in many languages, there are syntactic/morphological restrictions constraining the form of non-sentential strings used to perform various speech acts like clarifications/corrections/etc. (Ginzburg 2012; Gregoromichelaki 2012). Therefore, syntax/semantics must be involved in their licensing. Moreover, all such speech acts can be perfectly processable well before any sentential or propositional unit has been delivered by standard grammars or any informative intention-grounding pragmatic inference has been derived:

(14.3)   A: Er, the doctor
    B: Chorlton?
    A: Chorlton, mhm, he examined me, erm, he, he said now they were on about a slight [shadow] on my heart.
                       [BNC: KPY 1005–1008]

For many other cases, just abandoning syntactic/semantic accounts and relegating the analysis to pragmatics doesn't help. This is because the phenomenon illustrated in (14.1) earlier and below, so-called split utterances (SUs), involves syntactic/semantic constraints operating across shifts of contextual parameters, e.g. speaker/hearer roles. For example, (14.4) involves a split between a preposition and its complement and (14.5) a split between determiner and noun:[1]

(14.4)   JACK: I just returned
         KATHY: from…
         JACK: Finland.   [Lerner 2004]

(14.5)   A: I need a a…
         B: mattock. For breaking up clods of earth.   [BNC]

Such split dependencies can be arbitrarily complex. (14.6) splits apart both a dependency between the left-peripheral *wh*-form and the associated object 'gap' position of *axe* as well as the auxiliary and verb; (14.7) separates the negative polarity *any of the saliva kits* from A's initiating utterance on which it is dependent across B's intervention, while simultaneously being construed as an extension of B's intervention:

(14.6)   A: Which unit are we thinking we should…
         B: axe? None.

(14.7)   A: Has every female gymnast handed in
         B: her blood sample?
         A: or even any of the saliva kits?

But SU data are also problematic for all syntactic/semantic frameworks that rely on linear-order independent, bottom-up licensing of syntactic/semantic constituency and dependencies (see e.g. Hornstein et al. 2005; cf. Putnam 2009, 2010; Osborne et al. 2011). Given that such frameworks rely on a notion of 'sentence' or 'phrase' (see e.g. Collins 2003, 2007) as the minimal units that can be interpreted, they must necessarily resort to either an assumption of ellipsis regarding each substring or a supplementary competence/performance division of labour (Kobele 2016; cf. Kempson et al. 2017, 2019) in order to account for such data, if at all.

An ellipsis account is not viable since encoded deletion operations will have to be postulated for any partial string, for example, missing subjects in English:

(14.8)   HESTER COLLYER: It's for me.
         MRS ELTON THE LANDLADY: And Mr. Page?

---

[1] Such phenomena are also beyond the reach of analyses like Barton (1990) and Barton and Progovac (2005) since these accounts, despite their welcome pioneering contribution, concentrate and rely exclusively on predefined, well-formed non-sentential constituents and not the role of incremental licensing.

HESTER COLLYER: is not my husband. But I would rather you
continue to think of me as Mrs. Page.

[from *The Deep Blue Sea* (film)]

Beyond postulating ellipsis, resorting to a distributed competence/performance account not only does not deliver a parsimonious explanation it also appears empirically inadequate. This is because the problems for syntactic/ semantic frameworks are not just due to the bottom-up licensing imposed by standard competence approaches. It is the very notion of syntactic constituency, mediating between pairings of phonological–semantic representations (Brody 2002), that gets in the way. This remains the case even when non-standard constituents are employed (Steedman 2000) since the SU-splits can occur at any point. Any constituency constraints included in the competence account preclude an intuitive systematic analysis of SUs as simple continuations, because even invoking shared structures that somehow splice together surface syntactic structures will, in many cases, result in ill-formed strings or incorrect interpretations:

(14.9)   A [SEEING B EMERGE FROM A SMOKE-FILLED KITCHEN]:
         Did **you** burn
         B [INTERRUPTING]: **myself**? No, fortunately not.

Moreover, note that SU partial strings are incrementally interpretable since they can be used to accomplish speech acts (see (14.8)) *necessarily* without any propositional enrichment (see (14.10)), otherwise their incompleteness will not be adequate as a parsimonious explanation for the triggering of the completion:

(14.10) PSYCHOLOGIST: And you left your husband because …
         CLIENT: we had nothing in common anymore

Even frameworks that integrate syntax/semantics and pragmatics within the grammar (Ginzburg 2012; Ginzburg et al. 2014) do not provide a unified account of all non-sentential cases since they separate out some 'fragments' to be treated as propositional, resolved through powerful coercion operations, and others as continuations either by the speaker ('self-repair') or the hearer ('completions', Poesio & Rieser 2010). The problem that permeates such accounts is the necessary encoding of higher-order speech-act characterisations (e.g. 'The speaker is asserting/querying/clarifying *x*') associated with the derivation of propositions for the licensing of each contextual switch in dialogue. However, this does not provide for the intuitive unified explanation of the phenomena, which, in our view, is the potential for top-down predictive, incremental, and interactive processing. The ability to incrementally set out and resolve dependencies by either interlocutor, instead of appealing to some constituency-defining competence, underlies the successful coordination of speaker/hearer actions displayed in (14.1)–(14.10). And this ability underpins monologue as well as dialogue, as evidenced by phenomena like parenthetical insertion:

(14.11)   Well, they dropped cards in *I suppose* the doors (Dehé 2014: 65)

(14.12)   Hi, and welcome to New Books in Sociology, a podcast where we interview authors of interesting and influential books in the field of, *you guessed it*, sociology...

[Sociology-Halperin]

Immediate, sub-sentential coordination among interlocutors, instead of the communication of codified constituent structures,[2] explains why interlocutors can achieve what from an analyst's external point of view can be described as propositional 'speech acts' without the interlocutors needing to process either full sentences or propositions. Regarding the mechanisms available to the interlocutors, such higher-order explicatures (e.g. 'The speaker is asserting/claiming/querying/requesting p') are not a necessary precondition for coordination.[3] For example, in (14.8) and (14.10) earlier, initiating a dependency is all that is needed to induce a resolving continuation by the other interlocutor. Interlocutors do not, in addition, need to infer/plan following higher-order speech acts/intentions (Gregoromichelaki et al. 2011, 2013a; see also Wilson & Wharton 2006). Meaningful coordination in interactive exchanges needs to be locally opportunistic (Clark 1996) so that efficiency requires no essential guidance by some preformed overarching plan by either participant. This is more evident in non-cooperative cases where seamless and timely intervention is perfectly possible without any necessary consideration of the intentions of the first speaker:

(14.13)   A: It's obvious from what he says (that)
              B: (that) you are wrong.

---

[2] Codified constituent structures occur, for example, in dialogue modelling where the grammar includes derivations of 'I am asking you whether you intended to utter x' for clarification requests.

[3] This is also argued within RT (Sperber & Wilson 1986/1995: 244) for specific speech-act characterisations. However, we go further in that we claim that not even a 'proposition expressed' is a necessary ingredient of coordination/communication and weak communicative acts like 'saying' (Sperber & Wilson 1986/1995: 247) need to be analysed not as deriving propositional schemata but as descriptions of the fundamental (turn-taking) procedures induced by the grammar (Eshghi et al. 2015; Gregoromichelaki & Kempson 2015; Gregoromichelaki 2017).

SU exchanges thus demonstrate the exercise of very basic human abilities, 'knowing how to go on' (Wittgenstein 1953: Section 150) in any process, so that even very young children participate – indeed SUs form the staple diet upon which they learn language, as displayed by the Old MacDonald nursery rhyme (see also Arnon et al. 2014):

(14.14) A: Old MacDonald had a farm, E-I-E-I-O and on that farm he had a
         B: cow
         A: and the cow goes
         B: moo

In conclusion, the seamless fluency with which interlocutors take on or hand over utterance responsibility presents a formidable challenge to current formalisms where syntax/semantics are defined as operating bottom-up with reference to constituents, with these then feeding into some extra-grammatical account of pragmatic inference. For these reasons, we turn now to a view of the grammar that essentially employs a view of syntax/semantics as goal-directed predictive action (procedures) for interactive coordination, not exchange of propositions, with no separation imposed between some putative grammatical, as opposed to extra-grammatical, context and structure.

14.3   Dynamic Syntax

Dynamic Syntax (Kempson et al. 2001; Cann et al. 2005) is a grammar architecture whose core notion is incremental interpretation of word sequences (comprehension) or linearisation of contents (production) relative to context. The Dynamic Syntactic engine, including the lexicon, is articulated in terms of goal-driven actions that are accomplished by giving rise to expectations of further actions, by processing contextual input, or by being abandoned as unviable in view of more competitive alternatives. Thus words, syntax and morphology are all modelled as 'affordances', opportunities for action that interlocutors can deploy to perform step-by-step a mapping from perceivable stimuli (phonological strings) to conceptual structure, or vice versa.

To illustrate, we display in (14.15)–(14.18) the (condensed) steps involved in the parsing of a long-distance dependency:

(14.15)

The task always starts with a set of probabilistically weighted predicted information states (we show only one and only the syntactically relevant part). Such states include routinised goals to build conceptual structures of some ontological type (e for entities in general, e_s for events, $e \rightarrow (e_s \rightarrow t)$ for predicates, etc.). In (14.15), the goal to build a proposition of type t is shown as a one-node tree with the goal *?Ty(t)* and the current focus of attention, the pointer ◊. The pointer at a node including a goal drives the prediction of further affordances/subgoals, expected to eventually satisfy the current goal either by the processing of (verbal) input (as a hearer) or by producing that input (as a speaker). For (14.15), one of the probabilistically licensed next steps for English (executed by lexical and general computational *macros* of actions) is illustrated next: a prediction that a structurally underspecified node (indicated by the dotted line) can be built and can accommodate the result of parsing/generating *who*. As illustrated here, temporary uncertainty about the eventual contribution of some element is implemented through *structural underspecification*. Initially unfixed tree-nodes model the retention of the contribution of the *wh*-element in a memory buffer until it can unify with some argument node in the upcoming local domain. Non-referential words like *who* and other semantically underspecified elements (e.g. pronominals, anaphors, auxiliaries, tenses) contribute *underspecified content* in the form of so-called *metavariables* (indicated in bold font), which trigger search for their eventual type-compatible substitution from among contextually salient entities or predicates.

General computational and lexically triggered macros then intersperse to develop a tree: in (14.16), the verb contributes both conceptual structure in the form of unfolding the tree further and fetching an ad hoc concept (indicated as *Hug'*) developed according to contextual restrictions,[4] as well as placeholder metavariables for time and event entities to be supplied by the context. Finally, the pointer ◊ is left at the argument node implementing the word-order restriction that the object needs to follow the verb in English:

(14.16)

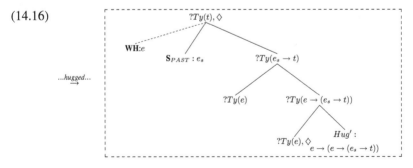

---

[4] For reasons of space, we present here a very simplistic view of conceptual content as atomic formulae; for more extensive views, see Wilson and Carston (2007); Carston (2012, 2013, 2016a); Cann and Kempson (2017); Gregoromichelaki (2017).

At this point, the word *Mary* can be processed to deliver a contextually determined individual (*Mary'*) at the argument node of the predicate. After this step, everything is in place for the structural underspecification to be resolved, namely, the node annotated by *who* can now unify with the subject node of the predicate, which results in a well-formed explicature representing the minimal content of an utterance of *Who hugged Mary?* in binary tree form:[5]

(14.17)

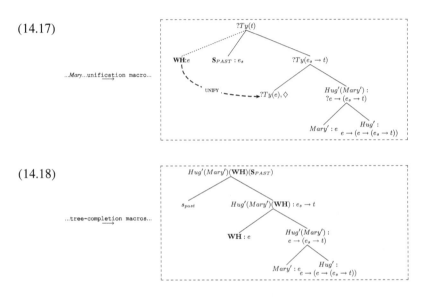

(14.18)

In this instance, processing a single speaker's utterance has ended with unresolved content, modelled as a metavariable needing substitution from context, the contribution of the *wh*-pronoun. The substitution of such a metavariable can be provided either by the same speaker (e.g. as in a rhetorical question, self-questioning/correction, etc.) or by the interlocutor. Besides trees, the complete model includes the full set of licensed next steps for partial trees currently entertained as live options, a record of activated entities/events/propositions, and contextual parameters like the utterance/ locutionary event, speaker-hearer roles, and times. All these elements constitute an *information state* (Hough 2014; Gregoromichelaki 2017). The information state tracks not only the shifting parameters of each word-utterance event serving for the interpretation of various indexical metavariables but also the actions used, recorded as traversals of paths in a graph display, and the processing paths that have been considered as probabilistically live

---

[5] For a fuller discussion of the framework, see Kempson et al. (2001); Cann et al. (2005); Eshghi et al. (2010, 2011, 2012, 2015); Kempson et al. (2016, 2017).

options but not eventually pursued (see e.g. Sato 2011; Hough 2014). Storing the action paths is necessary for the resolution of anaphora and ellipsis, especially 'sloppy' readings:

(14.19) A: John upset his mother.
          B: Harry too.

Maintaining abandoned options is required for the explicit modelling of conversational phenomena like clarification, self-/other-corrections, etc. but also for humorous effects and puns (Gregoromichelaki 2017).

The DS model assumes tight interlinking of NL perception and action. The predictions generating the sequence of trees above are equally deployed in comprehension and production. Comprehension involves the generation of predictions/goals and awaiting input to satisfy them, while production involves the deployment of action (verbalising) by the predictor themselves in order to satisfy their predicted goals. By imposing top-down predictive and goal-directed processing at all comprehension/production stages, interlocutor feedback is constantly anticipated and seamlessly integrated (Gargett et al. 2008, 2009; Purver et al. 2010; Eshghi et al. 2015; Gregoromichelaki 2017). At any point, either interlocutor can take over to realise such predicted goals. This can be illustrated in the sharing of the dependency constrained by the locality definitive of reflexive anaphors:

(14.20) MARY: Did **you** burn
          BOB: **myself**? No.

As shown in (14.20), a simplified version of (14.9), Mary starts a query involving an indexical metavariable contributed by *you* that is resolved by reference to the *Hearer'* contextual parameter currently occupied by *Bob'*:

(14.21)

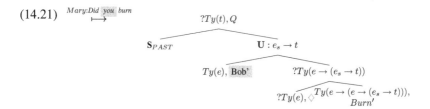

With the information state tracking the speaker/hearer roles as they shift sub-sententially, these roles are reset in the next step when Bob takes over the utterance. *Myself* is then uttered. Being a pronominal, it contributes a metavariable and, being a reflexive indexical, it imposes the restriction that the entity to substitute that metavariable needs to be a co-argument that bears the

Speaker' role. At this point in time, the only such available entity in context is again *Bob'*, which is duly selected as the substituent of the metavariable:

(14.22)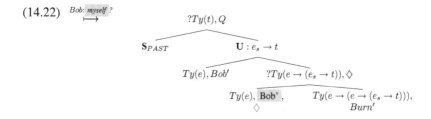

As a result, binding of the reflexive is semantically appropriate, and locality is respected even though joining the string as a single sentence would be ungrammatical. This successful result relies on the lack of a syntactic level of representation and the sub-sentential licensing of contextual dependencies which renders the fact that the utterance constitutes a joint action irrelevant for the wellformedness of the string. Concomitantly, coordination among interlocutors here can be seen, not as propositional inferential activity, but as the outcome of the fact that the grammar consists of a set of licensed complementary actions that speakers/hearers perform in synchrony (Gregoromichelaki et al. 2011, 2012; Gregoromichelaki 2013b; Gregoromichelaki & Kempson 2015). Due to sub-sentential step-by-step licensing, speakers are not required to plan propositional units, so hearers do not need to reason about propositional intentions. Given that parsing/production are predictive activities, a current goal in the information state may be satisfied by a current hearer, so that it yields the retrieval/provision of conceptual information that matches satisfactorily the original speaker's goals, as in (14.5)–(14.7), (14.9), or is judged to require some adjustment that can be seamlessly and immediately provided:

(14.23)   KEN: He said 'the married couple will walk- walk down the street and they will be all dressed up and people will come by with.hh
LOUISE: rice.
KEN: rice, petals or anything they think is suitable'. [Lerner (2004) modified]

However, especially in confrontational situations as in (14.13), there is no need to assume that the hearer expends any effort to recognise the speaker's intention since completion by the interrupting party is a means of avoiding having to achieve any such recognition. So, what the shift of theoretical perspective has achieved in making procedures central to the processing mechanism qua grammar is a shift in the burden of explanation. No longer do all communicative effects need to be explained inferentially by grammar-external higher-order inference operating on representations of speaker intentions; instead, the interactive 'mind-reading' effect emerges from production/parsing involving 'predictive processing',[6] defined within the grammar itself. However, we can go even further than this, to cases of alleged explicit metarepresentation, and see how such effects can be achieved within a grammar appropriately conceived.

14.4   Quotation: Metarepresentation or Demonstration?

As we saw earlier in (14.4), (14.8) and (14.10), perfectly intelligible moves in dialogue can be achieved simply by initiating a grammatical dependency which prompts either interlocutor to fulfil it without specific determination or identifiability of a given speech act/intention. In various other cases, though, the interlocutor completing somebody else's utterance might be perceived as offering the completion along with a query as to whether such a (meta) representation is what the other interlocutor would have said (e.g. (14.6)–(14.7)). There are further so-called 'metarepresentational'/echoing phenomena in cases of citation, quotation, reports, echoic uses/irony, and code-switching:

(14.24)   'Cities,' he said, 'are a very high priority.' [FrameNet]

(14.25)   **Wright** won't disclose how much the Nike deal is worth, saying only that 'they treat **me** well'. (The Face, 9–93:55) [De Brabanter 2010]

(14.26)   A doctor tells him [Gustave Flaubert] he is like a 'vieille femme hysterique' (TLS online: 18-12-1998) [De Brabanter 2010]

(14.27)   Alice said that life is 'difficult to understand'. [Cappelen & Lepore 1997]

(14.28)   Mary felt relieved. If Peter came tomorrow, she would be saved. [Recanati 2000]

Despite recent attempts to integrate such phenomena within standard grammars (e.g. Potts 2007b; Ginzburg & Cooper 2014; Maier 2014a,b), certain data are not amenable to appropriate treatment due to incrementality not being included as an explanatory factor within these formalisms. For example, as can be seen above, quotation can appear sub-sententially, and discontinuously, at any point, which means that contextual parameters characterising the utterance as echoic (Noh 1998, 2000; Wilson 2000) need to be able to shift incrementally at each word-by-word processing stage. Split utterances are one of the environments where quotation occurs frequently (Lerner 1991)

---

[6] Prediction is argued to be an essential part of human cognition in general (e.g. Friston 2010; Clark 2016).

due to the opportunity for co-constructing a joint perspective on some (actual or imaginary) speech/thought eventuality:

(14.29) CLINICIAN: So **I** watch this person being killed and then **I** go to bed and **I**'m you know lying there going, 'well'
PATIENT: 'did **I** hear something?' [Duff et al. 2007]

To analyse such cases, the grammar needs to include the resources that take into account embedded and sub-sentential context switches since such indexicals do not track the actual current speaker/hearer roles. Moreover, such sub-sentential switches include cases where the same structure can be employed both as expressing a speaker's own voice and as a subsequent quotation:

(14.30) JEM: Mary, whatever it is you think you know you mustn't speak of it. Not if you want to stay safe.
MARY: says the horse-thief. [BBC Transcripts, *Jamaica Inn*, Episode 1]

(14.31) A: SOMEONE is keen
B: says the man who slept here all night. [BBC Transcripts, *The A-Word*]

In all such cases, issues of 'footing' (Goffman 1979), namely, changes in perspectives and roles assumed by interlocutors, intersect with syntactic/semantic issues of direct/indirect speech constructions and speech-act responsibility and echoing (Goodwin 2007; Kempson et al. 2011; Gregoromichelaki 2013a; Gregoromichelaki & Kempson 2016). For these reasons, a unified account of the synergy of such NL devices to derive appropriate contents cannot be given within standard theories involving encapsulation and division of labour between semantics/pragmatics and syntax.

Gregoromichelaki (2017) argues that such global interactions are straightforwardly accounted for in DS due to its incremental modelling of context shifting, the potential for sharing of syntactic/semantic dependencies, and the fact that there is no requirement to derive a comprehensive propositional speech act. However, modelling the potential of partially assuming another speaker's role, being perceived as 'demonstrating' what somebody was going to say/think, and the 'metalinguistic' appearance of phenomena like the quoted strings in (14.32)–(14.34) might seem especially problematic for the DS approach that eschews syntactic representations at the level of strings:

(14.32) 'La neige est blanc' is well-formed/grammatical/correct.

(14.33) James says that 'Quine' wants to speak to us. [James thinks that McPherson is Quine, Recanati 2010]

(14.34) 'I talk better English than the both of youse!' shouted Charles, thereby convincing me that he didn't. [Partee 1973]

Unlike RT, as we saw, DS takes words/constructions as *affordances*, triggers for action, exploited by speakers/hearers to achieve coordination. This means that words/constructions are not defined as abstract code elements, expression types that are associated with referential/semantic values (representations).[7] With no expression types to serve as the semantic values of quotations (as metarepresentations), only mechanisms for processing stimuli, quotation thus offers a crucial test for the legitimacy of DS claims: when processing a quoted/ cited string, what happens within the quotation marks (or any other indications), if not metarepresentation (Wilson 2000), following DS assumptions?

Gregoromichelaki (2017) argues that these cases are also unproblematic for DS and need not be handled through metarepresentation as in RT,[8] even though (some of them) can be treated as echoic. This account employs the extended DS-TTR model (Purver et al. 2010; Hough 2014), which models conceptual structure as tree-structures annotated with so-called *record-types* (Type-Theory-with-Records, TTR, (Cooper 2012)), that is, complex type values modelling the fine-grained structure of concepts. The advantage of TTR is that types (concepts) and dependencies among them can be constructed ad hoc instead of being pre-specified in the model (following also Carston 2002; Cann & Kempson 2017). Through the subtyping mechanism, conceptual underspecification and progressive enrichment can be implemented formally. In combination with the incremental DS syntactic engine, DS-TTR then takes a *grammar* as just the time-linear procedures of conceptualising/manifesting, elaborating, and reasoning over contextually integrated stimuli (not necessarily linguistic ones). In turn, this now provides the potential to explicate the broader family of echoic/metalinguistic phenomena in a natural manner that conforms with intuitions and parallels the DS modelling of anaphora/ellipsis.

First, in order to model cases like (14.6)–(14.7) and (14.24)–(14.29), as well as mid-sentence code-switching in general, it is assumed that the predictions driving processing at each step are induced by variable categorisation/linearisation systems (*grammars*/idiolects) that can shift at each word-utterance stage. Such shifts are indicated by switching the value of the designated metavariable in the information state that keeps track of which and whose grammar is being employed at each sub-sentential stage (see also Recanati 2010: 256; Ginzburg & Cooper 2014). Next, consider the most challenging cases, namely, metalinguistic uses, for example (14.32), where an NL-string appears in a

---

[7] For a notion of 'representation' approximately compatible with the DS claims, see e.g. Egan (2014); Bickhard (2016); Wiese (2017). According to DS, representational abstractions of the actual mechanics of conversation may be involved in explicit reasoning that can ensue in cases of failure of the fundamentally subpersonal cognitive mechanisms, deception, manipulation, etc.

[8] Contra Wilson (2000), Gregoromichelaki (2017) argues that all such cases can be analysed as 'demonstrations', even metalinguistic cases, as long as an appropriate code-free conception of the grammar is adopted.

regular NP/DP position. Under DS assumptions, this will be a pointer position where the English grammar ($DS_{English}$) has already generated a prediction for the processing of a singular term, an entity type ($?Ty(e)$). However, the grammar does not specify how such an entity type is to be provided and there are always multiple ways to derive such contents. The explanation of how such content is derived here is based on the independent assumption that actions/procedures are first-class citizens in DS. This means that the subpersonal grammatical mechanisms include (also subpersonal) higher-order operations aggregating and (re-)running chunks of actions. This is needed, for example, in order to provide parallel but distinct contents in the anaphoric cases of 'sloppy readings' (see earlier (14.19)), deep anaphora, etc. The idea now is that the same mechanism can be used cataphorically for metalinguistic, echoic, and similar uses combined with two additional DS-TTR assumptions: (a) a grammar maps stimuli (eventualities) to conceptual types or vice versa, and (b) new types (concepts) can be constructed and manipulated ad hoc on-line by enriching the available TTR annotations.

Under these assumptions, (14.34) illustrates a case where the sequence of actions a speaker performs under the guidance of *some* grammar (here French) is isolated from the rest of the processing task (implemented by a change in contextual parameters) and conceptualised/'reified' as a subtype of the type 'entity' ($Ty(e)$), an eventuality entity ($Ty(e_s)$). This eventuality can then satisfy the predicted goal, ($?Ty(e)$), to be achieved on the node where the pointer resides following $DS_{English}$. By assumption, a grammar maps eventualities to conceptual categorisations, but in the usual case only the conceptual structure is retained long term while the actual action execution is stored separately and decays fast. For anaphora/ellipsis resolution, the grammar also includes instructions to build content from any type of stimulus. In (14.34), the speaker's performance, the speaker's actual execution of a sequence of DS_{French} actions (literally a 'demonstration' of a speech event), is performed while a $DS_{English}$ prediction for a singular term is in force. Thus, the performance itself becomes part of the conceptual structure derived with the predicted $DS_{English}$-type generated on-line as the performance unfolds. The rest of the string then, with the speaker having moved out of the DS_{French}-demonstration mode, delivers a content that characterises in some way the DS_{French}-demonstration event. This delivers the interpretation that the event of using the French grammar in this way can be characterised as in accordance with the speaker's grammaticality/correctness judgements.[9]

For the cases where the interpretation of the indexicals reflects an echoed utterance/thought event, e.g. (14.25), (14.27)–(14.29), (14.33)–(14.34),

---

[9] Note that DS_{French} is *not* part of the speaker's awareness. The grammaticality/correctness judgement refers to some approximation of the actual DS_{French}.

similarly, the relevant nodes where the strings in quotation marks are processed are annotated through demonstrations the speaker performs. The only addition to the previous process is that now the invoked action execution, besides a change in the grammar, also involves a shift in the values of contextual parameters which are now supplied by some salient utterance/thought event.

Cases of *direct quotation* where a verb, e.g. *say*, requires a complement presented as an echoed utterance/thought eventuality are analysed as cases where such a contextual switch has been grammaticalised. Such verbs initially introduce a metavariable as a placeholder for their complement. The substituent of this metavariable can be provided either cataphorically by a subsequent demonstration by the interlocutors, as in (14.23), or anaphorically by appropriating a previous utterance event (perhaps not intended as a demonstration at all, as in (14.30)–(14.31)), or both, as in (14.24).

Finally, given that DS-TTR does *not* license form–meaning correspondences but only provides for the parsing/generation of stimuli in context, the process of reifying the demonstration of some linguistic element to provide ad hoc content of another already predicted type on the tree can be extended to the processing of non-linguistic signals composed with linguistic ones as the conceptualisation of some experience that is being demonstrated:

(14.35) John saw the spider and was like 'ahh!' [in a scared voice]

(14.36) John was eating like [gobbling gesture with hands and face]

Arguably, the modelling of the availability of such potential goes a long way in providing a starting point for modelling the processes required both for language acquisition and language change, both of which involve iterative, interactive implementation of this potential.

14.5   Conclusion

The view of NLs as codes mediating a mapping between internally specified expression types and private representations of the world has been abandoned here to give way to a view where utterances are taken as goal-directed physical actions coordinating with equally goal-directed mental actions within and across speakers. Instead of assembling propositional representations of reality, such actions are aimed to locally and incrementally alter the affordances of the internal/external context for both one's self and one's interlocutors so that the next predicted action goals can unfold. Taking the non-representational RT notion of procedures (Wilson 2016) as the basic architectural constituent of NL grammars, actions can be seen to manipulate perceptual stimuli composed not only of 'words' and 'syntax' but also of non-linguistic elements like visual marks, prosody, gestures, gaze, etc. NL meaning, from this point of view, is a phenomenon that emerges at group level via interaction and is not determined through individual psychological processes. NL knowledge is then part of the ability to coordinate effective interaction with the environment, one's own self, or one's interlocutors. We believe that this non-modular, procedural definition of syntactic mechanisms removes one of the obstacles for integrating NL processing within a general sensorimotor account of higher cognitive functions (see e.g. Pulvermüller 2010; Gregoromichelaki et al. 2013b; Seth 2015; Pezzulo & Cisek 2016) as it avoids the necessity of the 'cognitive sandwich' (Hurley 2008) perspective. Furthermore, the necessity of assuming fine-grained interactional dynamics to account for meaningful engagements among agents and their environment indicates that the boundaries of individual cognition are fluid and indeterminate. Therefore, any account of individual psychological mechanisms will remain incomplete unless the distribution and complementarity of social cognitive processes are modelled in parallel (see also e.g. Bickhard 2009, 2016; Anderson 2014).

Acknowledgements

This chapter is part of an exploration of how basic RT insights could be extended to the concept of language itself, defining even syntax in terms of underspecification and incremental context-relative update. It comes with warmest thanks by the first author to Deirdre Wilson for her inspirational teaching and support, and by the second author to Deirdre for sustained friendship over many years. Grateful thanks are also due to two anonymous reviewers and the editors, in particular Robyn Carston, for valuable comments and advice.

Part III

Figurative Language and Layered Interpretations

15 Metaphor and Metonymy in Acquisition: A Relevance-Theoretic Perspective

Ingrid Lossius Falkum

15.1 Introduction

Although most accounts of figurative language distinguish between metaphor and metonymy, they are typically seen as closely related, complementary processes. Traditionally, metaphors such as (15.1) are seen as involving relations of resemblance (e.g., Marit is 'like' a parrot) and metonyms such as (15.2) real-world contiguity relations (e.g., between hats and people wearing them) (Ullmann 1962).

(15.1)   Marit is a *parrot*.

(15.2)   The *hat* is late for school today.

In relevance theory (Sperber & Wilson 1986/1995; Carston 2002; Wilson & Sperber 2004, 2012), where tropes such as metaphor and metonymy are seen as fundamentally communicative phenomena – a matter of language use – metaphor and metonymy have been taken to differ in the pragmatic mechanisms they exploit.[1]

An important recent development in relevance theory is the approach to lexical pragmatics, investigating how word meanings are interpreted and adjusted in accordance with speakers' context-specific expectations of relevance (Carston 1997, 2002; Wilson & Carston 2006, 2007). This account sees the activation of a linguistically encoded concept as the starting point for a pragmatic process of ad hoc concept construction, whose result is a concept that is either narrower or broader than the one encoded (or a combination of the two). Part of this proposal is a deflationary account of metaphor, which treats it as lying at the endpoint of a continuum of conceptual broadening, which also includes other 'loose uses' such as approximation, hyperbole and category extension (Sperber & Wilson 2008).

---

[1] This view is distinct from the widely influential cognitive linguistic account, where metaphor and metonymy are seen as properties of human thought processes, and metaphorical and metonymic uses in language as merely reflecting underlying conceptual structures (Lakoff & Johnson 1980; Lakoff 1987; Gibbs 1994, and many others).

The relevance-theoretic account has been very influential and has given rise to a host of theoretical and empirical research on lexical pragmatics and metaphor in recent years. Metonymy, however, has until quite recently been a somewhat neglected phenomenon in relevance theory. One notable exception is Papafragou's (1996) early account where she analysed metonymic uses as arising from a creative process of naming, that is, as a variety of metarepresentational use of language, distinct from metaphor.

Recently there has been some speculation within relevance theory as to whether metonymy could be brought within the scope of the recent approach to lexical pragmatics and analysed, together with metaphor, as a form of ad hoc concept construction (Carston 2010; Falkum 2011). A unified treatment of the two is tempting given the affinity between metonymy and ad hoc concept construction: both target individual words or phrases, contribute to the proposition expressed, and give rise to a continuum of literal and figurative cases.

In this chapter I approach the distinction between metaphor and metonymy from the perspective of language acquisition. Focusing on what we know about young children's early production of metaphors and metonyms, I argue in favour of maintaining the traditional distinction between the two. Although metonymy shares many characteristics with those language uses that involve ad hoc concept construction, and is often used, both in adult and child language, with communicative functions similar to those associated with metaphor, the developmental data suggests that they may rely on different pragmatic mechanisms.

The chapter is structured as follows. In Section 15.2, I briefly outline the relevance-theoretic account of metaphor and one proposal for a treatment of metonymy, and discuss some implications. In Section 15.3, I discuss the developmental literature on children's ability with metaphor and metonymy, focusing on data from production. I argue that while the cognitive processes underlying early metaphor production have much in common with ad hoc concept construction (Pouscoulous 2011; Wałaszewska 2011), early metonymic uses appear to rely on a different process in which salient associative relations are exploited for referential purposes to fill vocabulary gaps and/or to compensate for limited expressive ability (Wilson & Falkum 2014; Falkum et al. 2017).

15.2   Metaphor and Metonymy in Relevance Theory

Relevance theory takes intended speaker meanings to be derived inferentially from encoded linguistic meanings and assumes that there is a systematic gap between the two (Sperber & Wilson 1986/1995; Carston 2002; Wilson & Sperber 2004, 2012). In bridging this gap, the hearer has to construct appropriate hypotheses about (i) the intended explicit content of the utterance (*explicature*); (ii) the intended contextual assumptions (*implicated premises*), and (iii) the intended contextual assumptions (*implicated conclusions*) (Wilson & Sperber 2004). The hearer achieves this by following a path of least effort in considering interpretive hypotheses, and stopping when the interpretation he arrives at satisfies his expectations of relevance (Wilson & Sperber 2004: 613). Relevance is assessed in terms of the amount of effort invested to process an input and the positive cognitive effects the individual may derive from it (Sperber & Wilson 1986/1995). One of the pragmatic subtasks that the hearer must carry out in arriving at the explicit content of an utterance is to contextually adjust the meanings of individual words. Within relevance theory, this happens as a result of a process of ad hoc concept formation, which takes the encoded concept and a set of associated encyclopaedic assumptions as input, and outputs a concept with either a narrower or broader denotation than the one encoded, consistent with the hearer's occasion-specific expectations of relevance (Carston 1997, 2002; Wilson & Carston 2006, 2007). Consider (15.3)–(15.6):

(15.3)   Sally drives/walks/types *fast*.

(15.4)   The Earth is *round*.

(15.5)   Henrik turned *bald overnight*.

(15.6)   Marit is a *parrot*.

In (15.3), *fast* communicates different concepts depending on the verb it modifies, each of which would be narrower than the one linguistically encoded. In (15.4), *round* is used to express the ad hoc concept ROUND* ('approximately round'), and represents a small departure from the linguistically encoded concept. In (15.5) *bald* and *overnight* are both used hyperbolically and contribute to the interpretation that Henrik lost a lot of hair in a short period of time, and involve a larger departure from the linguistically encoded concepts. In the metaphorical use of *parrot* in (15.6), the construction of the ad hoc concept PARROT* represents a radical departure from the linguistically encoded concept, contributing to the interpretation that Marit tends to repeat what she has heard others say.

The proposal is that each of the examples in (15.3)–(15.6) are outcomes of a single pragmatic process of ad hoc concept formation that adjusts the meanings of individual words in different directions – narrowing in (15.3), different degrees of broadening in (15.4), (15.5) and (15.6) – in accordance with the speaker's expectations of relevance. Furthermore, cases such as (15.4)–(15.6) are seen as forming a continuum of broadening where approximation and metaphor lie at each extreme.

While metaphorical ad hoc concepts have been intensively studied within the relevance-theoretic framework in the last couple of decades, metonymy has received less attention. In an early relevance-theoretic account, Papafragou (1996) analysed metonymy as a variety of metarepresentational use of language involving the introduction of a novel name for a referent. She saw metonymy primarily as a way of economising on the processing effort required for assigning reference (e.g., 'The *hat* is late for school'), but also, secondarily, as a means of achieving cognitive effects that would not be communicated by any literal paraphrase, for instance, by allowing the speaker to express an attitude towards the metarepresented content (e.g., 'The *smelly breath* is approaching'). On Papafragou's account, the hearer must first recognise the metarepresentational use of the expression (by rejecting the 'literal' interpretation of the utterance), and use this as a starting point for deriving the speaker-intended metonymic referent.

This relevance-theoretic account takes metonymy to involve a pragmatic process which is distinct from that underlying metaphor. In Falkum (2011) I questioned the assumption that metonymy should involve the operation of an entirely different process, given the many similarities between metonymy and those language uses that result in ad hoc concept formation, and metaphor in particular. Like ad hoc concept formation, metonymy targets individual words or phrases, contributes to the proposition expressed (e.g., the proposition expressed by 'The *hat* is late for school today' has a person and not a hat as a constituent), and gives rise to a continuum of literal and figurative cases (e.g., from the literal '*Woolf* is a famous writer' to the conventionally metonymic '*Woolf* is on the top shelf' to the novel metonymy '*Woolf* is coming to the party', used to refer to a woman who is obsessed with Woolf's novels). And like ad hoc concept formation, metonymy appears to contribute a concept to the mental representation of the proposition expressed. Furthermore, metonymy and metaphor may serve similar communicative functions; both can be used as referential expressions and as predicates with similar effects, as in (15.7)–(15.8), and it is sometimes difficult to decide whether an expression is used metonymically or metaphorically, as in (15.9)–(15.10).

(15.7)   a. The *pretty face* just went out.
         b. The *pretty doll* just went out.

(15.8)   a. Maria is a *divine voice*.
         b. Maria is a *nightingale*. (examples from Papafragou 1996)

(15.9)   The primary goal of Olympic athletes is to *get on the podium*.

(15.10) The *new Woolf* is giving a public talk tomorrow.

In a discussion of so-called 'free' pragmatic enrichment Carston (2010) describes metonymic uses as a form of ad hoc concept formation:

> [M]etonymic uses present an interesting challenge since they seem to result in an *ad hoc* concept which contributes to explicature (truth-conditional content) but they are not instances of narrowing or broadening of the encoded lexical concept. (Carston 2010: 244)

However, Carston notes that it is not clear exactly how (or even whether) metonymy can be analysed within the general lexical pragmatic approach of relevance theory. As she points out, metonymy clearly does not involve narrowing (e.g., the individuals who wear hats do not constitute a subset of the set of hats) and it does not seem amenable to lexical broadening either. Compare the metaphor in (15.11) with the metonymic use in (15.12):

(15.11) Marit is a *parrot*.

(15.12) The *hat* is late for school today.

In interpreting the metaphor in (15.11), the hearer constructs the broadened ad hoc concept PARROT*, communicating 'someone who repeats other people's utterances' on the basis of encyclopaedic assumptions associated with the concept PARROT (e.g., some parrots can repeat human language). This ad hoc concept overlaps with the encoded concept, and includes actual parrots that satisfy the description and excludes those that do not.[2] However, if the metonymic expression *hat* in (15.12) were taken to communicate the ad hoc concept HAT*, paraphrasable as 'hat-wearing person', this concept would not be broader than the linguistically encoded concept in the sense of having a denotation that includes or overlaps with the linguistically specified one; rather, the concept communicated would be entirely different from the one encoded. That lexical broadening doesn't seem to work as an analysis of metonymic uses is perhaps even clearer if we look at metonymic uses of proper names. If metonymy were a pragmatic process that targeted and adjusted the linguistic meaning of an expression, it is not clear what entity it would operate on in the case of proper names, which arguably do not have any encoded semantic content. For ad hoc concept construction to work in these cases, a referent would have to be assigned to the proper name before the process can operate on a representation of this referent. While this might work for fully established cases such as *Woolf, Dostoyevsky* and so on, it is not clear that it would work in cases where the referent of a name is unknown to the hearer, as in '*Needham* is difficult to read' (Frisson & Pickering 2007) where an accessible interpretation would be

---

[2] This illustrates how metaphors often also involve an element of narrowing (Carston 1997).

'book(s) written by Needham', regardless of whether the hearer has ever heard about this author.

So however tempting it might be to bring metonymy within the scope of the current relevance-theoretic approach to lexical pragmatics and ad hoc concept formation, it is difficult to see how such an account would proceed: metonymy just isn't a case of lexical pragmatic *adjustment* as such. Rather, the concept communicated by a metonymic use is one whose denotation falls outside that of the lexically encoded concept and is linked to the latter via a contextually available association. One option might be to drop the assumption that ad hoc concept formation involves *adjusting* lexical meanings, and treat it as a more general process that turns encoded concepts into different concepts, whose denotations may or may not include or overlap with the ones encoded. One worry here would be that the account loses some of its explanatory appeal. Alternatively, we might drop the idea that metonymic uses communicate ad hoc concepts and assume that they involve a different sort of pragmatic process.

I will now look at metaphor and metonymy from the perspective of language acquisition. The data from children's early spontaneous productions are interesting for the discussion of the distinction between metaphor and metonymy because they suggest that the precursors of the two in development may not be the same. This, in turn, suggests that adult metaphorical and metonymic uses may also rely on different cognitive mechanisms.

15.3   Metaphor and Metonymy in Acquisition

15.3.1   *Comprehension of Metaphor and Metonymy*

By far the most research on figurative language acquisition has focused on children's ability to understand metaphor, a matter of contention in the developmental literature for several decades (for reviews, see Vosniadou 1987; Winner 1988/1997; Gibbs 1994; Pouscoulous 2011). Many early studies of children's metaphor comprehension concluded that this was a complex, late-emerging ability (e.g., Asch & Nerlove 1960; Billow 1975; Winner et al. 1976). However, more recent studies suggest that the lack of understanding was linked to the complexity of the tasks used and attest instead to the presence of an *early* metaphorical ability, with comprehension emerging during the preschool years, even as early as age 3 (Vosniadou et al. 1984; Vosniadou 1987; Pearson 1990; Özçaliskan 2005; Deamer 2013). Only a handful of studies have investigated children's metonymy comprehension, but they all point to an early-emerging ability with an onset around age 3 (Nerlich et al. 1999; Rundblad & Annaz 2010; Van Herwegen et al. 2013; Falkum et al. 2017). Thus, the developmental evidence to date suggests that metaphor and metonymy comprehension emerge around the same time in development, and may follow similar developmental trajectories, although further comparative studies are required to establish this. However, it is in production that the developmental data suggests a clearer distinction between metaphor and metonymy.[3]

15.3.2   Production of Metaphor and Metonymy

A number of studies have reported the occurrence of spontaneous metaphors in the speech of preschool children (Gardner et al. 1978; Winner et al. 1979, 1980; Billow 1981). One example is the 18-month-old boy who called a toy car a *snake* while twisting it up his mother's arm (Winner et al. 1979). Some further attested examples are given below:

(15.13) N (2 years old), called her father a *kiwi* after he had shaved his head and the hair had just started growing back. (Pouscoulous 2011)

(15.14) D (3;3) [points to his eyes, wide open]: Here are my *lights*. Now they *are on*. [then closes his eyes]. Now they *are off*. [reversal]. (Clark, unpublished diary data)

(15.15) V (4;0) [is playing with a toy plough truck]:
Se her. Den kan *åpne gapet sitt*, og den kan *lukke gapet sitt*.
('Look. It can *open its mouth*, and it can *close its mouth*').

(15.16) V (3;8) [is cold from being outside]:
Hvor lenge skal vi gå inn mamma? Jeg *visner*!
('When can we go inside, mummy? I'm *withering*!').

(15.17) V (3;11) [about something he wants his mother to forget]:
Du kan bare *kaste det ut* av hodet ditt.
('You can just *throw it out* of your head')

(15.18) V (4;10) [on the bus. We have passed many parked excavators along the roadside. Then we pass one that's at work]:
Se, en gravemaskin. En som er *levende*.
('Look, an excavator. One that's *alive*'). (Examples
(15.15)–(15.18) from Falkum, unpublished diary data)

---

[3] An anonymous reviewer questioned my choice to focus on production data, pointing out that these are often hard to interpret and typically thought to underestimate children's performance compared to comprehension data. While this is correct, I believe that for the study of figurative language acquisition there is much insight to be gained from early spontaneous production data, especially because controlled comprehension experiments may not be feasible with children at a very young age. However, the conclusions I draw here obviously rest on my interpretation of the production data.

Metonymy as such has not received much focus in the research on children's spontaneous productions, but the developmental literature contains a number of observations of early uses in which children exploit salient associative relations to get a referential meaning across, or to convey some information about the relationship between the referent and some other person, object, property or state. Here are some examples:

(15.19)   H (1;8) is enumerating the lamps in the house, pointing to the first two of them uttering *Light – mehr light*. When she gets to the third lamp, she utters *mehr – Mama*, intending to communicate that the third lamp is next to her mother's favourite chair (Leopold 1949)

(15.20)   H (0;11): *nose* for handkerchief (Werner & Kaplan 1963)

(15.21)   *Nonno* for grandfather's apartment building; *cat* for cat's usual location on top of the TV when absent; *nap* for crib blanket; *peepee* or *doodoo* for toilets, people on the toilet, or hearing the toilet flush (Rescorla 1980; children in her study were aged 1;0–1;8)

(15.22)   *cookie* for bag that had previously contained a cookie; *ball* for mother's tennis racquet (Huttenlocher & Smiley 1987; children in their study were aged 0;13–2;6)

(15.23)   M (1;6) [M wants Dad to turn on light, on which M had previously burned his hand]: *Au, au!* ('Ouch, ouch!'). (Falkum, unpublished diary data)

(15.24)   M (1;7): *Mama* for mother's bathrobe. (Falkum, unpublished diary data)

Such early apparently metaphorical and metonymic uses are sometimes mentioned in discussions of the phenomenon of *overextension* in lexical acquisition, that is, when a child is using a word for a broader range of referents than what is conventional in adult usage (Clark 1973; Bloom 1975; Anglin 1977; Barrett 1978, 1986; Bowerman 1980; Rescorla 1980; Wałaszewska 2011). The most frequently discussed cases of overextension are those based on perceptual similarity, for instance, when a child refers to the moon using the word *ball*, or uses *dog* to refer to any moving animal (Clark 1973). The hypothesis is that the child has overgeneralised the meanings of *ball* and *dog* to the broader categories of 'round things' and 'moving animals' on the basis of similarity of shape, movement, and so on.

Rescorla (1980: 326) distinguishes between three types of overextension: (i) *categorical overinclusions* involve the use of a word to communicate a concept close to the word's conventional meaning in some clear higher-order taxonomic category of adult usage (e.g., *robin* for birds, *car* for vehicles);

(ii) *analogical overextensions* are cases of similarity or analogy between the word's conventional meaning and the communicated meaning but these are not related in any clear categorical sense according to conventional taxonomy (e.g., *ball* for moon, *loud* for spicy food[4]), and (iii) *predicate statements* are based on contextual association, involving 'a word used not for its conventional referent but for a referent normally found in contiguity with it' (e.g., *doll* for usual location of doll in crib when absent).

Early metaphorical uses like (15.13)–(15.18) have been claimed not to qualify as 'real metaphors', comparable to those produced by adults, but to be more appropriately explained as analogical overextensions or instances of pretence, where the child already knows the term for an object but chooses to call it something else in the context of pretend play (Winner 1979; Winner et al. 1980; Vosniadou 1987; Gibbs 1994). The examples in (15.13)–(15.15) might be reanalysed as instances of pretence, while the ones in (15.16)–(15.18) might be reanalysed as overextensions. In the latter case, the hypothesis would be that the child has overgeneralised the meanings of *wither, throw out* and *alive* to broader categories on the basis of similarity or analogy with the conventional category, which would include events of becoming cold and suppressing thoughts for *wither* and *throw out* and moving inanimates for the category of things that are alive.

Overextensions and pretence are indeed sometimes difficult to distinguish from metaphor. As Pouscoulous (2011) notes, some of children's spontaneous non-conventional uses of language, which may seem metaphorical, are probably more appropriately analysed as cases of unintentional mislabellings (e.g., *loud* for spicy food). Others are difficult to distinguish from pretence, like the use of *mouth* in (15.15). However, it seems clear that the cognitive processes at work in overextension and pretence share common features with those enabling the production of fully fledged metaphors, and analysing all of children's early spontaneous uses as cases of unintentional mislabellings or pretence may underestimate their metaphorical abilities (Vosniadou 1987; Pouscoulous 2011).

When young children have not acquired the conventional term to express a particular meaning, one option they have available to them is to overextend the meaning of a word they have already learned (Clark 1978, 2009). In producing an overextension, the child chooses a word which she thinks 'fits' the target referent best, relying on this to guide the hearer in working out her communicative intention (Clark 1978). If overextension is a pragmatic strategy to fill vocabulary gaps, some early metaphorical uses might plausibly be seen

---

[4] M (1;11) [tastes a spicy Thai curry for the first time. Covers his ears with his hands]: *Øt!* (= the Norwegian adjective *høyt*, 'loud'). (Falkum, unpublished diary data).

as instances of a child trying out a new label for a given referent. The child might suspect that the label she has chosen is inappropriate but it is the best available option for her communicative purposes, one that will probably be sufficient to guide the hearer to her intended meaning (Pouscoulous 2011). Such cases of intentional misuses have a clear affinity with broadening and ad hoc concept formation: 'There is just one step to cross from deliberately extending the meaning of a term beyond the limits of its suspected literal sense to intentionally using an expression metaphorically' (Pouscoulous 2011: 65). While Pouscoulous calls such intentional misuses 'the perfect stepping stone for metaphor production' (Pouscoulous 2011: 68), Wałaszewska (2011) goes as far as treating them as genuine instances of broadened ad hoc concepts. But notice that the cognitive process underlying the production of unintentional mistakes such as *ball* for 'moon' or *loud* for 'spicy' is also closely related to the one enabling the production of broadened ad hoc concepts in the form of intentional misuses and fully fledged metaphors. In all three cases, a broader concept is constructed on the basis of encyclopaedic information associated with instances of the conventional denotation of the chosen expression.

With regard to pretence, the similarity between this process and metaphor has led scholars to suggest that some of the cognitive processes involved may the same, to the extent that if children are able to achieve one, they can also do the other (Vosniadou 1987; Pouscoulous 2011). One important parallel between metaphor and pretence is the presence of some form of analogy, where some properties of the literal denotation are shared with the metaphorical or fictional one. Another is the intentional use of non-literal labels, involving the conscious violation of adult category boundaries, which preschoolers do regularly in the context of pretend play. A plausible hypothesis, then, is that pretence is a precursor of metaphor, in which some of the same cognitive abilities are involved. However, an important difference between metaphor and pretence is that only metaphor is properly communicative, while a communicative context is not necessary for pretend play; thus, their functions are different (Pouscoulous 2011).

Early metonymic uses such as (15.19)–(15.24) have been discussed in the developmental literature as instances of overextension of the predicate statement type, but in contrast to the early 'metaphorical' uses, the connection with metonymy has not been drawn. On this view, the examples above would count as instances where the child has overgeneralised the meaning of the word to a heterogeneous categories of things, a so-called 'complexive category', based on a contiguity relation (Werner & Kaplan 1963; Bowerman 1980). For instance, *nose* in (15.20) would denote both noses and handkerchiefs, and *cat* in (15.21) both cats and their usual locations. However, the overextension analysis has been questioned on the basis that it seems implausible. For instance, Huttenlocher and Smiley (1987) discuss the examples in (15.22) of a child being observed seeing a cookie in a school bag, and uttering *cookie* when he later saw the same bag closed, and of another child uttering *ball* upon seeing his mother's tennis racquet. In these cases, they argue, it seems unlikely that the child genuinely thinks that cookies and school bags, or balls and tennis racquets, are instances of the same categories, as in true cases of overextension. Bloom (2000: 37) makes a similar observation:

Children have been observed to point to a cookie jar and say 'cookie'. One might say that this reflects a confound confusion: the child thinks that the word refers not only to cookies but to all cookie-related entities. But perhaps the child thinks that there is a cookie in the cookie jar, doesn't know the words for jar and in, and is expressing her thought in a sensible way.

Bloom's example illustrates that from the earliest stages of communication, children exploit salient associative relations in their productions to get their meanings across. When children lack the conventional term for an entity, they can refer to it by using a familiar term that refers to something that is saliently associated with that particular entity. Many of the early symbolic gestures infants make use of, both in the pre-linguistic stage and later in combination with one-word utterances, are based on associative relations between the gesture and the meaning represented. Examples are clapping hands for 'baseball game', smacking lips for 'food', peeling gesture for 'banana', pointing to the sky for 'airplane' and so on (Acredolo & Goodwyn 1988). Among the earliest referring expressions acquired by children are onomatopoeia such as *bow-wow* ('dog'), *vroom-vroom* ('vehicle'), *grrr* ('lion'), which, although they vary in degree of conventionality, are based on salient associative relations between the sound represented and the object being referred to. Arguably, early metonymic uses such as those in (15.19)–(15.24) have more in common with these processes than they have with overextension and metaphor, although their communicative function – to fill vocabulary gaps – is often the same.

In overextension and metaphor, the speaker uses an already acquired expression whose denotation shares some properties with the intended referent. In the case of unintentional mistakes, that is, genuine cases of overextension, the child falsely believes that the expression used also has the intended referent as part of its denotation. This is not ad hoc concept formation as such, but the process is similar in that the child has generalised, on the basis of some shared property (or properties), from a particular instance or category to a broader category. In intentional misuses, which give rise to some of the spontaneous metaphors reported in the developmental literature, the child has acquired the conventional meaning of the expression used, but not the one for the intended denotation. The category expressed by use of the term is deliberately extended to cover the intended denotation, taking encyclopaedic information associated with the denotation of the encoded expression (e.g., in (15.18) that 'things that are alive move') as input in forming the ad hoc concept (e.g., ALIVE*). It is possible to see this as a genuine case of broadening by ad hoc concept formation (Wałaszewska 2011).

Children's early metonymic uses are arguably different from this. In these uses the child does not plausibly believe that the expression chosen includes the target referent as part of its denotation, as in genuine overextension, nor does she extend its meaning on the basis of shared denotational properties, as in intentional misuses. Rather, she uses a familiar expression for an entity to refer to something that is for her saliently associated with that particular entity, relying on the hearer to make the connection between the two and identify her intended referent. Although these uses, where the child does not know or is unable to produce the conventional expression for the referent in question, are clearly different from metonymic uses by adults (which involve deliberate exploitation of a contextually salient association between two entities by use of a lexical term that conventionally refers to one of the entities to refer metonymically to the other), they too presuppose an ability to make use of salient associations between objects and events for the purpose of communication. This makes them, to use Pouscoulous's (2011) words, 'the perfect stepping stone to metonymy'.

15.4   Concluding Remarks

To sum up, I think the data from children's early spontaneous productions suggest that metaphor and metonymy may involve distinct pragmatic processes, although the similarities between them are many. While the cognitive processes underlying metaphor production share common features with those involved in the production of overextensions and pretence, early metonymic uses may be the outcome of a more basic process in which salient associative relations are exploited for referential purposes in making up for vocabulary gaps, and where an analysis in terms of the construction of 'complexive categories' – i.e., overextensions – does not seem plausible. This is arguably the same process that underlies many other early productions by children, including symbolic gestures and onomatopoeia, among others. However, both processes are inherently communicative: it is children's strong drive to communicate that leads them to choose expressions which they think 'fit' their target referents best, or are saliently associated with them, and rely on this to guide the hearer to their intended meanings. This is also what enables them to produce fully fledged metaphors and metonyms as they grow older.

Acknowledgements

This chapter is a small token of my gratitude to Deirdre Wilson, who introduced me to relevance theory when I was an MA student in pragmatics at UCL in

2004, and whose ideas about language and communication have been a great source of inspiration ever since. I thank Deirdre for her continuous support, generosity, warmth, humour and friendship. This chapter is based on many of her ideas about lexical pragmatics, and our ongoing joint work on metonymy.

This research was funded by a Young Research Talent Grant from the Research Council of Norway (project no. 240324). I would like to thank Robyn Carston, Billy Clark and Kate Scott for their support in writing this chapter and an anonymous referee for helpful feedback.

16 Relevance and Metaphor Understanding in a Second Language

Elly Ifantidou

16.1 Introduction

Studies on metaphor in a second language (L2) often assume that successful metaphor comprehension and production involve the ability to understand one entity in terms of another (see, for example, Cameron 2003; Littlemore & Low 2006; Littlemore 2008; Piquer-Píriz 2008; Li 2009; Low et al. 2010; Chung-hong Leung & Crisp 2011; Jin & Cortazzi 2011; Komorowska 2013; Miller 2013; Robisco Martín & Cuadrado Esclápez 2013). In these studies, scholars aim to build on the ability of participants to elicit mappings from a source to a target entity, by connecting, for example, the expression *to have a certain viewpoint* to the conceptual metaphor UNDERSTANDING IS SEEING (Golden 2010). Beyond the conceptual metaphor paradigm (Lakoff & Johnson 1980; Littlemore & Taylor 2014), little evidence exists on L2 metaphoric interpretation.

My aim in this chapter is to show that metaphor comprehension in L2 is less structured and less bound up with conventionally expressed conceptual metaphors than standardly assumed. Adopting a relevance-theoretic approach, I will argue that metaphors trigger an optimally relevant interpretation which is activated by an emotional response to the situation represented by the metaphor. Emphasis will be placed on discussing second language learners' preference for metaphors when asked to choose which of a range of inferential routes have guided them in arriving at particular interpretations. I will suggest that the emotional response extends to all metaphors, as predicted by Carston's account (2010). The questions I would like to raise relate to assumptions about the processing load incurred by metaphors. If metaphors are costly, as suggested by comprehension difficulties (Vosniadou et al. 1984) and longer reading times (Gerrig & Healy 1983; Gregory & Mergler 1990; Noveck et al. 2001; Olkoniemi et al. 2016), would this extra effort make them more likely than other inferential tools to be identified by addressees as having played a role in interpretation? Recent experiments confirmed that metaphor familiarity correlated with decreased neural activity (Cardillo et al. 2012) whereas novelty is more likely related to higher processing effort (Bohrn et al. 2013). In the same vein,

Schmidt and Seger (2009) support the idea that unfamiliar, non-conventional metaphors, such as *Dictionaries are microscopes of words* (Schmidt & Seger 2009: 384), involve semantic features and relationships which are harder to identify. I am assuming that in English as a foreign language (EFL) settings, too, processing load is increased when encountering difficulty with the semantics of words used metaphorically (on processes affecting reading comprehension in L2, see Grabe and Stoller 2011). If, on the other hand, metaphors are as effortful to process as literal counterparts (Gibbs 1994, 2002; Weiland et al. 2014), the question remains whether metaphors would be preferred during interpretation over other inferential tools, namely evidentials, referring expressions and irony. I will suggest that non-native language users' preference for metaphors can be explained on a relevance-theoretic account in which metaphors are seen as instances of loose use[1] triggered by affective values of words in a context which is adjusted to the addressee's prior experience. As a result of automatic processing, familiar and conventional metaphors may elicit concrete interpretations, as in example (16.1). The less familiar metaphors I am interested in elicit an array of schematic interpretations which rely on imagery and emotions as much as on propositional content, as illustrated by interpretations received from participants of this study in example (16.2):[2]

(16.1)   *roots of catastrophe* lie in the policies of governments ⇒ causes of catastrophe

(16.2)   a type of *warfare* which *triggered a special repugnance* from countries which regard themselves as upholding moral standards ⇒
   a. war brings out a particular reaction
   b. war has always caused opposition and aversion
   c. war which will dishonour countries with high moral standards
   d. 'dirty' warfare is considered especially immoral
   e. Western countries should pay closer attention to the war in Syria
   f. got a positive behaviour from these countries
   g. got help from these countries

(16.2a–g) make manifest stronger and weaker implications, some of which are not licensed by the linguistic context, e.g. d–g. Could these be types of imagistic, autobiographical, or emotional reactions to the topic of the metaphor? I will sketch an answer in Section 16.5.

---

[1] My analysis in terms of loose use (and lexical narrowing and broadening in relevance-theoretic terms) does not involve the more recent account in terms of *ad hoc concepts* that assumes the replacement or adjustment of literal lexical meanings.

[2] 'Conventional' does not necessarily imply 'familiar' in EFL contexts. Hence, the seemingly fairly conventional metaphor in (16.2) was the least familiar to the majority of the participants (86 per cent) in this study.

Despite traditional views on metaphors evoking non-propositional effects such as feelings, insights, images (see Burke 1757; Black 1954–1955; Davidson 1978/1984), less attention has been paid to the fact that as well as identifying a referent, metaphors trigger emotional responses such as affection or dislike. By adopting views first expressed in Burke (1757) and recently by Carston (2010), I will suggest that metaphors aid comprehension by being vehicles for emotions, especially in texts which impede accurate reading due to fragmented lexical meaning (De Bruyn 2012: 277). Emotions connect to their cognitive bases: perceptions, memories, previous experiences, imagining, beliefs. In effect, each type of emotion prompts a distinct type of evaluative judgement or attitude. Mary judges that the joke is funny because she is amused by it and Peter judges that the idea is untenable because he is made anxious by it (Deonna & Teroni 2012). I have argued elsewhere that fairly conventional metaphors (e.g. *Susan is an angel*, *My lawyer is a shark*) are commonly used by addressees as means of persuasion in an argument for or against specific claims (Ifantidou 2014: 95). I would like to suggest that metaphors can evoke justified emotions when processing linguistically underdetermined content, as in EFL settings. Next, I sketch two theoretical frameworks which have been extensively used to explain how metaphors are understood.

16.2   On Metaphor Understanding

In the experimental cognitive linguistic literature, the predominant question is whether metaphors are understood as conceptual mappings. Experimental work suggests that people are more likely to use source–target mappings when these are primed by a simile or an 'A is B' metaphor or when novel rather than conventional metaphors are used (Krennmayr 2011: 273–7). However, a body of psycholinguistic literature suggests that conceptual metaphors are automatically inferred when interpreting conventional metaphors (Gibbs 2015a). A related question is whether it makes a difference if people have time to think. Evidence from judgement studies shows that conceptual information is accessible when people can reflect on the appropriateness of conventional metaphors (e.g. *blow her top*, *bite his head off*). But evidence from reading and reaction time studies suggests that metaphors consistent with the intended conceptual mapping are not read faster (Glucksberg et al. 1993). In other words, to comprehend conventional metaphors, people do not necessarily resort to conceptual mappings.

As suggested above, ideas from cognitive linguistics (Lakoff & Johnson 1980) have informed experimental settings which rely on people's familiarity with conceptual schemata residing in memory and prior experience. For example, we understand the metaphorical expressions *winning*, *battle* and *defence* in a business text, and *construct*, *collapse*, *shaky* in arguments, by accessing the conceptual metaphors BUSINESS IS WAR and ARGUMENTS ARE

BUILDINGS, respectively. In other words, within cognitive linguistics, conceptual metaphors are seen as structuring the human mind by being pre-established and context-independent, hence systematic and recurring in language.

Relevance theory, on the other hand, is concerned with metaphor as contributing to verbal communication (Sperber & Wilson 2008: 84) rather than thought. On the relevance-theoretic account, language is merely evidence for an open array of interpretations which addressees freely derive from perception, memory or inference. I will next turn to a poetic metaphor discussed by Sperber and Wilson (2008), which illustrates the type of inferential processing I would like to discuss in Sections 16.3 and 16.5. As suggested in the introduction, metaphors may trigger an array of non-propositional effects (an experience or feeling) rather than a more or less definite, truth-evaluable propositional content. Consider the following metaphor, from Carl Sandberg's poem 'Fog':

(16.3)   The fog comes
          on little cat feet
          It sits looking
          over harbor and city

          on silent haunches
          and then moves on

According to Sperber and Wilson (2008), the interpretation of ON-LITTLE-CAT-FEET* is inferred by assigning to the movement of fog the properties of silence, smoothness, stealth, properties which are not part of the linguistically encoded meaning of the phrase 'on-little-cat-feet'. Combined with the following four lines, the phrase elicits a movement which seems relaxed yet tense, or mysterious. As Carston (2010) observes, in cases of 'extended' metaphors such as this, the open-ended array of effects is inferred as part of an aesthetic experience or an impression which readers retrieve by drawing on their sensorimotor experience and memory.

But what happens if single words used in metaphors are unknown? What processing route may addressees follow given their abilities and preferences? I will next turn to examples of linguistic and non-linguistic types of cultural human artefact which may be hard to pin down with accuracy and precision yet attract attention and evoke an aesthetic experience in which a personal and imagistic element play a dominant role.

16.3   Metaphors and 'Beyond-Meaning' Effects

Arguing against the idea of pre-established mappings, Sperber (1975) discussed the idea that we have considerable freedom to connect 'any two terms' whereby one becomes the symbol of the other in an inferential, meta-phorical relation. The 'symbolic use of figurative language' (Sperber 1975: 27) can be seen in Balzac's pairing between leaving one's hat in the lobby of a gambling house and the passion for gambling.[3] Sperber considers the connection between the fact of leaving one's hat in the lobby and a passion for gambling poorly motivated, circumstantial, and hence arbitrary. Given that 'the motiv-ation of symbols is [often] arbitrary ... any pairing at all may be motivated, but none may be predicted' (Sperber 1975: 28). For example, Balzac's meta-phor may evoke a series of symbolic representations which are conceivable but not generalisable: of the law (stripping the gambler of his hat), of respect (to those who will win his money), of self-loss (by analogy to hat loss) (Sperber 1975: 28). According to Sperber, these relations are as poorly motivated as the first relationship, and conceivable only because of a previously established arbitrary link: between leaving one's hat in the lobby of a gambling house and the passion for gambling. Symbolic relations are purposely ambiguous, fig-urative, imaginary, often motivated neither by logic nor natural resemblance, hence idiosyncratic. They are, in Sperber's terms, 'defective'[4] types of input to inferential processing which yield 'a potentially indefinite number of new metaphors, dream-like associations' rather than truth-evaluable propositions (Sperber 1975: 93, 103, 105, 141, 144).

That stimuli are sometimes defective, i.e. incomplete, or ambiguous albeit interpretable, has been postulated in neurological accounts of ambiguity.[5] Zeki (2004) argued that the brain is flexible enough to acquire knowledge from and assign meaning to ambiguous or incomplete stimuli such as abstract compositions, subtle paintings, unfinished geometrical figures and sculptures. Among several examples, Zeki discusses the girl's facial expression in Johannes Vermeer's *Girl with a Pearl Earring* as being inviting yet remote, chaste yet sensuous, annoyed yet pleased.

Incomplete, fragmented stimuli can be interpreted too. German art his-torian Johann Winckelmann depicted his ideal of Greek beauty with great detail and accuracy despite the badly damaged and incomplete fragment of the famous *Torso Belvedere*. His emotional response to a visual experience (North 2012: 5–6) allowed him to perceive it as 'the high ideal of ... mature manly years ... elevated to a state of divine contentment ... in apparent calm and stillness, which recall the blissful self-absorption of ideal youth ... charged by intimations of the naked physical power of a hero laying waste all that came in

---

[3] In the opening passage of Balzac's novel *La Peau de Chagrin*.

[4] 'Defective input' refers to conceptual representations which cannot be evaluated in terms of the way the world really is (Sperber 1975: 144).

[5] Ambiguity is here defined as 'uncertain, open to more than one interpretation, doubtful' (Oxford Dictionary of English) and on a neurobiological definition as 'an attribute that heightens sub-stantially the artistic and aesthetic merit of a work' (Zeki 2004).

his way' (Potts 1994: 179). The girl's face and the *Torso Belvedere* are compelling instances of how a subtle image and an incomplete fragment may receive one interpretation, the viewer's, at any given moment under the influence of memory and experience, despite the fact that there is no correct or ultimate meaning but several equally valid interpretations (Zeki 2004: 192).

In literary genres, the idea of schematic thoughts eliciting further sets of thoughts has been discussed with reference to poetic closure (Fabb 2016), and experimentally attested by Bohrn et al. (2013).[6] Fabb showed that an effortful process such as the end of a poem can be gratifying due to the uncertainty of the interpretation of a closure that creates a pleasurable aesthetic effect. In earlier work, Fabb (2002) argued that linguistic form is experienced as aesthetic when it is complex, indeterminate, ambiguous and contradictory, i.e. in tension with the content of the text on particular instances of written or spoken performance. In a functional magnetic resonance imaging (fMRI) experiment, Bohrn et al. (2013) isolated activations pertaining to an aesthetic experience by ruling out judgement making. The study supported the claim that reading is facilitated by an implicit aesthetic evaluation during which the neural correlates recruit the emotion system in a similar way to the aesthetic perception of visual art (Bohrn et al. 2013: 3). In other words, rewarding effects derived while reading tap into our semantic and aesthetic perceptual abilities alike. As Bohrn et al. observe, spontaneous aesthetic evaluation takes place independently of familiarity evaluation. This may mean that in cases of written text, fragmented (due to unfamiliar words) linguistic decoding can elicit an aesthetic or moral evaluation, e.g. pleasure/pain, goodness/badness, reward/aversion (Bohrn et al. 2013: 4). I will call these 'beyond-meaning' effects.

That emotions may sometimes take over lexical meaning is supported by neuroimaging experiments which suggest that the emotional aspects of words are processed rapidly and automatically with onset at 60–80 ms, whereas lexical access is taken to occur after 200 ms (Wang & Bastiaansen 2014). Such very early emotion effects suggest that emotion affects word processing pre-lexically, that is, before the lexical meaning is activated, or when a minimum degree of linguistic processing has taken place (Citron 2012; see also Dudschig et al. 2014; Htsu et al. 2015). Moreover, the neurophysiological evidence suggests that controlled word recognition is subserved by memory and affect (see Cato et al. 2004; Kuchinke et al. 2005; see also Schacht & Sommer 2009; Mar et al. 2011; Citron 2012).

Further evidence from neuroscience shows that metaphorical sentences activate emotion-related regions of the brain and are more emotionally evocative than their literal counterparts, mainly through their grounding from affective

---

[6] See Bohrn et al. (2013) for more experimental evidence on emotional reactions to literature/poetry.

experiences (Aziz-Zadeh & Gamez-Djokic 2016). This is the case with taste metaphors, such as those in example (16.4):

(16.4)   She looked at him *sweetly*.
His statements about marriage are *rotten*.
The break up was *bitter* for him.

The examples I discussed in this section have an aesthetic or symbolic value rather than a truth-evaluable content which truly or falsely represents worldly states, and they evoke emotional effects which in turn motivate acts of inference. The results presented next are in line with this type of evidence, in that metaphors attract addressees' attention and when non-fully propositional, elicit affective values of pleasure/displeasure and arousal.

16.4   Methodology

16.4.1   Rationale

The study set out to answer two questions related to metaphor comprehension. Firstly, why would metaphors be attractive to a significantly larger number of participants among a range of inferential tools offered as cues to interpretation? Secondly, why are metaphors plausibly interpreted when lexical meaning is not fully grasped?

16.4.2   Participants

Sixty native Greek speakers, undergraduate students (5 male, 55 female) of the Department of English Language and Literature, National and Kapodistrian University of Athens, Greece, age range 18 to 22, optionally took part in the study (spring 2016) for extra credit in the compulsory course *Genres in English*. Their performance in the Language Progress test (24_2_2016) (excellent score: 60) was relatively good ($M = 46, 2, SD = 9.7$). Relative to the score range, performances were distinguished in terms of language proficiency levels. The majority of participants were at C1–C2 level of language proficiency (62 per cent), and the fewest were at B1–B2 level (38 per cent).

16.4.3   Procedure – Materials

In testing preference for metaphors, two editorials were used from *The Wall Street Journal* ('Hope at last in Venezuela', www.wsj.com/articles/hope-at-last-in-venezuela-1449534184) and *The Guardian* ('The Guardian view on Venezuela's plight: both bad luck and bad management', www.theguardian.com/commentisfree/2016/may/19/the-guardian-view-on-venezuelas-plight-both-bad-luck-and-bad-management). In testing metaphor comprehension, a random selection of metaphors from twelve British and US broadsheet or electronic newspaper editorials were assessed for degree of similarity to Greek metaphors. Editorials were used as stimuli for having large numbers of novel, creative metaphors (Krennmayr 2011), and hence serving as better candidate-stimuli for unfamiliar metaphors in EFL. The editorials used did not differ when assessed for their metaphors' similarity to Greek metaphors by two linguists (the author and a colleague): the raters' evaluation on a 1–4 scale (1: no similarity, 2: moderate, 3: strong, 4: perfect similarity) did not differ ($X^2 = 0.984$, $df = 3$, *Sig. (2-sided)* = 0.805). Chi-square analysis showed that type of metaphor did not correlate with metaphors occurring in the editorials used ($X^2 = 12.407$, $df = 12$, *Sig. (2-sided)* = 0.414). Therefore, the texts did not vary in respect to the type of metaphors used.

In testing *preference* for metaphors, participants were asked to read two editorials on the same topic, evaluate the views put forward, and provide linguistic evidence that guided them in their search for the attitudes adopted. Linguistic evidence involved participants' choice among metaphors, evidentials, referring expressions and irony, and use of the selected inferential routes to justify the inferences retrieved. In testing metaphor *comprehension*, participants completed six tests, three of which were administered before and three after interventions. Interventions involved discussions of editorials and inferential tools, use of meta-language, written assignments and feedback offered in terms of explicit instruction. Interventions followed the pre-test and preceded the post-test.

Test 1 required participants to choose the correct interpretation of the metaphor from four options offered. Test 2 asked participants to identify the source concept, the target concept and a feature shared. Test 3 required participants to infer two implicatures derived from a metaphor. For each test, participants were asked to note unknown words. Participants were also asked to provide the meaning of unknown words.

16.5   Results – Discussion

On preference, Table 5 shows the frequency of metaphors selected and interpreted by participants compared to evidentials, referring expressions and irony during their search for linguistic evidence for or against particular claims put forward in editorials.

The difference is statistically significant ($t(59) = -2.049$, $p < 0.01$). In other words, metaphor was selected by a statistically significant greater number of participants compared to the other features. The second column shows number of instances of each feature in the two texts.

On comprehension, in Tests 1 and 3 participants performed at equal rates before and after interventions, respectively (Test 1: Mean score 7.13 and 7.12; Test 3: Mean score 5.8 and 6.0). In Test 2, participants scored lower before (Mean 5.0) but significantly higher (Mean 8.7, ($t(59) = -7.48$, $p < 0.01$))

Table 5 *Frequencies per feature selected by participants, and occurrences in stimuli texts*

	Selected by	Occurrences in editorials
	%	N
Metaphors	94	29
Evidentials	63	28
Referring expressions (to individuals or groups)	43	29
Irony	41	27

after interventions. In all tests, participants noted a considerable number of unknown words in the metaphors tested (before interventions: Test 1: 86%, Test 2: 48%, Test 3: 30%; after interventions: Test 1: 53%, Test 2: 33%, Test 3: 53%). When checking for correlations, it was shown that participants' scores in the six tests did not correlate with number of unknown words identified, which suggests that they interpreted correctly the metaphors regardless of the number of unknown words encountered. Given this evidence on participants' preference for, and competence in comprehension of, fragmented metaphors, I would like to concentrate on certain examples and provide a qualitative discussion of tendencies observed in participants' reactions to the metaphors tested. In discussing the evidence, I will use relevance theory's treatment of loose use and 'non-propositional' effects, such as emotions, images, sensorimotor processes, and their role in the interpretation of metaphors (see Wilson 2018).

In the following examples, readers risk interpreting metaphors which communicate fragmentary propositional meaning but are relevant enough to attract attention and encourage a search for inferred, non-propositional effects. The unknown words discussed in examples (16.5–16.8) were identified by the majority of participants (*repugnance* 86%, *crumbling* 74%, *plight* 68%, *grinding* 62%). In example (16.5) *repugnance* was identified as an unknown word and participants guessed that it indicated 'disgust, distaste, an undesirable reaction, less interest, reluctance, importance, reaction, dishonour'.

(16.5)   The world would be averting its gaze from a **warfare** which has always **triggered** a special **repugnance** from countries which regard themselves as upholding moral standards.

From left ('disgust') to right ('dishonour'), narrower and broader definitions were provided by participants, possibly primed by the contextual cues *averting its gaze* and *warfare*. However, certain meanings, such as 'dishonour' are not directly linked to the contextual cues, whereas others, such as 'disgust, distaste', coincided with the literal content of the word[7] reported as 'unknown'.

In example (16.6) *crumbling* was identified as an unknown word and was interpreted as 'breaking into pieces, becoming weaker' and 'weaker, troubled'.

(16.6)   But it could also lead to disaster, if the **crumbling regime** is
          replaced by the jihadist forces of the Islamic state or al-Qaeda,
          as already occurred in eastern Syria.

A narrow definition is given ('breaking into pieces'), which bypasses contextual cues: *disaster* and *replaced by* would trigger a broader interpretation along the lines of a 'defeated' or 'fallen' regime. The response 'troubled' (political situation) suggests that the participant has loosened the meaning of *crumbling*. It is a broader interpretation than the type of interpretation the linguistic cues *disaster* and *replaced by* would evoke.

In example (16.7) *plight* was identified as an unknown word and was defined as 'terrible situation, suffering and helplessness, crisis, situation, mass, a lot of people'.

(16.7)   The immigrants' **plight paints a horrific picture** of a regionwide
          network of human trafficking.

In the interpretation 'terrible situation, suffering' and 'helplessness', enrichment seems to narrow to certain aspects of contextual meaning: a *horrific picture* of *immigrants* may imply homelessness, discrimination, exploitation, death, but why helplessness and suffering? On a similar narrow interpretation, *plight* was interpreted as 'mass, a lot of people'. *The immigrants* could be two or more people with no indication in the linguistic context of how many they actually were. Why 'mass, a lot of people'? On the other hand, 'crisis' is a loose interpretation of *plight*. Given the contextual cue *horrific picture*, an interpretation along the lines of 'disaster, catastrophe' or 'tragedy' should be easier to retrieve. So why 'crisis'? Similarly, when interpreting *plight* as 'situation', participants broadened and toned down the meaning of the metaphorical word, as if ignoring the linguistic cues *horrific picture* and *human trafficking*.

A similar pattern seems to emerge in example (16.8):

(16.8)   For two years, the regime of Bashar al-Assad has appeared to have
          the upper hand in Syria's **grinding civil war**, thanks to the heavy
          intervention of Iranian-sponsored militias and criminal tactics.

For *grinding*, participants suggested the explanations 'grinder, shaking, harsh, tough, ongoing, cruel', where, apart from the literal meaning ('grinder'),

---

[7] See https://dictionary.cambridge.org/dictionary/english/repugnant.

broader interpretations which go beyond the linguistic cues were provided. Overall, the meanings obtained seem to approximate the literal content of the word used metaphorically (*repugnance*=disgust, *crumbling*=break down, *plight*=terrible situation, *grinding*=grinder), to be primed by contextual cues (*repugnance*=undesirable reaction, *grinding*=ongoing) or to ignore contextual cues (*repugnance*=dishonour; *plight*=situation, mass of people, *grinding*=widespread, poverty and damage, *crumbling*=troubled).

The wide range of meanings obtained raised the question of whether there was anything that they shared, which was perhaps not very obvious, and perhaps non-linguistic too. Using Bradley and Lang's (1999) norming of emotional ratings for a large number of English words, it turned out that the majority of participants used expressions which have negative or positive valence rates, and overall similar emotional ratings (if we also take into consideration arousal means). On a 1-to-9 scale rating of whether one feels happy or unhappy (valence) while reading individual words, the words used by 95 and 81 per cent of participants to define unknown words in pre- and post-intervention tests are of clearly negative and clearly positive affective value, as shown by the examples in Table 6.[8]

Based on this evidence, I would like to suggest that vague and indeterminate meanings of words used metaphorically are types of 'descriptively ineffable' meaning (see also Wharton & Strey this volume). For second language users, 'descriptively ineffable' meaning is impossible to represent conceptually due to its unfamiliar lexical content. Therefore, interpreting a metaphor will tap into participants' emotional reaction more than its propositional meaning. In other words, addressees seem to be attracted to metaphors because they derive non-propositional effects by drawing on their emotional attitude to the images and sensorimotor processes which metaphors evoke. This is supported by metaphor interpretations derived when lexical meaning is hard to pin down but relevant enough to trigger affective values in the form of high- or low-valence words used to describe fragmentary propositional meaning. Despite elliptical lexical content, processing effort is reduced because metaphors create a bond with the readers which is emotion-driven and often autobiographical too. Compared to evidentials, irony and referring expressions, metaphors attract readers' attention because they convey a certain import which can be broader than the notion of meaning in the sense that they trigger 'beyond-meaning' effects (images and emotions), and hence are able to evoke interpretive effects which are weakly communicated (i.e. neither anticipated nor endorsed by the

---

[8] I am not assuming that emotions are two-dimensional (see Fontaine et al. 2007; Scherer 2009) but that the interplay of two psychological primitives is preliminary evidence that at least two basic affective properties such as valence and arousal play a role in participants' interpretation of unknown words metaphorically used.

Table 6 *Emotional ratings for words used by participants to explain unknown words (Bradley & Lang 1999)*

	Valence Mean	Arousal Mean
broken (for *crumbling*)	3.05	5.43
trouble (for *crumbling*)	3.03	6.85
disgust (for *repugnance*)	2.45	5.42
crisis (for *plight*)	2.74	5.44
terrible (for *plight*)	1.93	6.27
helpless (for *plight*)	2.20	5.34
cruel (for *grinding*)	1.97	5.68
desire (for *repugnance*)	7.69	7.35
honour (for *repugnance*)	7.66	5.90
interest (for *repugnance*)	6.97	5.66
people (for *plight*)	7.33	5.94

communicator) (see Wilson 2018). These are not meanings or a message that addressees can easily bring to consciousness and define. They are emotional phenomena (aspects of words, values, states experienced) which, once evoked, help increase the rewarding effects conveyed and minimise the processing effort caused by descriptively ineffable types of language use. The overall evidence suggests that metaphor and emotion processing are tightly linked together, which may help develop a more realistic answer to how metaphorical uses of language are understood.

16.6   Conclusion

I have argued that metaphors are preferred as a tool of comprehension among a range of inferential routes and that they are plausibly interpreted when propositional meaning is not fully recoverable. This is supported by the finding that participants more frequently retrieved metaphors from newspaper editorials when also given a choice among evidentials, irony and referring expressions. Based on the test results for metaphor, I suggested that unfamiliar words in metaphors may function like trails left by previously experienced situations in which words may have been learnt, heard or spoken. As a result, single words may trigger images, sensorimotor processes and emotional attitudes experienced at the time. As noted by Deonna and Teroni (2012), emotions are not always directed at propositions but at episodes, such as episodic memory and sensory imagining. It is in virtue of awareness of a salient experiential feeling that we apprehend the world in evaluative terms, e.g. of the significance or pleasantness of events for our well-being and goal achievement. Fragmented metaphors are similar to Johann Winckelmann's fragment of *Torso Belvedere*, the extended metaphor in Carl Sandburg's poem *Fog* or Johannes Vermeer's *Girl with a Pearl Earring*, whereby incomplete, subtle and unusual, or ambiguous stimuli invite different interpretations, only one of which is retrievable at any given moment. Building on the relevance-theoretic view that acts of linguistic communication provide blueprints for an open array of interpretations derived from perception, memory or inference helps to accommodate the data I have focused on here and to account for it within a more comprehensive model of metaphoric competence as applied to second language pragmatics.

Acknowledgements

This chapter is a modest token of my deep gratitude for the inspiration, support and friendship that Deirdre Wilson has so generously given me over the years.

The author wishes to express her gratitude to the audiences of the *15th IPrA* (Belfast) and the *1st Beyond Meaning* (Athens) international conferences, for thought-provoking comments. Special thanks to Anne Bezuidenhout, Nigel Fabb, Anna Hatzidaki, Tzeni Liontou, Louis de Saussure, Goni Togia, Tim Wharton and Deirdre Wilson for stimulating discussions, and to the editors of this volume for constructive suggestions. Of course, all inadequacies remain those of the author.

17 Component Processes of Irony Comprehension in Children: Epistemic Vigilance, Mind-Reading and the Search for Relevance

Tomoko Matsui

17.1 Introduction

Comprehension of irony may be characterised by the recognition of a substantial gap between what the speaker said and what the speaker intended to communicate by an utterance. Often, the speaker of an ironical utterance implicitly highlights this contrast by the use of particular tone of voice, facial expressions and gestures such as head shaking (Utsumi 2000; Bryant & Fox Tree 2005). Once the hearer has recognised the incongruity between what he had expected to hear from the speaker, given a certain conversational context, and what he actually heard, the next phase of irony comprehension, geared towards filling the gaps, begins. Pragmatic models of irony comprehension are constructed on the basis of how the hearer's recognition of incongruity during on-line comprehension will yield an ultimate understanding of the speaker's attitude and intentions (Gibbs 1986; Kreuz & Glucksberg 1989; Wilson & Sperber 1992; Kumon-Nakamura et al. 1995).

Existing developmental studies suggest that understanding of irony develops in a piecemeal fashion. They also indicate that comprehension of irony may require several different abilities. Winner and Leekam (1991) found that children between 5 and 7 years can distinguish ironical utterances from lies on the basis of discourse context, but not on the basis of ironical tone of voice. More recently, Filippova and Astington (2008) have shown that only children who are capable of identifying the discrepancy between the meaning of the utterance and the speaker's intentions behind it could understand the speaker's ironic intentions and attitudes. Bryant (2012) suggests that children are sensitive to a variety of signals of irony early on, but unlike adults, they are not capable of integrating these signals to yield understanding of the intentions and attitudes of the speaker.

Within the framework of relevance theory, Wilson (2009) suggests that comprehension of irony and that of deliberate lies are analogous in many ways and both processes are likely to involve 'epistemic vigilance' and mind-reading abilities. Sperber and his colleagues have claimed that success in standard

231

false-belief tasks is linked to the child's developing capacity for epistemic vigilance: the capacity to defend oneself against being accidentally or intentionally misinformed by communicators (Sperber et al. 2010). Currently, however, little is known about how children's developing epistemic vigilance contributes to their general pragmatic interpretations. To date, one study has claimed that epistemic vigilance is involved in the understanding of intentional deception (Mascaro & Sperber 2009) and another suggests that it may be required in understanding verbal irony (Wilson 2009).

According to Wilson, the crucial difference between deliberate lies and ironical utterances is how the speaker manipulates the expression of her attitude. In deliberate lies, the speaker's attitude is intentionally concealed, while in irony, it is intentionally communicated. The speaker of a deliberate lie expresses a proposition that she believes to be false, and intends to conceal her belief from the hearer. The speaker of irony, on the other hand, expresses a proposition that they believe to be false, and intends to share this with the hearer through the expression of a dissociative attitude towards it.

In the following, I will take up Wilson's suggestion and consider how epistemic vigilance and mind-reading ability play a role in children's understanding of a speaker's intentions in irony. First, I will consider how epistemic vigilance and mind-reading abilities may contribute to children's understanding of tacitly conveyed speaker's intentions and attitudes in irony. On the basis of existing developmental studies, I will then suggest that children's interpretation of irony as a deliberate lie may be best accounted for by the interaction between processes that identify how the utterance achieves relevance, their already functioning epistemic vigilance, and a mind-reading ability to infer the speaker's intentions.

Existing developmental studies indicate that an ability to understand that verbal irony is echoic, i.e. that the speaker is expressing his dissociative attitude towards an attributive thought mentioned by the utterance, takes time to develop through adolescence (Dyck et al. 2001; Kaland et al. 2008). I will suggest that adult-like understanding of verbal irony as being echoic requires sophistication in the search for relevance which is supported by both higher-order mind-reading abilities and epistemic vigilance to integrate incongruities among linguistic, paralinguistic and contextual information. I will also discuss the possibility that effort-demanding higher-order mind-reading may be short-circuited if the hearer recognises the speaker's ironic intent and dissociative attitude on the basis of evaluation and integration of a variety of implicit clues the speaker has provided, which, of course, is the function of epistemic vigilance.

17.2   Development of Irony Understanding

Overall, existing studies on children's understanding of irony suggest that adult-like understanding is achieved relatively late in development, sometime during middle childhood and adolescence. Due to the scarcity of studies on development during adolescence, however, here I will mainly consider findings on children's understanding of irony during middle childhood (6 to 11 years old).

Most developmental studies on irony comprehension explain children's comprehension of irony in terms of their higher-order mental-state understanding. They suggest that irony comprehension requires not a single psychological process but several different processes, each of which requires different socio-cognitive abilities. For example, Hancock et al. (2000) suggest a two-stage model of comprehension of irony on the basis of Ackerman's proposal (Ackerman 1983). First, the hearer understands the speaker's belief about the situation under discussion. Second, once the hearer has understood the speaker's belief, he then infers the speaker's pragmatic intent or attitude. The authors claim that the first process requires first-order mind-reading ability and the second process, the second-order equivalent. Past research on development of mind-reading ability (or 'theory of mind') has revealed that by 5 years of age, children have acquired the concept of belief and can think and talk not only about true beliefs but also about beliefs that are false (Bartsch & Wellman 1995). Children come to understand first-order false beliefs around 5 years of age, and second-order false beliefs sometime between 6 and 8 years (Perner & Wimmer 1985). Thus, just like the sequential order assumed in the development of mental-state understanding, Hancock and colleagues claim that there is a sequential order in the understanding of the speaker's beliefs, intentions and attitudes behind ironical utterances. Hancock et al. also suggest a causal relation between the two processes: accurate understanding of the speaker's belief about the situation enables the hearer to infer the speaker's intent or attitude.

More recent studies confirm the suggested relation between the first-order mind-reading abilities and understanding of the speaker's beliefs about the situation in ironical utterances. By 7 years of age, children understand that the speaker of an ironical utterance does not believe what the utterance describes (Filippova & Astington 2008). Understanding of a speaker's beliefs developmentally precedes understanding of the speaker's intent (Pexman & Glenwright 2007). The relation between second-order mind-reading ability and understanding of a speaker's intent or attitude communicated by irony has also been demonstrated by many studies (Winner & Leekam 1991; Happé 1993; Sullivan et al. 1995). As mentioned earlier, however, a few studies report that children over 9 years old have a tendency to interpret ironical utterances as lies (Demorest et al. 1984; Winner et al. 1987). Winner and Leekam (1991) suggest that children find the speaker's second-order intention behind lies (i.e. the speaker intends that the hearer believes P) easier to understand than the second-order intention behind irony (i.e. the speaker intends that the hearer does not believe P). The question of why this is the case, however, has not been fully addressed so far. I will come back to this point later.

Furthermore, children who interpret irony as a lie do not understand the speaker's dissociative attitude. In order to tap into children's ability to understand the speaker's attitude in irony, existing studies typically use a question asking whether the speaker was *nice* or *mean* when he spoke sarcastically (Dews et al. 1996; Hancock et al. 2000; Pexman & Glenwright 2007). As Wilson (2013) points out, asking children whether the speaker is nice or mean is too simplistic and is not the best way to test their ability to recognise the speaker's mocking, contemptuous or critical attitude. In any case, these studies demonstrated that less than 50 per cent of children (the average age is 8; 7 in Pexman & Glenwright 2007) answered that the speaker of irony was mean rather than nice. So it appears that for children around 8 and 9, understanding a speaker's dissociative attitude is rather difficult.

17.3   The Role of Epistemic Sensitivity, Mind-Reading Ability and the Search for Relevance in Comprehension of Irony

Now let's consider the development of children's understanding of irony in terms of epistemic vigilance, mind-reading ability and the search for relevance. When there is a discrepancy among different aspects of an utterance, e.g. among lexical, prosodic or contextual information, the hearer will take it as a sign of inconsistency or incoherence. Sensitivity to signs of inconsistency or incoherence is considered to be the function of epistemic vigilance (Sperber et al. 2010). So sensitivity to a variety of implicit cues to the speaker's intentions and attitudes in irony are likely to be part of the function of epistemic vigilance, too.

Existing studies on the development of epistemic vigilance reveal that from an early age, children show sensitivity to a variety of social cues indicating the speaker's knowledge, confidence, motivation and competence (Matsui & Miura 2009; Matsui & Yamamoto 2013). For example, children demonstrate their sensitivity to signs of trustworthiness of the speaker (i.e. epistemic vigilance towards the source of information) by 3 years of age (e.g. Clément et al. 2004; Matsui et al. 2009, 2016a). Children also become sensitive to the truthfulness of information (i.e. epistemic vigilance towards the content of information) at around 4 years of age (Mascaro & Sperber 2009). They understand that a lie is a false statement without grasping that it is intentionally false (Wimmer et al. 1984). As children get older, their degree of vigilance becomes more sophisticated. Unfortunately, however, just like existing studies on the development of mind-reading abilities, investigation of the development of epistemic vigilance between middle childhood and adolescence (say, between 9 and 18 years old) is currently missing. So in the following, on the basis of the existing findings about children's attentional biases in interpreting irony, I speculate on how epistemic vigilance and the mind-reading abilities of a typical 9-year-old function during the interpretation of irony.

As discussed earlier, when discourse context and utterance meaning are not congruent, 9-year-olds tend to interpret the utterance as a lie, i.e. that the speaker intends that the hearer believes what he says (Demorest et al. 1983, 1984; Winner et al. 1987; Capelli et al. 1990). Younger children (e.g. 6-year-olds in Ackerman (1983) and in Demorest et al. (1983)) tend to interpret an ironical utterance as sincere, i.e. that the speaker believes what he said and so intends that the hearer believes it. Although these errors are often explained by the notion of lexical bias, these cases are actually conceptually different. Six-year-olds who interpret an ironical utterance as sincere may not yet be fully able to use their second-order mind-reading ability. They may also believe that the speaker is benevolent but incompetent. Nine-year-olds, by contrast, are also capable of using their second-order mind-reading ability to interpret the ironical utterance as a lie. They understand that the speaker who tells a deliberate lie is competent but has malevolent intentions.

The question here is why 9-year-olds interpret irony as lying despite their capabilities (a) to assess the truthfulness of information and (b) to understand the speaker's second-order intentions. I would like to suggest one possible answer on the basis of a relevance-theoretic hypothesis of how the hearer's interpretive processes function. According to Sperber et al., the speaker's communicative behaviour activates two distinct processes in the hearer. One is geared to assessing the trustworthiness of the speaker, and the other geared to identifying the relevance of what is communicated (Sperber et al. 2010). Here let us speculate on how the two processes may operate in the mind of a 9-year-old when interpreting irony. On the basis of existing findings about children's epistemic vigilance (e.g. sensitivity to true vs. false information) and mind-reading ability, 9-year-olds are probably aware that paying attention to and processing information which the speaker not only knows is false but also wants the hearer to confirm as false is totally pointless for the hearer. In other words, these children are already epistemically quite vigilant and see that openly false information is irrelevant or even harmful for the hearer and so he should not process it. Such intuitive awareness about relevance in children is based on the process for assessing the truthfulness of the information as well as the process geared to identifying its relevance.

Importantly, unlike adults, 9-year-olds are not yet fully aware that openly false information may communicate some other information that *is* relevant to the hearer. Having heard irony, adults are able to infer that the speaker intentionally communicated false information and so will continue searching for relevance until they find the interpretation intended by the speaker. In the case of irony, the relevant information includes the speaker's dissociative attitude towards what is described by the utterance. For children, however, the idea that the speaker is communicating false information intentionally in order to communicate something more important is quite hard to grasp. In fact, even for adults, the idea that deliberately false information may communicate some other relevant information is counter-intuitive: they too quite often misinterpret irony as lying (Demorest et al. 1984; Creusere 1999).

So, for 9-year-olds, who have already acquired the concept of intentional deception, it is easier to interpret the speaker who communicates false information as lying than to interpret that speaker as wanting the hearer to acknowledge the falsity of the information. In the case of intentional deception, the speaker communicates false information (just as in irony) but it is not openly false to everyone (unlike irony): for deception to succeed, the speaker conceals from the hearer his own belief that it is false. I suggest that 9-year-olds' hypotheses about how false information can achieve relevance is likely to be based on their understanding of intentional deception. They may think that as long as the hearer believes that the utterance is true, what is communicated may have some relevance to him. In other words, they may think that communicated information *should at least be presented as true so that the hearer finds it relevant*. What I would like to suggest here is that 9-year-olds' interpretation of irony as a deliberate lie is not the result of a careless mistake or a casual choice but is the output of the joint processes of their developing epistemic vigilance, mind-reading abilities, and the process geared to identifying how information achieves relevance.

17.4   Children's Attentional Biases in Irony Comprehension

Children's developing comprehension of irony has also been examined in terms of their attentional biases. Children's attentional biases are closely related to their developing epistemic vigilance. During utterance comprehension, particular verbal or non-verbal clues may become more salient and effective to the hearer than others in the process of selecting the interpretation intended by the speaker. When there are discrepancies between utterance meaning, discourse context, and prosodic information, for example, the hearer may prioritise a particular discrepancy and use it to infer the speaker's intention, while more or less ignoring other discrepancies. It has been shown that for adults, ironical prosody (which is typically incongruent with utterance meaning) is likely to be the most salient clue in interpreting ironical utterances (Creusere 1999).

For children, however, it takes many years to become competent in taking prosody as an effective clue for irony. Existing studies suggest that at around 8 years of age, children come to make use of prosodic cues to infer the speaker's ironical intent (Ackerman 1981; Capelli et al. 1990). What clues, then, do children younger than 8 typically use in order to infer the speaker's ironical intent? Some studies suggest that young children have a strong 'lexical bias': when there is an 'affective' discrepancy between lexical content and what prosody indicates in the utterance, lexical content is prioritised in interpretation (Friend & Bryant 2000). For example, if a young child hears the utterance 'Fantastic job!' said in an angry voice, the child will pay more attention to the lexical content than the prosodic information in the utterance and interpret it as a compliment.

Children are found to show another attentional bias in the interpretation of irony. Aguert et al. demonstrated that upon hearing a pseudo-utterance with meaningless syllables accompanied by mismatching prosody and discourse context (either a combination of positive prosody and negative discourse context, or of negative prosody and positive discourse context), children at or younger than 7 years relied more on discourse context to determine the speaker's feeling behind the utterance. They call this type of preference 'contextual bias' (Aguert et al. 2010). It is at around 9 years of age that children start to pay equal attention to both prosody and discourse context. For adults, on the other hand, prosody is the most effective clue for inferring the speaker's feeling behind the utterance.

Therefore, another possible line of explanation for 9-year-olds' interpretation of irony as deliberate lying is based on their inability to use prosodic information as a clue to infer the speaker's attitude. Existing studies suggest that for adults, affective prosody accompanying an utterance is the most effective clue from which to infer the speaker's intentions and the attitudes it communicates. If so, it is reasonable to assume that if children acquired adult-like sensitivity to the prosody accompanying irony, then it would provide them with a stepping stone to understanding the speaker's dissociative attitude and intention (i.e. the speaker does not intend that the hearer believes what he says). In other words, once children start paying more attention to the prosodic information, it should become easier for them to realise that the utterance is echoic, i.e. the speaker is expressing an attributed thought and communicating his own dissociative attitude to it, and that the utterance achieves relevance in that way. Until around 10 years of age, however, upon hearing an utterance in which prosodic and lexical information are incongruent, it is difficult for children to pay attention to both types of information and to integrate them to find the intended interpretation of utterance (Friend 2000). According to Aguert et al. (2013), sensitivity to prosodic indications of the speaker's emotions and attitudes communicated by an utterance increases during middle childhood and adolescence. On the basis of these existing studies, it is unlikely that 9-year-olds are able to use prosodic information to infer the speaker's dissociative attitude communicated by irony.

Of course, adults are also capable of interpreting irony without relying on prosodic cues. Adults are equipped with higher-order metarepresentational abilities and can use them to infer the intentions and attitudes of the speaker. That adults use their higher-order metarepresentational abilities to interpret irony has been confirmed by neuropsychological studies. One recent study using functional magnetic resonance imaging (fMRI) demonstrated the extensive activation of a higher-order mind-reading network (right and left temporoparietal junctions, medial prefrontal cortex (MPFC) and prefrontal cortex) as well as the left inferior frontal gyrus (IFG), which is considered to contribute to integration between language and higher-order mind-reading, during irony comprehension (Spotorno et al. 2012). Other studies also report that the MPFC, which is considered to be a part of the neural basis of mind-reading, is activated during the comprehension of irony (Uchiyama et al. 2006; Wang et al. 2006; Shibata et al. 2010).

Little is known, however, about the neural basis for integrating prosodic information during the comprehension of irony. Matsui and colleagues conducted an fMRI experiment to investigate the neural underpinning of irony comprehension in an auditory modality (Matsui et al. 2016b). The behavioural data revealed that affective prosody (either positive or negative) facilitated interpretation of irony. There was a significant interaction between context and prosody: irony perception was enhanced when positive prosody was used in the context of a bad deed or, vice versa, when negative prosody was used in the context of a good deed. The corresponding interaction effect was observed in the rostro-ventral portion of the left IFG corresponding to Brodmann's Area (BA) 47. Interestingly, unlike the study by Spotorno and colleagues, they didn't find activation of the theory-of-mind network during on-line comprehension of irony. There are many potential reasons why this is the case: for example, the story used in the experiment may have been too simple or too short for adults to make use of higher-order mind-reading, as suggested by Spotorno et al. (2012). An interesting possibility is that during on-line comprehension of irony, effortful higher-order mind-reading might be short-circuited, whenever possible, because of the preference for frugal information processing. Prosodic information is the most salient and effective clue for adults to infer the speaker's intentions and attitudes in irony comprehension. So maybe irony accompanied by salient affective prosody is more likely to induce such a short-circuit than irony in a written form. Conversely, interpretation of irony in a written modality is more likely to require higher-order mind-reading than that in an auditory modality. These intriguing possibilities need to be tested in future research.

17.5   Final Remarks

The question of how children understand lies and irony has attracted the attention of developmental researchers. However, in the field of developmental psychology in general, investigation of children's understanding of a speaker's intentions and attitudes in communication remains scarce. Still, the connection between higher-order mind-reading abilities and children's understanding of lies and irony has been widely supported in the field. What is urgently needed is much more research not only on general socio-cognitive development but also on development of pragmatic abilities through late-middle childhood and adolescence. As mentioned in this chapter, relatively little is currently known about socio-cognitive development during late-middle childhood and adolescence, despite recent neuropsychological findings that our social cognition continues to develop during this period (Blakemore & Choudhury 2006; Vetter et al. 2014). I believe that relevance theory can provide an adequate theoretical framework to predict and explain not only the mechanisms of communication among adults, but also the development of pragmatic abilities across childhood and adolescence. For example, as Wilson (2013) suggests, a relevance-theoretic account of irony predicts that the most important developmental achievement in terms of successful comprehension of irony by the hearer is to understand that the utterance is echoic: the speaker is expressing an attributed thought and communicating his own dissociative attitude to it. On the basis of the existing studies reviewed in this chapter, I assume that the understanding of an utterance as echoic becomes possible some time between adolescence and adulthood. What contributes to such understanding is currently unknown, though continuing development of higher-order metarepresentational abilities and executive functions are likely contributors. I would suggest that adult-like sophistication and flexibility in the search for relevance is also involved in recognition of an utterance as echoic. As briefly illustrated in this chapter, 9-year-olds' identification of how irony achieves relevance is constrained by their inability to find the connection between false information and the speaker's dissociative attitude. There is no doubt that more developmental research using relevance theory as a theoretical framework is needed to reveal the development of pragmatic abilities throughout the lifespan.

Acknowledgements

Knowing Deirdre has been a motivating experience, and a defining one for me. Her passion for research, teaching and writing has continued to inspire me ever since I met her as a naive young PhD student at UCL in the early 1990s. I thank her for being such a great role model, mentor, friend and confidante.

I am grateful to the editors of this volume and an anonymous reviewer for constructive comments on an earlier version of this chapter.

18   Allegory in Relation to Metaphor and Irony

Christoph Unger

18.1   Introduction

Relevance theory as developed by Dan Sperber and Deirdre Wilson has broken with the long-standing tradition of assuming that verbal utterances essentially fall into two kinds: literal and figurative (or tropes). Sperber and Wilson argue that figurative utterances do not constitute a natural class.

Metaphor and irony, for instance, function in fundamentally different ways. At the same time, metaphors have much in common with certain non-figurative utterances such as approximations (Sperber & Wilson 1986/1995, 1990, 2008), and irony has much in common with non-figurative utterances echoing, with approving propositional attitudes, thoughts of others (Sperber & Wilson 1986/1995, 1990; Wilson & Sperber 1992, 2012: 123–45). This break with tradition has resulted in the abandonment of the old strategy (codified for instance in John Searle's principle of expressibility, Searle 1969: 20) to build explanatory theories of language use on the study of literal language first, assuming that figurative utterances can ultimately be reduced to meaning-equivalent literal ones. The claim that comprehending tropes requires no cognitive competences apart from those independently necessary to process literal utterances also has important implications for the study of rhetoric. It means that rhetorical competence is inherent in the competence required to comprehend ostensive communication. Consequently, rhetoric does not have a distinctive subject matter (Wilson & Sperber 2012: 96); rather, the study of rhetorical competence reduces to the study of pragmatic competence.

However, the trope of allegory seems to raise questions about this relevance-theoretic approach to figurative language, because allegories convey a literal meaning *alongside* a figurative one in a way that mutually reinforces these interpretations. Both figurative and non-figurative interpretations seem to be required for allegory but not for metaphor and irony. In this paper, I will develop the argument advanced in Unger (2017, 2018) that relevance theory can nevertheless account for the interpretation of allegory as a trope[1] without having to postulate any additional mechanism. This account argues that allegories are processed in the same way as fictions, the processing of which involves the mind's capacity to process multi-layered intentions (Sperber & Wilson 1987b; Wilson 2011c). Since the communicative intention as defined in relevance theory is a two-layered informative intention, this capacity is required to process ostensive communication in general. Moreover, there is no clear dividing line between allegory, which has been classified in classical rhetoric as a trope, and fiction, which is not usually regarded as a trope. Therefore, a closer inspection of allegory within a relevance-theoretic account of communication reveals that, rather than posing a challenge to relevance theory's outlook on rhetoric, it provides additional support for it.

The argument is structured as follows. In Section 18.2 I briefly review the relevance-theoretic account of a pragmatic mechanism central to the comprehension of metaphors. In Section 18.3 I review a pragmatic mechanism behind the comprehension of irony. Section 18.4 reviews the properties of allegory as discussed in literary theory and discusses to what extent these observations challenge the relevance-theoretic approach to rhetoric. The main argument is developed in Section 18.5 and runs as follows: Allegory shares with fiction the property that it communicates on multiple layers. On a first layer, a narrative is conveyed that ostensibly fails to satisfy the audience's expectations of relevance. This layer is embedded in a second one where the audience's expectations of relevance are satisfied by considering a range of implications of the narrative on the first layer. In the case of allegory, these implications amount to weak implicatures of the narrative on the first layer that interpretively resemble some traits of that narrative. In the case of fiction, the second-layer implications may have a looser relation to the first-layer narrative. Since multi-layered communication falls naturally within the scope of ostensive communication as defined in relevance theory, no additional cognitive mechanism needs to be postulated for processing allegories.

18.2   Mechanism 1: Ad hoc Concept Construction and the Comprehension of Metaphor

Consider the following examples:

(18.1)   MICHAEL (ON THE PHONE): Congratulations on your new home! What's it like?
          JANE: It's a mansion. In fact, it's the old Seward Mansion.

---

[1] For some initial remarks about how this relevance-theoretic account of allegory as a trope may relate to allegorese, i.e. allegory as an interpretion method, see Unger (2018).

(18.2)   MICHAEL: I'm glad you've got a bungalow, not that tiny flat you lived
in before.
JANE: Yes, *it's a mansion.*

(18.3)   MICHAEL: You have a huge, gorgeous house!
JANE: Yes, it's a mansion.

In each of these examples, the word *mansion* is used in different ways: literally in (18.1), as a hyperbole in (18.2), and as a metaphor in (18.3). Over the last thirty years or so, relevance theorists have argued that the comprehension of such utterances involves the ability of the human mind to construct new ad hoc concepts in the comprehension process, on the basis of linguistically encoded concepts (for an overview, see e.g. Carston 2002; Wilson & Sperber 2002; Wilson & Carston 2007 and Sperber & Wilson 2008). This process is constrained by expectations of relevance and may be applied to the above examples as follows:

(18.4)   **Relevance expectation:** Jane is going to describe the character, size, location, interior and exterior of her family's new home.
Contextual assumption: A named, historic home built by a wealthy family is unique.
Explicature: JANE'S NEW HOME IS A MANSION.

Comment: The word *mansion* is used to communicate the concept MANSION (denoting named historic homes), the concept that the word *mansion* encodes.[2]

(18.5)   **Relevance expectation:** Jane will comment positively on the size of her family's new home.
Contextual assumption: A mansion is a kind of house.
Contextual assumption: A mansion is a large house.
Contextual assumption: A large house feels spacious.
Contextual assumption: Jane and her family experience their new home as spacious.
Explicature: Jane's new home is a MANSION*.
Implicature: Jane's family feels good in their new house.

Comment: The word *mansion* communicates an ad hoc concept MANSION* denoting big houses in general. This ad hoc concept is constructed on the basis of the concept MANSION encoded by the

---

[2] An anonymous reviewer pointed out that, strictly speaking, lexical adjustment may also occur in such cases of 'literal' meaning, so that an ad hoc concept MANSION* is constructed, an ad hoc concept that is based on a concept template encoded by the word *mansion* and that refers to named historic homes. For ease of exposition, I do not go into these details here, but see Carston (2012) for discussion.

word *mansion* in order to warrant an implicature that satisfies relevance expectations. This use of the word *mansion* is interpreted as a hyperbole.

(18.6)   **Relevance expectation:** Jane will make a positive comment on Michael's compliment about the beauty of her house.
Contextual assumption: A mansion has many grand rooms and appointments.
Contextual assumption: Mansions are beautiful and luxurious.
Explicature: JANE'S NEW HOME IS A MANSION**.
Implicature: Jane believes that their house is beautiful and luxurious.

Comment: the word *mansion* communicates an ad hoc concept MANSION** denoting beautiful houses. This ad hoc concept is constructed on the basis of the concept MANSION encoded by the word *mansion* in order to warrant an implicature that satisfies relevance expectations. The word *mansion* is interpreted as a metaphor.

In all cases, the interpretation accepted as the one intended by the communicator is the first one that is easily accessible and that satisfies the expectations of relevance raised in the communication event. In (18.4), the hearer arrives at a literal interpretation, in (18.5), an interpretation of the utterance as hyperbole, and in (18.6), an interpretation of the utterance as a metaphor. Neither hyperbolic nor metaphorical interpretations involve the recovery of a literal interpretation as a step in the procedure. The prediction is that when the intended interpretation is a figurative one, the audience will typically only entertain the intended figurative interpretation. There is no requirement to access a literal interpretation.

18.3   Mechanism 2: Interpretive Resemblance, Metarepresentations and the Comprehension of Irony

Over the last thirty years or so, Deirdre Wilson and Dan Sperber have developed the *echoic use theory of irony* (Sperber & Wilson 1981, 1986/1995, 1990; Wilson & Sperber 1992, 2012). I will outline this account briefly here. This account is based on the notion of *interpretive use*. An utterance is used interpretively if it is used to metarepresent another representation by way of resembling it with regard to its logical properties. Resemblance in logical properties is called *interpretive resemblance*. The metarepresented representation may be a public one (e.g. an utterance), a private one (a thought, a mental representation), or an abstract one (e.g. a sentence type). An interpretively used utterance is relevant in virtue of the metarepresentation relation. However, this metarepresentation may be relevant in different ways. In reported speech, for instance, the relevant point is that the utterance is attributed to some other communicator (or to the communicator at a different time). An example of such an *attributive interpretive use* is (18.7).

(18.7)   MICHAEL: So you went to look at the property yesterday. The house
is a mansion, it said in the advertisement. How did you like it?
JANE: Well, *'the house is a mansion'* – that's what they wrote. But all
we saw was a neglected, tumbledown structure with a sagging roof
and a rotting foundation.

Here, Jane is quoting (part of) the advertisement and making clear that she does not commit to the accuracy of the content of the metarepresented utterance. Having understood Jane's utterance along these lines, Michael arrives at an interpretation that satisfies his expectations of relevance.

However, utterances may also metarepresent other representations for purposes other than merely reporting what someone has said or thought. For instance, communicators may want to metarepresent someone's thought or utterance in order to simultaneously convey an attitude towards the propositional content of the metarepresented representation. If an utterance is designed to achieve relevance in this way, Sperber and Wilson (1986/1995: 238) describe this as an *echoic use* of the utterance. Echoic use is a subtype of attributive use. Examples of echoically used utterances are the italicised units in (18.8)–(18.10).

(18.8)   MICHAEL: So you went to look at the property yesterday. The house
is a mansion, it said in the advertisement. How did you like it?
JANE (DISMISSIVELY): *The house is a mansion, indeed!* – If you
consider a tiny bungalow with a small front yard a mansion!

(18.9)   MICHAEL: So you went to look at the property yesterday. The house
is a mansion, it said in the advertisement. How did you like it?
JANE (EXCITEDLY): *The house is a mansion!* In fact, it's the
old Seward Mansion! – No stately home could be more well-kept.

(18.10)   MICHAEL: So you went to look at the property yesterday. The house
is a mansion, it said in the advertisement. How did you like it?
JANE: *The house is a mansion?* Rubbish! It was just a neglected,
tumbledown structure with a sagging roof and a rotting foundation.

In all these examples, Michael must, in addition to recognising that Jane is metarepresenting the advertisement and that she does not commit to the truthfulness of the metarepresented content, understand Jane as implicitly communicating an attitude. Otherwise, Michael could not understand Jane's utterance as a relevant answer. In other words, Michael must recognise that Jane is using her utterance echoically. Of these, only (18.8) would usually be taken to be an example of verbal irony. This is because the propositional attitude conveyed is of a *dissociative* kind, in contrast to (18.9), where the attitude is an approving one, and in contrast to (18.10), where the dissociative attitude is explicitly conveyed. The dissociative attitude conveyed may be one of a range of attitudes from mild, humorous dissociation to ridicule and scorn, perhaps including anger. There is thus no clear-cut boundary between non-ironic attitudes and ironic ones; rather, there is a continuum of echoic uses ranging from ones expressing supportive attitudes through various degrees of dissociation to angry disavowal. Wilson and Sperber (2012: 95–6) also discuss the case of Shakespeare's play *Julius Caesar*, where Mark Antony says four times that *Brutus is an honourable man*, each time with a slightly different attitude, the first time with a conciliatory attitude, then with an increasingly scornful attitude each time. Again, the conclusion is that there are important continuities between literal and figurative utterances in the sense that the same cognitive mechanisms are involved in their comprehension. With regard to irony and positive attitude echoes, the cognitive mechanism involved is the competence to comprehend echoic uses of language.

Thus, the basic cognitive mechanism involved in irony is actually shared with a wide range of non-figurative utterances, not only with echoic uses of a non-dissociative kind, but also with non-echoic attributive interpretive uses of utterances. It is the human mind's ability to process interpretive uses of utterances that is the basis for our ability to engage in verbal irony and in similar non-figurative types of verbal exchanges.

Summarising the arguments of the last two sections, we find that we can affirm the generalisations in (18.11) and (18.12):

(18.11) Neither figurative language use nor literal language use is a natural kind:
    a. There is a continuum between non-figurative language uses and instances that could be classified as employing the trope of metaphor, with no clear boundary between them. Therefore, metaphor cannot be clearly defined.
    b. Utterances typically classified as instances of the trope irony share many properties with a range of utterance types that are not standardly classified as tropes or figurative language. Therefore, irony cannot be clearly defined.

(18.12) Metaphor and irony involve different cognitive mechanisms:
    a. Metaphor involves competence in ad hoc concept construction.
    b. Irony involves competence in processing interpretive use, which in turn requires competence in processing interpretive resemblance relations.

These findings strongly suggest that the notion of figurative language is not a natural kind, because it can only be delimited in an arbitrary fashion and cross-cuts utterances involving different cognitive mechanisms in comprehension. Moreover, neither intuitions about literary or about figurative language use play an essential role in pragmatic processing; considerations of relevance alone are sufficient.

18.4   Allegory: A Fly in the Ointment

Consider the following examples of allegory. On the face of it, they appear to contradict the claim that intuitions about literary or figurative language use play no role in pragmatic processing:

(18.13) When you walk through a storm, hold your head up high. (Line from the song 'You'll Never Walk Alone', www.kopleft.com/youll-never-walk-alone-lyrics-and-history/)

(18.14) You can't put the toothpaste back in the tube. (Proverb, example 10a from Wilson 2012)

(18.15) No use crying over spilled milk. (Proverb, example 10b from Wilson 2012)

Such utterance types occur frequently in everyday communication, but usually not in situations where the addressee is walking on a road in stormy weather, or wondering what to do with toothpaste he has accidentally squeezed out of the tube, or spilled a bottle of milk. In other words, these examples involve figurative language. Yet the literal meaning is very clear in the sense that the scenes portrayed are easily imaginable states of affairs in some possible world. Moreover, grasping the figurative meaning appears to involve grasping the literal meaning and drawing relevant inferences from states of affairs described to the utterance situation at hand. In other words, the literal meaning and the figurative meaning are both essential for comprehending these utterances. At the same time, the literal and figurative meanings are easily distinguishable, and the figurative meaning does not 'take over' or replace the literal meaning. This contrasts with metaphors such as (18.3): the utterance *The house is a mansion* neither communicates the proposition THE HOUSE IS A HISTORIC NAMED HOUSE, nor is the recovery of this proposition necessary to comprehend the intended explicature.

Classical rhetoric identified this kind of language use as allegory, the standard definition of which was formulated by Quintilian: 'Allegory … either presents one thing in words and another in meaning, or else something absolutely opposed to the meaning of the words' (Butler 1922: 8.6.44). Quintilian distinguishes three types of allegories: a first which involves extended metaphors as in (18.16), a second which does not involve metaphor at all, as in (18.17), and a third type in which pure allegory and metaphor are mixed, as in (18.18).

(18.16)   O ship, new waves will bear thee back to sea. What dost thou? Make the haven, come what may [Quintilian explains this example as follows: '... Horace represents the state under the semblance of a ship, the civil wars as tempests, and peace and good-will as the haven.'] (Hor.Od.i.xiv.1) (Butler 1922: 8.6.44)

(18.17)   What I marvel at and complain of is this, that there should exist any man so set on destroying his enemy as to scuttle the ship on which he himself is sailing. (Cicero, unknown speech) (Butler 1922: 8.6.47)

(18.18)   I always thought that Milo would have other storms and tempests to weather, *at least in the troubled waters of political meetings.*

Quintilian's classic definition is certainly not without its problems. Kurz (1997) reviews the issues in more detail and argues that literary theory has converged on a definition of allegory that takes another property of this trope as central: the insight that the literal meaning, which Kurz calls the *initial meaning*, is persistent and co-exists in the audience's mind with the figurative meaning. 'Allegory', writes Kurz (1997: 37), 'has a double meaning, but metaphor has not'. The point is not merely that the initial meaning of an allegory is transparent and persistent, but that the initial meaning, communicated by way of a direct speech act, simultaneously communicates an allegorical meaning by way of an indirect speech act, so that both the initial and allegorical meanings are coherent in themselves and interconnected in a mutually supportive way.

This perspective on allegory has the advantage that it provides a useful perspective on all kinds of allegory, not only on allegories based on extended metaphor. As examples (18.14) and (18.17) illustrate, non-metaphorical allegories are by no means an exception.[3] However, it also raises a question for the relevance-theoretic view that the non-figurative meaning plays no role in the interpretation of tropes. In the case of allegory, the optimally relevant interpretation contains *both* a non-figurative meaning ('initial meaning') and figurative implications.[4] Recovering the non-figurative meaning is a crucial stepping

---

[3] This also casts doubt on pragmatic accounts that seek to reduce allegory to extended metaphor and argue that the comprehension of allegory is based on the same mechanisms as the comprehension of metaphor. Examples of such accounts include Crisp (2008); Gibbs (2011, 2015b); Hamilton (2011). See Unger (2017) for a more detailed evaluation of some prominent accounts of this kind.

[4] Allegory is not the only fly in the ointment in regard to the persistence of literal meaning. Carston (2010) and Carston and Wearing (2011) point out similar observations with regard to highly imagistic and artistic metaphors, and Rubio Fernández (2007) provides experimental evidence that the literal meaning of metaphors remains activated in the audience's mind for

stone for the audience to infer the intended figurative meaning. However, the non-figurative meaning cannot be discarded after recovering the figurative interpretation; rather, it is necessary for achieving relevance to retain the non-figurative meaning alongside the figurative interpretation. This raises the question of whether relevance theory ought to recognise a third mechanism for interpreting non-literal utterances after all. Unger (2017, 2018) argues that, despite appearances, relevance theory can account for the interpretation of allegory without having to postulate any additional mechanism. In the next section, I review this proposal and discuss its implications for the relevance-theoretic view of rhetoric.

18.5   The Relevance of Multi-Layered Communication Acts: No Fly in the Ointment After All

Consider again example (18.17). Intuitively, we can interpret this utterance as a mini-narrative, in which an imaginary person, sailing on the same ship as his enemy, sinks that ship in order to destroy his enemy. This suggests that comprehending allegories has many things in common with comprehending fictional stories. Sperber and Wilson (1987b: 751) and Wilson (2012) have suggested ways for accounting for fictional narratives within relevance theory. The question is how fiction could be relevant in the sense of Sperber and Wilson (1986/1995), who define relevance in terms of positive cognitive effects, or in other words, true improvements of an individual's representation of the world. Sperber and Wilson (1987b) assume that communicators may communicate on various levels simultaneously. An author of a work of fiction communicates on a first layer a description in a story world. She then embeds this layer in a second one, where she intends the reader to gain positive cognitive effects by connecting the events of the story to her own personal experience in the real world. In Wilson's (2012) words, the story achieves 'internal' relevance in the story world on the first layer of communication, and 'external' relevance on the second. On the first layer of communication, the ostensive stimulus consists of the narrator's or characters' utterances, on the second layer, the ostensive stimulus consists in the author producing a story which – in the case of pure fiction – blatantly has no truth value in the real world. Unger (2006) discusses an example of a text that communicates on at least three layers. In each of these instances of multi-layered communication, it is the blatant failure to fully satisfy relevance expectations that causes the audience to process the

---

a long time. Space does not permit discussion of these findings in the light of the account of allegory proposed in the next section. Carston (2010) also discusses extended metaphor which plays a role in a common type of allegory and may be seen as having a blurry boundary with allegory.

communicative act at an additional layer until cognitive effects are achieved that satisfy the audience's relevance expectations (while not incurring gratuitous processing effort).[5]

Notice that this approach to layering in communication fits naturally into the design of relevance theory: verbal communication is an instance of *ostensive communication*. Ostensive communication occurs when a communicator produces an ostensive stimulus, which is a behaviour (or the trace of it in the form of e.g. writing on paper or audiovisual recording) that the audience can see as rational only by attributing to the communicator an intention to inform the audience of something (the *informative intention*) and to inform the audience that the communicator has this informative intention (the *communicative intention*) (Sperber & Wilson 1986/1995: 63). Ostensive stimuli may be simple in that they consist of simple gestures such as pointing to the sky, or of verbal utterances containing a single sentence. They may also be complex in the sense that they combine different kinds of behaviours, such as gestures and verbal utterances. In fact, the representation of a complete act of ostensive communication may be used as an ostensive stimulus in its own right. If it is, the represented act of ostensive communication serves as an ostensive stimulus for a second-level act of communication (Sperber & Wilson 1987b: 751).

Unger (2017) argues that the comprehension of allegories follows the same pattern: in producing an allegory, the communicator describes a situation or event in some fictional world, ostensibly failing to fully satisfy relevance expectations. This ostensive withholding of relevance functions as an ostensive stimulus on a second layer of communication. In order to satisfy relevance expectations on this level, the audience connects the situation described in the utterance to some accessible context in such a way as to satisfy the relevance expectations at hand. This is done by assuming that the intended positive cognitive effects on this second layer of communication *interpretively resemble* the contextual implications made manifest by the initial meaning (the fictional description). Consider (18.19), a slightly more up-to-date variant of (18.17):

(18.19)   [Peter is a member of parliament, and parliament is debating proposals for sanctions against a country whose economic policies have been threatening domestic industries. He believes that Michael's proposal goes too far, even potentially having negative effects on the domestic economy. He comments on Michael's proposal:]

---

[5] This does not mean that the audience always has to find out about the lack of relevance at the first layer the 'hard way', by running up against high processing costs not offset by cognitive effects. Rather, as an anonymous reviewer suggests, readers of fiction come to fiction knowing that it is fictional and are therefore prepared to look for multi-layered interpretations. Also, some allegorical as well as fictional interpretations may be salient in an early phase of the comprehension process. Still, in all these cases, the communicator makes it overt that relevance will not be satisfied on the first layer alone.

It blows my mind to find out that there are people who are so bent on destroying their enemies that they scuttle the ship on which they themselves are sailing.

The audience's manifest expectations of relevance are that Peter will comment on Michael's proposal and argue for his point of view. Yet explicitly he is describing a fictitious situation where some specific person is damaging a ship on which he is sailing, with the intention of hurting his enemies. This obviously does not satisfy the audience's expectations of relevance. However, the utterance is intelligible, that is, it is possible to comprehend the propositions expressed as well as some implications, so it is not completely irrelevant either. This in turn raises the expectation that Peter intends to communicate something on a second layer of communication, using the fiction portrayed in his utterance as a stimulus for the audience to acquire cognitive effects that satisfy their expectations of relevance. Thus, the second layer of communication creates the expectation that the 'story' of the man scuttling the ship on which he is sailing is the most relevant way for Peter to convey his thoughts on Michael's proposal. This in turn raises the expectation that Peter believes that there is significant overlap of implications from the 'story' and implicatures that he intends to convey. In other words, the 'initial meaning' of the allegorical utterance interpretively resembles the implicatures the communicator intends to convey to a relevant degree. Guided by these expectations, the audience can readily infer that Peter thinks that Michael's proposals are too strong, that they are harmful to the country's own interests, that they are dangerously self-destructive, etc.

This account of allegory requires no cognitive mechanisms apart from those independently required to account for the comprehension of ostensive communication, according to relevance theory: first, the capacity to process layered intentions, and second, the capacity to process interpretive resemblances between representations. Moreover, it suggests an explanation for the transparency and persistence of the 'initial meaning' in allegory: since allegory is an instance of a multi-layered communicative act, it is passed through the comprehension module several times, using the output of the first pass as an ostensive stimulus for the next one. Outputs of comprehension processes are sets of mental representations which are accessible to introspection and capable of being stored in memory. Metaphors, in contrast, involve ad hoc concept construction, a pragmatic process computed as one of the computations carried out during one pass through the comprehension module. These pragmatic processes are intuitive, unconscious computations, so that the individual inferential steps in these processes are neither available to introspection nor capable of being stored in memory. This is why the literal meaning plays no essential role in the comprehension of metaphor.

Although allegory and metaphor are, on this account, independent phenomena arising through different pathways of inferential computation, it is easy to see that they may be combined. Recall that allegories create the expectation of there being a relevant overlap of implications derivable from the 'initial meaning' and the implicatures the communicator intended to convey. The richer the manifest implications of the 'initial meaning', the richer is the set of manifest implicatures of the allegorical utterance, and the more likely it is that there is a large overlap in these sets of representations. This might explain Quintilian's intuition that allegories involving extended metaphors are the most widespread type of allegories.

My account of allegory claims that allegory is processed in the same way as fictional utterances. Yet not all fictions are allegories. Fiction is on the second layer communicating 'by *showing* what is possible or conceivable' (Sperber & Wilson 1987b: 751), whereas allegory is communicating an array of weak *implicatures* that interpretively resemble certain implications of the literal meaning.

If these considerations are right, it appears that there is no sharp dividing line between fiction and allegory. The difference is in how strongly manifest certain ways of relating the fictional world to the audience's expectations of relevance are as opposed to others. Thus, within the range of communicative acts involving multi-layered communication, there is a continuum of cases from ones that are traditionally classified as tropes (allegory) to cases that are not considered as such.

18.6   Conclusion

I have argued that the pragmatic processing mechanisms for allegory interpretation are the same as those required for processing fiction. These are mechanisms that are independently required for processing ostensive stimuli in general: the cognitive capacity to process layered intentions, and the capacity to process relations. Moreover, I have argued that among the ostensive stimuli that are processed in this way as stimuli involving multi-layered communication, there is a cline between ones that classical rhetoric has classified as tropes and ones that are not. This means that we find the same pattern with allegory as with metaphor and irony: comprehending these tropes requires no special mechanisms apart from those that are independently needed to process non-figurative language, and there is no sharp or principled dividing line between figurative and non-figurative utterances. Metaphor comprehension involves the mechanism of ad hoc concept construction, a mechanism that is also essential for comprehending hyperbole and approximations. Irony interpretation involves the mechanism of echoic use, which accounts for our ability to comprehend tacitly conveyed propositional attitudes, a competence that is also essential for processing cases of echoic use that do not amount to irony. Thus, a closer study of allegory reveals that rather than posing a problem for the relevance-theoretic approach to rhetoric, it is a phenomenon on which this approach can shed an interesting light.

Acknowledgements

With this chapter I want to express my deep gratitude for the encouragement, inspiration and support that Deirdre Wilson has given me over the years.

This research was partly supported by the Research Council of Norway as part of the project 'The Meaning and Function of Norwegian Tags (NOT)', Nr. 230782. I am grateful to two anonymous reviewers whose engaging, encouraging, and comprehensive comments have led to many improvements.

19 Slave of the Passions: Making Emotions Relevant

Tim Wharton and Claudia Strey

19.1 Introduction

> Reason is, and ought only to be the slave of the passions ... (Hume, Treatise of Human Nature (THN) 2.3.3)

Thus, Hume famously articulated a view of the relationship between rationality or reasoning on the one hand and emotions or 'passions' on the other. His insight was that rationality alone does not suffice to motivate an individual to engage in an act of reasoning. According to Hume, the motivation to do so comes only from the passions. Cognition and affect, thinking and feeling, reason and passion, which are often analysed as two opposing forces, work together in complex ways. Patricia Greenspan puts it like this:

> [Emotional] states are commonly thought of as antithetical to reason, disorienting and distorting practical thought. However, there is also a sense in which emotions are factors in practical reasoning, understood broadly as reasoning that issues in action. At the very least emotions can function as 'enabling' causes of rational decision-making ... insofar as they direct attention toward certain objects of thought and away from others. They serve to heighten memory and to limit the set of salient practical options to a manageable set, suitable for 'quick-and-dirty' decision-making. (2002: 206)

Given these observations, and given the fact that humans regularly communicate subtle information about their emotional states, it might be presumed that accounts of linguistic communication would include quite developed views on how these states are communicated. But for a range of reasons, most linguists working on meaning have persisted with the view that the mental processes behind reason and passions not only exist in two separate domains, but work entirely independently. Emotions and emotional communication receive relatively little attention.

It would be an oversimplification to suggest that this reflects a lazy, anti-affect bias. The view that emotion is antithetical to cognition has its roots in Socratic/Platonic philosophy, a tradition which, arguably, linguists have inherited. It is also a consequence of the philosophical foundations on which modern theories of semantics and pragmatics are built (Costa 2008). Both the formal, idealised language philosophy of Frege, Russell and Tarski, and the ordinary language philosophy of Austin, Searle and Grice took it that the truth conditions of a sentence, or what is 'meant' by an utterance in context, is a proposition *p*. As a result of this, and the fact that linguists, philosophers and pragmaticists have tended to stay close to those areas of meaning illuminated by semantics and logic, attention has been almost entirely focused on propositional meaning (Sperber & Wilson 2015); the vaguer aspects of communication, including descriptively ineffable emotional meanings that are too nebulous to be paraphrased in propositional, conceptual terms at all, have been left largely untouched.

In this chapter, we want to suggest that (what we loosely call) 'emotional communication' involves paradigm examples of those vaguer aspects of communication discussed in Sperber and Wilson (2015). As a result, we argue that the time has come to develop ways in which emotional communication might be better integrated within a pragmatic theory. As a first step in this direction, we ask three questions:

1. What are emotions (and what is their relationship with reasoning)?
2. What is communicated in cases of emotional communication?
3. *How* do we communicate emotional states?

The chapter is organised as follows. In Section 19.2 we address Question 1. We argue for a view of emotions which is consistent with Hume and which blends ideas from, on the one hand Rey (1980) and, on the other, Cosmides and Tooby (2000). We turn to Questions (2) and (3) respectively in Sections 19.3 and 19.4, recognising that the 'what' and 'how' questions are closely interlinked. We consider the descriptive ineffability of emotional communication and show how recent developments in relevance theory (Sperber & Wilson 2015; Wilson 2011b, 2016) mean it is uniquely capable of accommodating the vaguer aspects of communication. We pay particular attention to Sperber and Wilson's (2015) continua between showing and meaning$_{NN}$ and determinate and indeterminate showing and meaning$_{NN}$ and the newly articulated view of relevance-theoretic procedural meaning presented in Wilson (2016). Central to our thinking is the idea that the traditional relevance-theoretic notion of positive cognitive effect needs to be complemented by a new notion of *positive emotional effect* (Gutt 2013; Kolaiti 2015; Strey 2016).

19.2   Emotions and Reasoning

Even the word 'emotion' is problematic. During the seventeenth century, philosophers preferred 'passion' or 'affect', while eighteenth-century intellectuals used the word 'sentiment' (Schmitter 2014). A further problem stems from the strong rationalist tradition that emotion is something of minor importance, a property not of the 'soul', but of the body. Socratic/Platonic philosophy assumed that emotion interfered with reason, and that truth was achieved through the mind, not the senses. For Socrates, the mind was actually limited by emotions; Plato believed they were not to be trusted.

Hume refuted the idea that humans regulate their actions by reason alone. Hume's passions formed one part of a much more nuanced distinction between 'ideas' and 'impressions', which amounts roughly to the intuitive distinction between thinking and feeling. The second of these groups he divided into 'primary' and 'secondary' impressions. The first included the perception of physical sensations of, say, pleasure or pain, and the second included what Hume called impressions of 'reflection', which include passions. A useful way of thinking about this is to imagine the two arousal states we know as excitement and anxiety or fear. They have (broadly speaking) the same physical symptoms, and so as 'primary' impressions they can be regarded as very similar. However, once reflected upon, they lead to quite different passions. Elizabeth Radcliffe (1999: 113) remarks:

Since I am disposed to be fearful of heights, susceptible to vertigo, and so on, the representation of standing at the edge of the cliff is associated for me with the idea of discomfort. As a consequence of this association, when I come to the belief that I am actually standing at that location, I feel fear. But if I don't have these tendencies, but others, I might associate the idea of being at the cliff's edge with pleasure, and then I would feel joy at the view or at the sense of freedom I get standing there ... *The representation of the situation without a contribution from my emotional constitution doesn't affect me.*[1]

The view of emotions we articulate here owes a great deal to Hume. We follow Rey (1980), for whom full-fledged emotional states are distinguished from 'sensations' or 'feelings' by the fact that they involve an interaction between several elements: cognitive, qualitative and physiological. So the emotion we call 'sadness' is characterised as involving an interaction between a *cognitive* element – the belief that something which you would prefer not to happen is about to, or the knowledge that something has happened which you would prefer not to have happened; an (optional) *qualitative* element – that feeling of being 'down' (which we might experience without being able to introspect on and, indeed, might attempt to pretend doesn't exist); and a *physiological* element – chemical changes in the brain (in the case of sadness or depression, depletion of norepinephrine). Whilst full-fledged emotional states crucially involve cognitive as well as qualitative and physiological elements, 'feelings' or 'sensations' need not. The parallels with Humean passions are clear.[2]

---

[1] Italics in original.

[2] The parallels with the account offered in Damasio (2006) should also be clear, but with two important differences. The first is terminological: what Damasio calls 'feeling' we call

Cosmides and Tooby (2000) (see also Tooby & Cosmides 2008) explore human cognition within the framework of evolutionary psychology, according to which the mind's species-specific neural architecture evolved in response to adaptive problems faced by our ancestors. They define emotion as a kind of superordinate cognitive mechanism, the function of which is to regulate or mobilise cognitive sub-mechanisms responsible for perception and attention, goal choice, information-gathering, physiological changes and specialised types of inference. An individual experiencing the kind of physiological changes summarised above automatically becomes hyper-alert, prepared to pay a high degree of attention to perceptual inputs they may not normally even notice. They are equipped with an entirely newly defined set of goals, and directed to prioritised inferential processes. The language is very different but, again, this view of emotions clearly owes something to Hume's original conception.

19.3   Emotional Communication

19.3.1   Describing and Expressing

Let us begin by making a distinction between describing an emotion and expressing it directly. In (19.1) and (19.2) the speaker is using her words to describe the emotional state she is in. In (19.3) and (19.4) she is expressing it.

(19.1)   I'm scared!

(19.2)   I'm delighted!

(19.3)   Aaaaaaaargh! (With a terrified facial expression)

(19.4)   Yaaaaaaaay! (Jumping up and down)

One response to this distinction might be to suggest that even describing an emotion is, in a way, expressing it (albeit conceptualising it first). However, to the extent that this response is correct, the words in (19.1) or (19.2) can only be said to be expressing their emotion *indirectly*. Expressing an emotion directly never amounts to describing it: (19.1) and (19.2) convey truth-evaluable propositions; (19.3) and (19.4) convey nothing of the sort. Although it may reinforce emotional description (it's easy, for example, to imagine (19.1) being uttered with a terrified facial expression), what we define as 'emotional communication' does not itself 'describe' anything.

'emotion'. The second is more substantive in that we are proposing a more integrated view of emotion and rationality. We thank Costa (p.c.) for bringing our attention to this point.

More typically than not, emotional communication involves non-verbal behaviours. But even when conveyed through language, it remains non-truth-conditional and contributes to meaning in a manner somehow independent of that utterance. The truth conditions of Ralph's utterance to Jack of (19.5) in Golding's *Lord of the Flies* are specified by (19.6); the expressive dimension is not part of the truth-conditional content:[3]

(19.5)   You're a beast and a swine and a bloody, bloody thief!

(19.6)   Jack is a beast and a swine and a thief.

On its own, this non-truth-conditionality does not constitute a huge problem. There are a number of non-truth-conditional expressions which, over the past years, have been comfortably integrated within pragmatic theories. In relevance-theoretic terms, the non-truth-conditional discourse adverbial 'frankly' does not contribute to the proposition expressed by an utterance of (19.7) but, rather, communicates the higher-level explicature in (19.8).

(19.7)   Frankly, the match was one-sided.

(19.8)   The speaker is saying frankly that the match was one-sided.

The interjections 'wow!' and 'aha!' do not contribute to the proposition expressed by utterances of (19.9) and (19.11) but, rather, communicate the higher-level explicatures in (19.10) and (19.12):

(19.9)   Wow! Roger's won again!

(19.10) The speaker is delighted that Roger has won again.

(19.11) Aha! Andy's won!

(19.12) The speaker is surprised that Andy has won.

Accounts along these lines have made progress in our understanding of how interjections contribute to speaker meaning (see also Wałaszeska 2004; Padilla Cruz 2009a,b; for alternative analyses see Ameka 1992; Wilkins 1992; Foolen 1997; Kaplan 1999; Wierzbicka 2000; Potts 2007a,c; Blakemore 2011, 2013b; Strey 2016). However, the problem of descriptive ineffability remains. Is the

---

[3] An anonymous reviewer suggested that 'bloody, bloody' *does* in fact contribute to the truth conditions of (19.5), insofar as it leads to the construction of a (truth-evaluable) ad hoc concept THIEF* which is perhaps different to the concept THIEF expressed in an utterance of (19.6). We take this suggestion on board, and agree that such an ad hoc concept may indeed be constructed in interpreting an utterance of (19.5). However, we maintain that this ad hoc concept does not exhaust the expressive element of meaning to which we refer. The sheer repetition of 'bloody' does something else, something which works independently from the descriptive meaning, and is ineffable. For discussion of the distinction to which we refer, see Jackson (2016).

full range of what is conveyed by 'wow!' and 'aha!' truly exhausted by the propositional-attitude descriptions in (19.10) and (19.12)? Probably not. More needs to be said.

19.3.2   Ineffability and Procedures

When asked what a word such as 'dog' means, most people will respond with a definition: 'a kind of animal', 'a canine mammal'. But the meaning conveyed by other words is not so amenable to introspection. Consider the word 'but': what does 'but' mean? The same problem arises with words that directly express emotion, such as 'bloody'. In a series of papers on expressive meaning, Potts (2007c) reports that in a large number of interviews and surveys 'bastard' was only defined by one person as a 'vile, contemptible person'. It appears that while people will happily explain that the word is used to vent emotions, pinning down exactly what they mean is very hard to do.

Blakemore (1987, 2002) reassesses Grice's account of discourse connectives by introducing a distinction between *conceptual* and *procedural* encoding. Most words encode concepts, constituents of conceptual representations. Most of these contribute to the truth conditions of an utterance; they have logical properties, can act as input to inference rules, and are used to describe the world. Some words, however, do not map onto concepts. This is one reason we find it hard to say what they mean. Rather than encoding the constituents of conceptual representations, the function of such words is to constrain the inferential processes involved in constructing or manipulating these representations. They guide the comprehension process by indicating the general direction in which the intended meaning is to be sought, by narrowing the hearer's search space.

Wharton (2003b) argues that interjections share with discourse connectives and discourse particles the property of encoding procedural rather than conceptual information. On this approach, the function of the interjection 'wow!' in (19.9) is to facilitate the retrieval of a range of speech-act or propositional-attitude descriptions associated with expressions of surprise or delight. Wharton (2009) takes the idea further and proposes that smiles and other natural, spontaneous facial expressions are *natural codes*, which should be analysed as encoding procedural rather than conceptual information. Natural codes are behaviours which carry meaning that is 'natural' in the sense of Grice (1957), but are inherently communicative: i.e. the reason they have propagated among humans is that they carry information. On this approach, the function of facial expressions of surprise or delight would be to facilitate the retrieval of similar, strongly communicated propositional-attitude descriptions to those activated by the interjection 'wow!' in (19.9). But while the procedural nature of natural codes goes some way to accounting for their ineffability, it only goes so far.

19.3.3   Relevance, Meaning and Showing

As well as making what is being communicated impossible to put into words, the descriptive ineffability of emotional communication means it is also hard to fit within the model of inferential processes relevance theory employs. As Sperber and Wilson (1986/1995: 57) put it: 'No one has any clear idea how inference might operate over non-propositional objects: say, over images, impressions or emotions ...'. We share this doubt. Indeed, we do not believe that inference can 'operate over' emotions. But we will argue that it does not follow from this that they play no role in inference: if Hume is right that emotional states motivate acts of inference, it is but a small step to propose they influence them too.

Relevance theory differs from most accounts of pragmatics in a number of different ways. We suggest that two of these differences make it uniquely capable of developing an account in which emotional communication can be integrated. The first difference is that relevance theory proposes, contra-Grice, that the informative intention is not always analysable as an intention to communicate simply a single proposition and propositional attitude. Sometimes, Sperber and Wilson (2015: 125) suggest, whatever the intended import is, it 'cannot be rendered as a proposition at all'. The relevance-theoretic informative intention, then, is an intention 'to make manifest or more manifest to the audience a set of assumptions I' (Sperber & Wilson 1986/1995: 58). Assumptions may be manifest to different degrees. The more salient a manifest assumption, the more strongly it is manifest. Vague communication typically involves a marginal increase in the manifestness of a very wide range of weakly manifest assumptions, resulting in an increased similarity between the cognitive environments of communicator and audience.

The second difference is the line Grice (1957) famously drew between showing and non-natural meaning (meaning$_{NN}$). This has had substantial effects on the development of pragmatics: in general, pragmatists still focus on the notion of meaning$_{NN}$ and abstract away from cases of showing. In contrast to the many researchers who argue that the line should be drawn in a different place, Sperber and Wilson (1986/1995) argue the line should not be drawn at all. According to relevance theory, both showing and meaning$_{NN}$ are instances of overt intentional or *ostensive-inferential communication*, and rather than there being a cut-off between the two notions, there is a continuum of cases in between.

Sperber and Wilson (2015: 123) augment the original figure of the continuum-as-a-straight-line with a separate, orthogonal dimension, which allows them to accommodate the fact that what is shown or meant$_{NN}$ might be more or less determinate and, effectively, turns the straight line into a square (see Figure 1). The showing–meaning$_{NN}$ continuum is concerned with the directness of the

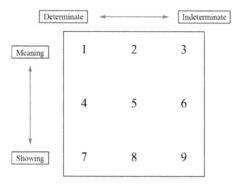

Figure 1 Two continua combined – indeterminate/determinate showing and meaning (Sperber & Wilson 2015)

evidence presented for the basic layer of information being communicated. Evidence is shown when the ostensive behaviour that points it out is direct, such as when I point to a church in the distance when my walking companion asks where we are heading. A coded response, such as an utterance of 'We're heading to Coombes Church', is indirect, and an example of meaning$_{NN}$.

The continuum between determinate and indeterminate import reflects the nature of the information that is being pointed out ostensively, whether shown or meant$_{NN}$. When I point to the church (showing), or respond 'We're heading to Coombes Church' (meaning$_{NN}$), the information being pointed out is highly determinate: a particular building. Poetic metaphors, on the hand, are cases of indeterminate meaning: what is meant is as descriptively ineffable as expressive meaning, too nebulous to be paraphrased at all.[4] Some cases of showing are indeterminate too. In the course of our walk, I stop and I breathe in the country air deeply, smile and turn my head ostensively in the general direction of the church. The view, the sounds and smells perceivable in my walking companion's physical environment will interact with her inferential abilities and her memories to alter her cognitive environment, making it possible for her to have further thoughts, memories and feelings similar to my own. What I intended to convey was merely an impression. I did not mean any one thing.

These two differences, we suggest, shed new light on how better to analyse some of the weaker, vaguer aspects of communication, including the communication of emotions, feelings and sensations. The change in the informative intention means that what is communicated might be vague and indeterminate. The two continua free us from the limitations imposed by the notion of determinate meaning. So, as well as the strongly communicated

---

[4] See Golding (2016) for an insightful exploration of the non-propositional effects of metaphor.

propositional-attitude descriptions activated by the interjection 'wow!' in (19.9), what is conveyed would also include an array of weakly implicated assumptions along the lines of the account sketched above.

Notice, however, that an array of weak implicatures is still, to some extent, a propositional account. Implicatures, no matter how weak, are still implicatures. And implicatures are propositions. If something really is too nebulous to be paraphrased in propositional terms, perhaps there are alternatives to attempting to paraphrase it as an array of yet further propositions. In the next section we propose an alternative.

19.4   Emotional Effects

19.4.1   Thought and Emotional Effects

Our alternative begins with a view of 'thought' that is perhaps different from the one standardly taken in relevance theory. Under this view, which is largely the one standardly provided by philosophers, thought involves, on the one hand, propositions (p) and, on the other, propositional attitudes such as 'believing that p', 'desiring that p' etc. In recent work developing a cognitive account of literature and art, Patricia Kolaiti (2015) treats thought in an interestingly different way. She argues that thought is a complex state, a mixture of causally interconnected conceptual and perceptual representations and that (for example) the aesthetic effects of literature and art cannot be properly explicated using the traditional relevance-theoretic notion of positive cognitive effect. She proposes that the notion be supplemented with a new notion of *positive perceptual effect*. As part of a justification for this move, Kolaiti points out that Sperber and Wilson themselves occasionally nod in the direction of the existence of ways of achieving relevance other than the three types of positive cognitive effects introduced in *Relevance*. Kolaiti cites Ramachandran and Hirstein's (1999) work on the neurology of aesthetic pleasure. They claim that engaging with certain types of images in certain types of ways is actually reinforcing and rewarding for the individual. It is good for us. What makes these perceptual effects positive is that they improve aspects of cognition. Might the notion of perceptual effects be useful in the analysis of emotional communication? It seems to us that the answer to this is no. Perception is a sensory phenomenon and, as we have seen in the previous sections, emotional states crucially involve the interplay between perception and cognition. We suggest another type of effect: *positive emotional effect*.

Sperber and Wilson suggest that one of the main pay-offs of ostensive communication is that it enhances the mutual cognitive environments of those engaging in it (in terms of shared thoughts/beliefs etc.). It does not seem too implausible a claim to suggest that the same may be true of emotional communication. Just as an awareness of the beliefs of others can have important consequences for successful interaction with them, so might an awareness of their emotions be beneficial also. Moreover, as the Radcliffe quote above illustrates, representations have little effect without a contribution from one's 'emotional constitution'.[5] In the next section we examine these emotional effects in more detail.

19.4.2   Emotion and Emotional Effects

The domain of relevance theory is ostensive-inferential communication and Wharton (2009) contains an extended defence of the claim that even spontaneous, natural behaviours (smiles, shivers) can be deliberately and openly shown (to a greater or lesser extent), which brings such behaviours within the realm of intentional communication. But just as utterances are complexes of non-natural and natural behaviours, both of which might be accounted for in terms of intentionality, so human interaction involves a great deal that goes on sub-attentively. Human interaction surely involves more than the interpretation of ostensive behaviour.

At all times, we are communicating information about our emotional state, attitudes, and evaluations of whatever we are currently confronting … Several of the nonverbal cues that reflect our internal state can be controlled consciously to some degree, but this will only occur if one directs one's conscious attention to the process of nonverbal encoding … We produce most of our nonverbal cues intuitively, without phenomenological awareness. (Lieberman 2000: 111)

Natural codes are being interpreted all the time, whether or not they are being deliberately shown. Lieberman's 'non-verbal encoding' is presumably linked to parallel processes of non-verbal *de*coding by an audience (an evolutionary account of the communication of the information to which Lieberman refers would be implausible in the absence of such processes). It is these codes that underpin the phenomenon psychologists call emotional contagion (Hatfield et al. 1994), in which not only is information about emotional states conveyed, but the states themselves are too.

Consider the following example. Andrew and Grace have arrived in a small village in France, quite late on a summer's evening. They book into a small hotel which, apart from the owner, appears to be pretty much deserted. Since it is August, they assume this is because during that month most people are away from the village on holiday. Andrew asks Grace if she thinks they are the only guests staying in the hotel. Grace replies:

(19.13)   I can hear footsteps in the room above us.

---

[5] For discussion of the problems associated with the stability of emotional communication, see Dezecache et al. (2013).

Grace's response interacts with existing assumptions Andrew is entertaining to yield the contextual implication in (9.14):

(19.14)   We are probably not the only guests staying in the hotel.

Let us change the context. Andrew and Grace live in a remote part of the countryside. There are no houses for miles around. The nearest building, some distance away, is a maximum-security prison. It is a stormy night and shortly before they go to bed they hear on the radio that a dangerous convict has escaped. In the middle of the night, Grace wakes Andrew and whispers (19.13) in a frightened tone of voice.

Let's pause and reconsider the discussion in Section 19.2. Tooby and Cosmides' idea is that an emotion is a superordinate cognitive mechanism, which exists to regulate or mobilise cognitive sub-mechanisms responsible for physiological changes, perception and attention, goal choice, information-gathering, specialised types of inference, etc. Given the new context, subconscious physiological changes over which they have little or no influence have put Andrew and Grace in a state of hyper-alertness. They feel the sensations these changes cause as those associated with fear, not just excitement, and are now acutely aware of their own emotional state. More than this, they are acutely aware of *each other's* emotional state (see Section 19.4.3).

Both Andrew and Grace will now automatically pay a high degree of attention to perceptual inputs they may not normally have even noticed: Is that rhythmic tapping really footsteps? Are there other things it might be? They are also equipped with a newly defined set of goals, in which safety is suddenly the most important of a range of new informational priorities: Can we get to the phone and call the police? Can we leave the house without the intruder noticing? Where are the car keys? But the motivation to reason in these particular ways comes from the way they feel: they have been directed to a course of reasoning, and to the derivation of the positive cognitive effects they are inferring, subconsciously, by their emotional state. The mental events that have *prompted* these particular courses of reasoning are not 'cognitive effects' in the sense of Sperber and Wilson's (1985/1996) – they are non-propositional, and do not necessarily rely on ostension to be communicated – but they are effects nonetheless: effects of the sensations and feelings Andrew and Grace are experiencing.

We call these effects *positive emotional effects*. Such effects are the bridges between, on the one hand, feelings and sensations and, on the other, cognition as traditionally construed. They prompt a range of particular inferential processes, and after having done so they do not simply disappear. They persist, working in tandem with the courses of reasoning they have motivated, and continuing to influence the hearer in the search for relevance. In this way, thinking and feeling, reason and passion, cognition and affect, which are often analysed as opposing forces, can be shown to work together in complex ways.

19.4.3   Procedures and Emotional Effects

Wilson (2011b) returns to the notion of procedural meaning and how it has developed over the years. She proposes some interesting changes. Originally, it was thought that the procedural meaning in a word such as 'but' existed to guide the hearer's path more easily to the intended interpretation. Building on Sperber et al.'s (2010) work on 'epistemic vigilance' – those cognitive strategies by which hearers avoid being either accidentally or intentionally misinformed – she proposes an interesting alternative in which the main function of discourse connectives would be not so much to guide the hearer's path as to trigger argumentative procedures which yield intuitions about evidential relations, and form part of the capacity for epistemic vigilance:

> The function of the procedural expressions in a language may be to activate … domain-specific procedures. In principle, these could be of any type at all, although in practice they are likely to be drawn from modules which play a significant role in linguistic communication: these include the modules (or sub-modules) involved in mindreading (Baron-Cohen 1995), emotion reading (Wharton 2003b, 2009), social cognition (Malle, 2004; Fiske & Taylor 2008), parsing and speech production (Levelt 1993), comprehension (Sperber & Wilson 2002) and so on. (Wilson 2011b: 17)

Co-evolving with the emotional mechanisms or procedures described above would have been emotion-*reading* mechanisms and procedures. These procedures are sub-attentive and unintentional and help us read emotional states, irrespective of whether those states are conveyed ostensively or non-ostensively. Panic does not spread through a crowd by virtue of each person in the crowd acting ostensively, any more than a flu epidemic is caused by everyone in a community deliberately coughing over the person next to them. It is these procedures that emotional communication exploits, and through which many emotional effects are communicated. The procedural information encoded by linguistic expressives, interjections, facial expressions, tone of voice and non-verbal behaviours generally not only puts the user into a state in which emotional procedures are highly activated, but, in doing so, makes it much more likely they will give rise to positive emotional effects in another. Just as there is no inferential route between, for example, 'so' and the procedure it encodes, so these behaviours have the effect of simply 'switching on' other mental states (some of which may be inferential heuristics).[6]

---

[6] Thanks to Christoph Unger (p.c.) for valuable input on this point.

19.5   Conclusion

We asked three questions:

1. What are emotions (and what is their relationship with reasoning)?
2. What is communicated in cases of emotional communication?
3. *How* do we communicate emotional states?

We have sketched a view of emotions that is consistent with Hume, but acknow-ledges recent work by Rey and Cosmides and Tooby. Emotions involve an interaction between several elements: cognitive, qualitative and physiological. They are superordinate cognitive mechanisms, and function to regulate cogni-tive sub-mechanisms responsible for perception and a range of other mental activities, among which are attention, information-gathering, physiological changes and specialised types of inference.

Emotional communication works on a number of different levels. Interjections, facial expression and affective tone of voice lead to the con-struction of higher-level explicatures and these (together with the proposition expressed by an utterance) lead to strong and weak implicatures by either pro-viding strong support for a single, determinate conclusion or marginally altering the strength or salience of a wide array of conclusions. But we have argued that these positive cognitive effects need to be supplemented by a new type of effect: *positive emotional effects*. The procedural information encoded by nat-ural codes puts the user into a state in which emotional procedures are highly activated, and these procedures are therefore much more likely to cause posi-tive emotional effects in another. Emotional communication is underpinned by the unconscious activation of both information about emotional states in others and, sometimes, the states themselves. In the latter case, the process is more a matter of 'contagion' than it is intentionally communicated.[7] Of course, if the hearer infers that, say, a natural behaviour has been used ostensively, it may well be selected by an audience using the relevance-theoretic comprehension procedure, in which case the standard inferential processes apply. But notice also that within the framework proposed by Sperber and Wilson (2015) what is shown can be highly indeterminate (in the vicinity of point 9 on Figure 1).

Inference does not operate over non-propositional objects. But it does not follow from that that non-propositional information does not influence the objects over which inference operates. While much emotional informa-tion may not be represented propositionally, it can still colour and flavour

---

[7] We are sure that there are close links between emotional effects, as presented here, and Kolaiti's (2015) notion of perceptual effects, particularly since the kind of responses we tend to asso-ciate with literature and art are often so strongly emotional. We aim to explore these links in future work.

the propositions themselves: writing an SMS message in upper case does not change its truth conditions, but it is not hard to imagine that it might influence how such a message is taken, or how it might shape the inferences someone draws from it. Inference is motivated by emotional states. These are the states that make inference happen, that make it worthwhile, that make us tick. We propose that not only do emotional states motivate acts of inference, they *influence* them. Reason is, and only ought to be, slave of the passions, and we hope the discussion above has gone some way to making emotions relevant.

Acknowledgements

The authors are grateful to Jorge Campos da Costa, Billy Clark, Florian Cova, Danny Dukes, Ernst-August Gutt, Elly Ifantidou, Patricia Kolaiti, Didier Maillat, Misha Müller, Steve Oswald, Louis de Saussure and Kate Scott for comments on an earlier draft. We would also like to thank two anonymous reviewers for their constructive criticisms which have greatly improved this chapter.

20 Adaptations as Communicative Acts: A Relevance-Theoretic Perspective

Anne Furlong

20.1 Introduction

The phenomenon of adaptation is universal, ubiquitous, and puzzling. Corrigan (2017: 23) notes that adaptation can be viewed from three perspectives: as a process, a product, or an act of reception. In every act of adaptation, a work in one medium is 'reconfigured or adjusted' in relation 'to one or more other texts or objects' (2017: 23). Generally speaking, the term 'adaptation' typically designates the resulting work. However, it applies also to the audience's engagement with the new text, as 'different works operate differently for different readers' (2017: 23). This chapter focuses primarily on the process and product of adaptation from a relevance-theoretic perspective, where, I argue, the role of the reader is crucial.

It is not obvious to many people why a literary[1] work that has succeeded in one form (or iteration) should be attempted in another. Albrecht-Crane and Cutchins (2013: 20) claim that 'adaptations … create a new text with its own manifold relationship to source text(s)', i.e., an adaptation communicates a set of assumptions (an interpretation) distinct from the set communicated by the source work. At the same time, an adaptation ostensively encourages the audience to utilise (some aspects of) the source as implicated premises in the context in which the new text is processed. Relevance theory provides a constrained account of context that allows for the broad spectrum of adaptive strategies, goals, and attitudes. We should be able to account for adaptations which succeed in the audience's estimation though departing in significant ways from the source, as we should also for those which retain many of the features of the source but implicitly critique or correct it.

My principal claim is that relevance theory provides a useful framework for understanding adaptations. The claim proceeds from my view that an adaptation is an act of communication like any other; consequently, relevance-theoretic principles, including the presumption of optimal relevance, apply

---

[1] Here I mean 'literary' in its broad cultural sense: a creative work, such as a novel or film that is highly valued because of its aesthetic properties or effects.

to adaptations as they do to other communicative acts. Given the crucial role of contextual assumptions in relevance theory, I argue that assumptions about the source work can form part of the context in which the writer intends an adaptation to be processed. Finally, adaptations relate to the source work in a number of ways; these can be accommodated and accounted for within a relevance-theoretic framework.

20.2   Some Issues in Adaptation

Every adaptation involves at least two texts: the source and an other. Scholars and critics have taken a number of approaches to sort out the relationship between them. Baetens (2005, 2010) and Meikle (2013) have examined economic and cultural aspects of adaptation. Albrecht-Crane and Cutchins's (2013) anthology takes a more historicising approach. Foundational works such as Bluestone (1957) and Chatman (1980), through to McFarlane (1996), Cahir (2006), and Hutcheon (2006), though primarily concerned with the reworking of novels into film, propose a range of theoretical frameworks to account for the production and reception of adaptation. All have been influenced by Dryden's 1683 (1913) division of translations (metaphrase, paraphrase, and imitation), which captures many intuitions about adaptation. He calls *metaphrase* 'turning an Author Word by Word, and Line by Line, from one Language into another'; *paraphrase* he defines as 'Translation with Latitude, where the Author is kept in view by the Translator, so as never to be lost, but his words are not so strictly follow'd as his sense [which is] amplified, but not alter'd'. Lastly, a translator embarked on *imitation* 'assumes the liberty, not only to vary from the words and sense but to forsake them both as he sees occasion; and taking only some general hints from the Original, to run division on the Ground-work, as he pleases'. Many contemporary theories of adaptation offer parallel or analogous categories.

So, for instance, Cahir (2006) proposes three modes of adaptation from text to film, explicitly calling them translations: literal, traditional, and radical, based on the degree to which a given adaptation 'reproduces the plot and all its attending details' (p. 16), or, in emphasising interpretation, presents the adaptation as 'a more fully independent work' (p. 17). Blankier (2014) reviews Leitch's (2003) taxonomy of adaptations, which overlaps and combines Cahir's (and Dryden's) divisions: celebration, adjustment, neoclassic imitation, colonisation, and analogue, depending on the adaptor's attitude towards the source. The various taxonomic systems are bewildering in their variety; and while any given descriptive system may illuminate a specific work, none has provided a satisfactory general account of adaptation. Despite their theoretical inventiveness and rigour, adaptation studies are hamstrung by considerations of fidelity, evaluation of the new work, and 'equivalence', i.e., attempting to identify the formal properties in the new work which function analogously to elements in the source.

Although fidelity is an inadequate criterion on which to evaluate or analyse adaptations, nevertheless the recognition of resemblance is fundamental to treating a text as an adaptation. Unless the audience notice some degree of resemblance between the source and the new work, they will not treat the new text as an adaptation at all. Once they become aware that a source text exists, and that it is manifestly intended to constitute part of the context in which the adaptation is interpreted, they are very likely to compare earlier and subsequent texts.

It is often assumed that the simple fact of resemblance explains how the audience knows what parts of the source text to select, and how these parts function in the new work. But resemblance per se places no constraints on the selection of context, nor does it explain why some works which are 'literal' (in Cahir's sense) can be highly critical of their sources, while others which seem to involve significant modification amount to mere 'celebrations' (in Leitch's). Relevance theory provides a global cognitive constraint that accounts for the selection and salience of those aspects of the source work which the adaptor encourages her audience to use in interpreting her text. In the following section, I highlight the specific features of relevance theory that help shed light on the construction of context in adaptations.

20.3   Relevance Theory: The Role of Context Construction

Relevance theory makes two fundamental claims about cognition and communication. It claims that 'human cognition tends to be organised so as to maximise relevance', and that 'every act of ostensive communication communicates a presumption of its own optimal relevance' (Sperber & Wilson 1986/1995: 260). 'Relevance' is a property (p. 261), and is quantifiable: something is relevant to the extent that the positive cognitive effects it produces are large, and to the extent that the cognitive effort needed to achieve these effects is small. The greater the positive cognitive effects that an utterance produces, the more relevant it is; and the more effort it takes to achieve these effects, the less relevant it is (pp. 122–32). Relevance thus involves a dynamic balance between effort and effect; when there are no longer adequate effects for the effort expended, we stop processing the text.

From a relevance-theoretic perspective, adaptations constitute interesting acts of communication. There is of course no guarantee that an audience will recognise that the new text is an adaptation. In that case, interpretation follows the standard relevance-theoretic comprehension procedure. But in the case of an adaptation that is recognised as such, the new work provides evidence for the intended interpretation by making manifest some degree of resemblance with the source, and encouraging the reader to retrieve parts of the earlier work which resemble aspects of the new one or to reproduce those parts in the context in which the adaptation is interpreted. In effect, the reader must use separate sets of assumptions that may be very similar, almost identical, to construct the context in which the new work is being processed. In relevance-theoretic terms, such extra effort seems counter-intuitive.

In an earlier paper (Furlong 2008), I argued that re-reading can be accounted for within a relevance-theoretic account in terms of additional cognitive effects gained by expanding the context to include assumptions derived from the previous interpretation. Re-readers may, I argued, pay attention to details missed on the first reading, extend the interpretive process (i.e., engage in non-spontaneous interpretation) in order to derive more implicatures, or aim at replicating a psychological or mental state resulting from reading. So, for example, a reader of *Little Dorrit* may, on a subsequent reading, make efforts to pay attention to metaphors of and allusions to imprisonment; he may derive new assumptions or extend existing lines of interpretation. Alternatively, the reader of Montgomery's *The Blue Castle* may re-read the novel, in parts or as a whole, to re-experience the improbable but satisfying conclusion.

I suggest that adaptations can be accounted for along similar lines. Unlike the re-reader, who voluntarily undertakes the work of replicating an earlier interpretation, the adaptor imposes this effort on her audience. The adaptor is not necessarily asking her audience to expend effort to produce new assumptions, or strengthen or eliminate existing ones (though that may be one outcome); nor is she positively aiming to replicate in a new medium the psychological or mental or emotional condition resulting from the reader's processing of the source work. Instead, she is encouraging the audience to select some part of the contextual assumptions in which the source work was processed, as well as their interpretation of it, as part of the context in which her own text is processed. The interpretation of an adaptation thus requires the audience to undertake a comparison, no matter how rough or perfunctory, because some degree of resemblance to (or fidelity with) the source work is essential to recognising the adaptor's intended interpretation, even if this is not required in order to evaluate it or judge its success. The question then becomes which assumptions are included in this new, expanded context, and what effects could possibly justify this increased effort. Relevance theory sheds light on how the selection is made, and suggests that an adaptation can achieve relevance only if it communicates assumptions and creates effects different from or at least in addition to those derivable from the source. I will deal with these issues separately, beginning with a consideration of context construction.

Sperber and Wilson (1986/1995: 137–8) contend that 'a crucial step in the processing of new information, and in particular of verbally communicated information, is to combine it with an adequately selected set of background assumptions – which then constitutes the context'. In the case of an adapted work, the issue concerns which aspects of the source text the audience is manifestly intended to entertain as part of the intended context. Given a source work of any level of complexity, the intended context appears both vast and unconfined: there seems in principle no limit to the degree to which the audience can incorporate material from the source.

In reality, many considerations constrain the construction of the intended context. There are limits on the investment of cognitive effort required to retrieve and combine information from the source, as well as on memory and attention. Nevertheless, the recognition that the new work is an adaptation means that the audience should retrieve from memory a selection of assumptions communicated by the source. The adaptation provides evidence as to which contextual assumptions derived from the source work the audience should incorporate into the context in which they interpret the adaptation. What limits that selection is the presumption of optimal relevance.

According to relevance theory, the presumption of optimal relevance is communicated by 'every act of ostensive communication' (Sperber & Wilson 1986/1995: 260):

The utterance is presumed to be

1. at least relevant enough to be worth the addressee's effort to process it, and
2. the most relevant one that is compatible with the speaker's abilities and preferences.
   (Sperber & Wilson 1986/1995: 270)

This raises the question of what makes an adaptation optimally relevant. As I suggest above, an adaptation cannot achieve relevance by replicating the effects of the source. Moreover, we must account for adaptations across a broad spectrum of resemblance, from virtual identity (Van Sant's putatively 'shot-for-shot'[2] remake of Hitchcock's *Psycho*), through textual fidelity alone (Branagh's film version of *Hamlet*), to reinvention (*House*, the CBS series based on Sherlock Holmes), and to inspiration (the film *She's the Man*, a contemporary inversion of *Twelfth Night*). In the following section, I show how a text that makes manifest significant portions of another text as part of the intended context can achieve optimal relevance.

20.4 Relevance Theory and Adaptation

In producing an adaptation, the communicator makes mutually manifest her intention to make manifest an extension of the immediately available context by retrieval of a similar context from the audience's memory, the context of

---

[2] Van Sant's 1998 movie does not, in fact, slavishly replicate every shot of the Hitchcock film. In a 2003 interview with Scott Tobias, the director admitted that an exact copy was impossible. In the course of filming, he added, 'Everything changed, because Hitchcock had an inimitable way of filmmaking.'

the source work. Although her utterance makes significant demands on the audience's cognitive resources, it requires no gratuitous effort to produce adequate positive contextual effects. The similarity of the contextual premises may result in some savings on the effort side; assumptions and especially interpretations retrieved from memory may entail less processing than engaging in a series of inferential operations over large and complex sections of text (especially multimodal works such as movies or operas). At the same time, the audience may well find that the slight differences between the old and new texts, and the clear distinctions in communicative goals between the first author and the adaptor, produce rich contextual effects. And since the adaptations I am here concerned with are complex works of narrative fiction, the positive contextual effects will include a very wide array of relatively weak implicatures, possibly including poetic effects. In fact, we should expect that it is precisely in giving rise to these weak implicatures that the adaptation achieves relevance: the lines of interpretation suggested by stronger or weaker resemblance can be extended indefinitely through ordinary non-spontaneous interpretation.

The communicative act of adaptation thus includes making manifest the relationship between the new work and its source. The adaptor encourages her audience to construct a context that includes assumptions communicated by the source work, the audience's interpretation of the source work, and the assumptions communicated by the adaptation. It is precisely this rich and complex context that invites readers to identify correspondences between the adaptation, the source, and other pre-existing treatments, and may partially account for the persistence of fidelity as an evaluative criterion long after it has been shown to be unhelpful. All of these claims follow from applying the relevance-theoretic account of communication to the phenomenon of adaptation, and treating the adaptation as a communicative act independent of the source.

But there is more to the process of adaptation than this. As I noted at the outset, adaptation theorists distinguish process, product, and reception. In a relevance-theoretic approach, I suggest, we might consider the adaptors, the texts, and the readers' interpretations their rough equivalents. Moreover, it is precisely the recognition that a text is manifestly adapted from a source work that triggers the expanded context construction and imposes increased effort on the audience. In the following paragraphs, I propose an account of the effects produced by this extra effort.

Every adaptation must be doing something different from (as well as in addition to) the source work. Some adaptations aim for 'equivalence' through transmediation;[3] so McFarlane (1996) argues that while some 'narrative

---

[3] 'Transmediation' refers to the practice of presenting a work in forms or media different from the source. Examples include film adaptations of text sources, musical settings of poems, paintings of scenes from operas, and so on. It can be very broadly construed; see Chouliaraki (2013) (journalism), Lavender (2017) (language arts education), and Mills (2011) (theatre studies).

elements' are 'amenable to display in film', others 'must find quite different equivalences' in the new medium. Audiences and theorists alike often assume that when adaptations ostensively aim for the highest levels of fidelity, the adaptor seeks to 'produce a [work] that will run parallel' to the source and 'have the same effect' on the audience (Christopher Priest discussing his goals as a noveliser of films, quoted in Baetens 2010: 67).

In fact, adaptations must do more than simply reproduce the effect of the original in a new setting, medium, or version if they are to achieve relevance: they must yield effects that could not be produced by the source work. The possibilities are very great indeed. An adaptor may communicate a new interpretation of the source; she may endorse the interpretation manifestly intended by the author; she may critique the source; she may extend the narrative by inventing events before or after the timeline of the source, or by developing minor or secondary characters and events; she may situate the characters and events in a different time, place, relation, or culture. In all these cases, and in general, fidelity is only one consideration among many, rather than a foundational evaluative criterion.

In contemporary Western culture, adaptation typically involves the transmediation of a text, most commonly resulting in a multimodal work such as a film. Here relevance is achieved as the adaptation presents evidence unavailable to a reader. No matter how rich and detailed a reader's interpretation may be, it is irreducibly interior, fundamentally private, and profoundly constrained by his imagination and experience. The moviegoer's cognitive environment, on the other hand, is substantially amplified by visual, aural, and somatic stimuli in addition to the linguistically provided evidence. Even an adaptation of the source material that hews closely to generally accepted interpretations offers the audience emotional and cognitive experiences distinct from those produced by reading. Transmediated adaptations can also move from screen to page. Successful novelisations of films achieve relevance in part by overcoming the constraints of time (one of the defining features of performance) while providing extended explanations of characters' motivations and states of mind, supplying authorial guidance, or explicating visual or other metaphors linguistically. Even while following the source work as exactly as conditions permit, successful adaptations can thus yield adequate positive cognitive effects without requiring gratuitous effort to achieve them.

Adaptations that do not involve a shift of medium present yet other prospects. Page-to-page adaptations frequently involve a change of perspective or narrator. So, e.g., Rhys's novel *Wide Sargasso Sea* retells the story of Jane Eyre from the mad wife's point of view. Remakes of films or new versions of older television involve cultural or historical shifts to appeal to specific target audiences, often for uncomplicated commercial reasons. They may also, as with Van Sant's remake of *Psycho*, communicate complex philosophical meditations on the nature of art.

Thus, adaptations provide evidence for the intended interpretation of the new work that exploits its resemblance, or debt, to the earlier text. As I have argued, an adaptation may, to varying degrees, endorse the source work, or criticise it, extend it, or even reject it. It may exploit the cultural capital of the source (whether 'literary' or not). Finally, if we extend the category of adaptation to include fanfic, then a new work may address what the adaptor regards as deficiencies in the source. Irrespective of the final form, all of these adaptations constitute communicative acts independent of the source. Crucially, the adaptor is not limited to or by the intended interpretation of the earlier text.

20.5   The Adaptor's Communicative Purpose

To suggest how this relevance-theoretic approach can resolve some of the dilemmas of adaptation studies, I consider here three cases of adaptation: one transmediated adaptation (book to film) and two novels. Each of them exploits the cultural capital of the source. The 1999 movie *Mansfield Park* and the novels *Mary Reilly* and *Florence and Giles* are based on well-known works of nineteenth-century fiction: *Mansfield Park*, *The Strange Case of Dr Jekyll and Mr Hyde*, and *The Turn of the Screw*. The audience is alerted to the adaptations' relationships to their sources in a number of ways, but it is only as they work through each adaptation that they can determine the adaptor's communicative goal. In each case, the adaptor makes strongly manifest her intention that the audience incorporate into the intended context assumptions drawn from their knowledge or interpretation of the source; her audience must be familiar with it if they are to arrive at the intended interpretation and experience the intended aesthetic effects.

20.5.1   Critical Reappraisal

Patricia Rozema's movie *Mansfield Park* (1999) adds new scenes and characters, and reinterprets the protagonist Fanny Price as a spirited proto-feminist and freethinker (rather than the downtrodden poor relation of the novel). At the same time, its adherence to external fidelity (names, setting, and historical detail) serves the director's goal, not of celebrating or re-creating the source, but of critiquing the economic and social oppression that supports the privileged lives of the main characters. The film, like the novel, is set during the first quarter of the nineteenth century; in both versions, the head of the Bertram household, where Fanny is a dependent and penniless cousin, derives his wealth from plantations in the West Indies.

But where Jane Austen is virtually silent on the slavery that underwrites the Bertrams' lavish and unproductive lives, Rozema interpolates scenes which suggest that both the father and his eldest son have indulged in sexual violence far from home. These new scenes serve to intensify the audience's awareness of the multiple fissures and hypocrisies in British society, such as the sexual double standards, the oppressive class system, and the commodification of women. The film ends, as does the novel, with Fanny presiding as chatelaine over panoramic views of the estate. This triumphant conclusion arises not, as in Austen, from the restoration and vindication of the existing social order, but out of the rehabilitation of the central character through her acknowledgement of her complicity and guilt.

Rozema's adaptation preserves much of the dialogue and setting of the earlier work, and the actors appear in period-appropriate costume. But where this level of faithfulness would typically reduce processing effort, I argue that Rozema has increased the cognitive load. Indeed, an audience familiar with Said's *Culture and Imperialism* will notice how closely Rozema's adaptation follows Said's handling of the novel. The references to Said, the interpolated scenes, and the radical changes to Fanny's actions and attitudes prompt detailed comparison of the film with Austen's novel, and this combination of new and given information significantly expands the intended context. Under these circumstances, the adaptation cannot achieve relevance as a simple transmediation. Instead, the viewer is encouraged to develop an interpretation that accounts for the differences by working out the director's communicative act: here, a pointed criticism of the source text. By making use of the novel as a social document, the director indicts not only the society depicted in Austen's text but also, to some degree, the writer herself and those who have read the novel uncritically.

20.5.2   Experimentation

John Harding's *Florence and Giles* occupies an intermediate position between celebration and critique. Harding makes slight alterations to names and places, reverses the birth order of the children in Henry James's work (*The Turn of the Screw*), and portrays the governess as both murderous and unstable. The adaptation seems primarily to be an experiment in mind style. Florence, the first-person narrator, gives the reader direct access to her thoughts, which take unusual linguistic form:

Blithe House is a great barn, a crusty stone mansion of many rooms, so immense it takes my little brother, Giles, who is as fast of limb as he is not of wit, three minutes and more to run through its length, a house uncomfortabled and shabbied by prudence, a neglect of a place, tightly pursed ... leaked and rotted and mothed and rusted ...

James's rendering of the mind style of his first-person narrator, the unnamed governess, is far more subtle, though also suggestive of a singular narrative mind:

I remember the whole beginning as a succession of flights and drops, a little seesaw of the right throbs and the wrong. After rising, in town, to meet his appeal, I had at all events a couple of very bad days – found myself doubtful again, felt indeed sure I had made a mistake.

James exercises precise control over the narrative; readers follow every movement of the governess's agonised descent into near-madness, so closely that it is virtually impossible to determine whether the events she describes are real or the product of her imagination. Unlike the psychologically distressed governess of *The Turn of the Screw*, however, Florence is rational and her mind is clear; her verbal inventiveness functions as a counterpart to James's stylistic virtuosity, not as integral to the interpretation of the work.

The results are mixed: the adaptation makes heavy cognitive demands on the reader, repaying this effort primarily in the reader's emotional or critical response to Florence's style. Her peculiar thought style (her speech is unremarkable) does not contribute to a richer interpretation: nothing accounts for Florence's odd syntax, and her expressions shed no additional light on the events or themes of Harding's novel. Some readers take pleasure in the writer's playfulness, but a number of reviewers reported simple frustration.

As with Rozema's film, Harding's book encourages the audience to retrieve substantial amounts of textual information from the source work, including plot, character, and setting. And like Rozema, Harding introduces salient alterations that draw the reader's attention as they note similarities and differences. Unlike Rozema, however, Harding forces the reader to pay attention to fine-grained detail, both in the unusual syntax and morphology, and in the minute, constant modifications to the story. Such intense scrutiny must produce significant increases in positive cognitive effects to achieve relevance; the new narrative stance, the coarser solution to the mystery of the previous governess's death, and above all, the peculiarity of Florence's language impose formidable demands. I suggest that the frustration expressed by some reviewers may be the result of their deeper knowledge of James's novella, which increased the processing effort by virtue of the greater contextual information available to them without producing adequate contextual effects: they developed no new insights into James's novella, and Harding's stylistic innovations added little literary value. Readers with only a passing familiarity are less likely to manipulate such large contexts; for them, Harding's primary communicative act – linguistic experimentation inspired by, indebted to, and parasitic on *The Turn of the Screw* – proved sufficiently relevant.

20.5.3   Fanfic

Valerie Martin's (2013) novel *Mary Reilly* (marketed as a 'parallel novel') makes few changes to Stevenson's horror classic (*Dr Jekyll and Mr Hyde*), instead relying on the complexities of the source text to supplement the modest effects of her novel. The source work supplies a structure onto which Martin projects romanticised views of Stevenson's protagonist through the eyes of a remarkable but overlooked young woman, an underservant in Jekyll's household who is the novel's narrator. This work is less ambitious than Rozema's or Harding's; a mass-market historical novel, it exploits the cultural capital of the source text to raise the prestige of a standard romantic fantasy.

Fanfic adaptations function in part as *eisegesis* (treating public texts as private or personal communication) and in part as celebration and extension of the source. As eisegetical interpretation, fanfic demonstrates the source's impact on the adaptor; in addition, it extends an admired and much-loved text by explicating or adding contextual information not provided by the author, but compatible with the information provided by the source. Martin's adaptation conforms to the template of much fanfic: it relies on the extension of an established fictional world into which some version of the author is projected, but the philosophical focus of the earlier work (an exploration of the human psyche) shifts in the new text towards the merely personal (the resolution of a shopworn romantic drama). I suggest that, contrary to the cases discussed above, with *Mary Reilly* the resemblance to Stevenson's novella decreases processing effort. As before, much of the contextual information will be available to the target audience, but here the reader is not put to the task of close comparison to achieve the intended effects.

20.6   Conclusion

An adaptation can fall anywhere on the spectrum of faithfulness, from identity through adequate resemblance, to the faintest of echoes. It may exploit critical or emblematic elements of the source work without ostensively referring to it. There is no correlation between the kind or extent of fidelity (and literariness, or aesthetic charge, or prestige), and the adaptor's communicative goals. Some adaptations endorse the work on which they are based, while others rely on the reputation of the source to legitimise the new enterprise. All adaptations are, then, independent communicative acts. As such, their relationship to their source works can be accommodated within a relevance-theoretic framework which can help partially resolve the vexed question of faithfulness. Some degree of resemblance between the old work and the new is necessary if the audience is to recognise the latter as an adaptation. In the best cases, the new work succeeds not only in its own right – as a comment, a celebration, a re-creation, or a rejection – but also by augmenting the audience's experience of the source.

What is the point of adaptation? If it were only to repeat what was already known, there would be none. In fact, even a modest, relatively literal, and deeply faithful adaptation will be a new and independent communicative act, and may be a highly creative one as well.

Acknowledgements

In a life governed by serendipity, I am most grateful for the chances that led me to Deirdre Wilson. Her patience, guidance, kindness, and high expectations sustained me during the long years of my doctoral work. She remains the source I return to, with deepest respect and admiration, as I pursue my own adaptations.

My thanks also to the anonymous referees for their encouraging responses and their fine-grained, keen-eyed criticism.

References

Ackerman, B. P. (1981). Young children's understanding of a speaker's intentional use of a false utterance. *Developmental Psychology* 17: 472–80.

(1983). Form and function in children's understanding of ironic utterances. *Journal of Experimental Child Psychology* 35: 487–508.

Acquaviva, P. (2014). Roots, concepts, and word structure: On the atoms of lexical semantics. In: F. Rainer, W. U. Dressler, F. Gardani & H. C. Luschutzky (eds.) *Morphology and Meaning*. John Benjamins, pp. 49–70.

Acredolo, L. & Goodwyn, S. (1988). Symbolic gesturing in normal infants. *Child Development* 59: 450–66.

Aguert, M., Laval, V., Le Bigot, L. & Bernicot, J. (2010). Understanding expressive speech acts: The role of prosody and situational context in French-speaking 5- to 9-year-olds. *Journal of Speech, Language, and Hearing Research* 53: 1629–41.

Aguert, M., Laval, V., Lacroix, A., Gil, S. & Le Bigot, L. (2013). Inferring emotions from speech prosody: Not so easy at age five. *PLoS ONE* 8(12): e83657. doi:10.1371/journal.pone.0083657.

Aikhenvald, A. Y. (2004). *Evidentiality*. Oxford University Press.

(2010). *Imperatives and Commands*. Oxford University Press.

(2014). The grammar of knowledge in typological perspective. In: A. Y. Aikhenvald & R. M. W. Dixon (eds.) *The Grammar of Knowledge*. Oxford University Press, pp. 1–51.

Albrecht-Crane, C. & Cutchins, D. (2013). Introduction: New beginnings for adaptation studies. In: C. Albrecht-Crane & D. Cutchins (eds.) *Adaptation Studies: New Approaches*. Fairleigh Dickinson University Press, pp. 11–22.

Alcázar, A. & Saltarelli, M. (2014). *The Syntax of Imperatives*. Cambridge University Press.

Allott, N. (2008). *Pragmatics and Rationality*. PhD thesis, University of London.

(2013). Relevance theory. In: A. Capone, F. Lo Piparo & M. Carapezza (eds.) *Perspectives on Linguistic Pragmatics*. Springer, pp. 57–98.

(2017). Metarepresentation. In: A. Barron, Y. Gu & G. Steen (eds.) *The Routledge Handbook of Pragmatics*. Routledge, pp. 295–309.

Altmann, G. T. M. & Kamide, Y. (1999). Incremental interpretation at verbs: Restricting the domain of subsequent reference. *Cognition* 73(3): 247–64.

Altmann, G. T. M. & Steedman, M. (1988). Interaction with context during human sentence processing. *Cognition* 30(3): 191–238.

Ameka, F. (1992). Interjections: The universal yet neglected part of speech. *Journal of Pragmatics* 18: 101–18.

Anderson, L. & Lepore, E. (2013a). Slurring words. *Noûs* 47(1): 25–48.

  (2013b). What did you call me? Slurs as prohibited words. *Analytic Philosophy* 54(3): 350–63.

Anderson, M. J. (2014). *After Phrenology: Neural Reuse and the Interactive Brain.* MIT Press.

Anglin, J. M. (1977). *Word, Object, and Conceptual Development.* W. W. Norton.

Anscombre, J.-C. & Ducrot, O. (1977). Deux *mais* en français? *Lingua* 43: 23–40.

Antony, L. (2003). Rabbit-pots and supernovas: On the relevance of psychological data to linguistic theory. In: A. Barber (ed.) *Epistemology of Language.* Oxford University Press, pp. 47–68.

Aoun, J. & Choueiri, L. (2000). Epithets. *Natural Language & Linguistic Theory* 18: 1–39.

Arad, M. (2005). *Roots and Patterns: Hebrew Morpho-Syntax.* Springer.

Arnon, I., Casillas, M., Kurumada, C. & Estigarribia, B. (eds.). (2014). *Language in Interaction: Studies in Honor of Eve V. Clark* (Vol. 12). John Benjamins.

Asch, S. & Nerlove, H. (1960). The development of double function terms in children: An exploratory investigation. In: B. Kaplan & S. Wapner (eds.) *Perspectives in Psychological Theory: Essays in Honor of Heinz Werner.* International Universities Press, pp. 47–60.

Atlas, J. D. & Levinson, S. C. (1981). It-clefts, informativeness and logical form: Radical pragmatics (revised standard version). In: P. Cole (ed.) *Radical Pragmatics.* Academic Press, pp. 1–61.

Aziz-Zadeh, L. & Gamez-Djokic, V. (2016). The interaction between metaphor and emotion processing in the brain. *Emotion Review* 8(3): 275–6.

Bach, K. (2006). Review of C. Potts 'The Logic of Conventional Implicatures'. *Journal of Linguistics* 42(2): 490–5.

  (2018). Loaded words: On the semantics and pragmatic of slurs. In: D. Sosa (ed.) *Bad Words.* Oxford University Press.

Baetens, J. (2005). Novelization, a contaminated genre? *Critical Inquiry* 32: 43–60.

  (2010). Expanding the field of constraint: Novelization as an example of multiply constrained writing. *Poetics Today* 31(1): 51–79.

Baillargeon, R., Scott, R. M. & Bian, L. (2016). Psychological reasoning in infancy. *Annual Review of Psychology* 67(1): 159–86.

Banfield, A. (1982). *Unspeakable Sentences.* Routledge & Kegan Paul.

Barceló, A. & Stainton, R. J. (2016). Cuasi-Factivos. *Elenkhos* 1(1): 65–88.

Barner, D. & Bachrach, A. (2010). Inference and exact numerical representation in early language development. *Cognitive Psychology* 60(1): 40–62.

Barner, D., Brooks, N. & Bale, A. (2011). Accessing the unsaid: The role of scalar alternatives in children's pragmatic inference. *Cognition* 118(1): 84–93.

Barnhart, R. K. (1988). *Chambers Dictionary of Etymology.* Chambers Harrap.

Baron-Cohen, S. (1995). *Mindblindness.* MIT Press.

Barrett, M. D. (1978). Lexical development and overextension in child language. *Journal of Child Language* 5: 205–19.

  (1986). Early semantic representations and early word usage. In: S. A. Kuczaj II & M. D. Barrett (eds.) *The Development of Word Meaning: Progress in Cognitive Development Research.* Springer, pp. 39–67.

Barton, E. (1990). *Nonsentential Constituents.* John Benjamins.

Barton, E. & Progovac, L. (2005). Nonsententials in Minimalism. In: R. Elugardo & R. Stainton (eds.) *Ellipsis and Non-Sentential Speech*. Springer, pp. 71–93.

Bartsch, K. & Wellman, H. M. (1995). *Children Talk about the Mind*. Oxford University Press.

Bauer, L. (1978). *The Grammar of Nominal Compounding with Special Reference to Danish, English and French*. Odense University Press.

(1983). *English Word Formation*. Cambridge University Press.

Beck, D. M. & Lavie, N. (2004). Look here but ignore what you see: Effects of distractors at fixation. *Journal of Experimental Psychology: Human Perception and Performance* 31: 592–607.

Begby, E. (2017). Language from the ground up: A study of Homesign communication. *Erkenntnis* 82: 693–714.

Bergen, L. & Grodner, D. J. (2012). Speaker knowledge influences the comprehension of pragmatic inferences. *Journal of Experimental Psychology: Learning, Memory, and Cognition* 38(5): 1450–60.

Berthonneau, A. M. & Kleiber, G. (1993). Pour une nouvelle approche de l'imparfait: l'imparfait, un temps anaphorique méronomique. *Langages* 112: 55–73.

Bezuidenhout, A. (2004). Procedural meaning and the semantics/pragmatics interface. In: C. Bianchi (ed.) *The Semantics/Pragmatics Distinction*. CSLI, pp. 101–31.

Bianchi, C. (2014). Slurs and appropriation: An echoic account. *Journal of Pragmatics* 66: 35–44.

Bickhard, M. H. (2009). The interactivist model. *Synthese* 166(3): 547–91.

(2016). The anticipatory brain: Two approaches. In: V.C. Müller (ed.) *Fundamental Issues of Artificial Intelligence*. Springer, pp. 259–81.

Billow, R. M. (1975). A cognitive developmental study of metaphor comprehension. *Developmental Psychology* 11(4): 415–23.

(1981). Observing spontaneous metaphor in children. *Journal of Experimental Child Psychology* 31: 430–55.

Black, M. (1954–1955). Metaphor. *Proceedings of the Aristotelian Society* 55: 273–94.

Blakemore, D. (1987). *Semantic Constraints on Relevance*. Blackwell.

(1992). *Understanding Utterances: An Introduction to Pragmatics*. Blackwell.

(2002). *Relevance and Linguistic Meaning: The Semantics and Pragmatics of Discourse Markers*. Cambridge University Press.

(2009). Parentheticals and point of view in free indirect style. *Language and Literature* 18(2): 129–53.

(2010). Communication and the representation of thought: The use of audience-directed expressions in free indirect thought representations. *Journal of Linguistics* 46(3): 575–99.

(2011). On the descriptive ineffability of expressive meaning. *Journal of Pragmatics*. 43: 3537–50.

(2013a). Voice and expressivity in Free Indirect Thought representations: Imitation and representation. *Mind & Language* 28(5): 579–605.

(2013b). *The Expressive Meaning of Racial Epithets: Towards a Non-Unitary Account of Expressive Meaning*. University of Brighton College of Arts and Humanities – Lectures in Language and Linguistics: 11 December 2013.

(2015). Slurs and expletives: A case against a general account of expressive meaning. *Language Sciences* 52: 22–35.

Blakemore, D. & Gallai, F. (2014). Discourse markers in free indirect style and interpreting. *Journal of Pragmatics* 60: 106–20.

Blakemore, S.-J. & Choudhury, S. (2006). Development of the adolescent brain: Implications for executive function and social cognition. *Journal of Child Psychology and Psychiatry* 47: 296–312.

Blankier, M. (2014). Adapting and transforming 'Cinderella': Fairy-tale adaptations and the limits of existing adaptation theory. *Interdisciplinary Humanities* 31(3): 108–23.

Blochowiak, J. & Grisot, C. (2018). The pragmatics of descriptive and metalinguistic negation: Experimental data from French. *Glossa: A Journal of General Linguistics* 3(1): 50.

Bloom, L. (1975). *One Word at a Time*. Mouton.

Bloom, P. (2000). *How Children Learn the Meaning of Words*. MIT Press.

 & Markson, L. (2001). Are there principles that apply only to the acquisition of words? *Cognition* 78: 89–90.

Bluestone, G. (1957). *Novels into Film: A Critical Study*. The Johns Hopkins Press.

Bohn, M., Call, J. & Tomasello, M. (2015). Communication about absent entities in great apes and human infants. *Cognition* 145: 63–72.

Bohrn, I. C., Altmann, U., Lubrich, O., Menninghaus, W. & Jacobs, A. M. (2013). When we like what we know: A parametric fMRI analysis of beauty and familiarity. *Brain and Language* 124: 1–8.

Boisvert, D. & Ludwig, K. (2006). Semantics for nondeclaratives. In: E. Lepore & B. C. Smith (eds.) *The Oxford Handbook of Philosophy of Language*. Oxford University Press, pp. 864–93.

Bosch, P. (2001). Against the identification of anaphora and presupposition. In: J. van Kuppevelt & R. Smith (eds.) *Proceedings of the Second SIGdial Workshop on Discourse and Dialogue*, pp. 1–4. Aalborg, Denmark. Available at: http://aclweb.org/anthology/W/W01/W01-1604.pdf.

Botha, R. P. (1982). On 'the Galilean style' of linguistic inquiry. *Lingua* 58(1): 1–50.

Bott, L. & Noveck, I. A. (2004). Some utterances are underinformative: The onset and time course of scalar inferences. *Journal of Memory and Language* 51(3): 437–57.

Bowerman, M. (1980). The structure and origin of semantic categories in the language learning child. In: M. L. Foster & S. Brandes (eds.) *Symbol as Sense*. Academic Press, pp. 277–99.

Bradley, M. M. & Lang, P. J. (1999). *Affective Norms for English Words (ANEW): Instruction Manual and Affective Ratings*. Technical Report C-1, The Center for Research in Psychophysiology, University of Florida.

Breheny, R. (1996). Pro-active focus. *UCL Working Papers in Linguistics* 8: 1–42.

 (1998). Interface economy and focus. In: V. Rouchota & A. H. Jucker (eds) *Current Issues in Relevance Theory*. John Benjamins, pp. 105–40.

 (2006). Communication and folk psychology. *Mind & Language* 21(1): 74–107.

 (2011). Experimentation-based pragmatics. In: W. Bublitz & N. Norrick (eds.) *Handbook of Pragmatics* (Vol. 1: Foundations of Pragmatics). De Gruyter Mouton, pp. 561–86.

Breheny, R., Katsos, N. & Williams, J. (2006). Are generalised scalar implicatures generated by default? An on-line investigation into the role of context in generating pragmatic inferences. *Cognition* 100: 434–63.

Breheny, R., Ferguson, H. J. & Katsos, N. (2013). Taking the epistemic step: Toward a model of on-line access to conversational implicatures. *Cognition* 126(3): 423–40.

Brennan, J. & Pylkkänen, L. (2008). Processing events: Behavioral and neuromagnetic correlates of aspectual coercion. *Brain and Language* 106(2): 132–43.

Brody, M. (2002). On the status of representations and derivations. In: S. D. Epstein & T. Daniel Seely (eds.) *Derivation and Explanation in the Minimalist Program*. Blackwell, pp. 19–41.

Brucart, J. M. (2012). Copular alternation in Spanish and Catalan attributive sentences. *Revista de Estudos Linguísticos da Univerdade do Porto* 7: 9–43.

Bryant, G. A. (2012). Is verbal irony special? *Language and Linguistics Compass* 6(11): 673–85.

Bryant, G. A. & Fox Tree, J. E. (2005). Is there an ironic tone of voice? *Language and Speech* 48(3): 257–77.

Bucciarelli, M., Colle, L. & Bara, B. G. (2003). How children comprehend speech acts and communicative gestures. *Journal of Pragmatics* 35(2): 207–41.

Büring, D. (2003). On d-trees, beans, and b-accents. *Linguistics and Philosophy* 26(5): 511–45.

   (2007). Semantics, intonation and information structure. In: G. Ramchand & C. Reiss (eds.) *The Oxford Handbook of Linguistic Interfaces*. Oxford University Press, pp. 445–68.

   (2016). Focus, questions and givenness. In: K. von Heusinger, E. Onea & M. Zimmermann (eds.) *Questions in Discourse*. Brill.

Burke, E. (1757). *A Philosophical Enquiry into the Origin of Our Ideas of the Sublime and the Beautiful*. R. & J. Dodsley.

Burton-Roberts, N. (1989). *The Limits to Debate*. Cambridge University Press.

Butler, H. E. (ed.) (1922). *Quintilian. With an English Translation*. Harvard University Press.

Cahir, L. (2006). *Literature into Film: Theory and Practical Approaches*. McFarland.

Caink, A. & Clark, B. (eds.) (2012). Inference and implicature in literary interpretation. *Special Issue of Journal of Literary Semantics* 41(2): 99–191.

Camacho, J. (2012). *Ser* and *estar*: The Individual/Stage level distinction and aspectual predication. In: J. I. Hualde, A. Olarrea & E. O'Rourke (eds.) *The Handbook of Spanish Linguistics*. Blackwell, pp. 453–76.

Cameron, L. (2003). *Metaphor in Educational Discourse*. Continuum.

Camp, E. (2013). Slurring perspectives. *Analytic Philosophy* 54: 330–49.

Cann, R. & Kempson, R. (2017). What do words do for us? *Dialectica* 71: 425–60.

Cann, R., Kempson, R. & Marten, L. (2005). *The Dynamics of Language*. Elsevier.

Capelli, C. A., Nakagawa, N. & Madden, C. M. (1990). How children understand sarcasm: The role of context and intonation. *Child Development* 61(6): 1824–41.

Cappelen, H. & Lepore, E. (1997). Varieties of quotation. *Mind* 106: 429–50.

Cardillo, E. R., Watson, C. E., Schmidt, G. L., Kranjec, A. & Chatterjee, A. (2012). From novel to familiar: Tuning the brain for metaphors. *NeuroImage* 59: 3212–21.

Carlson, G. (1977). *Reference to Kinds in English*. PhD thesis, University of Massachusetts, Amherst.

   (2006). 'Mismatches' of form and interpretation. In: V. van Geenhoven (ed.) *Semantics in Acquisition*. De Gruyter, pp. 19–36.

Carnap, R. (1950). *Logical Foundations of Probability*. University of Chicago Press.

Carpenter, P. A. & Just, M. A. (1975). Sentence comprehension: A psycholinguistic processing model of verification. *Psychological Review* 82(1): 45–73.

Carruthers, P. (2003). Moderately massive modularity. *Royal Institute of Philosophy Supplement* 53: 67–89.

Carston, R. (1995). Quantity maxims and generalized implicature. *Lingua* 96: 213–44.

(1996). Metalinguistic negation and echoic use. *Journal of Pragmatics* 25: 309–30.

(1997). Enrichment and loosening: Complementary processes in deriving the proposition expressed? In: E. Rolf (ed.) *Pragmatik*. VS Verlag für Sozialwissenschaften, pp. 103–27.

(1998a). Negation, 'presupposition' and the semantics/pragmatics distinction. *Journal of Linguistics* 34: 309–50.

(1998b). Informativeness, relevance, and scalar implicature. In: R. Carston and S. Uchida (eds.) *Relevance Theory: Applications and Implications*. Benjamins, pp. 179–236.

(2002). *Thoughts and Utterances: The Pragmatics of Explicit Communication*. Blackwell.

(2010). Metaphor: Ad hoc concepts, literal meaning and mental images. *Proceedings of the Aristotelian Society* CX(3): 295–321.

(2012). Word meaning and concept expressed. *The Linguistic Review* 29(4): 607–23.

(2013). Word meaning, what is said and explicature. In: C. Penco and F. Domaneschi (eds.) *What Is Said and What Is Not*. CSLI Publications, pp. 175–204.

(2016a). The heterogeneity of procedural meaning. *Lingua* 175–176: 154–66.

(2016b). Underspecified word meaning, pragmatics and the lexicon. Plenary talk at the conference *Between (Stable) Meanings and (Unstable) Interpretations*, Uniwersytet Jagiellonski, Kraków, 15–16 September, 2016.

(forthcoming) Lexical innovation, word meaning and the lexicon.

Carston, R. & Uchida, S. (eds.) (1998). *Relevance Theory: Applications and Implications*. John Benjamins.

Carston, R. & Wearing, C. (2011). Metaphor, hyperbole and simile: A pragmatic approach. *Language and Cognition* 3(2): 283–312.

Cartwright, N. (1983). *How the Laws of Physics Lie*. Clarendon Press.

(1999). *The Dappled World: A Study of the Boundaries of Science*. Cambridge University Press.

Casartelli, D. (2017). *The Interaction of Negation and Epistemic Modality. A Pragmatic Approach*. MA thesis, University of Geneva.

Cato, M. A., Crosson, B., Gökçay, D., Soltysik, D., Wierenga, C., Gopinath, K., Himes, N., Belanger, H., Bauer, R. M., Fischler, I. S., Gonzalez-Rothi, L. & Briggs, R. W. (2004). Processing words with emotional connotation: An fMRI study of time course and laterality in rostral frontal and retrosplenial cortices. *Journal of Cognitive Neuroscience* 16(2): 167–77.

Cave, T. (2016). *Thinking with Literature: Towards a Cognitive Criticism*. Oxford University Press.

Chafe, W. & Nichols, J. (eds.) (1986). *Evidentiality: The Linguistic Coding of Epistemology*. Ablex.

Chapman, S. & Clark, B. (eds.) (2014). *Pragmatic Literary Stylistics*. Palgrave Macmillan.

(in press). *Pragmatics and Literature*. John Benjamins.

Chatman, S. (1980). What novels can do that films can't (and vice versa). *Critical Inquiry* 7(1): 121–40.

Chevallier, C., Wilson, D., Happé, F. & Noveck, I. (2010). Scalar inferences in Autism Spectrum Disorders. *Journal of Autism and Developmental Disorders* 40(9): 1104–17.

Chevallier, C., Noveck, I., Happe, F. & Wilson, D. (2011). What's in a voice? Prosody as a test case for the Theory of Mind account of autism. *Neuropsychologia* 49: 507–17.

Chierchia, G. (2004). Scalar implicatures, polarity phenomena, and the syntax/ pragmatics interface. In: A. Belleti (ed.) *Structures and Beyond: The Cartography of Syntactic Structures* (Vol. 3). Oxford University Press, pp. 39–103.

Chierchia, G., Crain, S., Guasti, M., Gualmini, A. & Meroni, L. (2001). The acquisition of disjunction: Evidence for a grammatical view of scalar implicatures. In: A. H.-J. Do, L. Domínguez & A. Johansen (eds.) *Proceedings of the 25th Annual Boston University Conference on Language Development*. Cascadilla Press, pp. 157–68.

Chierchia, G., Fox, D. & Spector, B. (2009). Hurford's constraint and the theory of scalar implicatures. In: P. Egré & G. Magri (eds.) *Presuppositions and Implicatures. Proceedings of the MIT-Paris Workshop*. MIT Working Papers in Linguistics, pp. 47–62.

Chomsky, N. (1959). A review of B. F. Skinner, 'Verbal Behavior', 1957. *Language* 35: 26–58.

(1970). Remarks on nominalization. In: R. Jacobs and P. Rosenbaum (eds.) *Readings in English Transformational Grammar*. Ginn & Co, pp. 184–221.

(1975). *Reflections on Language*. Pantheon Books.

(1978a). A theory of core grammar. *Glot* 1: 7–26.

(1978b). Interview with Sol Saporta. *Washington State University, Dept. of Linguistics Working Papers in Linguistics*, Supplement 4: 1–26.

(1980). *Rules and Representations*. Columbia University Press.

(1983). Things no amount of learning can teach: Noam Chomsky interviewed by John Gliedman. *Omni* 6(11). Available at: www.chomsky.info/interviews/198311--.htm. Accessed 8 November 2018.

(1991). Linguistics and cognitive science: Problems and mysteries. In: A. Kasher (ed.) *The Chomskyan Turn*. Basil Blackwell, pp. 26–55.

(1992a). Explaining language use. *Philosophical Topics* 20: 205–31.

(1992b). Language and interpretation: Philosophical reflections and empirical enquiry. In: J. Earman (ed.) *Inference, Explanation and Other Frustrations: Essays in the Philosophy of Science*. University of California Press, pp. 99–128.

(1995). *The Minimalist Program*. MIT Press.

(1996). *Powers and Prospects*. South End.

(2002). *On Nature and Language*. Cambridge University Press.

(2006). *Language and Mind*. Cambridge University Press.

Chouliaraki, L. (2013). Re-mediation, inter-mediation, trans-mediation. *Journalism Studies* 14(2): 267–83.

Chung-hong Leung, D. & Crisp, P. (2011). Cantonese and English bodies do talk: A cross-cultural, metaphor-metonymy study on body-part idioms. In: L. Jin & M. Cortazzi (eds.) *Researching Chinese Learners: Skills, Perceptions and Intercultural Adaptations*. Palgrave Macmillan, pp. 43–66.

Cipria, A. & Roberts, C. (2000). Spanish *imperfecto* and *pretérito*: Truth conditions and *Aktionsart* effects in a Situation Semantics. *Natural Language Semantics* 8: 297–347.

Citron, F. M. M. (2012). Neural correlates of written emotion word processing: A review of recent electrophysiological and hemodynamic neuroimaging studies. *Brain and Language* 122: 211–26.

Clark, A. (2016). *Surfing Uncertainty: Prediction, Action, and the Embodied Mind*. Oxford University Press.

Clark, E. V. (1973). What's in a word? On the child's acquisition of semantics in his first language. In: T. E. Moore (ed.) *Cognitive Development and the Acquisition of Language*. Academic Press, pp. 65–110.

(1978). Strategies for communicating. *Child Development* 49: 953–9.

(2009). *First Language Acquisition*. Cambridge University Press.

Clark, E. V. & Clark, H. H. (1979). When nouns surface as verbs. *Language* 55: 767–811.

Clark, H. H. (1996). *Using Language*. Cambridge University Press.

Clark, H. H. & Carlson, T. B. (1982). Hearers and speech acts. *Language* 58(2): 332–73.

Clark, H. H. & Chase, W. G. (1972). On the process of comparing sentences against pictures. *Cognitive Psychology* 3(3): 472–517.

Clément, F., Koenig, M. & Harris, P. (2004). The ontogeny of trust. *Mind & Language* 19: 360–79.

Clifton, C. & Frazier, L. (2012). Discourse integration guided by the 'question under discussion.' *Cognitive Psychology* 65: 352–79.

Collins, J. (2003). Expressions, sentences, propositions. *Erkenntnis* 59(2) : 233–62.

(2007). Syntax, more or less. *Mind* 116(464): 805–50.

Comrie, B. (1985). *Tense*. Cambridge University Press.

(1986). Tense in indirect speech. *Folia Linguistica* 20: 265–96.

Cooper, R. (2012). Type theory and semantics in flux. In: R. Kempson, N. Asher & T. Fernando (eds.) *Handbook of the Philosophy of Science* (Vol 14: Philosophy of Linguistics). Elsevier, pp. 271–323.

Corazza, E. (2005). Epithets qua attributive anaphors. *Journal of Linguistics* 41: 1–32.

Cormack, A. & Smith, N. (in prep). *Categorial Minimalism: Syntax, Semantics and the Language of Thought*.

Corrigan, T. (2017). Defining adaptation. In: T. Leitch (ed.) *The Oxford Book of Adaptation Studies*. Oxford University Press, pp. 23–35.

Cosmides, L. & Tooby, J. (2000). Evolutionary psychology and the emotions. In: M. Lewis, & J. Haviland-Jones (eds.) *Handbook of Emotions*. Guilford Press, pp. 91–115.

Costa, J. C. (2008). *A Relevância da Pragmática na Pragmática da Relevância*. EDIPUCRS.

Creusere, M. A. (1999). Theories of adults' understanding and use of irony and sarcasm: Applications to and evidence from research with children. *Developmental Review* 19: 213–62.

Crisp, P. (2008). Between extended metaphor and allegory: Is blending enough? *Language and Literature* 17(4): 291–308.

Croom, A. (2008). Racial epithets: What we say and mean by them. *Dialogue* 51: 34–45.

(2011). Slurs. *Language Sciences* 33: 343–58.

(2014a). The semantics of slurs: A refutation of pure expressivism. *Language Sciences* 41: 227–42.

(2014b). Slurs, stereotypes, and in-equality: A critical review of 'How Epithets and Stereotypes are Racially Unequal'. *Language Sciences* 44: 1–16.

Csibra, G. & Gergely, G. (2009). Natural pedagogy. *Trends in Cognitive Sciences* 13(4): 148–53.

Dalton, P. & Lavie, N. (2004). Auditory attentional capture: Effects of singleton distractor sounds. *Journal of Experimental Psychology: Human Perception and Performance* 30(1): 180–93.

Damasio, A. (2006). *Descartes' Error: Emotion, Reason and the Human Brain.* Random House Vintage.

Davidson, D. (1970). Mental events. In: L. Foster & J. W. Swanson (eds.) *Experience and Theory.* University of Massachusetts Press, pp. 79–101.

(1978/1984). What metaphors mean. *Critical Inquiry* 5(1): 31–47. Reprinted in his 1984 *Inquiries into Truth and Interpretation.* Oxford University Press, pp. 245–64.

(1986). A nice derangement of epitaphs. In: E. Lepore (ed.) *Truth and Interpretation: Perspectives on the Philosophy of Donald Davidson.* Blackwell, pp. 433–46.

Davies, E. (1986). *The English Imperative.* Croom Helm.

Deamer, F. (2013). *An Investigation into the Processes and Mechanisms Underlying the Comprehension of Metaphor and Hyperbole.* PhD thesis, University College London.

De Brabanter, P. (2010). The semantics and pragmatics of hybrid quotations. *Language and Linguistics Compass* 4(2): 107–20.

De Bruyn, F. (2012). 'Expressive uncertainty': Edmund Burke's theory of the sublime and eighteenth-century conceptions of metaphor. In: K. Vermeir & M. F. Deckard (eds.) *The Science of Sensibility: Reading Burke's Philosophical Enquiry.* Springer, pp. 265–82.

Declerck, R. (1991). *Tense in English: Its Structure and Use in Discourse.* Routledge.

Degen, J. & Tanenhaus, M. (2015). Processing scalar implicature: A constraint-based approach. *Cognitive Science* 39: 667–710.

Dehé, N. (2014). *Parentheticals in Spoken English: The Syntax–Prosody Relation.* Cambridge University Press.

de Marchena, A., Eigsti, I.-M., Worek, A., Ono, K. E. & Snedeker, J. (2011). Mutual exclusivity in autism spectrum disorders: Testing the pragmatic hypothesis. *Cognition* 119(1): 96–113.

Demorest, A., Silberstein, L., Gardner, H. & Winner, E. (1983). Telling it as it isn't: Children's understanding of figurative language. *British Journal of Developmental Psychology* 1: 121–34.

Demorest, A., Meyer, C., Phelps, E., Gardner, H. & Winner, E. (1984). Words speak louder than actions: Understanding deliberately false remarks. *Child Development* 55: 1527–34.

Dendale, P. & Tasmowski, L. (eds.) (2001). Evidentiality (special issue). *Journal of Pragmatics* 33(3).

Deonna, J. A. & Teroni, F. (2012). *The Emotions: A Philosophical Introduction.* Routledge.

De Saussure, L. & Sthioul, B. (2005). Imparfait et enrichissement pragmatique. In: P. Larrivée & E. Labeau (eds.) *Nouveaux développements de l'imparfait.* Rodopi, pp. 103–20.

de Swart, H. (1998). Aspect shift and coercion. *Natural Language and Linguistic Theory* 16: 347–85.

(2011). Mismatches and coercion. In: C. Maienborn, K. von Heusinger & P. Portner (eds.) *Semantics: An International Handbook of Natural Language Meaning.* De Gruyter, pp. 574–97.

Deutsch, W. & Pechmann, T. (1982). Social interaction and the development of definite descriptions. *Cognition* 11(2): 159–84.

de Villiers, P. A., de Villiers, J., Coles-White, D. J. & Carpenter, L. (2009). Acquisition of relevance implicatures in typically-developing children and children with autism. In: J. Chandlee, M. Franchini, S. Lord & G. M. Rheiner (eds.) *Proceedings of the 33th Annual Boston University Conference on Language Development*. Cascadilla Press, pp. 121–32.

Dews, S., Winner, E., Kaplan, J., Rosenblatt, E., Hunt, M., Lim, K., McGovern, A., Qualter, A. & Smarsh, B. (1996). Children's understanding of the meaning and functions of verbal irony. *Child Development* 67: 3071–85.

Dezecache, G., Mercier, H. & Scott-Phillips, T. (2013). An evolutionary approach to emotional communication. *Journal of Pragmatics* 59(B): 221–33.

Dickens, C. (2011). *The Complete Works of Charles Dickens*. Delphi.

Diesendruck, G. & Markson, L. (2001). Children's avoidance of lexical overlap: A pragmatic account. *Developmental Psychology* 37(5): 630–41.

Dominicy, M. & Franken, N. (2002). Speech acts and relevance theory. In: D. Vanderveken & S. Kubo (eds.) *Essays in Speech Act Theory*. John Benjamins, pp. 263–84.

Doron, E. (1991). Point of view as a factor of content. In: S. K. Moore & A. Z. Wyner (eds.) *Proceedings of the 1st Conference on Semantics and Linguistic Theory (SALT 1)*.

Downing, P. (1977). On the creation and use of English compound nouns. *Language* 53: 810–42.

Drożdżowicz, A. (2015). *Investigating Utterance Meaning: Essays in the Epistemology of Language*. PhD thesis, University of Oslo.

  (2016). Speakers' intuitions about meaning provide empirical evidence: Towards experimental pragmatics. In: M. Hinton (ed.) *Evidence, Experiment, and Argument in Linguistics and the Philosophy of Language*. Peter Lang, pp. 65–90.

Dryden, J. (1913). Preface concerning Ovid's Epistles. In: J. Sargeaunt (ed.) *The Poems of John Dryden*. Oxford University Press.

Ducrot, O. (1984). *Le Dire et le Dit*. Minuit.

Dudschig, C., de la Vega, I. & Kaup, B. (2014). Embodiment and second-language: Automatic activation of motor responses processing spatially associated L2 words and emotion L2 words in a vertical Stroop paradigm. *Brain and Language* 132: 14–21.

Duff, M. C., Hengst, J. A., Tranel, D. & Cohen, N. J. (2007). Talking across time: Using reported speech as a communicative resource in amnesia. *Aphasiology* 21(6–8): 702–16.

Dupré, J. (1993). *The Disorder of Things: Metaphysical Foundations of the Disunity of Science*. Harvard University Press.

Dyck, M. J., Ferguson, K. & Schochet, I. M. (2001). Do autism spectrum disorders differ from each other and from non-spectrum disorders on emotion recognition tests? *European Child & Adolescent Psychiatry* 10(2): 105–16.

Eckardt, R. (2006). *Meaning Change in Grammaticalization: An Enquiry into Semantic Reanalysis*. Oxford University Press.

Egan, F. (2014). How to think about mental content. *Philosophical Studies*, 170(1): 115–35.

Eiteljoerge, S., Pouscoulous, N. & Lieven, E. (2016). Some pieces are missing: Scalar implicatures in children. Paper presented at the 41st Annual Meeting of the Boston University Conference on Language Development, Boston, MA.

Epley, N., Morewedge, C. K. & Keysar, B. (2004). Perspective taking in children and adults: Equivalent egocentrism but differential correction. *Journal of Experimental Social Psychology* 40(6): 760–8.

Escandell-Vidal, V. (2018a). Evidential commitment and feature mismatch in Spanish *estar* constructions. *Journal of Pragmatics* 128: 102–15.

(2018b). *Ser y estar* con adjetivos. Afinidad y desajuste de rasgos. *Revista Española de Lingüística* 48: 57–114.

Escandell-Vidal, V. & Leonetti, M. (2011). On the rigidity of procedural meaning. In: V. Escandell-Vidal, M. Leonetti & A. Ahern (eds.) *Procedural Meaning: Problems and Perspectives*. Emerald, pp. 81–102.

Escandell-Vidal, V., Leonetti, M. & Ahern, A. (eds.) 2011. *Procedural Meaning: Problems and Perspectives*. Emerald.

Eshghi, A., Healey, P. G. T., Purver, M., Howes, C., Gregoromichelaki, E. & Kempson, R. (2010). Incremental turn processing in dialogue. In: *Proceedings of the 16th Annual Conference on Architectures and Mechanisms for Language Processing (AMLAP)*, York, UK, September 2010.

Eshghi, A., Purver, M. & Hough, J. (2011). *Dylan: Parser for Dynamic Syntax*. Technical report, Queen Mary, University of London.

Eshghi, A., Hough, J., Purver, M., Kempson, R. & Gregoromichelaki, E. (2012). Conversational interactions: Capturing dialogue dynamics. In: L. Borin & S. Larsson (eds.) *From Quantification to Conversation*. College Publications, pp. 325–49.

Eshghi, A., Howes, C., Gregoromichelaki, E., Hough, J. & Purver, M. (2015). Feedback in conversation as incremental semantic update. In: *Proceedings of the 11th International Conference on Computational Semantics (IWCS 2015), Queen Mary University of London, UK* April 2015, pp. 261–71.

Evans, J. S. (2008). Dual-processing accounts of reasoning, judgment, and social cognition. *Annual Review of Psychology* 59: 255–78.

Fabb, N. (2002). *Language and Literary Structure*. Cambridge University Press.

(2016). Processing effort and poetic closure. *International Journal of Literary Linguistics* 5(4): 1–22.

Falkum, I. L. (2011). *The Semantics and Pragmatics of Polysemy: A Relevance-Theoretic Account*. PhD thesis, University College London.

(2015). The how and why of polysemy: A pragmatic account. *Lingua* 157: 83–99.

Falkum, I. L., Recasens, M. & Clark, E. V. (2017). The moustache sits down first: On the acquisition of metonymy. *Journal of Child Language* 44(1): 87–119.

Faller, M. (2002). *Semantics and Pragmatics of Evidentials in Cuzco Quechua*. PhD thesis, Stanford University.

Fernald, T. (1999). Evidential coercion: Using individual-level predicates in stage-level environments. *Studies in the Linguistic Sciences* 29: 43–63.

Filippova, E. & Astington, J. W. (2008). Further development in social reasoning revealed in discourse irony understanding. *Child Development* 79(1): 126–38.

Fischler, I., Bloom, P. A., Childers, D. G., Roucos, S. E. & Perry, N. W. (1983). Brain potentials related to stages of sentence verification. *Psychophysiology* 20(4): 400–9.

Fiske, S. T. & Taylor, S. E. (2008). *Social Cognition: From Brain to Culture*. McGraw-Hill.

Flaubert, G. (2013). *Complete Works of Gustave Flaubert*. Delphi.

Fodor, J. A. (1975). *The Language of Thought*. Crowell.

(1983). *The Modularity of Mind: An Essay on Faculty Psychology*. MIT Press.

(1998). *Concepts*. Clarendon Press.

(2002). The lexicon and the laundromat. In: P. Merlo and S. Stevenson (eds.) *The Lexical Basis of Sentence Processing*. John Benjamins, pp. 75–84.

(2005). Reply to Steven Pinker 'So how does the mind work?' *Mind & Language* 20(1): 25–32.

Fontaine, J. J., Scherer, K. R., Roesch, E. B. & Ellsworth, P. C. (2007). The world of emotions is not two-dimensional. *Psychological Science* 18(12): 1050–7.

Foolen, A. (1997). The expressive function of language: Towards a cognitive semantic approach. In: S. Niemeier & R. Dirven (eds.) *The Language of Emotions*. John Benjamins, pp. 15–31.

Foppolo, F., Guasti, M. T. & Chierchia, G. (2012). Scalar implicatures in child language: Give children a chance. *Language Learning and Development* 8(4): 365–94.

Fowler, A. (1989). A new theory of communication. *London Review of Books* 11(7): 16–17.

Francis, E. J. & Michaelis, L. A. (eds.) (2003). *Mismatch: Form-Function Incongruity and the Architecture of Grammar*. CSLI Publications.

Franke, M. (2011). Quantity implicatures, exhaustive interpretation, and rational conversation. *Semantics and Pragmatics* 1: 1–82.

Fretheim, T. (2014). Et relevansteoretisk blikk på likheter og ulikheter mellom partiklene *da* og *altså* [A relevance-theoretic view of similarities and differences between the particles *da* and *altså*]. *Norsk Lingvistisk Tidsskrift* 32(2): 197–256.

(2015a). Grammatikalisering av adverbet *gjerne* i ulike norske varieteter. [Grammaticalisation of the adverb *gjerne* in different varieties of spoken Norwegian.] *Norsk Lingvistisk Tidsskrift* 33(1): 3–48.

(2015b). A relevance-theoretic perspective on the Norwegian utterance-final particles *da* and *altså* compared to their English counterpart *then*. In: S. Hancil, A. Haselow & M. Post (eds.) *Final Particles*. Walter de Gruyter, pp. 249–84.

(2016). The speaker's derivational intention. In: M. Padilla Cruz (ed.) *Relevance Theory: Recent Developments, Current Challenges and Future Directions*. John Benjamins, pp. 33–58.

(2017). The pragmatics of 'Yes' and 'No'. In: S. Assimakopoulos (ed.) *Pragmatics and Its Interfaces*. Mouton, pp. 175–200.

Friend, M. (2000). Developmental changes in sensitivity to vocal paralanguage. *Developmental Science* 3: 148–62.

Friend, M. & Bryant, J. B. (2000). A developmental lexical bias in the interpretation of discrepant messages. *Merrill-Palmer Quarterly* 46(2): 342–69.

Frisson, S. & Pickering, M. J. (2007). The processing of familiar and novel senses of a word: Why reading Dickens is easy but reading Needham can be hard. *Language and Cognitive Processes* 22(4): 595–613.

Friston, K. (2010). The free-energy principle: A unified brain theory? *Nature Reviews Neuroscience*, 11(2): 127.

Furlong, A. (2008). You can't put your foot in the same river once: Relevance stylistics and repetition. *Proceedings of The State of Stylistics, 26th Annual Meeting of the Poetics and Linguistics Association*. Rodopi, pp. 283–302.

Gagné, C. & Shoben, E. (1997). Influence of thematic relations on the comprehension of modifier-noun combinations. *Journal of Experimental Psychology: Learning, Memory and Cognition* 23: 71–87.

García Fernández, L. & Camus Bergareche, B. (eds.) (2004). *El pretérito imperfecto*. Gredos.

Gardner, H., Winner, E., Bechhofer, R. & Wolf, D. (1978). The development of figurative language. In: K. E. Nelson (ed.) *Children's Language* (Vol. 1). Gardner Press, pp. 1–38.

Gargett, A., Gregoromichelaki, E., Howes, C. & Sato, Y. (2008). Dialogue-grammar correspondence in Dynamic Syntax. In: *Proceedings of the 12th SemDial (LonDial)*, London.

Gargett, A., Gregoromichelaki, E., Kempson, R., Purver, M. & Sato, Y. (2009). Grammar resources for modelling dialogue dynamically. *Journal of Cognitive Neurodynamics*, 3(4), 347–63.

Garrett, E. (2001). *Evidentiality and Assertion in Tibetan*. PhD thesis, UCLA.

Gazdar, G. (1979). *Pragmatics: Implicature, Presupposition, and Logical Form*. Academic Press.

Gerrig, R. J. & Healy, A. F. (1983). Dual processes in metaphor understanding: Comprehension and appreciation. *Journal of Experimental Psychology: Learning, Memory and Cognition* 9: 667–75.

Geurts, B. (2007). Really fucking brilliant. *Theoretical Linguistics* 33(2): 207–214.

(2010). *Quantity Implicatures*. Cambridge University Press.

(2018). Convention and common ground. *Mind & Language* 33(2): 115–29.

Gibbs, R. W. (1986). On the psycholinguistics of sarcasm. *Journal of Experimental Psychology: General* 115(1): 3–15.

(1994). *The Poetics of Mind*. Cambridge University Press.

(2002). A new look at literal meaning in understanding what is said and implicated. *Journal of Pragmatics* 34(4): 457–86.

(2011). The allegorical impulse. *Metaphor and Symbol* 26(2): 121–30.

(2015a). Do pragmatic signals affect conventional metaphor understanding? *Journal of Pragmatics* 90: 77–87.

(2015b). The allegorical character of political metaphors in discourse. *Metaphor and the Social World* 5(2): 264–82.

Gigerenzer, G. & Todd, P. M. (1999). *Simple Heuristics That Make Us Smart*. Oxford University Press.

Gigerenzer, G., Hertwig, R. & Pachur, T. (2011). *Heuristics: The Foundations of Adaptive Behavior*. Oxford University Press.

Ginzburg, J. (1996). Interrogatives: Questions, facts and dialogue. In: S. Lappin & C. Fox (eds.) *The Handbook of Contemporary Semantic Theory*. Blackwell, pp. 359–423.

(2012). *The Interactive Stance: Meaning for Conversation*. Oxford University Press.

Ginzburg, J. & Cooper, R. (2014). Quotation via dialogical interaction. *Journal of Logic, Language and Information* 23(3): 287–311.

Ginzburg, J., Fernández, R. & Schlangen, D. (2014). Disfluencies as intra-utterance dialogue moves. *Semantics and Pragmatics* 7(9): 1–64.

Glucksberg, S., Brown, M. & McGlone, M. S. (1993). Conceptual metaphors are not automatically accessed during idiom comprehension. *Memory and Cognition* 21: 711–19.

Goffman E. (1979). Footing. *Semiotica* 251–2: 1–30.

Golden, A. (2010). Grasping the point: A study of 15-year-old students' comprehension of metaphorical expressions in schoolbooks. In: G. Low, Z. Todd, A. Deignan & L. Cameron (eds.) *Researching and Applying Metaphor in the Real World*. John Benjamins, pp. 35–61.

Golding, A. (2016). *Metaphor in the Embodied Mind: Beyond the Propositionality of Figurative Language.* PhD thesis, University of Brighton, UK.

Goldin-Meadow, S. (2005). *The Resilience of Language.* Psychology Press.

Gómez, J. C. (1996). Ostensive behavior in great apes: The role of eye contact. In: A. E. Russon, K. A. Bard & S. Taylor Parker (eds.) *Reaching into Thought: The Minds of the Great Apes.* Cambridge University Press, pp. 131–51.

Goodwin, C. (2007). Interactive footing. In: E. Holt. & R. Clift (eds.) *Reporting Talk: Reported Speech in Interaction.* Cambridge University Press, pp. 16–46.

Gough, P. (1966). The verification of sentences: The effects of delay of evidence and sentence length. *Journal of Verbal Learning and Verbal Behavior* 6: 492–6.

Grabe, W. & Stoller, F. (2011). *Teaching and Researching Reading.* Pearson.

Green, G. M. (1976). Main clause phenomena in subordinate clauses. *Language* 52: 382–97.

Greenspan, P. (2002). Practical reasoning and emotion. In: A. Mele & P. Rawlings (eds.) *Rationality.* Oxford University Press.

Gregoromichelaki, E. (2012). Review of J. Ginzburg (2012) *The Interactive Stance. Folia Linguistica* 47(1): 293–316.

(2013a). Clitic left dislocation and clitic doubling: A dynamic perspective on left-right asymmetries in Greek. In: G. Webelhuth, M. Sailer & H. Walker (eds.) *Rightward Movement in a Comparative Perspective.* John Benjamins, pp. 321–68.

(2013b). Grammar as action in language and music. In: M. Orwin, C. Howes & R. Kempson (eds.). *Language, Music and Interaction.* College Publications.

(2017). Quotation in dialogue. In: P. Saka & M. Johnson (eds.) *The Semantics and Pragmatics of Quotation.* Springer, pp. 195–255.

Gregoromichelaki, E. & Kempson, R. (2015). Joint utterances and the (split-) turn-taking puzzle. In: A. Capone & J. Mey (eds.) *Interdisciplinary Studies in Pragmatics, Culture and Society.* Springer, pp. 703–43.

(2016). Reporting, dialogue, and the role of grammar. In: A. Capone, F. Kiefer & F. Lo Piparo (eds.) *Indirect Reports and Pragmatics.* Springer, pp. 115–50.

Gregoromichelaki, E., Kempson, R., Purver, M., Mills, G. J., Cann, R., Meyer-Viol, W. & Healey, P. G. T. (2011). Incrementality and intention-recognition in utterance processing. *Dialogue and Discourse,* 2(1): 199–233.

Gregoromichelaki, E., Kempson, R. & Cann, R. (2012). Language as tools for interaction: Grammar and the dynamics of ellipsis resolution. *The Linguistic Review* 29(4): 563–84.

Gregoromichelaki, E., Kempson, R., Howes, C. & Eshghi, A. (2013a). On making syntax dynamic: The challenge of compound utterances and the architecture of the grammar. In: I. Wachsmuth, J. P. de Ruiter, P. Jaecks & S. Kopp (eds.) *Alignment in Communication: Towards a New Theory of Communication.* John Benjamins, 58–85.

Gregoromichelaki, E., Cann R. & Kempson, R. (2013b). Coordination in dialogue: Subsentential speech and its implications. In: L. Goldstein (ed.) *Brevity.* Oxford University Press.

Gregory, M. E. & Mergler, N. L. (1990). Metaphor comprehension: In search of literal truth, possible sense, and metaphoricity. *Metaphor and Symbolic Activity* 5: 151–73.

Grice, H. P. (1957). Meaning. *Philosophical Review* 66: 377–88.

(1967[1989]). Logic and conversation: William James lectures. In: H. P. Grice (1989) *Studies in the Way of Words*. Harvard University Press, pp. 1–143.

(1975). Logic and conversation. In: P. Cole and J. L. Morgan (eds.) *Syntax and Semantics: Speech Acts* (Vol. 3). Academic Press, pp. 41–58.

(1981). Presupposition and conversational implicature. In: P. Cole (ed.) *Radical Pragmatics*. Academic Press, pp. 183–98. Reprinted in his (1989) *Studies in the Ways of Words*. Harvard University Press, pp. 269–82.

(1989). *Studies in the Way of Words*. Harvard University Press.

Grigoroglou, M. & Papafragou, A. (2016). Acquisition of pragmatics. In: R. Clark & M. Aronoff (eds.) *Oxford Research Encyclopedia of Linguistics*. Oxford University Press.

Grodner, D., Klein, N., Carbary, K. & Tanenhaus, M. (2010). 'Some', and possibly all, scalar inferences are not delayed: Evidence for immediate pragmatic enrichment. *Cognition* 116: 42–55.

Groenendijk, J. & Stokhof, M. (1984). *Studies on the semantics of questions and the pragmatics of answers*. In: F. Landman & F. Veltman (eds.) *Varieties of Formal Semantics*. Foris, pp. 143–70.

Guasti, M. T., Chierchia, G., Crain, S., Foppolo, F., Gualmini, A. & Meroni, L. (2005). Why children and adults sometimes (but not always) compute implicatures. *Language and Cognitive Processes* 20(5): 667–96.

Gutt, E.-A. (2013). How does the affective relate to ostensive-inferential communication? Unpublished draft, available at: www.saunalahti.fi/~ehmgutt. Accessed 8 November 2018.

Hamilton, C. (2011). Allegory, blending, and censorship in modern literature. *Journal of Literary Semantics* 40(1): 23–42.

Hancock, J. T., Dunham, P. J. & Purdy, K. (2000). Children's comprehension of critical and complimentary forms of verbal irony. *Journal of Cognition & Development* 1: 227–48.

Happé, F. G. E. (1993). Communicative competence and theory of mind: A test of relevance theory. *Cognition* 48: 101–19.

Harnish, R. M. (1994). Mood, meaning and speech acts. In: S. Tsohatzidis (ed.) *Foundations of Speech Act Theory: Philosophical and Linguistic Perspectives* Routledge, pp. 407–59.

Haspelmath, M. & Sims, A. (2013). *Understanding Morphology*. Routledge.

Hatfield, E., Cacioppo, J. & Rapson, R. (1994). *Emotional Contagion*. Cambridge University Press.

Hauser, M., Chomsky, N. & Fitch, W. T. (2002). The faculty of language: What is it, who has it, and how did it evolve? *Science* 298: 1569–79.

Hedger, J. (2012). The semantics of racial slurs: Using Kaplan's framework to provide a theory of derogatory epithets. *Linguistic and Philosophical Investigations* 11: 74–84.

(2013). Meaning and racial slurs: Derogatory epithets and the semantics/pragmatics interface. *Language and Communication* 33: 205–13.

Heggstad, L. (1963). *Gamalnorsk Ordbok* [Old Norse Dictionary]. Det Norske Samlaget.

Hirschberg, J. (1985). *A Theory of Scalar Implicature*. PhD thesis, University of Pennsylvania.

Hobart, R. E. (1934). Free will as involving determination and inconceivable without it. *Mind* 43(169): 1–27.

Hochstein, L., Bale, A., Fox, D. & Barner, D. (2014). Ignorance and inference: Do problems with Gricean epistemic reasoning explain children's difficulty with scalar implicature? *Journal of Semantics* 33(1): 107–35.

Hom, C. (2008). The semantics of racial epithets. *Journal of Philosophy* 105(8): 416–40.

Hooper, J. B. (1975). On assertive predicates. In: J. P. Kimball (ed.) *Syntax and Semantics* (Vol 4). Academic Press, pp. 91–124.

Hopper, P. J. & Traugott, E. C. (1993). *Grammaticalization.* Cambridge University Press.

Horn, L. R. (1972). *On the Semantic Properties of the Logical Operators in English.* PhD thesis, Indiana University.

(1984). Toward a new taxonomy for pragmatic inference: Q-based and R-based implicature. In: D. Schiffrin (ed.) *Meaning, Form, and Use in Context: Linguistic Applications.* Georgetown University Press, pp. 11–42.

(1985). Metalinguistic negation and pragmatic ambiguity. *Language* 61(1): 121–74.

(1989). *A Natural History of Negation.* University of Chicago Press.

Hornsby, J. (2001). How to think about derogatory words. In: P. French & H. Wettstein (eds.) *Figurative Language. Midwest Studies in Philosophy* 25. Blackwell, pp. 128–41.

Hornstein, N. (1990). *As Time Goes By: Tense and Universal Grammar.* MIT Press.

Hornstein, N., Nunes, J. & Grohmann, K. (2005). *Understanding Minimalism.* Cambridge University Press.

Hough, J. (2014). *Modelling Incremental Self-Repair Processing in Dialogue.* PhD thesis, Queen Mary, University of London.

Htsu, C.-T., Jacobs, A. M., Citron, F. M. M. & Conrad, M. (2015). The emotion potential of words and passages in reading Harry Potter: An fMRI study. *Brain and Language* 142: 96–114.

Huang, Y. (2000). *Anaphora: A Cross-Linguistic Study.* Oxford University Press.

Huang, Y. T. & Snedeker, J. (2009). Online interpretation of scalar quantifiers: Insight into the semantics-pragmatics interface. *Cognitive Psychology* 58(3): 376–415.

Hurley, S. L. (2008). The shared circuits model (SCM): How control, mirroring, and simulation can enable imitation, deliberation, and mindreading. *Behavioral and Brain Sciences* 31(1): 1–58.

Hutcheon, L. (2006). *A Theory of Adaptation.* Routledge.

Huttenlocher, J. & Smiley, P. (1987). Early word meanings: The case of object names. *Cognitive Psychology* 19: 63–89.

Hyland, K. (1998). *Hedging in Scientific Research Articles.* John Benjamins.

Ifantidou, E. (2001). *Evidentials and Relevance.* John Benjamins.

(2014). *Pragmatic Competence and Relevance.* John Benjamins.

Jackendoff, R. (1972). *Semantic Interpretation in Generative Grammar.* MIT Press.

(1997). *The Architecture of the Language Faculty.* MIT Press.

(2010). *Meaning and the Lexicon: The Parallel Architecture 1975–2010.* Oxford University Press.

Jackson, R. (2016). *The Pragmatics of Repetition, Emphasis and Intensification.* PhD thesis, University of Salford, UK.

Jacobs, A. T. (2002). Appropriating a slur: Looping in the African American usage of *nigga*. *M/C Journal: A Journal of Media and Culture* 5(4).

Jary, M. (2010). *Assertion.* Palgrave.

(2011). Assertion, relevance and the declarative mood. In: V. Escandell-Vidal, M. Leonetti & A. Ahern (eds.) *Procedural Meaning: Problems and Perspective.* Emerald, pp. 267–89.

Jary, M. & Kissine, M. (2014). *Imperatives*. Cambridge University Press.
  (2016). When terminology matters: The imperative as a comparative concept. *Linguistics* 54(1): 119–48.
Jeshion, R. (2013). Expressivism and the offensiveness of slurs. *Philosophical Perspectives* 27: 307–35.
Jin, L. & Cortazzi, M. (2011). More than a journey: 'Learning' in the metaphors of Chinese students and teachers. In: L. Jin & M. Cortazzi (eds.) *Researching Chinese Learners: Skills, Perceptions and Intercultural Adaptations*. Palgrave Macmillan, pp. 67–92.
Jones, M. & Love, B. (2011). Bayesian fundamentalism or enlightenment? On the explanatory status and theoretical contributions of Bayesian models of cognition. *Behavioural and Brain Sciences* 34: 169–231.
Kahneman, D. (2011). *Thinking, Fast and Slow*. Farrar, Straus and Giroux.
Kaland, N., Calleson, K., Moller-Nielsen, A., Mortensen, E. L. & Smith, L. (2008). Performance of children and adolescents with Asperger syndrome or high-functioning autism on advanced theory of mind tasks. *Journal of Autism and Developmental Disorder* 38: 1112–23.
Kalsang, K., Garfield, J. Speas. M. & DeVilliers, J. (2013). Direct evidentials, case, tense and aspect in Tibetan: Evidence for a general theory of the semantics of evidentials. *Natural Language and Linguistic Theory* 31(2): 517–61.
Kamide, Y., Altmann, G. T. M. & Haywood, S. L. (2003). The time-course of prediction in incremental sentence processing: Evidence from anticipatory eye movements. *Journal of Memory and Language* 49: 133–56.
Kampa, A. & Papafragou, A. (2017). Gricean epistemic reasoning in 4-year-olds. In: G. Gunzelmann, A. Howes, T. Tenbrink & E. J. Davelaar (eds.) *Proceedings of the 39th Annual Conference of the Cognitive Science Society*. Cognitive Science Society, pp. 2362–5.
Kaplan, D. (1989). Demonstratives. In: J. Almog, J. Perry & H. Wettstein (eds.) *Themes from Kaplan*. Oxford University Press, pp. 481–566.
  (1999). *What Is Meaning? Explorations in the Theory of Meaning as Use*. Manuscript, University of California, Los Angeles.
Karttunen, L. (1971). Some observations on factivity. *Papers in Linguistics* 5: 55–69.
Kasher, A. (1991). Pragmatics and Chomsky's research program. In: A. Kasher (ed.) *The Chomskyan Turn*. Basil Blackwell, pp. 122–49.
Katsos, N. & Bishop, D. V. M. (2011). Pragmatic tolerance: Implications for the acquisition of informativeness and implicature. *Cognition* 120(1): 67–81.
Kaup, B., Yaxley, R. H., Madden, C. J., Zwaan, R. & Lüdtke, J. (2007). Experiential simulations of negated text information. *The Quarterly Journal of Experimental Psychology* 60: 976–90.
Kehler, A. & Rohde, H. (2016). Evaluating an expectation-driven QUD model of discourse interpretation. *Discourse Processes* 54(3): 219–38.
Kempson, R., Meyer-Viol, W. & Gabbay, D. (2001). *Dynamic Syntax: The Flow of Language Understanding*. Blackwell.
Kempson R., Gregoromichelaki, E. & Howes, C. (2011). *The Dynamics of Lexical Interfaces*. CSLI Publications.
Kempson, R., Cann, R., Gregoromichelaki, E. & Chatzikyriakidis, S. (2016). Language as mechanisms for interaction. *Theoretical Linguistics* 42(3–4): 203–76.
  (2017). Action-based grammar. *Theoretical Linguistics* 43(1–2): 141–67.

Kempson, R., Gregoromichelaki, E., Eshghi, A. & Hough, J. (2019). Ellipsis in dynamic syntax. In: J. van Craenenbroeck & T. Temmerman (eds.) *The Oxford Handbook of Ellipsis*. Oxford University Press.

Kissine, M. (2013). *From Utterances to Speech Acts*. Cambridge University Press.

Kobele, G. M. (2016). Actual language use and competence grammars. *Theoretical Linguistics* 42(3–4): 277–90.

Kolaiti, P. (2015). The poetic mind: A producer-oriented approach to literature and art. *Journal of Literary Semantics* 45(1): 23–44.

Kolaiti, P. & Wilson, D. (2014). Corpus analysis and lexical pragmatics: An overview. *International Review of Pragmatics* 6: 211–39.

Kölbel, M. (2003). Faultless disagreement. *Proceedings of the Aristotelian Society* 104: 53–73.

Komorowska, H. (2013). Metaphor in education. In: K. Droździał-Szelest & M. Pawlak (eds.) *Psycholinguistic and Sociolinguistic Perspectives on Second Language Learning and Teaching*. Springer, pp. 57–72.

Kratzer, A. (1988). Stage-level and individual-level predicates. In: Krifka, M. (ed.) *Genericity in Natural Language*. SNS-Bericht, pp. 247–84.

(1995). Stage-level and individual-level predicates. In: G. Carlson & F. J. Pelletier (eds.) *The Generic Book*. University of Chicago Press, pp. 125–76.

Krennmayr, T. (2011). *Metaphor in Newspapers*. LOT Dissertation Series, 276. LOT.

Kreuz, R. J. & Glucksberg, S. (1989). How to be sarcastic: The echoic reminder theory of verbal irony. *Journal of Experimental Psychology: General* 118(4): 374–86.

Krifka, M. (1999). Additive particles under stress. *Proceedings of SALT 8*. CLC Publications, pp. 111–28.

Kuchinke, L., Jacobs, A. M., Grubich, C., Võ, M. L.-H., Conrad, M. & Manfred, H. (2005). Incidental effects of emotional valence in single word processing: An fMRI study. *NeuroImage* 28: 1022–32.

Kumon-Nakamura, S., Glucksberg, S. & Brown, M. (1995). How about another piece of pie: The allusional pretense theory of discourse irony. *Journal of Experimental Psychology: General* 124(1): 3–21.

Kuno, S. (1980). The scope of the question and negation in some verb-final languages. *Chicago Linguistic Society* 17: 155–69.

Kurz, G. (1997). *Metapher, Allegorie, Symbol*. Vandenhoeck und Ruprecht.

Ladd, R. D. (1981). A first look at the semantics and pragmatics of negative questions and tag questions. In: *Papers from the Seventeenth Regional Meeting of the Chicago Linguistic Society*. Chicago Linguistics Society, pp. 164–71.

Lakoff, G. (1987). *Women, Fire, and Dangerous Things: What Categories Reveal about the Mind*. University of Chicago Press.

Lakoff, G. & Johnson, M. (1980). *Metaphors We Live By*. University of Chicago Press.

Lapata, M. (2002). The disambiguation of nominalizations. *Computational Linguistics* 28: 357–88.

Lasnik, H. (1989). *Essays on Binding and Anaphora*. Kluwer.

Lavender, A. (2017). The internet, theatre, and time: Transmediating the theatron. *Contemporary Theatre Review* 27(3): 340–52.

Lavie, N. & De Fockert, J. (2005). The role of working memory in attentional capture. *Psychonomic Bulletin & Review* 12(4): 669–74.

Lawrence, D. H. (1971/1920). *Women in Love*. Heinemann.

Lee, H. S. (1991). *Tense, Aspect, and Modality: A Discourse-Pragmatic Analysis of Verbal Affixes in Korean from a Typological Perspective*. PhD thesis, UCLA.

(1999). A discourse-pragmatic analysis of the committal *-ci* in Korean: A synthetic approach to the form-meaning relation. *Journal of Pragmatics* 31: 243–75.

Lee, K. (1993). *A Korean Grammar on Semantic Pragmatic Principles*. Hankuk Munhwasa.

Leitch, T. (2003). Twelve fallacies in contemporary adaptation theory. *Criticism* 45(2): 149–71.

Leonetti, M. (1994). *Ser* y *estar*: estado de la cuestión. *Barataria* 1: 182–205.

(2004). Por qué el imperfecto es anafórico. In: L. García Fernández & B. Camus Bergareche (eds.) *El imperfecto*. Gredos, pp. 481–507.

Leonetti, M. & Escandell-Vidal, V. (2003). On the quotative readings of Spanish imperfecto. *Cuadernos de Lingüística* 10: 135–54.

Leopold, W. F. (1949). *Speech Development of a Bilingual Child*. Northwestern University Press.

Lepore, E. & Stone, M. (2015). *Imagination and Convention*. Oxford University Press.

Lerner, G. H. (1991). On the syntax of sentences-in-progress. *Language in Society* 20: 441–58.

(2004). On the place of linguistic resources in the organization of talk-in-interaction: Grammar as action in prompting a speaker to elaborate. *Research on Language and Social Interaction* 37(2): 151–84.

Levelt, W. (1993). *Speaking: From Intention to Articulation*. MIT Press.

Levin, B., Glass, L. & Jurafsky, D. (2014). Corpus evidence for systematicity in English compounds. Paper presented at *Sinn und Bedeutung 19*, Georg August University at Göttingen, 15–17 September 2014.

Levinson, S. C. (1983). *Pragmatics*. Cambridge University Press.

(1988). Putting linguistics on a proper footing: Explorations in Goffman's participation framework. In: P. Drew & A. Wootton (eds.) *Goffman: Exploring the Interaction Order*. Polity Press, pp. 161–227.

(1995). Three levels of meaning: Essays in honor of Sir John Lyons. In: F. R. Palmer (ed.) *Grammar and Meaning*. Cambridge University Press, pp. 90–115.

(2000). *Presumptive Meanings: The Theory of Generalized Conversational Implicature*. MIT Press.

Levy, R. (2008). Expectation-based syntactic comprehension. *Cognition* 106(3): 1126–77.

Lewis, D. (1979). Attitudes de dicto and de se. *The Philosophical Review* 88(4): 513–43.

Li, F. T. (2009). *Metaphor, Image, and Image Schemas in Second Language Pedagogy*. Lambert Academic Publishing.

Lieber, R. (2011). A lexical semantic approach to compounding. In: R. Lieber & P. Štekauer (eds.) *The Oxford Handbook of Compounding*. Oxford University Press, pp. 78–104.

Lieberman, M. (2000). Intuition: A social-cognitive neuroscience approach. *Psychological Bulletin* 126: 109–37.

Littlemore, J. (2008). The relationship between associative thinking, analogical reasoning, image formation and metaphoric extension strategies. In: M. S. Zanotto, L. Cameron & M. C. Cavalcanti (eds.) *Confronting Metaphor in Use: An Applied Linguistic Approach*. John Benjamins, pp. 199–222.

Littlemore, J. & Low, G. D. (2006). Metaphoric competence, second language learning and communicative language ability. *Applied Linguistics* 27(2): 268–94.

Littlemore, J. & Taylor, J. R. (2014). *The Bloomsbury Companion to Cognitive Linguistics*. Bloomsbury Academic.

Losee, J. (1980). *A Historical Introduction to the Philosophy of Science*. Oxford University Press.

Loukusa, S., Leinonen, E. & Ryder, N. (2007). Development of pragmatic language comprehension in Finnish-speaking children. *First Language* 27(3): 279–96.

Low, G., Todd, Z., Deignan, A. & Cameron, L. (eds.) (2010). *Researching and Applying Metaphor in the Real World*. John Benjamins.

Lucas, M. (1987). Frequency effects on the processing of ambiguous words in sentence contexts. *Language and Speech* 30(1): 25–46.

Lust, B. (2006). *Child Language: Acquisition and Growth*. Cambridge University Press.

Lyons, J. (1977). *Semantics*. Cambridge University Press.

MacDonald, M. C., Pearlmuttter, N. J. & Seidenberg, M. S. (1994). Lexical nature of syntactic ambiguity resolution. *Psychological Review* 101(4): 676–703.

Maguire, P., Wisniewski, E. & Storms, G. (2010). A corpus study of semantic patterns in compounding. *Corpus Linguistics and Linguistic Theory* 6: 49–73.

Maienborn, C. (2005). A discourse-based account of Spanish *ser/estar*. *Linguistics* 43(1): 155–80.

Maier, E. (2014a). Mixed quotation: The grammar of apparently transparent opacity. *Semantics & Pragmatics* 7(7): 1–67.

(2014b). Language shifts in free indirect discourse. *Journal of Literary Semantics* 43(2): 143–67.

Malle, B. (2004). *How the Mind Explains Behavior: Folk Explanations, Meaning and Social Interaction*. MIT Press.

Mar, R. A., Oatley, K., Djikic, M. & Mullin, J. (2011). Emotion and narrative fiction: Interactive influences before, during, and after reading. *Cognition and Emotion* 25(5): 818–33.

Marantz, A. (2001). *Words*. Unpublished ms, MIT.

(2013). Verbal argument structure: Events and participants. *Lingua* 130: 152–68.

Marín, R. (2004). *Entre ser y estar*. Arco/Libros.

(2010). Spanish adjectives within bounds. In: P. Cabredo Hofherr & O. Matushansky (eds.). *Formal Analyses in Syntax and Semantics*. John Benjamins, pp. 307–32.

(2015). Ser y estar. In: J. Gutiérrez-Rexach (ed.) *Enciclopedia de Lingüística Hispánica* (Vol. 2). Routledge, 13–24.

Markson, L. & Bloom, P. (1997). Evidence against a dedicated system for word learning in children. *Nature* 385(27): 813–15.

Martin, F. (2008). Deux types de stage-level predicates. *Langages* 169: 111–28.

Martin, V. (2013). *Mary Reilly*. Vintage.

Mascaro, O. & Sperber, D. (2009). The moral, epistemic and mindreading components of children's vigilance towards deception. *Cognition* 112: 367–80.

Matsui, T. & Miura, Y. (2009). Children's understanding of certainty and evidentiality: Advantage of grammaticalised forms over lexical alternatives. In: S. Fitneva & T. Matsui (eds.) *Evidentiality: A Window into Language and Cognitive Development*. Wiley, pp. 49–62.

Matsui, T. & Yamamoto, T. (2013). Developing sensitivity to the sources of information: Early use of the Japanese quotative particles *tte* and *to* in mother–child conversation. *Journal of Pragmatics* 59: 5–25.

Matsui, T., Rakoczy, H., Miura, Y. & Tomasello, M. (2009). Understanding of speaker certainty and false-belief reasoning: A comparison of Japanese and German preschoolers. *Developmental Science* 12: 602–13.

Matsui, T., Yamamoto, T., Miura, Y. & McCagg, P. (2016a). Young children's early sensitivity to linguistic indications of speaker certainty in their selective word learning. *Lingua* 175–176: 83–96.

Matsui, T., Nakamura, T., Utsumi, A., Sasaki, A. T., Koike, T., Yoshida, Y., Harada, T., Tanabe, H. C. & Sadato, N. (2016b). The role of prosody and context in sarcasm comprehension: Behavioral and fMRI evidence. *Neuropsychologia* 87: 74–84.

Mazzarella, D. (2013). 'Optimal relevance' as a pragmatic criterion: The role of epistemic vigilance. *UCL Working Papers in Linguistics* 25: 20–45.

  (2015). Politeness, relevance and scalar inferences. *Journal of Pragmatics* 79: 93–106.

McCawley, J. D. (1999). Participant roles, frames, and speech acts. *Linguistics and Philosophy* 22(6): 595–619.

McElree, B., Pylkkänen, L., Pickering, M. J. & Traxler, M. J. (2006). A timecourse of enriched composition. *Psychonomic Bulletin and Review* 31(1): 53–9.

McFarlane, B. (1996). *Novel to Film. An Introduction to the Theory of Adaptation.* Clarendon Press.

McMullin, E. (1985). Galilean idealization. *Studies in History and Philosophy of Science Part A* 16(3): 247–73.

Meikle, K. (2013). Rematerializing adaptation theory. *Literature/Film Quarterly* 41(3): 174–83.

Miller, B. (2013). Metaphor, writer's block and the *Legend of Zelda*: A link to the writing process. In: R. Colby, M. S. S. Johnson & R. Shultz Colby (eds.) *Rhetoric/Composition/Play through Video Games.* Palgrave Macmillan, pp. 99–111.

Miller, J. & Weinert, R. (1998). *Spontaneous Spoken Language: Syntax and Discourse.* Oxford University Press.

Millikan, R. (2004). *The Varieties of Meaning: The 2002 Jean Nicod Lectures.* MIT Press.

Mills, K. (2011). 'I'm making it different to the book': Transmediation of young children's multimodal and digital texts. *Australasian Journal of Early Childhood* 36(3): 56–68.

Milsark, G. (1974). *Existential Sentences in English.* PhD thesis, MIT.

Moeschler, J. (2010). Negation, scope and the descriptive/metalinguistic distinction. *Generative Grammar in Geneva* 6: 29–48.

  (2011). Causal, inferential and temporal connectives: Why *parce que* is the only causal connective in French. In: S. Hancil (ed.) *Marqueurs discursifs et subjectivité.* PUPH, pp. 97–114.

  (2013). How 'logical' are logical words? Negation and its descriptive vs. metalinguistic uses. In: M. Taboada & R. Trnavac (eds.) *Nonveridicality and Evaluation. Theoretical, Computational and Corpus Approaches.* Brill, pp. 76–110.

  (2016). Where is procedural meaning? Evidence from discourse connectives and tenses. *Lingua* 175–176: 122–38.

(2018). A set of semantic and pragmatic criteria for descriptive vs. metalinguistic negation. *Glossa: A Journal of General Linguistics* 3(1): 58.

Morisseau, T., Davies, C. & Matthews, D. (2013). How do 3- and 5-year-olds respond to under- and over-informative utterances. *Journal of Pragmatics* 59: 26–39.

Murphy, G. (1988). Comprehending complex concepts. *Cognitive Science* 12: 529–62.

Nadig, A. S. & Sedivy, J. C. (2002). Evidence of perspective-taking constraints in children's on-line reference resolution. *Psychological Science* 13(4): 329–36.

Nerlich, B., Clarke, D. D. & Todd, Z. (1999). 'Mummy, I like being a sandwich'. Metonymy in language acquisition. In: K. Panther & G. Radden (eds.) *Metonymy in Language and Thought*. John Benjamins, pp. 361–83.

Nicolle, S. (2015). Diachronic change in procedural semantic content. *Nouveaux Cahiers de Linguistique Française* 32: 133–48.

Nieuwland, M. S. & Kuperberg, G. R. (2008). When the truth is not too hard to handle: An event-related potential study on the pragmatics of negation. *Psychological Science* 12: 1213–18.

Nikolaeva, I. (1999). The semantics of Northern Khandy evidentials. *Journal Societé Finno-Ougrinne* 88: 131–59.

Ninan, D. (2014). Taste predicates and the acquaintance inference. In: T. Snider, S. D'Antonio & M. Weigand (eds.) *Proceedings of Semantics and Linguistic Theory (SALT)* 24: 290–309.

Noh, E.-J. (1998). Echo questions: metarepresentation and pragmatic enrichment. *Linguistics and Philosophy* 21: 603–28.

(2000). *Metarepresentation: A Relevance Theory Approach*. John Benjamins.

(2016). The Korean sentence-final suffix *-ci*: An epistemic marker vs. a metarepresentational marker. *Korean Journal of Linguistics* 41(2): 267–87.

Noh, E.-J., Choo, H. & Koh, S. (2013). Processing metalinguistic negation: Evidence from eye-tracking experiments. *Journal of Pragmatics* 57: 1–18.

North, J. H. (2012). *Winckelman's 'Philosophy of Art: A Prelude to German Classicism*. Cambridge Scholars Publishing.

Noveck, I. A. (2001). When children are more logical than adults: Experimental investigations of scalar implicature. *Cognition* 78(2): 165–88.

Noveck, I. A. & Sperber, D. (eds.) (2004). *Experimental Pragmatics*. Palgrave Macmillan.

(2007). The why and how of experimental pragmatics: The case of 'scalar inferences'. In: N. Burton-Roberts (ed.) *Advances in Pragmatics*. Palgrave, pp. 184–212.

Noveck, I. A., Bianco, M. & Castry, A. (2001). The costs and benefits of metaphor. *Metaphor and Symbol* 16: 109–21.

Olkoniemi, H., Ranta, H. & Kaakinen, J. K. (2016). Individual differences in the processing of written sarcasm and metaphor: Evidence from eye movements. *Journal of Experimental Psychology: Learning, Memory, and Cognition* 42 (3): 433–50.

O'Neill, D. K. (1996). Two-year-old children's sensitivity to a parent's knowledge state when making requests. *Child Development* 67(2): 659–77.

O'Neill, D. K. & Topolovec, J. C. (2001). Two-year-old children's sensitivity to the referential (in)efficacy of their own pointing gestures. *Journal of Child Language* 28: 1–28.

Osborne, T., Putnam, M. & Gross, T. M. (2011). Bare phrase structure, label-less trees, and specifier-less syntax. Is Minimalism becoming a dependency grammar? *The Linguistic Review* 28(3): 315–64.

Özçaliskan, S. (2005). On learning how to draw the distinction between physical and metaphorical motion: Is metaphor and early emerging cognitive and linguistic capacity? *Journal of Child Language* 32: 291–318.

Ozturk, O. & Papafragou, A. (2015). The acquisition of epistemic modality: From semantic meaning to pragmatic interpretation. *Language Learning and Development* 11(3): 191–214.

Padilla Cruz, M. (2009a). Might interjections encode concepts? More questions than answers. *Lodz Papers in Pragmatics* 5(2): 241–70.

(2009b). Towards an alternative relevance-theoretic approach to interjections. *International Review of Pragmatics* 1(1): 182–206.

(ed.) (2016). *Relevance Theory: Recent Developments, Current Challenges and Future Directions*. John Benjamins.

Palmer, F. R. (1974). *Semantics*. Cambridge University Press.

Panagiotidis, P. (2014a). A minimalist approach to roots. In: P. Kosta et al. (eds.) *Minimalism and Beyond: Radicalizing the Interfaces*. John Benjamins, pp. 287–303.

(2014b). Indices, domains and homophonous forms. *Theoretical Linguistics* 40(3/4): 415–27.

Papafragou, A. (1996). On metonymy. *Lingua* 99: 169–95.

(2006). From scalar semantics to implicature: Children's interpretation of aspectuals. *Journal of Child Language* 33(4): 721–57.

Papafragou, A. & Musolino, J. (2003). Scalar implicatures: Experiments at the semantics–pragmatics interface. *Cognition* 86(3): 253–82.

Papafragou, A. & Skordos, D. (2016). Scalar implicature. In: J. Lidz, W. Snyder & J. Pater (eds.) *Oxford Handbook of Developmental Linguistics*. Oxford University Press, pp. 611–29.

Papafragou, A. & Tantalou, N. (2004). Children's computation of implicatures. *Language Acquisition* 12(1): 71–82.

Papafragou, A., Fairchild, S., Cohen, M. & Friedberg, C. (2017a). Learning words from speakers with false beliefs. *Journal of Child Language* 44(4): 905–23.

Papafragou, A., Friedberg, C. & Cohen, M. (2017b). The role of speaker knowledge in children's pragmatic inferences. *Child Development* 89(5): 1642–56.

Partee, B. (1973). The syntax and semantics of quotation. In: S. R. Anderson & P. Kiparsky (eds.) *A Festschrift for Morris Halle*. Holt, Rinehart, and Winston, pp. 410–18.

Pearson, B. Z. (1990). The comprehension of metaphor by preschool children. *Journal of Child Language* 17(1): 185–203.

Pearson, H. (2013). A judge-free semantics for predicates of personal taste. *Journal of Semantics* 30(3): 103–54.

Pérez Jiménez, I., Leonetti, M. & Gumiel-Molina, S. (eds.) (2015). *New Perspectives on the Study of* Ser *and* Estar. John Benjamins.

Perner, J. & Wimmer, H. (1985). 'John thinks that Mary thinks that…': Attribution of second-order beliefs by 5- and 10-year-old children. *Journal of Experimental Child Psychology* 39: 437–71.

Perry, J. (1979). The problem of the essential indexical. *Noûs* 13(1): 3–21.

Peters, D. (2014). What elements of successful scientific theories are the correct targets for 'selective' scientific realism? *Philosophy of Science* 81(3): 377–97.

Pexman, P. M. & Glenwright, M. (2007). How do typically developing children grasp the meaning of verbal irony? *Journal of Neurolinguistics* 20: 178–96.

Pezzulo, G. & Cisek, P. (2016). Navigating the affordance landscape: Feedback control as a process model of behavior and cognition. *Trends in Cognitive Sciences* 20(6): 414–24.

Phelan, M. (2014). Experimental pragmatics: An introduction for philosophers. *Philosophy Compass* 9(1): 66–79.

Pickering, M. J., McElree, B., Frisson, S., Chen, L. & Traxler, M.J. (2006). Underspecification and aspectual coercion. *Discourse Processes* 42(2): 131–55.

Piñango, M. M., Zurif, E. & Jackendoff, R. (1999). Real-time processing implications of aspectual coercion at the syntax-semantics interface. *Journal of Psycholinguistic Research* 28(4): 395–414.

Piquer-Píriz, A. M. (2008). Reasoning figuratively in early EFL: Some implications for the development of vocabulary. In: F. Boers & S. Lindstromberg (eds.) *Cognitive Linguistic Approaches to Teaching Vocabulary and Phraseology*. Mouton de Gruyter, pp. 219–40.

Platzack, C. & Rosengren, I. (1997). On the subject of imperatives: A minimalist account of the imperative clause. *Journal of Comparative Germanic Linguistics* 1(3): 177–224.

Poesio, M. & Rieser, H. (2010). Completions, coordination, and alignment in dialogue. *Dialogue and Discourse* 1(1): 1–89.

Potts, A. (1994). *Flesh and the Ideal Winckelman: The Origins of Art History*. Yale University Press.

Potts, C. (2005). *The Logic of Conventional Implicatures*. Oxford University Press.
  (2007a). The expressive dimension. *Theoretical Linguistics* 33(2): 165–97.
  (2007b). The dimensions of quotation. In: P. Jacobson & C. Barker (eds.) *Direct Compositionality*. Oxford University Press, pp. 405–31.
  (2007c). The centrality of expressive indices. *Theoretical Linguistics* 33(2): 255–68.
  (2012). Conventional implicature and expressive content. In: C. Maienborn, K. von Heusinger, & P. Portner (eds.) *Semantics: An International Handbook of Natural Language Meaning* (Vol. 3). Mouton de Gruyter, pp. 2516–36.

Potts, C. & Roeper, T. (2006). The narrowing acquisition path: From expressive small clauses to declaratives. In: L. Progovac, K. Paesani, E. Casielles & E. Barton (eds.) *The Syntax of Nonsententials: Multi-Disciplinary Perspectives*. John Benjamins, pp. 183–201.

Pouscoulous, N. (2011). Metaphor: For adults only? *Belgian Journal of Linguistics* 25: 51–79.
  (2013). Early pragmatics with words. In: F. Liedke & C. Schulze (eds.) *Beyond the Words: Content, Context and Inference*. De Gruyter Mouton, pp. 149–71.

Pouscoulous, N., Noveck, I. A., Politzer, G. & Bastide, A. (2007). A developmental investigation of processing costs in implicature production. *Language Acquisition* 14(4): 347–75.

Preissler, M. A. & Carey, S. (2005). The role of inferences about referential intent in word learning: Evidence from autism. *Cognition* 97: B13–23.

Pullum, G. & Wilson, D. (1977). Autonomous syntax and the analysis of auxiliaries. *Language* 53: 741–88.

Pulvermüller, F. (2010). Brain embodiment of syntax and grammar. *Brain and Language* 112(3): 167–79.

Purver, M., Gregoromichelaki, E., Meyer-Viol, W. & Cann, R. (2010). Splitting the
    I's and crossing the *you*'s: Context, speech acts and grammar. In: *Proceedings of
    SemDial 2010 (PozDial)*, Poznan, Poland.
Pustejovsky, J. (1993). Type coercion and lexical selection. In: J. Pustejovsky (ed.)
    Semantics and the Lexicon. Reidel, pp. 73–94.
    (2011). Coercion in a general theory of argument selection. *Linguistics* 49(6): 1401–31.
Putnam, H. (1978). *Meaning and the Moral Sciences*. Routledge & Kegan Paul.
Putnam, M. T. (ed.). (2009). *Towards a Derivational Syntax: Survive-Minimalism*. John
    Benjamins.
    (ed.). (2010). *Exploring Crash-Proof Grammars*. John Benjamins.
Querido, A. (1976). The semantics of copulative constructions in Portuguese. In: M.
    Luján & F. Hensey (eds.) *Current Studies in Romance Linguistics*. Georgetown
    University Press, pp. 343–66.
Radcliffe, E. (1999). Hume on the generation of motives: Why beliefs alone never
    motivate. *Hume Studies* 25(1 & 2): 101–22.
Radford, A. (2004). *Minimalist Syntax: Exploring the Structure of English*. Cambridge
    University Press.
Rahman, J. (2012). The n word: Its history and use in the African American community.
    Journal of English Linguistics 40: 137–71.
Ramachandran, V. & Hirstein, W. (1999). The science of art: A neurological theory of
    aesthetic experience. *Journal of Consciousness Studies* 6(6–7): 15–51.
Reboul, A. (2015). Why language really is not a communication system: A cognitive
    view of language evolution. *Frontiers in Psychology* 6: Article 1434.
    (2017). Is implicit communication a way to escape epistemic vigilance? In:
    S. Assimakopoulos (ed.) *Pragmatics at Its Interfaces*. De Gruyter, pp. 91–112.
Reboul, A., Delfitto, D. & Fiorin, G. (2016). The semantic properties of free indirect
    discourse. *Annual Review of Linguistics* 2: 255–71.
Recanati, F. (2000). *Oratio Recta, Oratio Obliqua*. MIT Press.
    (2004). *Literal Meaning*. Cambridge University Press.
    (2010). *Truth-Conditional Pragmatics*. Oxford University Press.
    (2012). *Mental Files*. Oxford University Press.
Regier, T. (2005). The emergence of words: Attentional learning in form and meaning.
    Cognitive Science 29: 819–65.
Reichenbach, H. (1947). *Elements of Symbolic Logic*. Free Press.
Reinhart, T. (1995). *Interface Strategies*. OTS Working Papers.
    (2004). The processing cost of reference set computation: acquisition of stress shift
    and focus. *Language Acquisition* 12(2): 109–55.
Rescorla, L. (1980). Overextension in early language development. *Journal of Child
    Language* 7: 321–35.
Rey, G. (1980). Functionalism and the emotions. In: A. Rorty (ed.) *Explaining Emotions*.
    University of California Press, pp. 163–98.
    (2003). Chomsky, intentionality and a CRTT. In: L. M. Antony & N. Hornstein (eds.)
    Chomsky and His Critics. Blackwell, pp. 105–39.
Roberts, C. (1996/2012). Information structure in discourse: Towards an integrated
    formal theory of pragmatics. In: J.-H. Yoon & A. Kathol (eds.) *Papers in Semantics
    (Working Papers in Linguistics 49)*. The Ohio State University. Reproduced with
    minor amendments in *Semantics and Pragmatics* 5(6): 1–69.

Robisco Martín, M. M. & Cuadrado Esclápez, G. (2013). Metaphor and genre: An approach to improve the learning process of English for aeronautics. *Revista Española de Lingüística Aplicada* 1: 209–28.

Roby, D. (2007). *Aspect and the Categorisation of States. The Case of* Ser *and* Estar *in Spanish*. PhD thesis, University of Texas at Austin.

Romero, M. & Han, C.-Y. (2004). On negative yes–no questions. *Linguistics & Philosophy* 27(5): 609–58.

Rouchota, V. & Jucker, A. (eds.) (1998). *Current Issues in Relevance Theory*. John Benjamins.

Rubio Fernández, P. (2007). Suppression in metaphor interpretation: Differences between meaning selection and meaning construction. *Journal of Semantics* 24(4): 345–71.

Rundblad, G. & Annaz, D. (2010). Development of metaphor and metonymy comprehension: Receptive vocabulary and conceptual knowledge. *British Journal of Developmental Psychology* 28: 547–63.

Russell, B. (2012). *Probabilistic Reasoning and the Computation of Scalar Implicatures*. PhD thesis, Brown University.

Sabbagh, M. A. & Baldwin, D. A. (2001). Learning words from knowledgeable versus ignorant speakers: Links between preschoolers' theory of mind and semantic development. *Child Development* 72(4): 1054–70.

Sadock, J. (1998). On the autonomy of combination morphology. In: S. Lapointe, D. Brentari & P. Farrell (eds.) *Morphology and Its Relation to Phonology and Syntax*. CSLI Publications, pp. 161–87.

Sato, Y. (2011). Local ambiguity, search strategies and parsing in Dynamic Syntax. In: Kempson, R., Gregoromichelaki, E. & Howes, C. (eds.) *The Dynamics of Lexical Interfaces*. CSLI Publications, pp. 201–28.

Sauerland, U. (2004). Scalar implicatures in complex sentences. *Linguistics and Philosophy* 27: 367–91.

    (2012). The computation of scalar implicatures: Pragmatic, lexical or grammatical? *Language and Linguistics Compass* 6: 36–49.

Schacht, A. & Sommer, W. (2009). Emotions in word and face processing: Early and late cortical responses. *Brain and Cognition* 69: 538–50.

Scherer, K. R. (2009). Emotion theories and concepts (psychological perspectives). In: D. Sander & K. R. Scherer (eds.) *The Oxford Companion to Emotion and the Affective Sciences*. Oxford University Press, pp. 145–51.

Schlenker, P. (2004). Context of thought and context of utterance: A note on free indirect discourse and the historical present. *Mind & Language* 19: 279–304.

Schmerling, S. F. (1982). How imperatives are different, and how they aren't. In: R. Schneider, K. Tuite & R. Chameltzy (eds.) *Chicago Linguistic Society: Parasession on Nondeclaratives*, pp. 202–18.

Schmidt, G. L. & Seger, C. A. (2009). Neural correlates of metaphor processing: The roles of figurativeness, familiarity and difficulty. *Brain and Cognition* 71 (3): 375–86.

Schmitter, A. M. (2014). 17th and 18th century theories of emotions. In: E. Zalta (ed.) *The Stanford Encyclopedia of Philosophy*. Available at: https://plato.stanford.edu/entries/emotions-17th18th/. Accessed 8 November 2018.

Schulze, C., Grassmann, S. & Tomasello, M. (2013). 3-year-old children make relevance inferences in indirect verbal communication. *Child Development* 84(6): 2079–93.

Schwarzschild, R. (1999). GIVENness, AvoidF and other constraints on the placement of accent. *Natural Language Semantics* 7(2):141–77.

Scott, K. (2015). The pragmatics of hashtags: Inference and conversational style on Twitter. *Journal of Pragmatics* 81: 8–20.

(2018). Hashtags work everywhere: The pragmatic functions of spoken hashtags. *Discourse, Media & Context* 22: 57–64.

Scott-Phillips, T. (2015). *Speaking Our Minds*. Palgrave Macmillan.

Searle, J. R. (1969). *Speech Acts: An Essay in the Philosophy of Language*. Cambridge University Press.

Selkirk, E. (1984). *Phonology and Syntax: The Relation between Sound and Structure*. MIT Press.

Sellars, W. (1953). Inference and meaning. *Mind* 62(247): 313–38.

(1954). Some reflections on language games. *Philosophy of Science* 21(3): 204–28.

Seth, A. K. (2015). The cybernetic Bayesian brain. In: T. Metzinger & J. M. Windt (eds.) *Open MIND: 35(T)*. MIND Group, doi: 10.15502/9783958570108.

Shibata, M., Toyomura, A., Itoh, H. & Abe, J.-I. (2010). Neural substrates of irony comprehension: A functional MRI study. *Brain Research* 1308: 114–23.

Simons, M. (2007). Observations on embedding verbs, evidentiality, and presupposition. *Lingua* 117(6): 1034–56.

Skordos, D. & Papafragou, A. (2016). Children's derivation of scalar implicatures: Alternatives and relevance. *Cognition* 153: 6–18.

Smith, N. & Allott, N. (2016). *Chomsky: Ideas and Ideals*. Cambridge University Press.

Smith, N. & Tsimpli, I. (1995). *The Mind of a Savant: Language Learning and Modularity*. Blackwell.

Smith, N. & Wilson, D. (1979). *Modern Linguistics: The Results of Chomsky's Revolution*. Penguin.

Soames, S. (1977). Review of *Presupposition* by David E. Cooper and *Presuppositions and Non-Truth-Conditional Semantics* by Deirdre Wilson. *The Philosophical Review* 86(2): 274–8.

Sohn, H.-M. (1999). *The Korean Language*. Cambridge University Press.

Southgate, V., Chevallier, C. & Csibra, G. (2010). Seventeen-month-olds appeal to false beliefs to interpret others' referential communication. *Developmental Science* 16: 907–12.

Speas, M. (2010). Evidentials as generalized functional heads. In: A. M. DiSciullo & V. Hill (eds.) *Edges, Heads and Projections: Interface Properties*. John Benjamins, pp. 127–50.

Speas, P. (2008). On the syntax and semantics of evidentials. *Language and Linguistics Compass* 2(5): 940–65.

Spector, B. (2006). Scalar implicatures: Exhaustivity and Gricean reasoning. In: M. Aloni, A. Butler & P. Dekker (eds.) *Questions in Dynamic Semantics*. Elsevier, pp. 229–54.

Sperber, D. (1975). *Rethinking Symbolism*. Cambridge University Press.

(ed.) (2000). *Metarepresentations: An Interdisciplinary Perspective*. Oxford University Press.

Sperber, D. & Wilson, D. (1981). Irony and the use–mention distinction. In: P. Cole (ed.) *Radical Pragmatics*. Academic Press, pp. 295–318. Reprinted in: Steven Davies (ed.) 1991: *Pragmatics: A Reader*. Oxford University Press, pp. 550–63.

(1986/1995). *Relevance: Communication and Cognition*. Blackwell. Second edition with Postface 1995.

(1987a). Précis of 'Relevance: Communication and Cognition'. *Behavioral and Brain Sciences* 10(4): 697–710.

(1987b). Presumptions of relevance. *Behavioral and Brain Sciences* 10(4): 736–53.

(1990). Rhetoric and relevance. In: J. Bender & D. Wellbery (eds.) *The Ends of Rhetoric: History, Theory, Practice*. Stanford University Press, pp. 140–56. Reprinted in Wilson, D. & Sperber, D. 2012: *Meaning and Relevance*. Cambridge University Press, pp. 84–96.

(1996). Fodor's frame problem and relevance theory (reply to Chiappe & Kukla). *Behavioral and Brain Sciences* 19(3): 530–2.

(1997). Remarks on relevance theory and the social sciences. *Multilingua* 16(2/3): 145–51.

(2002). Pragmatics, modularity and mind-reading. *Mind & Language* 17(1–2): 3–23.

(2005). Pragmatics. In: F. Jackson & M. Smith (eds.) *The Oxford Handbook of Contemporary Philosophy*. Oxford University Press, pp. 468–501.

(2008). A deflationary account of metaphor. In: R. W. Gibbs (ed.) *The Cambridge Handbook of Metaphor and Thought*. Cambridge University Press, pp. 84–108.

(2015). Beyond speaker's meaning. *Croatian Journal of Philosophy* 44: 117–49.

Sperber, D., Clément, F., Heintz, C., Mascaro, O. Mercier, H., Origgi, G. & Wilson, D. (2010). Epistemic vigilance. *Mind & Language* 25(4): 359–93.

Spotorno, N., Koun, E., Prado, J., Van Der Henst, J. B. & Noveck, I. A. (2012). Neural evidence that utterance-processing entails mentalizing: The case of irony. *NeuroImage* 63(1): 25–39.

Stainton, R. J. (2006). *Words and Thoughts*. Oxford University Press.

Stalnaker, R. (1979). Assertion. In: P. Cole (ed.) *Syntax and Semantics* (Vol. 9). Academic Press, pp. 315–32.

Steedman, M. (2000). *The Syntactic Process*. MIT Press.

Stephenson, T. (2007). Judge dependence, epistemic modals, and predicates of personal taste. *Linguistics & Philosophy* 30: 487–525.

Stiller, A. J., Goodman, N. D. & Frank, M. C. (2015). Ad-hoc implicature in preschool children. *Language Learning and Development* 11(2): 176–90.

Strey, C. (2016). *The Language of Emotions: An Ostensive-Inferential Study*. PhD thesis, Pontifical University Catholic of Rio Grande do Sul.

Sullivan, K., Winner, E. & Hopfield, N. (1995). How children tell a lie from a joke: The role of second-order mental state attributions. *British Journal of Developmental Psychology* 13: 191–204.

Tanenhaus, M. K., Spivey-Knowlton, M. J., Eberhard, K. M. & Sedivy, J. C. (1995). Integration of visual and linguistic information in spoken language comprehension. *Science* 268(5217): 1632–4.

Tian, Y. & Breheny, R. (2015). *Representing Polar Questions and Inferring States of Inquiry*. Oral Presentation. Xprag, Chicago, USA.

Tian, Y., Breheny, R. & Ferguson, H. (2010). Why we simulate negated information: A dynamic pragmatic account. *The Quarterly Journal of Experimental Psychology* 63(12): 2305–12.

Tian, Y., Ferguson, H. & Breheny, R. (2016). Processing negation without context: Why and when we represent the positive argument. *Language, Cognition and Neuroscience* 31(5): 683–98.

Tobias, S. (2003). Interview: Gus Van Sant. The A./V. Club. Available at: https://film.avclub.com/gus-van-sant-1798208262. Accessed 9 November 2018.

Tooby, J. & Cosmides, L. (2008). The evolutionary psychology of the emotions and their relationship to internal regulatory variables. In: M. Lewis, J. M. Haviland-Jones & L. F. Barrett (eds.) *Handbook of Emotions*. Guilford Press, pp. 114–37.

Traugott, E. C. & Dasher, R. B. (2005). *Regularity in Semantic Change*. Cambridge University Press.

Tribushinina, E. (2012). Comprehension of relevance implicatures by pre-schoolers: The case of adjectives. *Journal of Pragmatics* 44(14): 2035–44.

Uchiyama, H., Seki, A., Kageyama, H., Saito, D. N., Koeda, T., Ohno, K. & Sadato, N. (2006). Neural substrates of sarcasm: A functional magnetic-resonance imaging study. *Brain Research* 1124(1): 100–10.

Ullmann, S. (1962). *Semantics: An Introduction to the Science of Meaning*. Blackwell.

Unger, C. (2006). *Genre, Relevance and Global Coherence: The Pragmatics of Discourse Type*. Palgrave Macmillan.

(2012). Procedural semantics, metarepresentation, and some particles in Behdini Kurdish. *Lingua* 122: 1613–35.

(2017). Towards a relevance theory account of allegory. In: A. Piskorska & E. Wałaszewska (eds.) *From Discourse to Morphemes: Applications of Relevance Theory*. Cambridge Scholars Publishing, pp. 152–174.

(2018). Cognitive pragmatics and multi-layered communication: Allegory in Christian religious discourse. In: P. Chilton & M. Kopytowska (eds.) *Religion, Language, and the Human Mind*. Oxford University Press.

Utsumi, A. (2000). Verbal irony as implicit display of ironic environment: Distinguishing ironic utterances from nonirony. *Journal of Pragmatics* 32: 1777–806.

van Berkum, J. J. A., Brown, C., Zwitserlood, P., Kooijman, V. & Hagoort, P. (2005). Anticipating upcoming words in discourse: Evidence from ERPs and reading times. *Journal of Experimental Psychology: Learning, Memory, and Cognition* 31(3): 443–67.

Van Herwegen, J., Dimitriouc, D. & Rundblad, G. (2013). Development of novel metaphor and metonymy comprehension in typically developing children and Williams syndrome. *Research in Developmental Disabilities* 34(4): 1300–11.

van Kuppevelt, J. (1996). Inferring from topics. *Linguistics & Philosophy* 19: 393–443.

van Rooij, R. & Schulz, K. (2004). Exhaustive interpretation of complex sentences. *Journal of Logic, Language and Information* 13: 491–519.

van Rooy, R. (2003). Questioning to resolve decision problems. *Linguistics and Philosophy* 26: 727–63.

Vendler, Z. (1957). Verbs and times. *The Philosophical Review* 66(2): 143–60.

Verbuk, A. & Shultz, T. (2010). Acquisition of relevance implicatures: A case against a rationality-based account of conversational implicatures. *Journal of Pragmatics* 42(8): 2297–313.

Vetter, N. C., Weigelt, S., Dohnel, K., Smolka, M. N. & Kliegel, M. (2014). Ongoing neural development of affective theory of mind in adolescence. *Social Cognitive and Affective Neuroscience* 9: 1022–9.

Vicente, A. (2018). Polysemy and word meaning: an account of lexical meaning for different kinds of content words. *Philosophical Studies* 175(4): 947–68.

von Fintel, K. (2001). Would you believe it? The King of France is back! (Presupposition and truth-value intuitions). In: A. Bezuidenhout & M. Reimer (eds.) *Description and Beyond*. Oxford University Press, pp. 269–96.

Vosniadou, S. (1987). Children and metaphors. *Child Development* 58(3): 870–85.

Vosniadou, S., Orthony, A., Reynolds, P. C. & Wilson, P. T. (1984). Sources of difficulty in the young child's understanding of metaphorical language. *Child Development* 55(4): 1588–606.

Waggoner, J. E. & Palermo, D. S. (1989). Betty is a bouncing bubble: Children's comprehension of emotion-descriptive metaphors. *Developmental Psychology* 25(1): 152–63.

Wałaszewska, E. (2004). What to do with response cries in relevance theory? In: E. Mioduszewska (ed.) *Relevance Studies in Poland* (Vol. 1). University of Warsaw, pp. 119–29.

  (2011). Broadening and narrowing in lexical development: How relevance theory can account for children's overextensions and underextensions. *Journal of Pragmatics* 43: 314–26.

Wang, A. T., Lee, S. S., Sigman, M. & Dapretto, M. (2006). Developmental changes in the neural basis of interpreting communicative intent. *Social Cognitive and Affective Neuroscience* 1(2): 107–21.

Wang, L. & Bastiaansen, M. (2014). Oscillatory brain dynamics associated with the automatic processing of emotion in words. *Brain and Language* 137: 120–9.

Wason, P. (1961). Response to affirmative and negative binary statements. *British Journal of Psychology* 52: 133–42.

  (1965). The contexts of plausible denial. *Journal of Verbal Learning Verbal Behavior* 4(1): 7–11.

Weiland, H., Bambini, V. & Schumacher, P. B. (2014). The role of literal meaning in figurative language comprehension: Evidence from masked priming ERP. *Frontiers in Human Neuroscience* 8: 583.

Weinberg, A. (2002). Semantics in the spin cycle: Competence and performance criteria for the creation of lexical entries. In: P. Merlo and S. Stevenson (eds.) *The Lexical Basis of Sentence Processing*. John Benjamins, pp. 85–93.

Weinberg, S. (1976). The forces of nature. *Bulletin of the American Academy of Arts and Sciences* 29(4): 13–29.

Werner, H. & Kaplan, B. (1963). *Symbol Formation: An Organismic-Developmental Approach to Language and the Expression of Thought*. John Wiley & Sons.

Wharton, T. (2003a). Natural pragmatics and natural codes. *Mind & Language* 18(5): 447–77.

  (2003b). Interjections, language and the 'showing-saying' continuum. *Pragmatics and Cognition* 11: 39–91.

  (2009). *Pragmatics and Non-Verbal Communication*. Cambridge University Press.

Wichmann, A. (2004). The intonation of *please*-requests: A corpus-based study. *Journal of Pragmatics* 36(9): 1521–49.

Wierzbicka, A. (2000). The semantics of human facial expression. *Pragmatics and Cognition* 8(1): 147–83.

Wiese, W. (2017). What are the contents of representations in predictive processing? *Phenomenology and the Cognitive Sciences* 16(4): 715–36.

Wilkins, D. (1992). Interjections as deictics. *Journal of Pragmatics* 18: 119–58.

Williamson, T. (2009). Reference, inference and the semantics of pejoratives. In: J. Almog & J. Lionardi (eds.) *The Philosophy of David Kaplan*. Oxford University Press, pp. 137–59.

Wilson, D. (1970). If that. *Linguistic Inquiry* 1: 369–73.

  (1975). *Presuppositions and Non-Truth-Conditional Semantics*. Academic Press.

(1991). *Slave of the Passions*. Picador.

(1998–9). *Non-Truth-Conditional Semantics: Mood Indicators I*. Lecture notes, Dept. Phonetics & Linguistics, University College London.

(2000). Metarepresentation in linguistic communication. In: D. Sperber (ed.) *Metarepresentations: An Interdisciplinary Perspective*. Oxford University Press, pp. 411–48. Reprinted in: D. Wilson & D. Sperber, *Meaning and Relevance*. Cambridge University Press, pp. 230–58.

(2003). Relevance theory and lexical pragmatics. *Italian Journal of Linguistics* 15: 273–91.

(2005). New directions for research on pragmatics and modularity. *Lingua* 115(8): 1129–46.

(2009). Irony and metarepresentation. *UCL Working Papers in Linguistics* 21: 183–226.

(2011a). Parallels and differences in the treatment of metaphor in relevance theory and cognitive linguistics. *Intercultural Pragmatics* 8(2): 177–96.

(2011b). The conceptual–procedural distinction: Past, present and future. In: V. Escandell-Vidal, M. Leonetti & A. Ahern (eds.) *Procedural Meaning: Problems and Perspectives*. Emerald, pp. 3–31.

(2011c). Relevance and the interpretation of literary works. *UCL Working Papers in Linguistics* 23: 69–80.

(2012). *Relevance and the Interpretation of Literary Works*. Talk presented at EPICS V: Relevance Theory: Recent Developments, Current Challenges and Future Directions. Seville, Spain, March 2012.

(2013). Irony comprehension: A developmental perspective. *Journal of Pragmatics* 59: 40–56.

(2016). Reassessing the conceptual–procedural distinction. *Lingua* 175–6: 5–19.

(2017). Irony, hyperbole, jokes and banter. In: J. Blochowiak, C. Grisot, S. Durriemann & C. Laenzlinger (eds.) *Formal Models in the Study of Language: Applications in Interdisciplinary Contexts*. Springer, pp. 201–20.

(2018). Relevance theory and literary interpretation. In: T. Cave & D. Wilson (eds.) *Reading Beyond the Code: Literature and Relevance Theory*. Oxford University Press, pp. 185–204.

Wilson, D. & Carston, R. (2006). Metaphor, relevance and the 'emergent property' issue. *Mind & Language* 21(3): 404–33.

(2007). A unitary approach to lexical pragmatics: Relevance, inference and ad hoc concepts. In: N. Burton-Roberts (ed.) *Pragmatics*. Palgrave, pp. 230–59.

(2008). Metaphor and the 'emergent property' problem: A relevance-theoretic treatment. *The Baltic International Yearbook of Cognition, Logic and Communication* 3: 1–40.

Wilson, D. & Falkum, I. L. (2014). Metonymy and relevance. Paper presented at the *Workshop on Relevance, Literariness and Style*, Middlesex University, London.

(2015). Explaining metonymy. Talk presented at the conference on *New Developments in Linguistic Pragmatics*, Lodz, Poland, April 2015.

(forthcoming). *Explaining Metonymy*.

Wilson, D. & Kolaiti, P. (2017). Lexical pragmatics and implicit communication. In: P. Cap & M. Dynel (eds.) *Implicitness: From Lexis to Discourse*. John Benjamins, pp. 147–75.

Wilson, D. & Sperber, D. (1981). On Grice's theory of conversation. In: P. Werth (ed.) *Conversation and Discourse*. Croom Helm, pp. 155–78.

(1986). Pragmatics and modularity. In: A. Farley, P. Farley & K.-E. McCullough (eds.) *Chicago Linguistic Society 22, Parasession on Pragmatics and Grammatical Theory*. Chicago Linguistics Society, pp. 67–84.

(1988a). Mood and the analysis of non-declarative sentences. In: J. Dancy, J. M. E. Moravcsik & C. C. W. Taylor (eds.) *Human Agency: Language, Duty and Value*. Stanford University Press, pp. 77–101.

(1988b). Representation and relevance. In: R. Kempson (ed.) *Mental Representation: The Interface between Language and Reality*. Cambridge University Press, pp. 133–53.

(1992). On verbal irony. *Lingua* 87: 53–76.

(1993). Linguistic form and relevance. *Lingua* 90: 1–25.

(1998). Pragmatics and time. In: R. Carston & S. Uchida (eds.) *Relevance Theory: Applications and Implications*. John Benjamins, pp. 1–22.

(2002). Truthfulness and relevance. *Mind* 111: 583–632.

(2004). Relevance theory. In: L. R. Horn & G. Ward (eds.) *Handbook of Pragmatics*. Blackwell, pp. 607–32.

(2012). *Meaning and Relevance*. Cambridge University Press.

Wilson, D. & Wharton, T. (2006). Relevance and prosody. *Journal of Pragmatics* 38(10): 1559–79.

Wilson, R. A. (2004). What computations (still, still) can't do: Jerry Fodor on computation and modularity. In: M. Ezcurdia, R. Stainton & C. D. Viger (eds.) *New Essays in the Philosophy of Language and Mind: Supplementary Issue 30 of the Canadian Journal of Philosophy*. University of Calgary Press, pp. 407–25.

Wimmer, H., Gruber, S. & Perner, J. (1984). Young children's conception of lying: Lexical realism-moral subjectivism. *Journal of Experimental Child Psychology* 37: 1–30.

Winner, E. (1979). New names for old things: The emergence of metaphoric language. *Journal of Child Language* 6(3): 469–91.

(1988/1997). *The Point of Words: Children's Understanding of Metaphor and Irony*. Harvard University Press.

Winner, E. & Leekam, S. R. (1991). Distinguishing irony from deception: Understanding the speaker's second-order intention. *British Journal of Developmental Psychology* 9: 257–70.

Winner, E., Rosenstiel, A. K. & Gardner, H. (1976). The development of metaphoric understanding. *Developmental Psychology* 12(4): 289–97.

Winner, E., McCarthy, M., Kleinman, S. & Gardner, H. (1979). First metaphors. In: D. Wolf (ed.) *Early Symbolization: New Directions for Child Development*. Jossey-Bass, pp. 29–41.

Winner, E., McCarthy, M. & Gardner, H. (1980). The ontogenesis of metaphor. In: R. P. Honeck & R. R. Hoffman (eds.) *Cognition and Figurative Language*. Lawrence Erlbaum Associates, pp. 341–61.

Winner, E., Windmueller, G., Rosenblatt, E., Bosco, L., Best, E. & Gardner, H. (1987). Making sense of literal and nonliteral falsehood. *Metaphor & Symbolic Activity* 2: 13–32.

Wisniewski, E. J. & Gentner, D. (1991). On the combinatorial semantics of noun pairs: Minor and major adjustments to meaning. In: G. B. Simpson (ed.) *Understanding Word and Sentence*. Elsevier, pp. 241–84.

Wittgenstein, L. (1953). *Philosophical Investigations*, trans. G. E. M. Anscombe. Blackwell.

Woodward, A. L. & Markman, E. M. (1998). Early word learning. In: W. Damon (ed.) *Handbook of Child Psychology* (Vol. 2: Cognition, Perception, and Language). Wiley, pp. 371–420.

Zanuttini, R. (2008). Encoding the addressee in the syntax: Evidence from English imperative subjects. *Natural Language and Linguistic Theory* 26: 185–218.

Žegarac, V. (1990). Relevance theory and the meaning of the English progressive. *UCL Working Papers in Linguistics* 1: 19–30.

Zeki, S. (2004). The neurology of ambiguity. *Consciousness and Cognition* 12: 173–96.

Zufferey, S. (2015). *Acquiring Pragmatics: Social and Cognitive Perspectives.* Routledge.

Zuo, B. (2017). *La négation et ses emplois spéciaux en chinois mandarin. Négation explétive, métaconceptuelle, métalinguistique et double négation.* PhD thesis, University of Geneva.

Author Index

Subject Index